Electronic Aids to Navigation
Position Fixing

D1033595

Electronic Aids to Navigation

Position Fixing

L. Tetley I. Eng., F.I.E.I.E., M.R.I.N.

Principal Lecturer in the Information Systems Division
Southampton Institute of Higher Education

D. Calcutt M. Sc., C. Eng., M.I.E.E.

Senior Lecturer in the Faculty of Engineering,
Portsmouth Polytechnic

VK
560
T36
1991

Edward Arnold
A division of Hodder & Stoughton
LONDON MELBOURNE AUCKLAND

RASMUSON LIBRARY
UNIVERSITY OF ALASKA-FAIRBANKS

© 1991 L. Tetley and D. Calcutt

First published in Great Britain 1986 as *Electronic Aids to Navigation*
Reprinted 1988
First published as *Electronic Aids to Navigation: Position Fixing* 1991

British Library Cataloguing in Publication Data

Tetley, L.
  Electronic aids to navigation: Position fixing.
  I. Title   II. Calcutt, D.
  629.04

  ISBN 0-340-54380-9

All rights reserved. No part of this publication may be reproduced
or transmitted in any form or by any means, electronically or
mechanically, including photocopying, recording or any
information storage or retrieval system, without either prior
permission in writing from the publisher or a licence permitting
restricted copying. In the United Kingdom such licences are issued
by the Copyright Licensing Agency: 90 Tottenham Court Road,
London W1P 9HE.

Typeset in 10/11 Times Roman by Brian Smith Partnership, Bristol
Printed in Great Britain for Edward Arnold, a division of Hodder
and Stoughton Limited, Mill Road, Dunton Green, Sevenoaks, Kent
TN13 2YA by St Edmundsbury Press Ltd, Bury St Edmunds,
Suffolk, and bound by Hartnolls Ltd, Bodmin, Cornwall.

Preface

Readers will find that this, the second edition of Electronic Aids to Navigation, has been extensively rewritten and enlarged to include new systems and technology. Each chapter has been reviewed and new material has been included in the high technology areas of satellite navigation and integrated navigation. Two further chapters have been included which deal with the Global Maritime Distress and Safety System (GMDSS), a subject which will affect the lives of all international mariners in the next decade, and NAVTEX. Nevertheless, even though technology is becoming ever more sophisticated it would be a serious error to ignore the human link in the electronic chain of action. It is the ship's captain or navigating officer who bears the responsibility for position fixing.

Position fixing is now easily achieved by the use of one of the hyperbolic systems described in the chapter dealing with Decca, Loran-C and Omega. Each of the systems described, however, possesses limiting factors which cause fix accuracy to be less than perfect. For more precise position fixing, data received from orbiting satellites is processed, by a microcomputer, to determine the position of a ship to within 100 metres. In many cases fix accuracy surpasses this figure and may be better than 10 metres.

L.S.I. technology has been directly responsible for the development and production of miniaturized equipment. Miniaturization has in turn led to the production of low cost equipment which is more reliable than was possible a decade ago. Ten years ago, to compute a fix, a satellite navigation receiver required a computer the size of a small car. Today better quality equipment produces a more accurate fix from apparatus which is hardly bigger than a domestic transistor radio. In future it is likely that the overall size of equipment will remain static but the processing capability will be increased enabling the apparatus to encompass many of the mundane tasks of ship management. The reduced size and cost of modern electronic navigation equipment has brought complex apparatus within easy reach of the small boat owner. Although this book is aimed at the merchant navy officer, it will also appeal to small craft owners who wish to improve their understanding of current systems.

Modern electronic apparatus is increasingly becoming microprocessor based. Electronic navigation equipment is no exception. Although in many cases specific manufacturers' equipment has been depicted, where possible each system has been described with microprocessor applications in mind. Some of the equipments described are not microprocessor controlled but have been included because of their widespread use. The principle of operation is the same regardless of the use of a microprocessor.

Readers will find that system descriptions will also apply to many other types of apparatus which are controlled by a dedicated microcomputer.

Radar, Automatic Radar Plotting Aids (ARPA) and maritime communications systems are all discussed in depth in the companion volume to this publication, *Electronic Aids to Navigation: Radar and Communications*. The Radar and Communications volume is written on the same lines as this book with the technology of each system discussed in depth followed by the application of that technology to the task in hand.

L. Tetley I. Eng., F.I.E.I.E., M.R.I.N.
D. Calcutt M.Sc., C.Eng., M.I.E.E.

Acknowledgements

A book of this complexity owes much to the cooperation of various individuals and equipment manufacturers.

Firstly we would like to thank the Magnavox Advanced Products & Systems Co Ltd, who initially supplied extensive information on satellite systems and equipment. It was from this data that an embryo of an idea grew into this publication. In many cases we have had no personal contact with individuals but despite this they gave freely of their time when information was requested.

We are extremely grateful for the assistance that the following individuals and organizations gave during the writing of this book. We are particularly indebted to those organizations who permitted us to reproduce copyright material.

Our thanks go to the following individuals:

Mr Frank Cody
Miss D. Heyzer
Mr T. Fujino
Mr Thomas A. Stansell
Mr R. G. Stevens
Mr Clive Burnell-Jones
Mr S. Buckley
Mr M. J. Quee

Mr John Vince
Mr R. L. Hill
Mr J. Bloss
Mr David Baxter
Mr Steve Dempsey
Mr F. G. Farnham
Dr A. G. Johns
Mr Paul Machin
Mr A Adib

and to the following organizations:

Krupp Atlas-Elektronik
Koden Electronics Company Ltd
Frank Cody Electronics Ltd
Racal Marine Electronics Ltd
Rediffusion Radio Systems
S.G. Brown Ltd
Hawker Siddeley
S.T.C. International Marine Ltd
Zilog UK Ltd
The U.S. Defense Mapping Agency
The Hydrographer of the Royal Navy

Magnavox Advanced Products &
Systems Co
Racal Decca Controls Ltd
Salen UK Marine Services Ltd
Sal Jungner Marine
Simrad Trading A/S
Sperry Ltd
Walker Marine Instruments Ltd
The International Maritime
Organization (IMO)
Ocean Voice & INMARSAT

The following figures have been taken from the IMO publication 'Global Maritime Distress and Safety System' and are reproduced with the kind permission of the International Maritime Organization, London:

Figure 11.1, page 353; figure 11.2, page 356; figure 11.3, page 358;
figure 11.4, page 360; figure 11.7, page 364; figure 12.1, page 367;
figure 12.2, page 368; figure 12.3, page 369.

Last, but by no means least, we would like to thank Pamela, my wife, and Janet, Dave Calcutt's daughter for their efforts in typing the original manuscript.

Contents

1
Sonar navigation

SONAR (SOund Navigation And Ranging) is the acronym established to identify those equipments which rely for their operation on relfected acoustic energy in water. However, the term is widely used to identify all modern systems which propagate acoustic or electromagnetic energy into sea water to determine a vessel's speed or the depth of water under the keel. This book is not concerned with those specialized sonar techniques which are used for identifying submerged objects, either fish or submarines. A navigator in the Merchant Navy is interested only in the depth of the water beneath the vessel, an indication of the speed of his ship and the distance run. The first section of this chapter deals with the characteristics and problems which arise from the need to propagate energy in sea water.

1.1 The characteristics of sound in sea water

The effects of the environment on acoustic energy must be understood because sonar systems rely on the accurate measurement of reflected energy or a precise measurement of time. These effects can be summarized as follows:

1. **Attenuation**
   A variable factor related to the transmitted power, the frequency of transmission, salinity of the sea water and the reflective surface of the sea bed.
2. **Frequency of transmission**
   This will vary with the system, i.e. echosounding or doppler speed log.
3. **Salinity of sea water**
   A variable factor which affects both the velocity of the acoustic wave and its attenuation.
4. **Velocity of sound in salt water**
   This is precisely $1505 \, \mathrm{m \, s^{-1}}$ at 15°C at atmospheric pressure. Most echo sounding equipment is calibrated at $1500 \, \mathrm{m \, s^{-1}}$.
5. **Reflective surface of the sea bed**
   The amplitude of the reflected energy varies with the consistency of the sea bed.
6. **Angle of incidence of propaged beam**
   The closer the angle to vertical the greater will be the energy reflected by the sea bed.
7. **Noise**
   Either inherent noise or that produced by one's own transmission causes the signal to noise ratio to degrade and thus weak echo signals may be lost in noise.

Attenuation and choice of frequency

The frequency of the acoustic energy transmitted in a sonar system is of prime importance. To produce a narrow directive beam of energy, the radiating transducer is normally large in relation to the wavelength of the signal. Therefore, in order to produce a reasonably sized transducer which emits a narrow beam, a high transmission frequency needs to be used. The high frequency will also improve the signal to noise ratio in the system because ambient noise occurs at the lower end of the frequency spectrum. Unfortunately the higher the frequency used the greater will be the attenuation as shown in figure 1.1. The choice of transmission frequency is therefore a compromise between transducer size, freedom from noise and minimal attenuation. Frequencies in the band between 15 kHz and 60 kHz are typical for echo sounders fitted to large vessels. A high power is transmitted from a large magnetostrictive transducer to indicate great depths with low attenuation. Small light craft use echo sounders which transmit in the band 200 kHz to 400 kHz. This enables compact electrostrictive or ceramic transducers to be used on a boat where space is limited. Speed logs use frequencies in the range 300 kHz to 1 MHz depending upon their design and are not strictly sonar devices in the true definition of the sense.

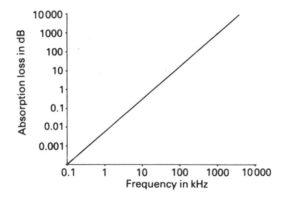

Fig. 1.1 A typical linear graph produced by plotting absorption loss against frequency. Salinity of the sea water is 3.4% at 15 °C

Another energy loss is caused by beam "spreading" which is independent of fixed parameters such as frequency, but depends upon distance between the transducer and the sea bed. Temperature also affects absorption. As temperature decreases, attenuation decreases. The effect of temperature is small and in most cases can be ignored.

Consistency of the sea bed

The reflective property of the sea bed changes with its consistency. The main types of sea bed and the attenuation which they cause are listed below. The measurements were made with an echo sounder transmitting 24 kHz from a magnetostrictive transducer.

Consistency	Attenuation
Soft mud	15 dB
Mud/Sand	9 dB
Sand/Mud	6 dB
Sand	3 dB
Stone/Rock	1 dB

These figures quoted are typical and are intended to be a guideline only. In practice there should be sufficient power in the transmitted signal to overcome these losses.

Salinity, pressure and the velocity of the acoustic wave

Since an echo sounder operates by precisely calculating the time taken for a pulse of energy to travel to the sea bed and return, any variation in the velocity of the acoustic wave from the accepted $1500\,\text{m s}^{-1}$ will cause an error in the indicated depth. The speed of acoustic waves in sea water varies with temperature, pressure and salinity. The graph, figure 1.2 illustrates the speed variation caused by changes in the salinity of sea water. Normal salinity is approximately 3.4%. As salinity increases, speed increases producing a depth indication which is too shallow. In practice errors due to salinity changes would not be greater than 0.5%. The error can be ignored except when the vessel transfers from sea water to fresh water in which case the indicated depth will be 3% greater than the actual depth. The variation of speed with pressure or depth is indicated by the graph in figure 1.3. It can readily be seen that the change is slight, and is normally only compensated for in apparatus fitted on survey vessels. Seasonal changes affect the level of the thermocline and thus there is a small annual velocity variation. However, this is very small and can be ignored.

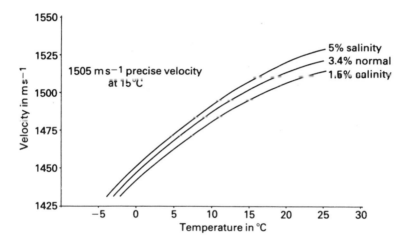

Fig. 1.2 Graph showing that the velocity of acoustic energy is affected by both the temperature and the salinity of sea water

Noise

Noise present in the sea adversely affects the performance of sonar equipment. Water noise has two main causes.
(a) the steady ambient noise caused by natural phenomena and
(b) variable noise caused by the movement of shipping and the scattering of one's own transmitted signal (reverberation).
Figure 1.4 illustrates that the amplitude of the ambient noise remains constant as range increases, whereas both the echo amplitude and the level of reverberation noise decrease linearly with range. Scattering increases and reverberation noise amplitude falls more slowly than the echo signal amplitude, however, because of beam spreading. Ambient noise is produced in numerous ways. It also possesses different characteristics at different frequencies and varies in behaviour with varying natural conditions such as rainstorms. Rain hitting the surface of the sea can cause a tenfold increase in the noise level at the low frequency (approx 10 kHz) end of the spectrum. Low frequency noise is also increased,

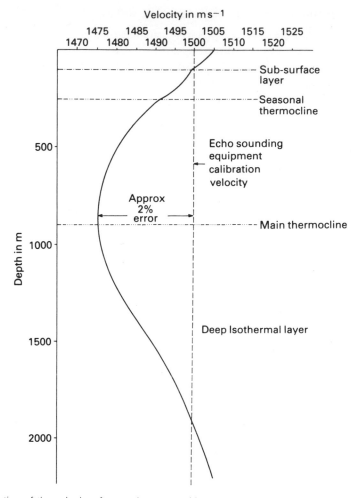

Fig. 1.3 Variation of the velocity of acoustic waves with pressure

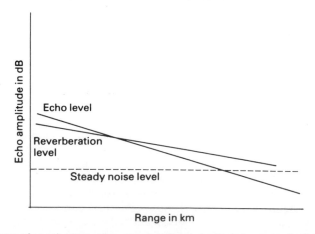

Fig. 1.4 Comparison of steady state noise, reverberation noise and signal amplitude

particularly in shallow water, by storms or heavy surf. Biological sounds produced by some forms of aquatic life are also detectable by the more sensitive types of equipment.

The steady amplitude of ambient noise produced by these and other factors affects the signal to noise ratio of the received signal and can in some cases lead to a loss of the returned echo. Signal to noise ratio can be improved by transmitting more power. This may be done by increasing the pulse repetition rate or increasing the amplitude or duration of the pulse. Unfortunately such an increase, which improves signal to noise ratio, leads to an increase in the amplitude of reverberation noise. Ambient noise is produced in the lower end of the frequency spectrum. By using a slightly higher transmitter frequency and a limited bandwidth receiver it is possible to reduce the effects of ambient noise significantly.

Reverberation noise is the term used to describe noise caused by one's own transmission. The noise is caused by a "back scattering" of the transmitted signal. It differs from ambient noise in the following ways:

(a) Its amplitude is directly proportional to the transmitted signal.
(b) Its amplitude is inversely proportional to the distance from the target.
(c) Its frequency is the same as that of the transmitted signal.

The signal to noise ratio cannot be improved by increasing transmitter power because reverberation noise is directly proportional to the power in the transmitted wave. Also it cannot be attenuated by improving receiver selectivity because the noise is at the same frequency as the transmitted wave. Furthermore reverberation noise increases with range because of increasing beamwidth. The area covered by the wavefront progressively increases causing a larger area from which back scattering will occur. This means that reverberation noise does not decrease in amplitude as rapidly as the transmitted signal. Ultimately therefore reverberation noise amplitude will exceed the signal noise amplitude, as shown in figure 1.4, and the echo will be lost. The amplitude of both the echo and reverberation noise decreases linearly with range. However, because of beam spreading, back scattering increases and reverberation noise amplitude falls more slowly than the echo signal amplitude.

Three totally different "sccattering" sources cause reverberation noise to be produced. Surface reverberation, as the name suggests, is caused by the surface of the ocean and is particularly troublesome during rough weather conditions when the surface is turbulent. Volume reverberation refers to the interference caused by beam scattering due to suspended matter in the ocean. Marine life, prevalent at depths between 200 and 750 metres, can cause this type of interference. Bottom reverberation depends upon the nature of the sea bed. Solid sea beds, such as hard rock, will produce greater scattering of the beam than silt or sandy sea beds. Beam scattering caused by a solid sea bed is particularly troublesome in fish finding systems because targets close to the sea bed can be lost in the scatter.

1.2 The transducer

The transducer is a converter of energy. RF energy, when applied to a transducer assembly, will cause the unit to oscillate at its natural resonant frequency. If the transmitting face of the assembly is placed in contact with, or close to, sea water the oscillations will cause acoustic waves to be transmitted in the water. Any reflected acoustic energy will cause a reciprocal action to take place. If the reflected energy comes into contact with the transducer face natural resonant oscillations will again be produced. These oscillations will in turn cause a minute e.m.f. to be created which can then be amplified by the receiver to produce the necessary data for display.

Three types of transducer construction are available, although only the first two have

been found to be sufficiently robust and reliable to be generally used. The three types
are: magnetostrictive, electrostrictive and piezo-electric resonators. both the
electrostrictive and the piezo-electric resonator types are constructed from piezo-electric
ceramic materials, and the two should not be confused.

Electrostrictive transducers

Certain materials, such as Rochelle salt and quartz, exhibit pressure electric effects when
they are subjected to mechanical stress. This phenomenon is particularly outstanding in
the element lead zirconate titanate, the material which is widely used for the construction
of the sensitive element in modern electrostrictive transducers. Such a material is termed
ferro-electric because of its similarity to ferro-magnetic materials.

The ceramic material contains random electric domains which when subjected to
mechanical stress will line up to produce a p.d. across the two plate ends of the material
section. Alternatively if a voltage is applied across the plate ends of the ceramic crystal
section its length will be varied. Figure 1.5 illustrates these phenomena.

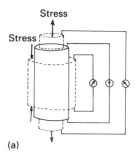

(a)

Fig. 1.5a An output is produced when a piezo-electric
ceramic cylinder is subjected to stress

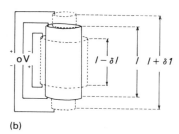

(b)

Fig. 1.5b A change of length takes place if a voltage is
applied across the ends of a piezo-electric ceramic cylinder

The natural resonant frequency of the crystal slice is inversely proportional to its
thickness. At high frequencies therefore the crystal slice is brittle, making its use in areas
subjected to large stress factors impossible. This is a problem if the transducer is to be
mounted in the forward section of a large merchant vessel where pressure stress can be
intolerable particularly in heavy weather. The fragility of the crystal also imposes limits
on the transmitter power which can be used because mechanical stress is directly related
to power. The power restraints thus established make the electrostrictive transducer
unsuitable for use in echo sounding apparatus where grreat depths need to be indicated.
In addition, the low transmission frequency requirement of an echo sounder means that
such a transducer crystal slice would have to be very thick. The crystal slice is stressed
by a voltage applied across its ends, thus the thicker the crystal slice, the greater is the
voltage required to stress it which in turn leads to insulation problems.

   The electrostrictive transducer is only fitted on large merchant vessels when the power transmitted is low and the frequency is high. This combination of factors is present in Doppler speed log systems.

   A Doppler speed log transducer is therefore an electrostrictive type and when fitted to a large vessel needs to be carefully constructed to withstand heavy pounding and stress. Such a transducer is manufactured by mounting two crystal slices in a sandwich of two stainless steel cylinders. The whole unit is pre-stressed by inserting a stainless steel bolt through the centre of the active unit as shown in figure 1.6. A change of length takes place if a voltage is applied across the ends of a piezo-electric ceramic cylinder. The bolt is insulated from the crystal slices by means of a PVC collar and the whole cylindrical section is made waterproof by means of a flexible seal. The bolt tightens against a compression spring which enables the crystal slices to vary in length, under the influence of the RF energy, whilst still remaining mechanically stressed. This method of construction is widely used on the electrostrictive transducers used in the Merchant Navy. For smaller vessels where the external stresses are not so severe the simpler piezo-electric resonator is used.

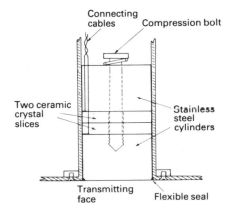

Fig. 1.6 Construction of a ceramic electrostrictive transducer

Piezo-electric resonator

This type of transducer makes use of the flexible qualities of a crystal slice. If the ceramic crystal slice is mounted in such a way that it is able to flex at its natural resonant frequency, acoustic oscillations can be produced. The action is again reciprocal. If the ceramic crystal slice is mounted at its corners only, and is caused to flex by an external force, a small p.d. will be developed across the ends of the element. This phenomenon is widely used in industry for producing such things as electronic cigarette lighters and fundamental crystal oscillator units for digital watches. However, a ceramic crystal slice used in this way is subject to the same mechanical laws as have previously been stated. The higher the frequency of oscillation, the thinner the slice needs to be and the greater the risk of fracture due to external stress or overdriving.

Magnetostrictive transducers

Figure 1.7 shows a bar of ferromagnetic material around which is wound a coil. If the bar is held rigid and a large current is passed through the coil, the resulting magnetic field produced will cause the bar to change in length. The change, which is only slight, may be an increase or a decrease in length depending upon the material used for construction. For

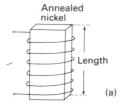

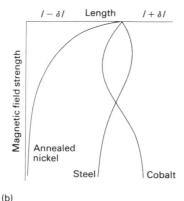

Fig. 1.7(a) A bar of ferromagnetic material around which is wound a coil

Fig. 1.7(b) Relationship between magnetic field strength and change of length

(b)

maximum change of length annealed nickel has been found to be the optimum material and consequently this is used extensively in the construction of marine transducers. As the a.c. through the coil increases to a maximum in one direction, the annealed nickel bar will reach its maximum construction length ($l - \delta l$). With the a.c. at zero the bar returns to normal (l). The current now increases in the opposite direction causing the bar once again to constrict ($l - \delta l$). The frequency of resonance is therefore twice that of the applied a.c. This frequency doubling action is conteracted by applying a permanent magnet bias field produced from an in-built permanent magnet. The phenomenon which causes the bar to change in length under the influence of a magnetic field is called 'magnetostriction', and in common with most mechanical laws possesses the reciprocal quality. When acoustic vibrations cause the bar to constrict, at its natural resonant frequency, an alternating magnetic field will be produced around the coil. A minute alternating current is caused to flow in the coil and a small e.m.f. is generated which is then amplified and processed by the receiver as the returned echo.

The annealed nickel bar is constructed of laminated strips bonded together with an insulating material in the same way as a low frequency transformer because of magnetic hysteresis and eddy current losses. Figure 1.8 illustrates the construction of a typical magnetostrictive transducer unit. The transmitting face is at the base of the diagram.

Magnetostrictive transducers are extremely robust which makes them ideal for use in large vessels where heavy sea pounding could destroy an unprotected electrostrictive type. They are extensively used with echo sounding apparatus because at the low frequencies used they can be constructed to an acceptable size and will handle the large power requirement of a deep sounding system. However, above approximately 100 kHz, magnetic losses increase causing their efficiency to fall to below the normal 40%. Above this frequency electrostrictive transducers are normally used.

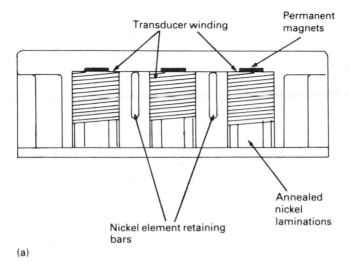

Fig. 1.8(a) Cross-section of a magnetostrictive transducer (courtesy of Marconi International Marine Co. Ltd.)

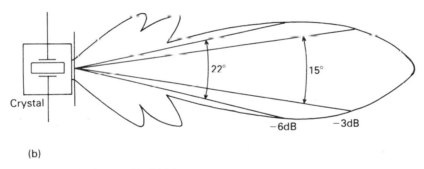

Fig. 1.8(b) Transmission beam with sidelobes

Transducer siting

The decision of where to mount the transducer must not be made in haste. It is vital that the active face of the transducer is close to, or in contact with, the water. The unit should be mounted well away from areas close to turbulence which will cause noise. Areas close to propellers or water outlets must be avoided.

Aeration is undoubtedly the biggest problem encountered when transducers are wrongly installed. Air bubbles in the water, for whatever reason, will pass close to the transducer face and act as a reflector of the acoustic energy.

As a vessel cuts through the water severe turbulence is created. Water containing vast quantities of air bubbles is forced under and along the hull. The bow wave is aerated as it is forced above the surface of the sea, along the hull. The wave falls back into the sea approximately one third of the length of the vessel from the bow. A transducer mounted aft of the position where the bow wave re-enters the sea, would suffer badly from the problems of aeration. Mounting the transducer ahead of this point, even in the bulbous bow, would be ideal. It should be remembered, however, that at some stage maintenance may be required and a position in the bulbous bow may be inaccessible.

A second source of aeration is that of cavitation. The hull of a vessel is seldom smooth. Any indentations or irregularities inthe hull shape will cause air bubbles to be produced which may lead to aeration of the transducer face. Hull irregularities are impossible to predict as they are not a feature of the vessel's design.

1.3 The echo sounder

In its simplest form, the echo sounding apparatus is purely a timing and display system which makes use of a transmitter and a receiver to measure the depth of water beneath a vessel. Acoustic energy is transmitted perpendicularly from the transducer to the sea bed. Some of the transmitted energy is reflected and will be received by the transducer as an echo. It has been previously stated that the velocity of sound waves in sea water is accepted as 1500 metres per second. Knowledge of this fact and the ability to precisely measure the time delay between transmission and reception, provides an accurate indication of the water depth.

$$\text{Distance travelled} = \frac{\text{velocity} \times \text{time}}{2}$$

where
velocity $= 1500\,\text{m s}^{-1}$ in salt water,
    time = time taken for the return journey in seconds,
distance = depth beneath the transducer in metres.
Thus if the time taken for the return journey is one second, the depth of water beneath the transducer is 750 metres. If the time is 0.1 second the depth is 75 metres, and so on.

The transmitter and transducer, must be capable of delivering sufficient power and the receiver must possess adequate sensitivity to overcome all of the losses in the transmission medium (sea water and sea bed). It is the likely attenuation of the signal, due to the losses described in the first part of this chapter, which determines the specifications of the equipment to be fitted on a merchant vessel.

The transmission of acoustic energy for depth sounding, may take one of two forms:
(a) A continuous wave system, where the acoustic energy is continuously transmitted from one transducer. The returned echo signal is received by a second transducer and a phase difference between the two is used to calculate the depth.
(b) The pulse system, in which rapid short, high intensity pulses are transmitted and received by a single transducer. The depth is calculated by measuring the time delay between transmission and reception.
The latter system is preferred in the majority of applications. Both the pulse length (duration) and the pulse repetition frequency (PRF) are important when considering the function of the echo sounding apparatus.

Pulse duration

The pulse duration effectively determines the resolution quality of the equipment. This, along with the display method, enables objects close together in the water, or close to the sea bed, to be recorded separately. This factor is particularly important in fish finding apparatus where very short duration pulses (typically 0.25 or 0.5 ms) and fast paper speeds on the display are used.
The discrimination (D) between echoes is:

$$D = V \times l \quad \text{in metres.}$$

where V = the velocity of acoustic waves,

   l = pulse length

For a 0.5 ms pulse length:

$$D = 1500 \times 0.5 \times 10^{-3} = 0.75 \text{ metres}$$

For a 2 ms pulse length:

$$D = 1500 \times 2 \times 10^{-3} = 3 \text{ metres}$$

Obviously a short pulse length is superior when the objects to be displayed are close together in the water.

A short pulse length also improves the quality of the returned echo because reverberation noise will be less. Reverberation noise is directly proportional to the signal strength, therefore reducing the pulse length reduces signal strength which in turn reduces noise. Unfortunately, reducing the signal strength in this way reduces the total energy transmitted which limits the maximum depth from which satisfactory echoes can be received. Obviously, a compromise has to be made. Most equipments are fitted with a means whereby the pulse length can be varied with range. For shallow ranges, and for better definition, a short pulse length is used. On those occasions where great depths are to be recorded a longer pulse is transmitted.

Pulse repetition frequency (PRF)

For a given pulse length, the *PRF* effectively determines the maximum range which may be indicated. It is a measure of the time interval between pulses when transmission has ceased and the receiver is awaiting the returned echo.

The maximum indicated range can be determined by use of the following formula:

$$\text{Maximum range indication } (r) = \frac{v \times t}{2} \text{ in metres}$$

where

v = velocity of sound in sea water (1500 m s^{-1})

t = time between pulses in seconds.

If the *PRF* is one per second (*PRF* = 60) the maximum depth recorded is 750 metres.

If the *PRF* is two per second (*PRF* = 120) the maximum depth recorded is 375 metres.

The maximum display range should not be confused with the maximum depth. For instance, if the *PRF* is one per second the maximum display range is 750 metres. If the water depth is 850 metres, an echo will be returned after a second pulse has been transmitted and the range display has been returned to zero. The indicated depth would now be 100 metres. A system of "phased" ranges, where the display initiation is delayed for a pre-determined period after transmission overcomes this problem.

Transmission beamwidth

Acoustic energy is radiated vertically downwards from the transducer in the form of a beam of energy. As figure 1.8b shows the main beam is central to the transducer face and shorter side lobes will also be produced. The beamwidth must not be excessively narrow otherwise echoes may be missed particularly in heavy weather when the vessel is rolling. A low *PRF* combined with a fast ship speed can in some cases lead to the vessel 'running away' from the echo which could well be missed. In general, beamwidths measured at the half power points (-3dB) used for echo sounding apparatus are between 15 and 25 degrees. To obtain this relatively narrow beamwidth, the transducer needs to be constructed with a size equal to many wavelenfths of the frequency in use. This fact dictates that the transducer will be physically large for the lower acoustic frequencies used in echo sounding. To reduce the transducer size, and keep a narrow beamwidth, it is possible to increase the transmission frequency. However, the resulting signal attenuation negates this change and in practice a compromise must once again be reached between frequency, transducer size and beamwidth.

1.4 An echo sounding system

Marconi International Marine Co. Ltd's "Seahorse" echo sounder (figure 1.9) is typical of many of the echo sounders in use at sea today. It has two ranges, either manually or automatically selected, to permit depths to 1000 metres to be recorded. Unlike earlier apparatus which displayed depth in either feet or fathoms, modern echo sounders display depth in metres to comply with international chart marking regulations. The shallow range on the "Seahorse" is 100 metres and operates with a short pulse length of $200 \mu s$ whereas the 1000 metre range uses a pulse length of 2 ms. Display accuracy for the chart recorder is typically 0.5% producing indications accurate to ±0.5 m on the 100 m range and ±5 m on the deepest range. Depth accuracy is the same for the digital display. However, because digital resolution is 0.1%, display accuracy is improved to 1 m for the highest range and 0.1 m on the shallow range. The digital display operates continuously whether the chart is in operation or not.

Operation

The earlier part of this explanation is devoted to describing the equipment purely as a chart recorder and as such it is a good example of a basic echo sounding system.

Transmission is initiated, when chart recording has been selected, by an output pulse from the inductive proximity detector. A low voltage d.c. supply connected to this detector produces a magnetic field. This field is interrupted, and a pulse produced, by a metal block mounted on a gear wheel driven by the stylus motor. Initiation of the pulse coincides with the point at which the stylus marks the transmission mark at zero on the sensitive paper. The gear wheel carrying the metal block revolves once only for each complete revolution of the stylus drive mechanism. Hence one transmission pulse is initiated each time the stylus reaches the top of the chart paper. The initiation pulse triggers the chart pulse generator circuit which introduces a slight delay, pre-set on each range, to ensure that transmission occurs at the instant the stylus marks the zero indication on the recording paper. The system trigger pulse, thus produced, has three functions:
(a) to initiate the output timing monostable circuit,
(b) to operate the blanking pulse generator, and
(c) to synchronize the digital and processing circuits.

The transmit timing monostable determines the period during which the 24 kHz oscillator runs and thus fixes the pulse duration. Pulse length is increased when the deep range is selected by the range switch (not shown). Power contained in the transmitted signal is produced by the power amplifier stage, the output of which is coupled to the magnetostrictive transducer with the neon indicating transmission.

During transmission the receiver input is blanked to prevent the high energy pulse from causing damage to the input tuned circuits. The blanking pulse generator also initiates the swept gain circuit and inhibits the data pulse generator. During transmission, the swept gain control circuit holds the gain of the input tuned amplifier low. At cessation of transmission, the hold is removed permitting the receiver gain to gradually increase at a rate governed by an inverse fourth power law. This type of inverse gain control is necessary because echoes which are returned soon after transmission ceases are of large amplitude and are likely to overload the receiver. The echo amplitude gradually decreases as the returned echo delay period increases. Thus the swept gain control circuit causes the average amplitude of the echoes displayed to be the same over the whole period between transmission pulses. However, high intensity echoes returned from large reflective objects will produce a rapid change in signal amplitude and will cause a larger signal to be coupled to the logarithmic amplifier causing a more substantial indication to be made on the paper. The logarithmic amplifier and detector stage produce a d.c. output, the amplitude of which is logarithmically proportional to the strength of the echo signal.

In the chart recorder display, electro-sensitive paper is drawn horizontally beneath the stylus. The paper is tightly drawn over the earthed roller guides by a constant speed paper drive motor. Paper marking is achieved by applying a high voltage a.c. signal to the stylus which is drawn at 90 degrees to the paper movement, across the paper on top of the left hand roller. The paper is marked by burning the surface with a high voltage charge produced through the paper between the stylus and earth. Marking voltage is between 440 and 1100 V and is produced by the print voltage oscillator running at 2 kHz. Oscillator amplifier output is a constant amplitude signal, the threshold level of which is raised by the d.c. produced by a detected echo signal. Thus a high intensity echo signal will cause the marking voltage to be raised above the threshold level by a greater amount than would a detected small echo signal.

For accurate depth marking it is essential that the stylus tracking speed is absolutely precise. The stylus is drawn by a belt controlled by the stylus d.c. motor. Speed accuracy is maintained by a complex feedback loop and tachogenerator circuit.

Digital circuits

The digital display section contains the necessary logic to drive the integral three digit depth display, the alarm circuit and the remote indicators. Pulse repetition frequency (*PRF*) of the clock oscillator is pre-set so that the time taken for the three digit counter to count from 000 to 999 is exactly the same as that taken by the stylus to travel from zero to the maximum reading for the range in use. The counter output is therefore directly related to depth.

When the chart recorder is switched off, the digital processing section, and the transmitter, are triggered from the processor trigger pulse generator circuit. Both the transmit and receive sections work in the same way as previously described. A low logic pulse from the trigger pulse standardizing circuit synchronizes the logic functions.

The d.c. output from the receiver detector is coupled via a data pulse generator circuit to the interface system. Unfortunately in any echo sounder it is likely that unwanted echoes will be received due to ship noise, aeration or other factors. False echoes would be displayed as false depth indications on the chart and would be easily recognized. However, such echoes would produce instantaneous erroneous readings on the digital counter display which would not be so easily recognized. To prevent this happening echoes are stored in a data store on the processing board and only valid echoes will produce a reading on the display. Valid echoes are those which have shown the same depth for two consecutive sounding cycles. The data store, therefore, consists of a two stage counter which holds each echo for one sounding cycle and compares it with the next echo before the depth is displayed on the digital display. The display circuit consists of three digital counters which are clocked from the clock oscillator circuit. Oscillator clock pulses are initiated by the system trigger at the instant of transmission. The first nine pulses are counted by the lowest order decade counter which registers 1 through 9 on the display lease significant figure (*LSF*) element. The next clock pulse produces a 0 on the *LSF* display and clocks the second decade counter by one producing a figure 1 in the centre of

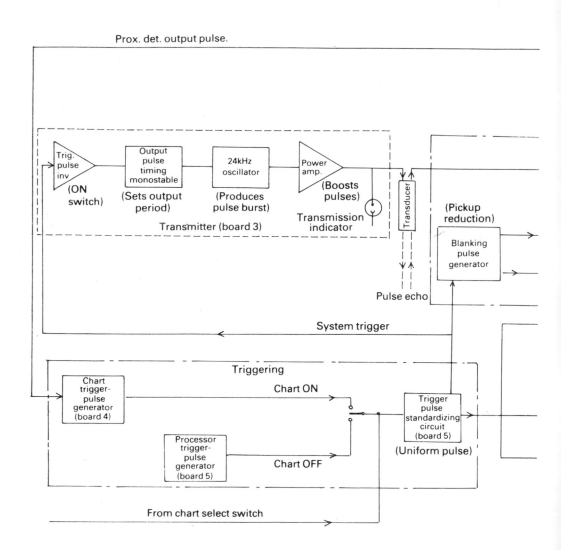

Fig. 1.9 A block schematic diagram of the Seahorse echo sounder (Courtesy of Marconi International Marine Co. Ltd.)

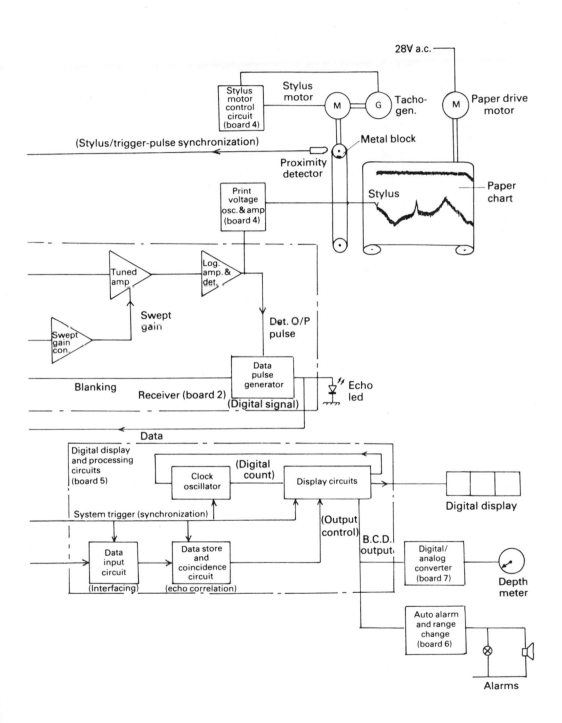

the display. This action continues, and if no echo is received, the full count of 999 is recorded when an output pulse from the counting circuit is fed back to stop the clock. Each time transmission takes place the counters are reset to zero and then enabled. This is not evident on the display because the data output from the counters is taken via latch which has to be enabled before data transfer can take place. Thus the counters are continually changing but the display data will only change when the latches have been enabled (when the depth changes). If an echo is received during the counting process, the count is stopped, and the output latches enabled, by a pulse from the data store. The new depth will now be displayed on the indicator and the counters reset at the start of the next transmission pulse. It is necessary that the clock pulse rate be directly related to depth. When the shallow (100 m) range is selected a high frequency is used. For the deep (1000 m) range the clock frequency is reduced by a factor of ten.

Depth information in BCD code from the display circuits is also coupled to a D to A converter, the output of which drives remote analog depth indicators. Auto depth alarm and range changing also operate from this code. Front panel thumbwheel switches enable a pre-set depth to be input. The BCD output of the counter is compared with the pre-set level. When the depth of water beneath the transducer is less than the selected depth an audible and visual alert is triggered. Automatic depth alarm is but one facility which illustrates how versatile an echo sounder can be once an echo pulse has been digitized.

1.5 Echo sounder apparatus display systems

There are numerous ways in which the depth indication can be displayed. Each system has its merits and each is popular with one or more sections of the maritime industry. In general each system is purely a timing circuit followed by the necessary processing circuitry to drive the display system. The five main systems in general use are briefly described here.

(a) The chart recorder

This is the most popular system of all because it provides a constant depth indication and a record of the depth data over a long period of time. Figure 1.9 illustrates the equipment necessary for the accurate operation of this system. The operation was described in the previous section. Overall depth accuracy depends upon the quality of the stylus motor speed control system. This type of display is expensive to produce and requires a supply of electro-sensitive chart recording paper.

(b) The digital display

Digital displays are gaining popularity because they are able to provide a clear and accurate indication of depth. Their only failing however is that they are unable to provide a past record of depth indication as with a chart recorder.

Any number of digits are possible in the display, but only three are necessary to provide a useful range of depth indications. Each of the seven segment display chips, in figure 1.10, has its cathode returned to chassis. The seven segment connections are driven by the outputs of a four bit binary decoder which decodes the output of the latch chip. IC1/2/3 are decade counters clocked from a master oscillator via the enable gate. The oscillatory frequency is directly related to the depth range selected. During the period between transmitted pulses the three counters must be capable of counting 999 clock pulses to register 999 on the display. If this number is exceeded without an echo being received, the display can be made to flash as an overrange warning. The logic circuitry for this operation

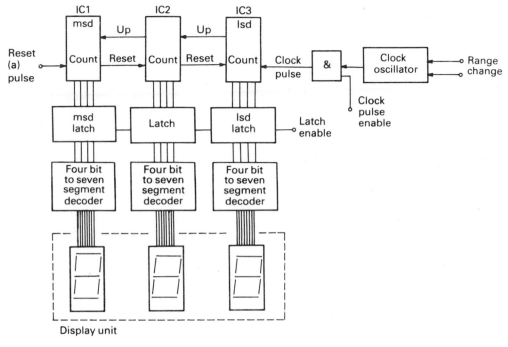

Fig. 1.10 Three digit display unit for an echo sounder

is not shown on the diagram. It should be noted that with the use of large scale integration (LSI) logic, figure 1.10 could be simplified by combining the count/latch decoders in one monolithic construction.

Sequence of Operation

As the transmitter fires, reset line (a) resets the counters to zero. The display is not affected, because the latches are not enabled, and will display the previous reading. Immediately after firing, the reset (a) pulse is removed and a clock enable pulse is applied to the AND gate. IC1, the least significant digit (lsd) counter commences counting the clock pulses. When a count of ten is reached the next decade counter is clocked via the UP line. This sequence continues with each of the three counters being clocked in decades until the returned echo is received. The processed echo signal produces a disable pulse to the enable input to the AND gate to prevent further clocking of the counters. The three latches are now enabled and the four bit data from each counter are decoded to produce a new depth indication on the display. The depth range is changed by changing the frequency of the clock oscillator. The deeper the range selected, the lower will be the clock frequency.

Digital display circuits will differ in design depending upon a number of factors but each will operate in a way similar to the one described here.

(c) The rotating l.e.d. display

This type of display is inexpensive and is therefore popular with small craft operators. The overall accuracy of this type of display, shown in figure 1.11, is dependent upon the speed precision of the servo system and the quality of the range calibration on the outer edge of the circular display. The servo system accurately rotates an arm on which is mounted three

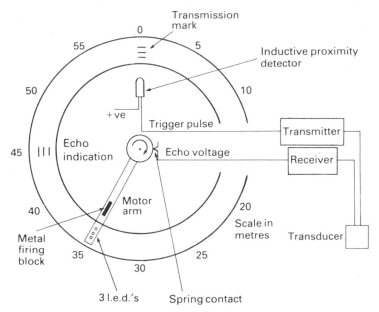

Fig. 1.11   Rotating light emitting diode display

light emitting diodes and a metal block. Each time the arm is at zero the block interrupts the magnetic field of the proximity detector to produce the transmitter trigger pulse. A small feedback pulse, caused by signal breakthrough into the receiver, is coupled via the spring contact to the three l.e.d.s causing them to light and indicate that transmission has taken place. At some time during one revolution of the servo arm, the amplified echo signal produces a voltage pulse to cause the l.e.d.s to illuminate to indicate the depth. If the depth is greater than the range selected, the echo willl return after the transmitter has fired a second time. A false indication will therefore be produced.

Servo motor speed is changed with range. The slower the sped of rotation, the greater the range. This type of display is used extensively on small boat installations.

(d) Analog l.e.d. display

The accuracy of this type of display is limited by the number of l.e.d.s used. For absolute accuracy large numbers of l.e.d.s would be required and for this reason the system is normally only used as a secondary display as shown in figure 1.12. Each l.e.d. in the display is connected in series with the d.c. supply to one of the outputs of a bistable counter. There must be one counter segment for each l.e.d. and therefore on the display shown forty-one counter segments are required.

Sequence of Operation
At an instant before the transmitter fires, the counter segment outputs controlling the l.e.d.s are set to logic 1. The transmitter pulse enables the master clock oscillator pulses to be connected via a logic gate to clock the counter. The first bistable now changes state and the resulting logic 0 causes the first l.e.d. to light indicating that transmission has taken place. Each successive clock pulse clocks the next bistable lighting each of the l.e.d.s in turn until the returned echo processed signal disables the clock pulse and stops the operation. The frequency of the clock oscillator must be such that forty-one clock pulses are

Fig. 1.12 A combination digital and linear l.e.d. display system (Courtesy of SIMRAD)

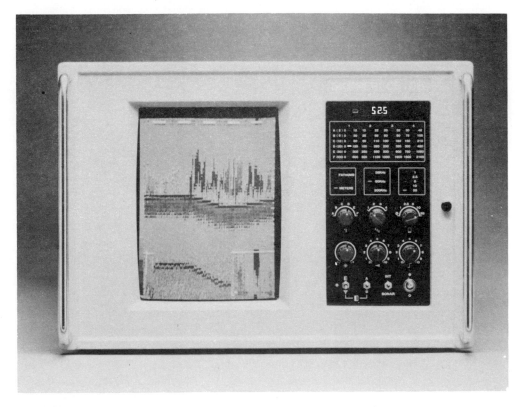

Fig. 1.13 An echo sounder with a visual display unit

produced in the period between transmission pulses. To increase the depth indication from 100 to 1000 metres simply requires that the clock oscillator frequency be divided by a factor of ten. The display should not be used when absolute accuracy is required. With forty l.e.d.s in the display, each l.e.d. indicates 2.5 metres on the 100 metre range and 25 metres on the 1000 metre range. To improve display accuracy more l.e.d.s would be required.

(e) The visual display unit (VDU)

Figure 1.13 shows the complicated display produced on the cathode ray tube face of the latest type of echo sounding apparatus. The system utilizes the technology developed for the "Space Invaders" type amusement machines. The apparatus is therefore extremely complex, expensive and unnecessary on those installations where an indication purely of depth is required. The display is favoured by the fishing industry where its versatility makes it ideal for fish finding situations. Once the echo, or echoes, have been processed and digitized they may be displayed in many different colours and arrangements. The experienced fisherman can recognize individual large fish, or other objects, simply by their shape and colour on the display. Colour is a function of echo intensity. The display can be split and enlarged to reveal small echoes which would otherwise have been lost in noise. The future of VDU displays is very bright. However, for purely bottom finding apparatus they are too expensive.

2
Speed measurement

2.1 Introduction

Speed measurement has always been of the utmost importance to the navigator. The accuracy of a dead reckoning position plotted after a long passage without star sights being taken, is dependent to a great extent upon a sound knowledge of the vessel's heading and speed. Modern navigators no longer fix the ship's position by dead reckoning alone. They are now able to use one or more of the many excellent electronic position fixing systems which have become available over the past decade. However, each electronic navigation system is only able to compute a precise position if it has available a number of parameters, one of which is the vessel's speed. The safety of the ship, and those on board, can be placed in jeopardy by incorrect data received from a speed log. Consider a modern vessel fitted with an Automated Radar Plotting Aid (ARPA) interfaced to the gyro-compass and speed log. If the speed log output is in error, the microprocessing section of the radar equipment receives the wrong speed data, related to time, when predicting the closest point of approach (CPA) to another vessel. In this case a potential collision situation could quickly arise.

Both safety and finance are factors which could be affected by an incorrectly calibrated speed log fitted to a VLCC. Should the speed of a VLCC (over 200 000 tons) exceed $10^{-2}\,\mathrm{m\,s^{-1}}$ (approx. ¼ knot) when the anchor is dropped, there is a great danger that both anchor and chain may be lost and consequently the vessel may run into danger. It is essential therefore that the navigator is provided with an extremely accurate indication of his vessel's speed at all times.

To be of value, the speed of an object must always be measured relative to some other point. At sea, speed may be measured relative to either the sea bed (ground reference speed) or to the water flowing past the hull (water reference speed). Both of these types of speed measurement are possible and both have their place in modern navigation.

The Pitot pressure tube log and the electromagnetic log provide speed indications with reference to water flowing past the log sensors. This type of speed information is vital when calculating the vessel's position by dead reckoning only. Similarly the same speed data are required by the satellite navigation receiver when, *between satellite fixes*, the microprocessor calculates the vessel's position by dead reckoning.

However, when a satellite fix is being computed the sat-nav receiver requires an input of ground reference speed to ensure that the satellite's altitude can be precisely computed and the fix accurately made.

Both the acoustic correlation type and the Doppler frequency shift type speed logs provide information on speed with reference to the sea bed. Where the depth exceeds about 200 metres both types of log measure speed by information returned from a barrier layer approximately 20 metres below the keel of the ship. This can, however, be considered to be ground reference speed.

This chapter deals with four types of log, all of which are in general use on board modern merchant ships.

2.2 The electromagnetic speed log

The em speed log works on Michael Faraday's well documented principle of measuring the flow of a fluid past a sensor by means of electromagnetic induction. The operation relies upon the principle that any conductor which is moved across a magnetic field will have induced into itself a small e.m.f. Alternatively, the e.m.f. will also be induced if the conductor remains stationary and the magnetic field is moved with respect to it. Assuming that the magnetic field remains constant, the amplitude of the induced e.m.f. will be directly proportional to the speed of movement. In a practical installation, the conductor into which the e.m.f. is developed, is the sea water flowing past the sensor.

The magnetic field is produced by a solenoid which may project into the water or be fitted flush with the hull. As the vessel moves, the sea water (the conductor) moving through the magnetic field has a small e.m.f. induced into it. This minute e.m.f., the amplitude of which is dependent upon the rate of cutting the magnetic lines of force, is detected by two small electrodes set into the outer casing of the sensor.

Figure 2.1 illustrates a solenoid with a magnetic field and a conductor connected in the form of a loop able to move at right angles to the field. If the conductor is moved in the direction shown, an e.m.f. will be produced across the inductor. In the case of an electromagnetic speed log, the conductor is sea water passing through the magnetic field. Fleming's Right Hand Rule shows that the generated e.m.f. is at right angles to the magnetic field (H). Induced current flowing in the conductor will produce an indication of the e.m.f. on the meter. If we assume that the energizing current for the solenoid is d.c. the induced e.m.f. is:

$$\text{e.m.f.} = \beta l v$$

where β = the induced magnetic field
l = the length of the conductor, and
v = the velocity of the conductor.

β is approximately equal to H the magnetic field strength. Therefore:

$$\text{e.m.f.} = Hlv \quad \text{assuming no circuit losses.}$$

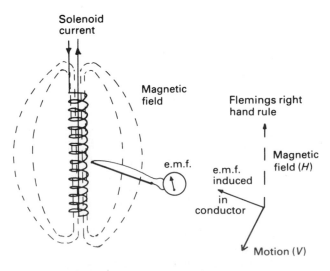

Fig. 2.1 Effect of moving a conductor through a magnetic field

To reduce the effects of electrolysis and make amplification of the induced e.m.f. easier, an a.c. is used to generate the magnetic field. The magnetic field strength H now becomes $H_m \sin \omega t$ and the e.m.f. induced is

$$\text{e.m.f.} = H_m l v \sin \omega t$$

If the strength of the magnetic field and the length of the conductor both remain constant then:

$$\text{e.m.f.} \simeq \text{velocity}$$

Figure 2.2 illustrates that the changes of e.m.f. brought about by changes in velocity produce a linear graph and thus a linear indication of the vessel's speed. The e.m.f. thus produced is very small but, if required, may be made larger by increasing the energizing current, or the number of turns, of the solenoid.

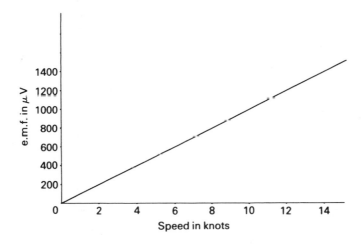

Fig. 2.2 Relationship between the vessel's speed and the output from the sensors

The following points should be noted:
(a) The a.c. supply to the solenoid produces inductive pick-up between the coil and the signal leads. This in turn produces a "zero" error which must be compensated for by "backing off" the zero setting of the indicator on calibration.
(b) The induced e.m.f. is very small (for reasonable amplitudes of energizing current) typically $100 \, \mu V$ per knot.
(c) The induced e.m.f. and hence the speed indication will vary with the conductivity of the water.
(d) The device measures the speed of the water flowing past the hull of the ship. This flow can vary due to the non-linearity of a hull design.
(e) Ocean currents may introduce errors.
(f) Pitching and rolling will affect the relationship between the water speed and the hull. Error due to this effect may be compensated for by reducing the sensitivity of the receiver. This can be done by damping out the oscillatory effect by using a C.R. circuit with a long time constant.
(g) Accuracy is typically 0.1% of the range in use, in a fore and aft direction and about 2% athwartships.

Figure 2.3 shows a typical sensor cutaway to reveal the solenoid and the pick-up electrodes. A speed translating system is illustrated in figure 2.4.

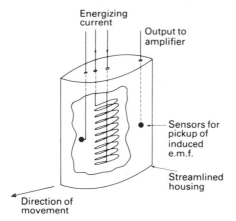

Energizing current

Output to amplifier

Sensors for pickup of induced e.m.f.

Streamlined housing

Direction of movement

Fig. 2.3 Constructional details of an electromagnetic log sensor

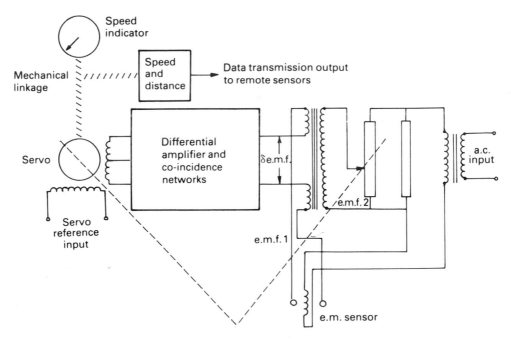

Speed indicator

Mechanical linkage

Speed and distance

Data transmission output to remote sensors

Servo

Differential amplifier and co-incidence networks

δe.m.f.

a.c. input

Servo reference input

e.m.f. 2

e.m.f. 1

e.m. sensor

Fig. 2.4 An e.m. speed log translating system

The small speed signal voltage e.m.f.1 from the sensor is applied to a differential transformer where it is compared with a reference voltage e.m.f.2 produced from a potentiometer across the input a.c. supply. The p.d. produced across the reference resistor provides the energizing current for the solenoid in the sensor.

If the signal voltage e.m.f.1 differs from the reference voltage e.m.f.2 an error signal voltage δe.m.f. will be produced. This error voltage is applied to the speed signal amplifier where it is amplified to produce enough power to drive the servo motor. The servo will turn, producing via the mechanical linkage, a reading of speed on the indicator. Also coupled to the servo shaft is the slider of the speed potentiometer which turns in the direction which will reduce the error voltage δ e.m.f. When this voltage becomes zero the servo ceases to turn. The speed indicator is stationary until the next error voltage δ e.m.f. is produced by a variation of the signal output e.m.f.1. Each time an error voltage δ e.m.f. is produced, the servo turns to cancel the error and thus balances the system.

An e.m. electronic speed log (see figures 2.5 and 2.6)

The potential developed across the transducer electrodes is proportional to magnetic field strength (and consequently the energizing current) and the flow velocity in the volume of water influenced by the field. The magnetic field strength is in no way stabilized against changes in ships mains, temperature, etc, but by effectively comparing the energizing current with the voltage at the electrodes, their ratio provides a measure of the ship's speed.

The input transformer T1 possesses a very high inductance and a step down ratio 5:1. This results in an input impedance, as seen by the pick-up electrodes, approaching 20 MΩ, which when compared with salt water can be considered an open circuit. Hence changes in salinity have no effect on the measured voltage and the resulting speed indication. A switched resistor chain (R1/R5) sets the gain of the overall amplifier in conjunction with resistor chain (R6/R10) which controls the amplitude of the feedback signal.

The output of IC1 is coupled, via IC2, which because of capacitive feedback (not shown), ensures that the circuit has a zero phase shift from T1 through T2, to the demodulator.

Demodulation is carried out by TR1/TR2 which are switched in turn from an a.c. reference voltage. This voltage is derived from a toroidal transformer monitoring the energizing current of the transducer. By driving TR1/TR2 synchronously, the phase relationship of the voltage detected by the electrodes determines the polarity of the demodulated signal. 0° and 180° phasing produce a positive or negative component. 90° and 270° produce no output and hence a complete rejection of such phase quadrature signals. The demodulated signal is applied to the Miller Integrator IC3 which in turn drives the current generator. Speed repeaters are current driven from this source.

Operation of the loop

With no vessel movement, there will be a zero signal at the input to IC1 and consequently a zero d.c. will appear at the multiplier chip input. No feedback signal is developed at the input to IC1. As the vessel moves ahead, the small signal applied to IC1 is processed through the electronic unit to produce a current flow through the speed repeaters and into the multiplier. There now exists an output from the multiplier, proportional to the speed repeater current and the "reference" voltage produced by the toroidal transformer monitoring the transducer energizing current. The a.c. voltage from the multiplier is fed back to IC1 in series with, and 180° out of phase with, the small signal at the secondary of T1. This a.c. signal rises slowly and eventually, with the time constant of the demodulator, is equal to the signal p.d. developed across T1. At this time the resultant signal applied to IC1 falls to zero and therefore the demodulator output remains at a constant figure. Any further change in speed results in an imbalance in the secondary of T1 producing a resultant a.c. signal to IC1. As a result, the demodulator output increases or decreases (faster or slower ship's speed) until the balance condition is restored. The speed repeaters will indicate the appropriate change of speed.

Distance integration

The speed current is passed through a resistive network on the distance integration board, in order that a proportional voltage may be produced for integration. Output of this board

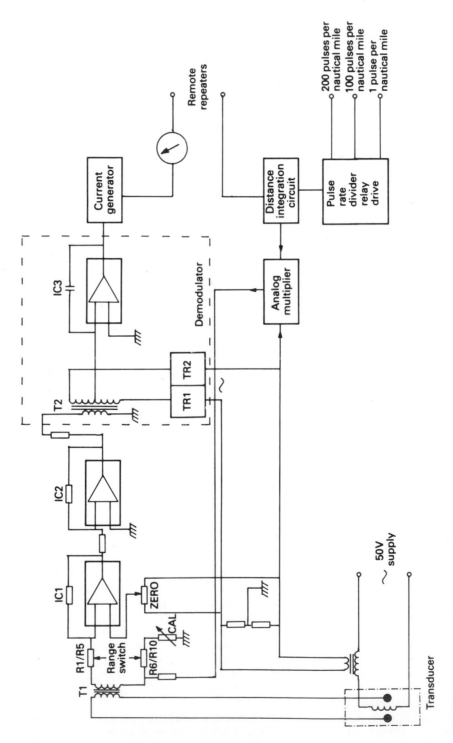

Fig. 2.5 A simplified diagram of the Walker EM4 electromagnetic log (Courtesy of Thomas Walker and Son Ltd.)

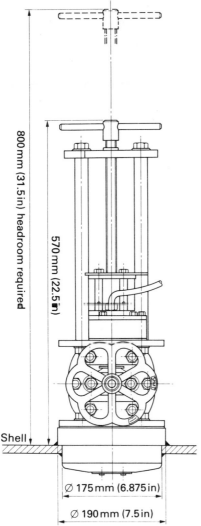

800 mm (31.5 in) headroom required

570 mm (22.5 in)

Shell

∅ 175 mm (6.875 in)

∅ 190 mm (7.5 in)

Fig. 2.6 The electromagnetic transducer assembly (Courtesy of Thomas Walker and Son Ltd.)

is a pulse train, the rate of which is proportional to the indicated speed. The 10 ms pulses are coupled to the relay drive board which contains the necessary logic to produce the following outputs: 200 pulses per nautical mile, 100 pulses per nautical mile and 1 pulse per nautical mile.

The log has been provided with a "test" facility. When switched to "test" the inputs to IC1 are re-arranged so that the feedback signal from the analog multiplier provides a signal, which when demodulated drives current through the speed repeaters indicating full speed.

2.3 The pressure tube log

When a tube, with an opening in its base, is vertically submerged in water a pressure proportional to the depth to which the tube is submerged will develop in the tube. If the tube is held stationary the pressure will remain constant and is termed **static** pressure. If the tube is now moved, whilst keeping the depth to which the tube is submerged constant, a second force called **dynamic** pressure is developed. The total pressure in the tube is therefore the sum of both the static and dynamic pressures.

If a second tube is installed close to the first in such a way that the static pressure is the same but there is no pressure increase due to movement then the basis for a pressure tube speed log has been achieved. This type of log, when installed on a vessel, causes a speed indication to be produced from a diaphragm contained in a pressure chamber. The diaphragm is made to move upwards due to unequal pressure forces developed in the two tubes when the vessel is moving. Figure 2.7 illustrates the basic operating principle of the diaphragm.

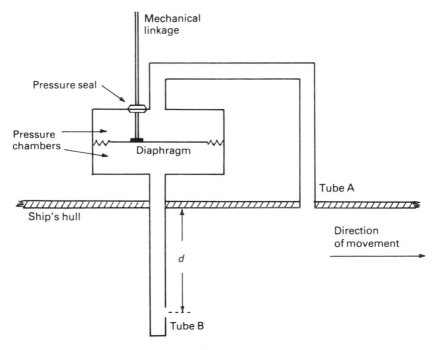

Fig. 2.7 Principle of a pressure tube type speed log apparatus

Tube A has a static pressure developed in it which is proportional to the vessel's draught. If there is no movement, a similar pressure is developed in tube B (subject to distance d). The diaphragm therefore comes under the influence of two almost equal and opposite pressures from which the display can be made to indicate zero. If the vessel now moves, in the direction shown, water will be forced into tube B producing a combined pressure in the lower half of the chamber equal to both the static and dynamic pressures. The difference in pressure, between upper and lower chambers, now forces the diaphragm upwards thus operating the mechanical linkage. Obviously the greater the speed of the vessel through the water, the more the diaphragm will move and the greater will be the speed indicated.

Unfortunately, the dynamic pressure developed in tube B, by the relative movement of water, is proportional to the square of the vessel's speed. Pitot's Law states that this pressure p is proportional to the square of the ship's speed v times the coefficient K.

$$p = K \times v^2$$

where K depends upon the tonnage, shape and speed of the ship, and the length of the protruding part of the Pitot tube beneath the ship (distance d).

This factor will produce a speed indication which is not linear, as shown in figure 2.8. Action must be taken to convert the non-linear diaphragm movement into a linear speed indication. In addition the assembly also produces a numerical indication of distance travelled through the water, which once again would be in error if it were derived from the non-linear dynamic pressure change.

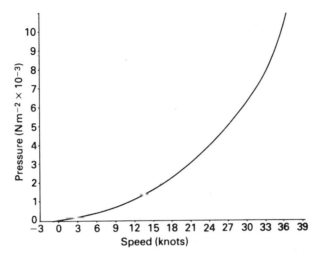

Fig. 2.8 Graph illustrating the non-linear increase in pressure with speed

Figure 2.9 is the basic mechanical diagram of the SAL Jungner Marine SAL24 Pitot type speed log which includes two repeating systems for speed and distance data transmission to remote indicators on the ship's bridge. This system has been superseded by the SAL24E which replaces much of the mechanical apparatus with electronics. The original log has been included because it is still in use on many vessels and is a fine example of a pressure type speed log system.

Method of operation

An increase in the vessel's speed will cause an increase in the dynamic pressure below the diaphragm in the pressure chamber (1). This causes the diaphragm to move upwards, pushing the pressure rod (2) and moving the lever (3) to the right on pivot (4). The upper end of the lever (3) moves the electric start contact (5) to the right to connect power to the reversible motor (6). The motor now turns causing the main shaft (7) to move the spiral cam (8) clockwise. This action tilts the lever (9), also pivoted on (4), to the left. The deflection stretches the main spring producing, via lever (3), a downward pressure on the diaphragm causing it to cease rising at an intermediate position. This is achieved when equilibrium has been established between the dynamic pressure, acting on the lower side of the diaphragm, and the counter pressure from the spring on the upper side. At this point the motor (6) stops and thus holds the spiral cam (8) in a fixed position indicating speed. This method of pressure compensation provides accurate indications of speed independent of alterations of the diaphragm caused by ageing.

The shape of the spiral cam (8) has been carefully calculated to produce a linear

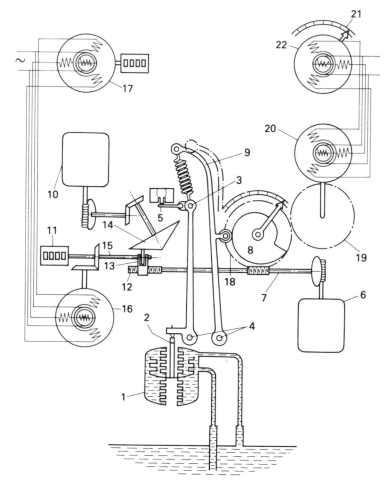

Fig. 2.9 Mechanical assembly of the SAL24 pressure log (Courtesy of SAL Jungner Marine)

1. pressure chamber
2. pressure rod
3. lever
4. pivot
5. electric start contact
6. reversible motor
7. main shaft
8. spiral cam
9. lever
10. constant speed motor
11. distance counter
12. screw spindle
13. friction wheel
14. distance cone
15. distance shaft
16. servo transmission system
17. servo transmission system
18. gear wheels
19. gear wheels
20. speed servo transmitter
21. remote speed indicator
22. servo receiver

indication of speed from the non-linear characteristic of the system. Also attached to the spiral cam is a second gearing mechanism which transfers the movement of the speed indicator to the three phase speed transmission system. An identical servo receiver is fitted in the remote speed repeater unit fitted on the ship's bridge and thus remote speed indication has been achieved.

Distance recording is achieved by using a constant speed motor (10) which drives, via friction gearing, the distance counter (11). The constant speed motor has been used in order that a distance indication may be produced which is independent of the non-linear characteristic of the system. The motor is started by contact (5) as previously described. The main shaft (7), whose angle of rotation is directly proportional to the speed of the ship, is fitted with a screw spindle (12). The rotation of the shaft causes a lateral displacement of the friction wheel (13). At zero speed, the friction wheel rests against the apex of the distance cone (14), whilst at maximum speed the wheel has been displaced along the cone to the rim. The distance indicator (11) is driven from the constant speed motor (10) via the cone. The nearer to the rim of the cone the friction wheel rides – the faster will be the distance indication drive.

Revolutions of the distance shaft (15) are transmitted to the remote distance indicator via the servo transmission system (16 & 7). Gear wheels (18 & 19) drive the speed servo transmitter (20) which operates the remote speed indicator (21) from the servo receiver (22).

The SAL 24E utilizes the same system of tubes, pressure tank and diaphragm to convert pressure variations due to speed, to electrical pulses suitable to drive the electronic circuits which replace much of the mechanical arrangement of the SAL 24 log. The distance integration mechanism with servo, cone and counter has been fully replaced by electronic circuitry. Figure 2.10 illustrates a typical installation of the Pitot system on board a vessel with a double bottom. The Pitot tube is encased in a sea-cock arrangement with valve control to enable the tube to be withdrawn, without shipping water, when the vessel goes alongside. A wingnut arrangement holds the tube in its withdrawn position. The static pressure opening is controlled by the use of a valve. Both dynamic and static pressures are transferred via air collectors and strainer valves to the pressure chamber. The strainer valves are designed to prevent water oscillations in the interconnecting pipes during operation. Such oscillations would cause the diaphragm to oscillate causing errors in the indication of speed.

Operation of SAL 24E

As previously described, when the vessel moves forwards, the dynamic pressure acting on the under side of the diaphragm causes it to move upwards forcing the pushrod upwards. In figure 2.11 this causes the pushrod arm assembly to move to the right on the pivot, increasing the tension on the spring assembly and producing an output from the differential transformer. This output is applied to the USER board, shown in figure 2.12, where it is processed to provide the drive for the speed servo control winding via a ± 24V switching amplifier. The servo now turns and rotates the cam assembly via gearing and the drive shaft. An increase in speed is now shown on the speed pointer. As the cam rotates it forces the balance arm to the left and tightens the spring until the pushrod arm and the diaphragm bellows are balanced. The cam is carefully designed so that the spring force is proportional to the square of the rotation angle and thus the non-linearity of the pressure system is counteracted. The speed potentiometer turns together with the speed pointer to provide an input to the UDIS board. This input produces various outputs enabling the system to be interfaced with other electronic equipment.

Distance board UDIS contains a precision voltage controlled oscillator the output of which is controlled by the gradient and zeroing circuit. The zeroing part of this circuit enables the equipment to be accurately calibrated for fittings on different types of vessel. The output from the speed potentiometer, in the mechanical unit, produces an increasing voltage gradient, of 0.1 V per knot, at the output of the gradient circuit to control the frequency of the VCO. The frequency of the VCO thus increases linearly with speed and after being divided by a factor of ten, provides outputs of 20 000 pulses per nautical mile. This output is subdivided on board UDCK to produce the required outputs of 200 pulses.

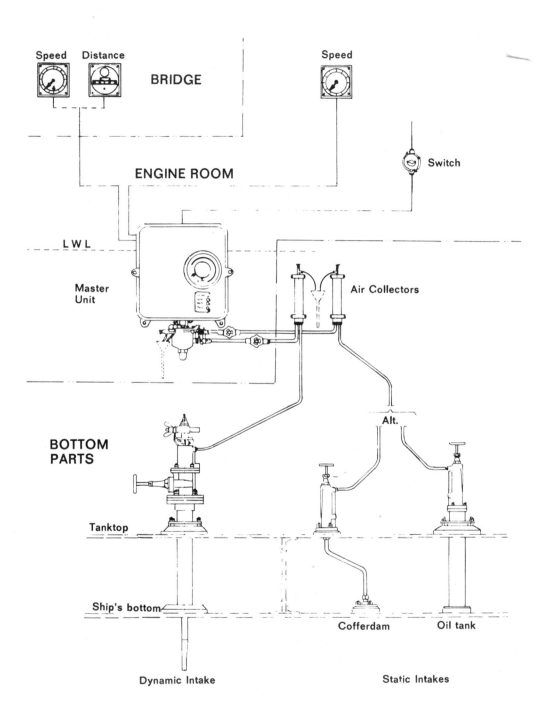

Fig. 2.10 A typical 'Pitot' pressure tube log installation (Courtesy of SAL Jungner Marine)

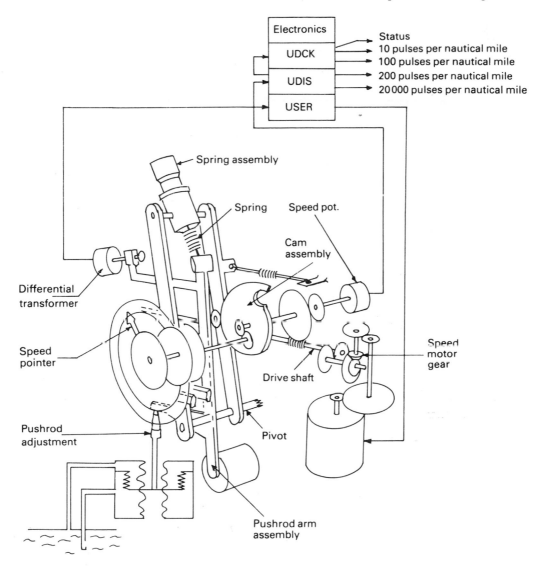

Fig. 2.11 The SAL 24E Pressure/Mechanical Assembly (Courtesy of SAL Jungner Marine)

per nautical mile, 100 pulses per nautical mile and 10 pulses per nautical mile to enable the system to be interfaced with other navigation equipment. The outputs of 0.1 V per knot are used to drive analog voltmeter type remote speed indicators. The 20 000 pulses per nautical mile output is used to provide information for the remote potentiometer servo type distance indicator on the ship's bridge.

Accuracy of the Pitot type speed log when correctly installed and calibrated is typically better than 0.75% of the range in use. However, the log cannot provide an indication of sideways movement of the vessel.

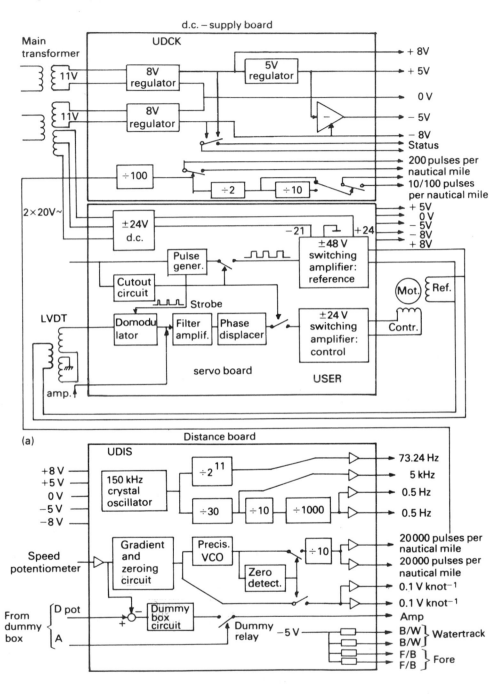

Fig. 2.12 Electronic diagram of the SAL 24E pressure speed log (Courtesy of SAL Jungner Marine)

2.4 Acoustic correlation log

Unlike the two previously described speed logs, which measure the vessel's speed with respect to water, the SAL-ACCOR log measures the speed with respect to the sea bed or to a water mass.

The log derives the vessel's speed by the use of a patented "Acoustic correlation" method. This is a way of combining the properties of sonic waves in sea water with a correlation technique. Speed measurement is achieved by bottom tracking to a maximum depth of 200 metres. If the bottom echo becomes weak or the depth exceeds 200 m, the system automatically switches to "water mass tracking" and will record the vessel's speed with respect to a water mass approximately 12 metres below the keel.

The transducer transmits pulses of energy at a frequency of 150 kHz from its two active piezo-ceramic elements which are arranged in the fore and aft line of the vessel (see figure 2.13). Each element transmits in a wide lobe perpendicular to the sea bed. As with an echo sounder, the transducer elements are switched to the receive mode after transmission has taken place. The sea bed, or water mass, reflected signals possess a time delay (T) dependent upon the contour of the sea bed as shown in figure 2.14. Thus the received echo is uniquely a function of the instantaneous position of each sensor element and the ship's speed. The echo signal, therefore, in one channel will be identical with that in the other channel but will possess a time delay as indicated in figure 2.14.

The time delay (T) can be presented:

$$T = 0.5 \times \frac{S}{v} \quad \text{in seconds}$$

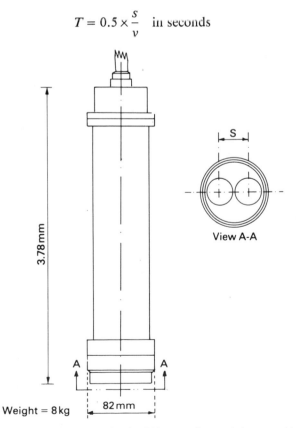

Weight = 8 kg

Fig. 2.13 Piezo-electric ceramic transducer for the SAL acoustic correlation speed log

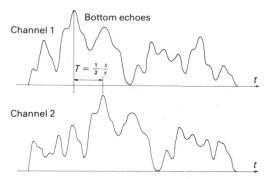

Fig. 2.14 Illustration of the time delay (*T*) between each channel echo signal

where
s = the distance between the receiving elements
v = the ship's velocity.

In the SAL-ACCOR log, the speed is accurately estimated by a correlation technique. The distance between the transducer elements (*s*) is precisely fixed, therefore when the time (*T*) has been determined, the speed of the vessel (*v*) can be accurately calculated.

It should be noted that the time delay (*T*) calculated is that between the two transducer echoes and **not** that between transmission and reception. Temperature and salinity, the variables of sound velocity in sea water, will not affect the calculation. Each variable has the same influence on each received echo channel. Consequently the variables will cancel.

It is also possible to utilize the time delay (*T*) between transmission and reception to calculate depth as is done in normal echo sounding apparatus. This provides an additional echo sounding facility on this apparatus.

In this case the depth (*d*) is:

$$R = \frac{T}{2} \times C \quad \text{in metres}$$

where
C = the velocity of sonic energy in sea waer (1500 m s^{-1})

Dimensions of the transducer active elements are kept to a minimum by the use of a high frequency and a wide lobe angle. A wide lobe angle (beamwidth) is used because echo target discrimination is not important in the speed log operation and has the advantage that the vessel is unlikely to "run-away" from the returned echo.

Some electronics are actually housed in the transducer assembly as shown in figure 2.15.

Operation

The power amplifier produces the transmitted power at the carrier frequency of 150 kHz, under the command of a pulse chain from the clock unit to initiate the sequence. Each receive channel must be identical if errors are to be avoided. The returned echoes are first amplified and then applied to sampling units. Each sampling unit effectively simplifies the echo signal to enable interconnection to be made, between transducer and main unit, without the risk of signal deterioration. As with other functions, sampling is commanded by the clock unit, which also provides a highly stable 150 kHz for the carrier frequency. This frequency is also used as a standard frequency for the other functions on the electronics board where it is divided to produce the 5 kHz needed to operate some of the speed indicators. As the name suggests, the administration block controls most of the electronic functions. This block initiates the transmit/receive cycle, determines whether the system selects B-track or W-track operation and supervises the speed and depth calculations. The unit is effectively a microprocessor and operates to a pre-determined program in much the same way as a microprocessor. Actual speed calculation takes place in the correlation block. The process extracts the time delay by correlating the sampled output of each channel.

The speed unit provides the following outputs to drive both speed and distance counters:

(a) an analog voltage, the gradient of which is 0.1 V per knot, to drive the potentiometer servo type speed indicators.

(b) a pulse frequency proportional to speed. The frequency is 200/36 pulses per second per knot. Pulses are gated into the digital counter by a 1.8 second gate pulse.

(c) a positive/negative voltage level to set the ahead/astern indication or the B track/W track indication.

(d) 2000 pulses per nautical mile to drive the stepping motor in the digital distance indicator.

The depth unit provides the following outputs to drive the depth indicators when the echo sounding facility is used:

(a) an analog voltage the gradient of which is $0.01\,\mathrm{V m^{-1}}$, to drive the analog depth indicator.

(b) negative pulses of $2\,\mathrm{ms\,m^{-1}}$, which are used to gate a 5 kHz standard frequency into the digital depth indicator.

(c) a positive/negative voltage level to cause the indicator to display 'normal operation' or 'overrange'.

When correctly installed and calibrated a speed accuracy of ± 0.1 knot is to be expected. Distance accuracy is quoted as 0.2%.

The SAL-ACCOR speed log can be made to measure the vessel's transverse speed with the addition of a second transducer set at 90 degrees to the first.

2.5 Doppler speed measurement

The phenomenon of Doppler frequency shift is often used to measure the speed of a moving object on which is situated a transmitter (see Appendix 2). Modern speed logs utilize this principle to measure the vessel's speed, with respect to the sea bed, with an accuracy approaching 0.2%.

If a sonar beam is transmitted dead ahead of a vessel, the reflected energy wave will have suffered a frequency shift (see figure 2.15(b)) the amount of which depends upon:

(a) the transmitted frequency,

(b) the velocity of the sonar energy wave,

(c) the velocity of the transmitter (the ship).

The frequency shift of the returned wave is:

$$fd = ft - fr \quad \text{in Hertz}$$

where ft = the transmitted wave frequency,

fr = the received wave frequency.

The Doppler shift formula, for a reflected wave, is given as:

$$fd = \frac{2v\,ft}{C} \quad \text{in Hertz}$$

where v = the velocity of the ship,

C = the velocity of the sonar wave ($1500\,\mathrm{m\,s^{-1}}$ in sea water)

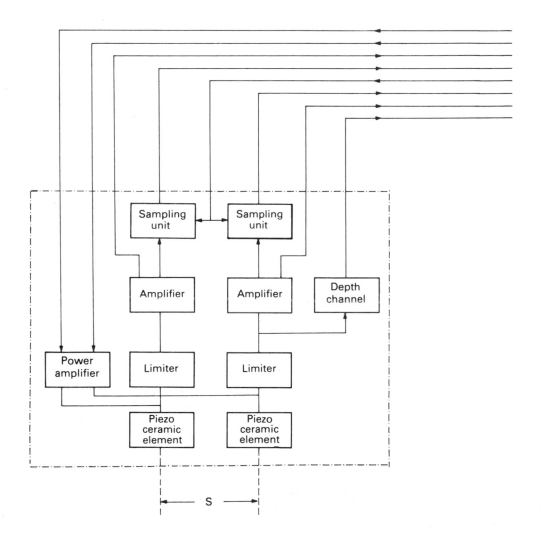

Fig. 2.15(a) Basic block diagram of the SAL-ACCOR acoustic correlation speed log

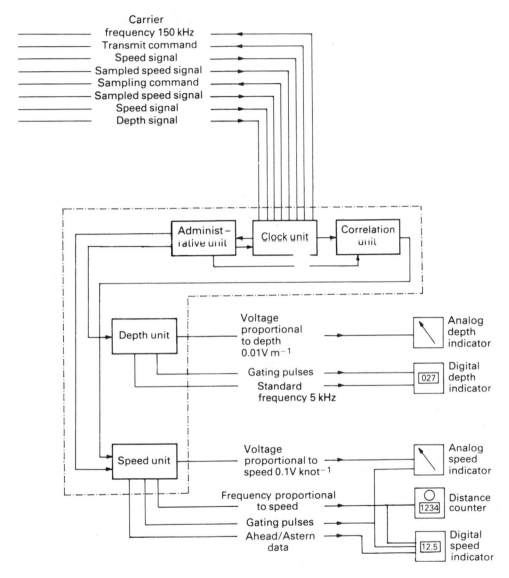

(Courtesy of SAL Junger Marine)

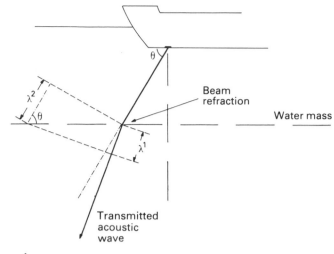

λ^1 = Wavelength after refraction
λ^2 = Wavelength before refraction

Fig. 2.15(b) Illustration of the change of wavelength which occurs as an acoustic wave crosses a watermass

Obviously there are no objects directly ahead of a vessel from which the acoustic wave can be reflected. The wave is therefore transmitted towards the sea bed, not vertically as with echo sounding, but ahead at an angle of 60 degrees to the horizontal. This angle has been found to be the optimum angle of incidence with the sea bed which will reflect a signal of sufficient strength to be received by the transducer. The shape of the sea bed has no effect on the frequency shift. Provided that the sea bed is not perfectly smooth, some energy will be reflected. The angle between the horizontal plane and the transmission must now be applied to the basic Doppler formula:

$$fd = \frac{2v\,\mathrm{ft}\cos\theta}{C} \quad \text{in Hertz}$$

Figure 2.16(a) illustrates this angle.
Using trigonometry:

$$\cos\theta = \frac{\text{Adjacent}}{\text{Hypotenuse}}$$

therefore:　　　　　　Adjacent $= C\cos\theta$　　(see figure 2.16(a))
For a propagation angle of 60 degrees $\cos\theta = 0.5$

$$\therefore fd = \frac{2v\,ft\,\cos\theta}{C} = \frac{v\,ft}{C}$$

It follows that if the angle changes the speed calculated will be in error because the angle of propagation has been applied to the speed calculation formula in this way. If the vessel is not in correct trim (or pitching in heavy weather) the longitudinal parameters will change and the speed indicated will be in error. To counteract this effect to some extent, two acoustic beams are transmitted, one ahead and one astern. The transducer assembly used for this type of transmission is called a "Janus" configuration after the ancient Roman

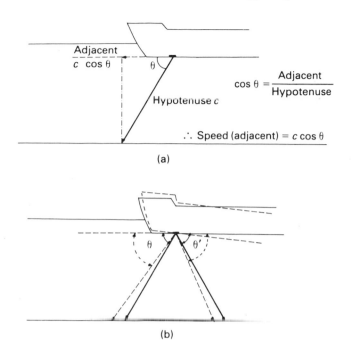

Fig. 2.16(a) Derivation of longitudinal speed using trigonometry
(b) The effect of pitching on the Janus transducer configuration

God who reputedly possessed two faces and was able to see into both the future and the past. Figure 2.16(b) illustrates the "Janus" assembly.

The Doppler frequency shift formula now becomes:

$$fd = \frac{2v\,ft}{C} + \cos\theta + \cos\theta)$$

($+ \cos 60° + \cos 60° = 1$) therefore the transmission angle can effectively be ignored.

As figure 2.16(b) shows, in heavy weather one angle increases as the other decreases almost cancelling the effects of pitching on the speed indication. Figure 2.17 illustrates the effect of the vessel's trim on the speed indication for two transducer arrangements. It can be seen that a three degree change of trim on a vessel in a forward pointing Doppler system will produce a 5% velocity error. With a Janus configuration transducer system the error is reduced to 0.2% but *not* fully eliminated.

The addition of a second transducer assembly set at right angles to the first one, enables dual axis speed to be indicated (Figure 2.18).

A precise indication of athwartships speed is particularly important on large vessels where the bow and stern sections may be drifting at different rates during docking manoeuvres.

Choice of frequency/transducer

As with echo sounding, the size of the transducer can be kept within reasonable limits by the use of a high frequency. This is particularly important in the situation where many elements are to be mounted in the same assembly. Unfortunately, as has already been discussed, attenuation losses increase exponentially with frequency. The choice of

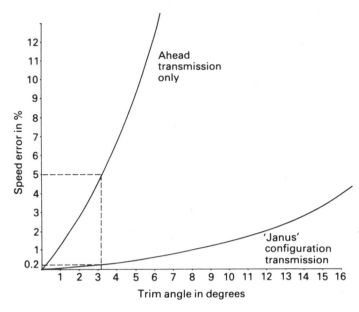

Fig. 2.17 Graph of speed error caused by variations of the vessel's trim

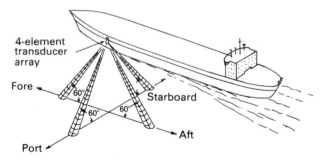

Fig. 2.18 Dual-axis velocity is measured by transmitting sonar pulses in four narrow beams toward the ocean bottom

frequency is once again a compromise between acceptable transducer size and the power requirements of the acoustic wave in order to overcome the signal losses due to the transmission media. Frequencies in the wide range 100 kHz to 1 MHz are typical.

The factor which has the greatest effect on speed accuracy is the velocity of the acoustic wave in sea water. Propagation velocity is determined by both the salinity and the temperature of the sea water through which the wave travels. However, velocity error due to these two factors can be virtually eliminated by mounting salinity and temperature sensors in the transducer array. Data from both sensors are processed to provide corrective information for the system. Alternatively the Krupp Atlas Alpha transducer system effectively counteracts the effects of salinity and temperature by the use of a phased beam.

ALPHA transducer array

The necessity of a tilted beam normally dictates that the transducer protrudes below the keel and therefore may suffer damage. It is possible to produce the required angle of propagation by the use of a number of flush fitting transducers. The Krupp Atlass Alpha (**A**tlas **L**ow Frequency **PH**ased **A**rray) multiple transducer 'Janus' assembly utilizes (4 × 18 = 72) flush fitting elements in each of the fore and aft positions. In theory any number of elements may be used, but the spacing of the elements must not exceed certain limits in order to keep unwanted sidelobes down to an acceptable level. Figure 2.19(a) illustrates part of the bow section of a vessel fitted with an Alpha transducer array. For clarity only a three element assembly is shown. If the three elements are fed with in-phase voltages the beam formed would be perpendicular. However, if the voltage to each element is phase delayed, in this case by 120 degrees, the main lobe is propagated at an angle θ which under these conditions is about 50 degrees. In this case the elements are fed with three sine waves each shifted clockwise by 120 degrees. For the 'Janus' configuration the same elements are alternately fed clockwise and counter clockwise. The Alpha system also overcomes the external factors which influence the velocity of acoustic waves in salt water and thus is able to counteract the unwanted effects of salinity and temperature change.

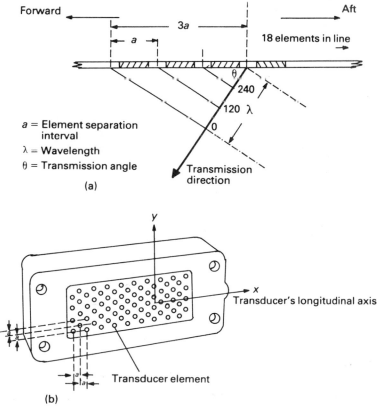

Fig. 2.19(a) Principle of the Alpha Transducer array
(b) A 72 element Alpha transducer array

The standard Doppler formula, from which velocity is calculated, comprises a number of parameters, two of which are variable. Ideally only the vessel's speed (v) should be the unknown factor in the formula. The velocity of acoustic waves (C) however, is also a variable. Since speed accuracy depends upon the accuracy of acoustic wave velocity in salt water it is advantageous to eliminate (*C*) from the formula.

$$fd = \frac{2v\,ft}{C}\cos\theta \tag{2.1}$$

With the Alpha system, the angle of propagation (*θ*) is a function of the velocity of acoustic waves because of the geometry and mode of activating the multiple elements. (Figure 2.19(a)). The angle of propagation is:

$$\cos\theta = \frac{\lambda}{3a} = \frac{C}{3a\,ft} \tag{2.2}$$

where a = the transducer element spacing and is therefore a fixed parameter.

$$\lambda = \frac{C}{ft} = \text{one acoustic wavelength in salt water.}$$

If equation (2.1) and equation (2.2) are now combined the Dopper frequency shift is:

$$fd = \frac{2v}{3a}$$

3a is a fixed parameter and therefore (*v*) is now the only variable.

As with echo sounding, two modes of operation are possible.

Continuous wave mode (CW)
Two transducers are used in *each* of the "Janus" positions. A continuous wave of acoustic energy is transmitted by one element and received by the second element. Received energy will have been reflected either from the sea bed, or, of the depth exceeds a predetermined figure (20 metres for the Simrad NL log), from a water mass approximately 6 metres below the keel. Problems can arise with CW operation particularly in deep water when the transmitted beam is caused to scatter by an increasing number of particles in the water. Energy due to scattering will be returned to the transducer in addition to the energy returned from the water mass. The receiver will become confused as the returned energy from the water mass becomes weaker due to the increasing effects of scattering. The speed indication is now very erratic and may fall to zero. The CW system is rarely used for this reason.

Pulse mode operation
To overcome the problems of the CW system, a pulse mode operation is used. This is virtually identical to that described previously for echo sounding where a high energy pulse is transmitted with the receiver off. The returned acoustic energy is received by the same transducer element which has been switched to the receive mode. In addition to overcoming the signal loss problem caused by scattering in the CW system, the pulse mode system has the big advantage that only half the number of transducers are required. It must be remembered that the system operates by measuring a *frequency difference* and not a time delay.

Comparison of the pulse and the CW systems
Pulse systems are able to operate in the ground reference mode at depths up to 300 metres (depending upon the frequency of the carrier used) and in the water track mode in any depth of water, whereas the CW systems are limited to depths of less than 60 metres. However, CW systems are superior in very shallow water, whereas the pulse system is limited by the PRF of the operating cycle. The pulse system requires only one transducer

(two for the Janus configuration) whereas separate elements are needed for CW operation. CW systems are limited by noise due to air bubbles from the vessel's own propeller particularly when going astern. Pulse system accuracy, although slightly inferior to the CW system, is constant for all operating depths of water. Accuracy of the CW system is better in shallow water but rapidly reduces as depth increases.

2.6 Simrad NL Doppler speed log

This log is typical of many of the speed logs in use in the Merchant Navy. The log provides accurate speed measurement in either a "Bottom Track" mode, when the depth of water below the keel is less than 20 metres, or in a "Water Track" mode if the water depth exceeds that figure.

The control unit (Figure 2.20(a))

Both trip and total distances travelled are displayed in digital form on the two mechanical counters of this unit. The operational controls are as follows:

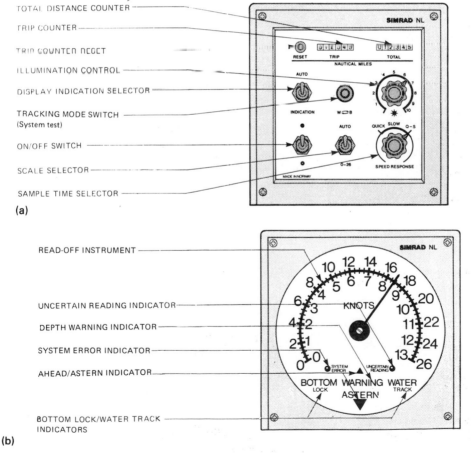

(a)

(b)

Fig. 2.20(a) Simrad NL control unit
(b) Simrad NL display unit

Display Indication Switch: In the "Auto" position: when operating in the W/T mode at speeds above 6.4 knots ahead, the speed scale is considered to be the most important and is therefore the only data displayed. At speeds below 6.4 knots the ahead pointer and W/T indicator are also illuminated. In position "Indication" ahead/astern and W/T & B/T indicators will be illuminated according to direction and mode.

Tracking Mode Switch: This permits quick changeover from the B/T mode to the W/T mode of operationn and vice versa. When switching on the unit, the log always commences in the B/T mode and automatically changes to W/T if, or when, the depth below the transducer exceeds 20 metres. If the optional test board is fitted, holding this switch depressed initiates a digital test sequence of the electronic receiving system. During this test the log will display an increasing speed to approximately 14 knots.

Scale Selector Switch: In the "Auto" mode, the range scale will automatically change as described in the circuit operation section. If the speed exceeds 25.6 knots, the log automatically switches to the lower scale 0 to 13 knots, the reading on which should be added to 25.6 knots for a true indication of speed.

Sample Time Selector: This three position switch enables the operator to select the system speed response most suitable for varying operational conditions.

(a) Quick: The log responds to swift fluctuations in speed due to the vessel pitching
(b) Slow: the normal operational mode
(c) Q–S: For use when there is excessive air in the water beneath the hull such as may be found during heavy weather.

The display unit

Figure 2.20 illustrates the main display unit and all the indications which the unit is able to produce.

Uncertain Reading Indicator: In the B/T mode l.e.d. will light intermittently when steep bottom contours or excessive air causes an indistinct returned echo. In the W/T mode the indicator lights when the returned echo signal is weak.

System Error Indicator: Will light if the transmitted pulse fails. If the test board is fitted this indicator lights if any of the d.c. power supplies, or the receiver, fails.

Depth Warning Indicator: Will flash if the depth below the transducer is less than 1 metre.

Operational Data

Carrier frequency	1 MHz
Speed accuracy	better than ± 2% above 5 knots. Within ± 0.1 knot below this figure
Minimum speed indication	0.1 knot
Distance accuracy	± 2%
Transducer beam width	3.5 degrees conical
Transducer tilt angle	60 degrees from the horizontal

Circuit operation in the water track mode (see figure 2.21)

The timing block contains a 16 MHz master crystal oscillator, the frequency of which is divided by sixteen to produce the transmitted carrier frequency. In the W/T mode, the transmission pulse period is 10 ms and is determined by the pulse length control circuitry. In the B/T mode the pulse length and the PRF are varied depending upon the depth of water detected. The timing unit is also responsible for generating the various timing sequences which control the main logic functions. Fore and Aft transmission is commanded by the

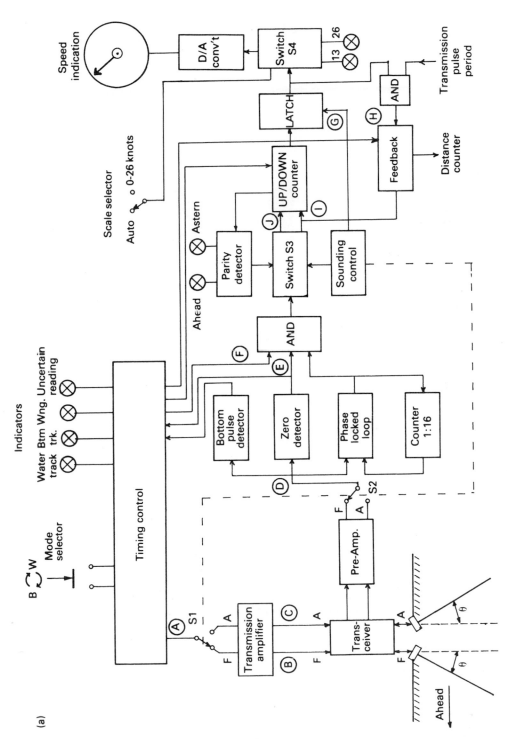

Fig. 2.21(a) Basic block diagram of the Simrad NL Doppler speed log

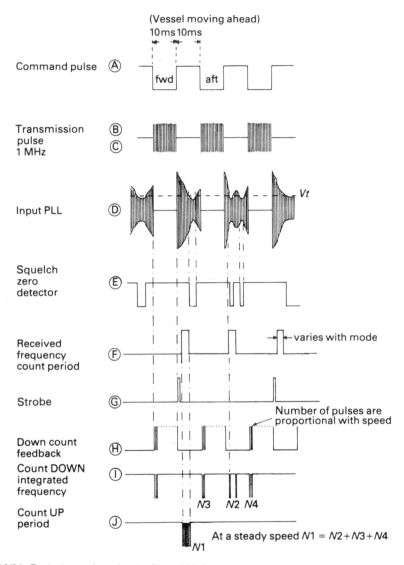

Fig. 2.21(b) Typical waveform for the Simrad NL log

sounding control circuit which switches S1, S2 and S3 to their required positions. Power in the W/T mode is 10 watts pulse power which is produced in the transceiver stage and directly coupled to the piezo ceramic Janus transducer assembly. Forward transmission is initiated before aft transmission. Received echo pulses (in the W/T mode from approximately 4 to 6 metres below the keel) will arrive at the transducer almost at the instant transmission ceases. The pulses are pre-amplified and applied to the switch S2 from where they are coupled to the following three detection circuits:

(a) The zero detector.
Output from this unit is a logic 1 for a normal detected signal level which exceeds a pre-set threshold voltage. If the signal level drops below the threshold, output from this circuit

falls to logic 0 to inhibit an output from the AND gate to the counter. This logic 0 is also applied to the timing board to operate the warning and/or uncertain reading indicators.

(b) Bottom pulse detector
If the sea bed is detected at a depth of less than 20 metres, output from this detector to the timing board causes the system to lock to bottom tracking.

(c) Phase locked loop
This forms the F.M. demodulator which detects the Doppler variation in frequency. This circuit also increases the received frequency by a factor of sixteen.

The AND gate produces an output of $16\,MHz \pm 16\,Fd$ when a zero detector pulse (E) (logic 1) arrives simultaneously with the receiver control internval pulse (F) from the master timing circuitry. Depending upon the inputs from the parity detector unit and the sounding control, the switch S3 will switch the inputs to the master counter to the state shown in the Table 2.1.

Table 2.1

Sounding control	Parity detector	
	Ahead	Astern
Ahead	up	down
Astorn	down	up

When the vessel moves ahead, the switch S3 firstly routes the forward transducer data (J) to the UP counter. The sounding control circuit then switches the aft data to the DOWN counter input. The difference between the two counts is proportional to the speed of the vessel. The resultant speed data are stored in the latch until the arrival of a strobe pulse (G) at the end of each count sequence. In order to reduce the deviation in the measured speed, the log calculates the average speed measured by a floating integration method. Floating integration is accomplished by returning the speed data through a feedback circuit to the DOWN input of the UP/DOWN counter. At a steady speed the count (N) will be equal on both the UP and DOWN counts, thus there will be no change in the indicated speed held in the latch logic circuitry of the D to A converter.

At a steady speed $N1 = N2 + (N3 + N4)$ as shown in figure 2.21(b). Under these conditions there will be no loading or resetting of the UP/DOWN counter. When the ahead speed changes, the difference between the UP and DOWN counts is proportional to the Doppler shift frequency. This difference is stored in the latch.

From the latch the speed data are applied to the nine bit logic switch S4. The switch selects the correct speed indication on the analog speed display. If the selector is in the auto position the logic circuit provides automatic switchover from the 0–13 knots scale to the 0 to 26 knots scale when the speed exceeds 12.8 knots. An automatic reciprocal action returns the indicator to 0–13 knots if the vessel's speed drops below 11.2 knots.

An analog voltage level (0–10 V) is produced by the D to A converter for speed indication.

Distance pulses are produced from the beedback circuit which contains a logic counter and a number of dividing circuits.

Multiple outputs are available as follows:
(a) 10 pulses per nautical mile to drive the internal digital distance indicator.
(b) 1 pulse per nautical mile for interfacing with extenal systems, and

(c) 200 pulses per nautical mile for interfacing with the satellite navigation receiver or radar.

2.7 The Krupp Atlas "Dolog" speed logs

Krupp Atlas speed logs have been developed, around the unique Alpha transducer array, to provide functions in addition to W/T and B/T speed indications. The Dolog 13D for instance is able to measure in addition to longitudinal speed, the transverse speed at both the bow and stern of the vessel. Transverse speed components are particularly useful during turning and docking manoeuvres as will be described later. Dologs utilize the Doppler frequency shift principle for their operation. However, because they operate at a lower carrier frequency than most Doppler speed logs, they are able to provide a speed indication in the B/T mode to greater depths. The control and display units of the Dolog 12D are illustrated in figure 2.22 and clearly show the versatility of the seven segment display and directional indicators. Analog displays may also be fitted if required. In

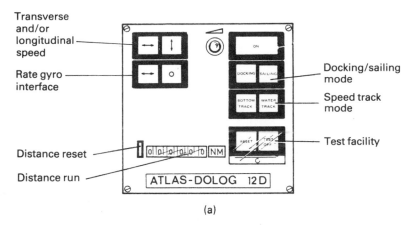

(a)

Fig. 2.22(a) Krupp Atlas Doppler log control unit

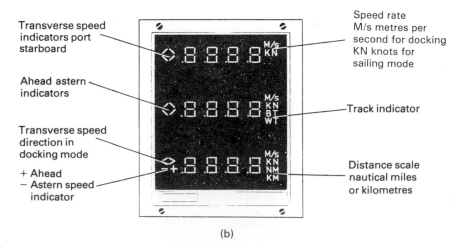

(b)

Fig. 2.22(b) Krupp Atlas Doppler log display unit

common with most Doppler speed logs, the Dologs are able to provide an indication of transverse speed when the vessel has been fitted with an additional transducer assembly at 90 degrees to the longitudinal assembly. Additionally it is possible to compute and display, in $m\,s^{-1}$, both bow and stern transverse movement during docking manoeuvres.

Brief technical details of the Krupp Atlas Dologs

Carrier frequency	100 kHz
Water track	If the depth exceeds 400 metres. The log tracks with reference to water mass approximately 10 to 30 metres below the keel.
Bottom track	To depths of approximately 400 metres.
Longitudinal speed accuracy	0.2% of measured value
Transverse speed accuracy	0.2% of measured value or 0.1 knot whichever is greater.
Transverse speed accuracy (stern)	0.2% depending upon rate gyro measurement
Distance accuracy	0.05 to 0.2% depending upon distance travelled
Longitudinal transducer breamwidth	6 degrees
Transverse transducer beamwidth	16 degrees
Beam deflection angle to the horizontal plane	Approximately 50 degrees
Transmission power	30 watts pulse

Speed vectors during a starboard turn manoeuvre
The Dolog 13D measures longitudinal and transverse speed, at the location of the transducers, by the Doppler principle. From this and the rate of turn, the transverse speed at other points of the ship can be computed and displayed. This facility is obviously invaluable to the navigator during difficult manoeuvres.

Figures 2.23(a) and (b) illustrate the speed vectors plotted from such data when turning to starboard without current effects, or a 4 knot current from the standard side. When the rudder is put hard over, the transverse speed indication vector (V_y) can point either to the side to which the rudder has been moved or to the other side. This will depend upon the longitudinal speed, the angular speed (rate of turn) and weather/tide conditions. If the longitudinal speed and transverse speeds at two points of the vessel are known, the ship's movement is completely determinable. In figure 2.23b, the bow transverse speed vector V_{3y} points to starboard, the direction of the ship's turning circle. In figure 2.23a however, V_{3y} points to port under the influence of the 4 knot current. The transverse speed development along the ship's length is represented by a dotted line (between V_{1y} and V_{3y}). The intersection of this line with the longitudinal axis produces a point at which the ship has longitudinal speed but no transverse speed. This point ($V_y = 0$) is normally roughly positioned in the fore third of the vessel if the ship is to turn along a circle about point M (the instantaneous centre of rotation). The effect of current from the starboard side causes point $V_y =$ to be outside the vessel and the ship is to turn around point M of figure 2.23a which is shifted forward relative to that of figure 2.23b. It is obvious therefore that an

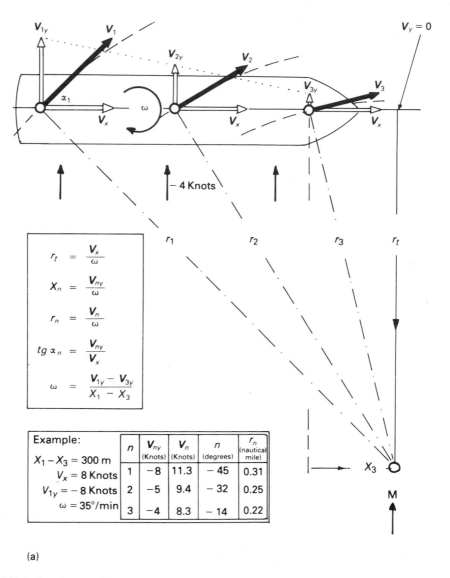

The equations shown in the figure:

$$r_t = \frac{V_x}{\omega}$$

$$X_n = \frac{V_{ny}}{\omega}$$

$$r_n = \frac{V_n}{\omega}$$

$$tg\,\alpha_n = \frac{V_{ny}}{V_x}$$

$$\omega = \frac{V_{1y} - V_{3y}}{X_1 - X_3}$$

Example:
$X_1 - X_3 = 300\ m$
$V_x = 8\ Knots$
$V_{1y} = -8\ Knots$
$\omega = 35°/min$

n	V_{ny} (Knots)	V_n (Knots)	n (degrees)	r_n (nautical mile)
1	−8	11.3	−45	0.31
2	−5	9.4	−32	0.25
3	−4	8.3	−14	0.22

(a)

Fig. 2.23(a) Speed vectors for a starboard turn with a four knot current (Courtesy of Krupp Atlas Elektronik)

accurate indication of transverse speeds at various points along the vessel enables the navigator to predict the movement of his ship.

Speed components with the rudder amidships
Figure 2.24 illustrates the effects of weather and current on the required heading of the vessel. The Dolog 12D is able to accurately measure the ship's speed in a longitudinal direction (V_x) and the transverse direction (V_y). The data derived from these measurements enables the navigator to predict the course to steer to optimize the performance of the vessel.

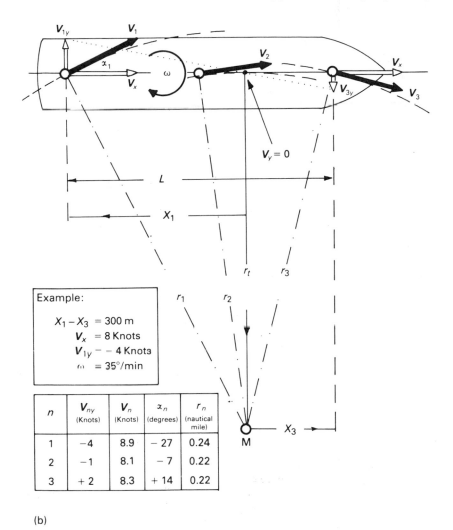

(b)

Fig. 2.23(b) Speed vectors for a starboard turn with no current (Courtesy of Krupp Atlas Elektronik)

By measuring both speed components (i.e. the velocity vector) it is possible to optimize the vessel's course by computing the drift angle:

$$\alpha = \arc \tan \frac{vy}{vx}$$

In the W/T mode this is the leeward angle (caused by wind) which is the angle between the "true course" (heading) and the CMG (course-made-good) through the water; in the B/T mode it is the angle due to wind and tidestream between the heading and the CMG over the ground. With the help of a two-component log the ship can be steered so that heading steered plus drift angle measured by the log results exactly in the intended chart course.

The transverse speed at the stern is computed from the transverse speed of the bow, the ship's rate of turn and the ship's length as follows:

$$V_{q2} = V_{q1} - \omega \cdot L$$

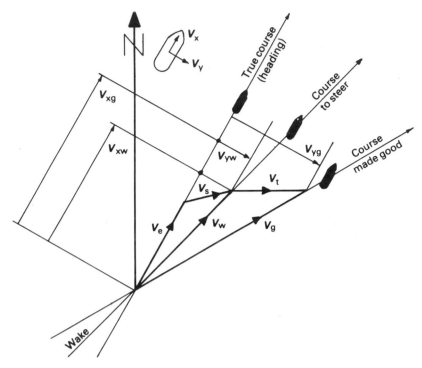

Fig. 2.24 External environmental effects on a vessel's track (Courtesy of Krupp Atlas Elektronik)

where
V_{q2} = stern transverse speed,
v_{q1} = bow transverse speed,
ω = rate of turn (angular velocity)
L = distance between bow and stern points of measurement.
By computing the stern transverse speed in this way the expense and problems involved in fitting a stern transverse transducer assembly have been overcome.

The above descriptions of vessel manoeuvres illustrate the versatility of a modern Doppler speed log of the Dolog type.

3
Decca navigator

The Decca Navigator is a hyperbolic navigation system arranged in chains comprising a central master and usually three outlying slaves. The four stations are arranged in pairs: master/red slave, master/green slave and master/purple slave. The stations transmit low frequency continuous wave (c.w.) signals and each pair produces a pattern of hyperbolic lines of position (LOP). These lines are overprinted on charts in the correct colour according to the pair used. The range of the system is typically 440 nautical miles (800 km) by day and 240 nautical miles (440 km) by night.

The receiver detects the line patterns and drives three indicators (decometers) which continuously and automatically display the numbers of the LOPs passing through the receiver. Each decometer reading gives a numbered LOP for the specified colour and the intersection of any two LOPs on the chart gives the position of the vessel containing the receiver.

3.1 System principles

Consider two transmitters radiating c.w. signals continuously (Figure 3.1). The waveforms shown are for an instant of time and are thus frozen. In practice the waveforms will be moving continuously at approximately $3 \times 10^8 \, \mathrm{m\,s^{-1}}$ in free space. If we assume that the phase of the transmission from each station is synchronized, then a receiver situated exactly half way between the transmitters at point A will receive the two signals in phase since the distance travelled by each transmitted wave is identical and the velocity of the wave in free space is assumed constant. If, however, the receiver is moved closer to, say, the master station, then the master and slave transmissions are no longer received in phase. Position B shows a point where the received transmissions are separated by exactly 180°

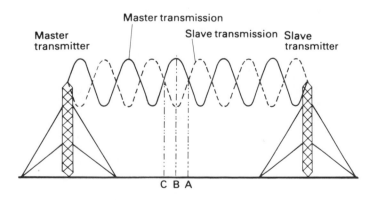

Fig. 3.1 Two transmitters radiating continuous wave signals

55

(antiphase). Position C shows a point where the receiver, having moved another 180° towards the master, is again receiving the two signals in phase. In moving from point A to point C the vessel, with the receiver, is said to have crossed one 'lane'. The width of the lane corresponds to one half-wavelength ($\lambda/2$) of the transmitted frequency.

A hyperbola is a line on which all points have a constant difference in distance from two fixed points, called the foci. It is possible therefore to plot LOPs for all receiver positions where received signals from master and slave transmitters (the foci) are in phase (Figure 3.2).

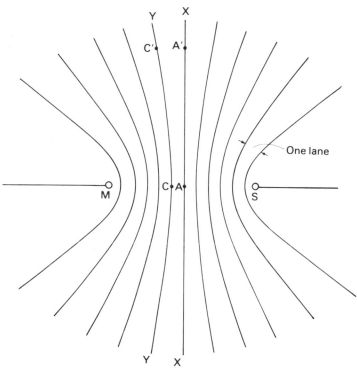

Fig. 3.2   A hyperbolic plot for a master/slave pair giving an indication of how the area between the stations may be divided into lanes

Thus the receiver in position A, referred to in figure 3.1, may be at any point on the line XX (for example, point A′) and similar the receiver in position C may be at any point along YY (for example, point C′).

It is the function of the decometer to indicate the actual phase difference experienced by the receiver as the vessel moves, say, from point A to point C. To traverse one lane, whether it is along the line joining the transmitters, called the baseline, or any other points on the specified LOPs, causes the decometer pointer to complete one revolution. By convention this rotation is clockwise if the vessel moves away from the master and towards the slave.

By using two master/slave pairs a second set of hyperbolae are obtained and the vessel's position found by the intersection of the relevant LOPs (Figure 3.3). Since the receiver is fitted with three decometers, each of which indicates a particular LOP for its master/slave pair, then any two decometer readings can be used to indicate the LOPs to be used on the chart. Information published by Decca gives an indication as to the most suitable pair of decometer readings to use, in a particular area for a particular chain, for greatest accuracy.

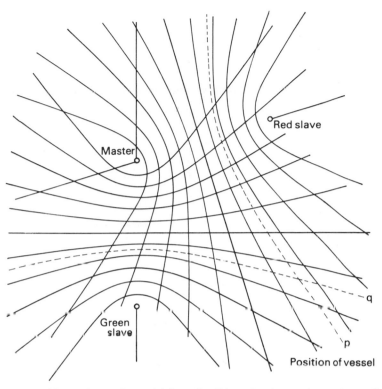

Fig. 3.3 Two master/slave pairs are shown. It follows that if the red and green decometer readings, in lanes and fractions of a lane (centilanes), give the lines 'p' and 'q' then the position of the vessel is given by the intersection of those two lines

3.2 Transmission frequencies

It has been assumed that the master and slave stations transmit the same frequency. However, if this were the case the two signals would merely combine in the receiver antenna and it would be impossible to separate them in the receiver in order to compare and obtain the phase difference between them. In practice the master and slave transmit on different frequencies which, however, have a specified relationship to each other, so that the receiver can derive a common frequency from each transmission by a process of frequency multiplication. Using the common comparison frequency the receiver can obtain the necessary phase difference between the two signals received (Figure 3.4). It can be seen from this diagram that the required comparison frequency in the receiver is 337.12 kHz while the master transmitter frequency is 84.28 kHz and the red slave transmitter frequency is 112.373 kHz. The two different transmission frequencies are thus easily received in the antenna, separated and each multiplied in a frequency multiplier circuit in the receiver to produce the common comparison frequency i.e.

$$84.28 \text{ kHz} \times 4 = 337.12 \text{ kHz and}$$
$$112.373 \text{ kHz} \times 3 = 337.12 \text{ kHz}$$

In fact the master and slaves for a particular chain radiate frequencies which are fixed multiples of a fundamental frequency "f".

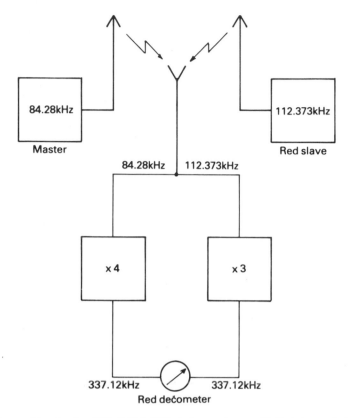

Fig. 3.4 The transmitters for the S.W. British (1B) chain are shown with their transmission frequencies

For the S.W. British chain (1B) the frequencies are:

$$
\begin{aligned}
\text{Master frequency} &= 6f = 84.28\,\text{kHz} \\
\text{Red slave frequency} &= 8f = 112.373\,\text{kHz} \\
\text{Green slave frequency} &= 9f = 126.419\,\text{kHz} \\
\text{Purple slave frequency} &= 5f = 70.233\,\text{kHz} \\
\text{where} \quad f \quad & \quad 14.0466\,\text{kHz}
\end{aligned}
$$

In practice all chains operate with a fundamental frequency close to the value of 14 kHz and master, red, green and purple slaves transmit on frequencies which are close to 84 kHz, 112 kHz, 127 kHz and 70 kHz respectively. The actual values used depend on the chain but in all cases the ratio of transmitted frequency of each station of the chain to the fundamental frequency used is fixed.

In order to maintain phase synchronization for signals transmitted from a master/slave pair it is normal for the slave to be 'triggered' by the master signal. In the event where transmission paths between master and slave may be unreliable and make this process difficult, atomic clocks may be used to produce phase-locked signals from master and slave. This requires careful monitoring and the control centre can make any corrections necessary to maintain the correct phase relationship.

3.3 Lane width

Since the decometer for a particular master/slave pair compares phase difference between two received signals at the comparison frequency then the indication that the vessel has crossed one lane i.e. covered one lane width, is related to that frequency.

Table 3.1 shows the transmission frequencies for the S.W. British chain (1B).

Fig. 3.1 Transmission frequencies for the S.W. British chain.

Station	Frequency (kHz)	Comparison Frequency (kHz)	Lane Width (metres)
Master	84.28 (6*f*)		
Red slave	112.373 (8*f*)	337.12 (24*f*)	444.4
Green slave	126.419 (9*f*)	252.84 (18*f*)	592.6
Purple slave	70.233 (5*f*)	421.399 (30*f*)	355.5

The lane width has been calculated assuming the velocity of the transmitted waves in free space to be $2.9965 \times 10^8 \,\mathrm{m\,s^{-1}}$. It should be noted that the lane width is half the wavelength of the comparison frequency. This can be seen in figure 3.1 where the vessel, in moving from point A to point C i.e. one lane width, has in fact traversed half a wavelength ($\lambda/2$ metres) of the comparison frequency used.

Another point worthy of note is that the lane width quoted in the table above is only valid along the baseline since, as figure 3.2 shows, the distance between points of zero phase difference increases away from the baseline. Compare the length A'C' in figure 3.2 with the length AC. The difference in lane width becomes more pronounced the closer a vessel approaches the baseline extension of either the master or slave transmitter. These differences in lane width do not invalidate the principle of position fixing using the Decca receiver since the decometer will indicate an actual position within a lane regardless of its width.

3.4 Zones and centilanes

Considering the Decca Mk. 21 receiver, the decometers have a single pointer which, as has already been stated, rotates one complete revolution to correspond to the vessel crossing one lane width. The scale, however, is marked in hundredths of a cycle to indicate centilanes (i.e. each lane has 100 centilanes). The centilane pointer is connected to a disc via a gearing chain and the disk is marked in lane numbers around its edge. There are 18, 24 or 30 numbers around this disc according to which decometer is considered (Table 3.2).

Table 3.2 List of markings for the Mk 21 receiver decometers.

Decometer	Zone letter	Lane number	Centilane number
Red	A–J	0–23	0–99
Green	A–J	30–47	0–99
Purple	A–J	50–79	0–99

The lane disc is in turn connected to a second disc which has marked around its periphery the zone letters A to J. The region between any master/slave pair is thus divided into zones starting with zone A at the master through to zone J; the zone letters are then repeated as necessary until the slave is reached.

Both the lane and zone discs are visible through a 'window' so that a zone, lane and centilane may be identified at any instant for each decometer.

Considering the red decometer, when the pointer makes one complete revolution (100 centilanes) the vessel has crossed one lane and the next lane number appears on the first disc. When the full 24 lanes have been crossed then the next zone letter appears on the second disc. It is possible that two lane numbers or two zone letters may appear in the window at the same time but it is a simple matter in practice to determine which of the two possible lane numbers or zone letters is the current one and which is the approaching one.

The lane numbers are 0 to 23 for the red decometer, 30 to 47 for the green decometer and 50 to 79 for the purple decometer. The use of separate lane numbers for each decometer enables a position fix to be determined simply by specifying a lane number without the need for a colour to be mentioned. This avoids possible confusion, especially in chart work.

3.5 Lane identification

It should be possible to set up the decometer lane indicators by noting the estimated position of the vessel on the lattice chart and correcting as necessary from new data as the vessel changes its position.

However, if it were possible to increase the wavelength of the comparison frequency used for a particular master/slave pair (i.e. lower the frequency of comparison) then a wider lane width pattern is obtained. In any lane the decometer pointer indicates which centilane the vessel is in with good accuracy and this is equally true for a wide lane. If the comparison frequency were reduced so that each wide lane corresponds to a normal zone then the centilane pointer would indicate with good accuracy which part of the wide lane (zone) the vessel is in. The receiver gives no indication of the zone and it is assumed that this information is readily available since at 100 miles from the stations the zones are approximately 20 miles wide and approximately 50 miles at the edge of the coverage.

Considering the master/red slave pair then for an increase in lane width to a zone width, the frequency of comparison must be reduced by a factor of 24 i.e. instead of 337.12 kHz it becomes $337.12/24 = 14.0466$ kHz i.e. the fundamental frequency f for that chain.

For the Mk. 21 receiver the fundamental frequency, used as the comparison frequency, is obtained by a system called Multipulse.

3.6 Multipulse lane identification

Signals known as Lane Identification (LI) signals are transmitted at regular intervals using transmissions from each of the four stations. The LI sequence commences with short bursts of transmission from each station in turn at intervals of 2½ seconds, followed by a 10 second interval and then repeated i.e. a series of three sets of signals per minute (see figure 3.5.).

For the master transmission all stations interrupt their transmissions for a short period and only the master transmits all four frequencies simultaneously. The receiver amplifies the four transmitted frequencies and uses the combined frequencies to produce the fundamental frequency (see figure 3.6).

An oscillator in the receiver, synchronized to the master transmission frequency ($6f$) during *normal* transmission provides the fundamental frequency via a frequency divider network (master frequency/6 = $6f/6$ = fundamental frequency f).

The frequency f obtained from the combined frequency transmission of the master is compared in phase to the frequency obtained via the oscillator and the result, after analog to digital conversion, is shown as a digital readout in lanes and tenths of a lane. The digital

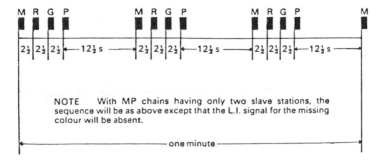

Fig. 3.5 Three multipulse Lane Identification Sequences

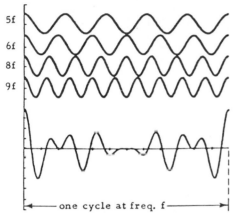

Fig. 3.6 The periodic multipulse transmission frequencies and the resultant sum

readout should be zero because any phase difference is the result of comparing the fundamental frequency derived from the *normal* master transmission with the *master* transmitter LI signals. If this is not the case then by pushing an LI zero button, the result may be set to zero.

The next LI transmission is from the red slave and it too transmits all four frequencies simultaneously. The receiver again combines these frequencies to produce a fundamental component which is again compared with the fundamental component derived from the oscillator divider network. The display will now indicate phase differences in lanes and tenths of a lane for the master/red slave pair.

The green and purple slave transmissions follow in sequence and will also give a digital readout. The master transmitter readout is recognized because the display flashes while this transmission is being received.

Some chains have only two slaves and if this is the case there is no LI signal for the missing colour.

The main advantage of multipulse (MP) is that the phase shift of one or more of the four transmitted frequencies, as a result of sky wave transmission, has little effect on the phase of the fundamental frequency derived from the combined frequencies. Thus with multipulse chains it is possible to achieve lane identification at greater ranges than usually is specified for the system.

3.7 The receiver

The basic block diagram of the Decca Navigator receiver is shown in figure 3.7. The chain transmission and receiver elements associated with the fine patterns are shown above the

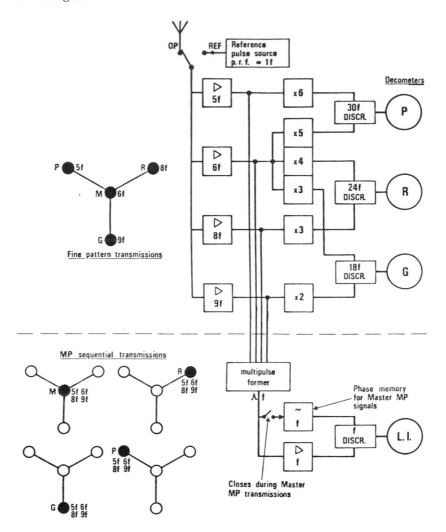

Fig. 3.7 Block diagram of a Decca Navigator Receiver of no particular mark

dotted line and those for lane identification, below. Typically the lane identification display is either a meter with three concentric scales covering one zone, or a digital/numerical readout. Superheterodyne principles have been used with the received four sets of frequencies being converted to intermediate frequencies by mixing with corresponding harmonics of a heterodyne frequency obtained, in the Mk. 21 receiver, from a synthesizer based on a single crystal oscillator operating at 436.907 kHz. This oscillator also provides timing outputs for the switching required in receiving LI transmissions. The phase difference between master and slave inputs at the intermediate frequency is unaltered from that of the r.f. at the receiver input.

The phases of respective pairs of common harmonics are compared, after frequency multiplication, in a discriminator. The output of the discriminator consists of d.c. currents proportional to the sine and cosine of the phase difference angle. These currents, fed to two coils mutually at right angles, causes a magnetic rotor to take up a position related to the phase angle. It is this rotor which positions the centilane pointer and, via gearing, the lane and zone indicator discs.

The function of the reference facility is to correct for possible differential phase errors in the receiver by applying a series of pulses at frequency, f, at the receiver input. Each pulse is short and sharp-sided to produce harmonics, corresponding to the transmitted Decca frequencies, which are essentially equal in amplitude and of fixed phase relationship. This reference input provides a phase datum so that the decometers should read zero in the absence of error. Any observed error may be restored to zero by adjustment of the appropriate zero control.

The receiver is divided into four main printed circuit boards with two smaller boards and a power unit which is interchangeable so as to cater for possible power supply variations. This modular type of construction is designed to facilitate repairs by rapid replacement of faulty boards with serviceable units (see figure 3.8).

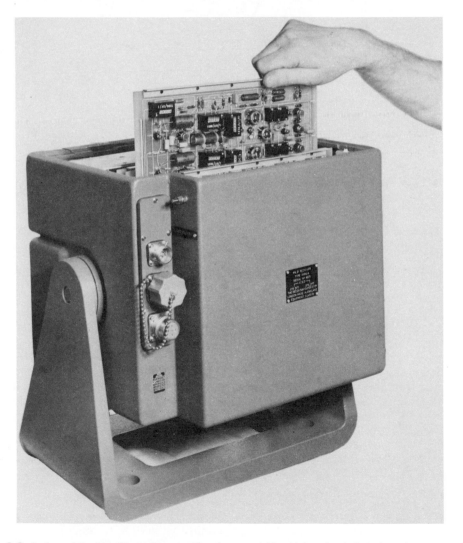

Fig. 3.8 A view of the Mk. 21 receiver showing the ease with which a plug-in board can be accessed

3.8 Decca chains

The first permanent navigation chain (the English chain (5B)) became operational in 1946 and subsequently other chains have been installed in Europe and other parts of the world as shown in the Decca coverage chart (Figure 3.9). At the time of writing there are 51 chains in operation, under construction or contracted for. A list of chains is shown in Table 3.3.

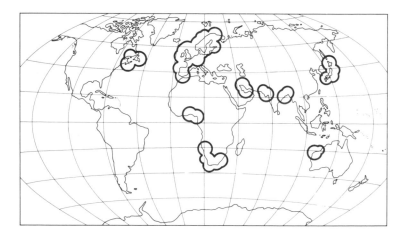

Fig. 3.9 Coverage of Decca chains in 1980. (For full details of individual chains see Table 3.3)

3.9 Decca frequencies

The master frequency of the first chain (5B) was chosen to be 85.00 kHz. Subsequent chains have had master frequencies centred around this value. Initially the chain spacing was chosen to be 180 Hz at the master frequency because of the very high selectivity of the Decca receiver and also because of the distance between chains the frequency separation between chains could be small. This was later reduced to 90 Hz to allow for more chains. Thus within the 2 kHz band width allowed for the master frequencies there are 21 possible sets of frequencies within the range using the 90 Hz spacing.

The original frequencies separated by 180 Hz are given code values with suffix B (i.e. 0B, 1B, 2B, etc) and the so called 'half frequencies' fit between the original frequencies and are separated from them by 90 Hz. These frequencies are given the code values with suffix E (i.e. 0E, 1E, 2E, etc). Further division was effected using frequencies 5 Hz below and 5 Hz above the 'B' values; these are designated by letters A and C respectively. In addition, frequencies 5 Hz below and above the 'E' values, coded D and F respectively, are used.

Table 3.4 shows the complete set of 'B' and 'E' frequencies allocated for master and slave transmissions while Table 3.5 shows the six sets of frequencies for the numerical group 5.

3.10 Accuracy

The Decca system is extremely accurate but there are errors and the system user should be aware of the possible errors and the corrections that need to be applied to minimize the effects. There are three possible causes of error:

Table 3.3 Current chain codes (August 1981)

Chain	Code	L.I. Signalling sequence	
List A—Chains in Operation			
South Baltic (Sweden)	0A/MP	MP†	
Vestlandet (Bergen, Norway)	0E/MP	MP†	
South West British	1B/MP	MP*	
South Persian Gulf (1981)	1C/MP	MP†	
Northumbrian	2A/MP	MP*	
East Newfoundland	2C/MP	MP*	
Holland	2E/MP	MP†	
Salaya (India West)	2F/MP	MP†	
North British	3B/MP	MP*	
Lofoten (Norway)	3E/MP	MP†	
German	3F/MP	MP*	
Port Hedland (W. Australia)	4A/MP	MP†	
Namaqua (South Africa)	4A/MP	MP†	
North Baltic	4B/MP	MP†	
North West Spanish	4C/MP	MP*	
Trondelag (Trondheim, Norway)	4E/MP	MP†	
English	5B/MP	MP*	See MENAS Notice 49/80
North Persian Gulf	5C/MP	MP*	and Admiralty Notice to
North Bothnian	5F/MP	MP†	Mariners 1003 (H3218/80).
Cape (South Africa)	6A/MP	MP†	
South Spanish	6A/MP	MP†	
Cabot Straits (Canada)	6B/MP	MP*	
North Scottish	6C/MP	MP*	
Bangladesh	6C/MP	MP*	
Tohoku (Japan)	6C/MP	MP†	
Gulf of Finland	6E/MP	MP†	
Danish	7B/MP	MP†	
Bombay (India West)	7B/MP	MP†	
Nova Scotia	7C/V	V1	
North Kyushu (Japan)	7C/MP	MP†	
Irish	7D/MP	MP†	
Finnmark (North Cape, Norway)	7E/MP	MP†	
Eastern Province (South Africa)	8A/MP	MP†	
French	8B/MP	MP*	
Calcutta (India East)	8B/MP	MP†	
Kanto (Japan)	8C/MP	MP†	
South Bothnian	8C/MP	MP†	
Dampier (W. Australia)	8E/MP	MP†	
Hebridean	8E/MP	MP†	
Lagos (Nigeria)	8F/MP	MP†	
Frisian Islands	9B/MP	MP*	
South West Africa	9C/MP	MP†	
Anticosti (Canada)	9C/MP	MP*	
Hokkaido (Japan)	9C/MP	MP†	
Helgeland (Polar Circle, Norway)	9E/MP	MP†	
Skagerrak	10B/MP	MP†	
Natal (South Africa)	10C/MP	MP†	
List B—Chains under Construction or Modernisation (see Admiralty Notice to Mariners for latest information)			
South East Nigeria	2B/MP	MP†	
Mid West Nigeria	3A/MP	MP†	
Shikoku (Japan)	4C/MP	MP†	
Hormuz	4D/MP	MP†	
Rivers (Nigeria)	7F/MP	MP†	

*/MP Chains may, infrequently, revert to V2 L.I. signalling for short periods.
Check Decca warnings and observe relevant operating procedure.
†These Chains are Multipulse only and do not have Mark V L.I.

Table 3.4 Decca chain frequency grouping in kHz. Nominal frequency (B) and 'half frequency' (E) groups. The 8.2*f* (orange) frequencies, not mentioned in the text, are used by airborne receivers to provide some identification. It is also used to transmit commands and data for chain control and surveillance

Chain code	1*f* (not radiated)	5*f* Purple	6*f* Master	8*f* Red	8.2*f* Orange	9*f* Green
0B	14.01750	70.0875	84.1050	112.1400	114.9435	126.1575
0E	14.03250	70.1625	84.1950	112.2600	115.0665	126.2925
1B	14.04667	70.2333	84.2800	112.3733	115.1827	126.4200
1E	14.06167	70.3083	84.3700	112.4933	115.3057	126.5550
2B	14.07667	70.3833	84.4600	112.6133	115.4287	126.6900
2E	14.09167	70.4583	84.5500	112.7333	115.5517	126.8250
3B	14.10750	70.5375	84.6450	112.8600	115.6815	126.9675
3E	14.12250	70.6125	84.7350	112.9800	115.8045	127.1025
4B	14.13750	70.6875	84.8250	113.1000	115.9275	127.2375
4E	14.15250	70.7625	84.9150	113.2200	116.0505	127.3725
5B	14.16667	70.8333	85.0000	113.3333	116.1667	127.5000
5E	14.18167	70.9083	85.0900	113.5433	116.2897	127.6350
6B	14.19667	70.9833	85.1800	113.5733	116.4127	127.7700
6E	14.21167	71.0583	85.2700	113.6933	116.5357	127.9050
7B	14.22750	71.1375	85.3650	113.8200	116.6655	128.0475
7E	14.24250	71.2125	85.4550	113.9400	116.7885	128.1825
8B	14.25750	71.2875	85.5450	114.0600	116.9115	128.3175
8E	14.27250	71.3625	85.6350	114.1800	117.0345	128.4525
9B	14.28667	71.4333	85.7200	114.2930	117.1507	128.5800
9E	14.30167	71.5083	85.8100	114.4130	117.2737	128.7150
10B	14.31667	71.5833	85.9000	114.5330	117.3967	128.8500

Table 3.5 Sample groups of Decca frequencies showing the relationship of A-B-C-D-E-F spot frequencies (in kHz) for one complete numerical group. The 8.2*f* frequencies are used by airborne receivers to provide zone identification. It is also used to transmit commands and data for chain control and surveillance

Chain code	1*f* (not radiated)	5*f* Purple	6*f* Master	8*f* Red	8.2*f* Orange	9*f* Green
5A	14.16583	70.8292	84.9950	113.3266	116.1590	127.4925
5B	14.16667	70.8333	85.0000	113.3333	116.1667	127.5000
5C	14.16750	70.8375	85.0050	113.3400	116.1735	127.5075
5D	14.18083	70.9042	85.0850	113.4467	116.2828	127.6275
5E	14.18167	70.9083	85.0900	113.4533	116.2897	127.6350
5F	14.18250	70.9125	85.0950	113.4600	116.2695	127.6425

1. Fixed error. Due to the actual hyperbolic LOPs, computed mathematically, being distorted in practice.
2. Reception of the transmitted signal by two possible paths, the ground wave and the skywave. The difference in the distance travelled by the two possible routes can lead to an incorrect decometer reading. The ground wave is the wanted path and the charts are prepared on the basis of reception via this path. The reception of signals via the skywave is a factor which limits the range of the system to 240 nautical miles by night in N. European latitudes but less nearer the equator.
3. Weather effects. The performance of the decometers and LI meter can be affected by snow or precipitation static and under these conditions greater care should be exercised in position fixing by taking frequent lane checks.

Fixed errors

The positions of the lattice lines on the Decca charts for each master/slave pair is based on the velocity of the radio waves from each station being constant. In fact the velocity of radio waves depends on the conductivity of the medium over which the wave is travelling and varies from land to sea. Such errors as caused by this mechanism of propagation are small and easily corrected. Pattern correction charts are available which give the necessary correction figure to be applied by addition (or subtraction) to the decometer reading (see figure 3.10). Where corrections are not quoted it should not be assumed that no errors exist; possibly no measurement of fixed error has been made for that area and the navigator should use his discretion as to whether to interpolate between quoted errors either side of the vessel's position or to assume less than absolute accuracy of the readings for that area.

Variable errors

The reception of a sky wave signal at the receiver causes interference with the wanted ground wave signal. The decometer is unable to distinguish between the two received signals and produces a reading which is the resultant of the two signals. The amount of variation from the phase difference produced purely by the ground wave signal depends on the phase and amplitude of the two waves. These parameters vary according to the time of day, the time of year and the position of the receiver on the surface of the earth. The resultant variable errors are complex and it is not possible to make 'sky wave correction' charts as for the fixed errors. However, it is possible to predict the errors in terms of statistical analysis as the percentage of time during which the variations would not exceed a certain value. A root mean square error criterion is used to give the likely degree of uncertainty of a Decca fix within the coverage area. This error depends, among other things, on the angle of 'cut' between the LOPs, the lane width on the baseline and the angle subtended by the baseline at the point of observation. The r.m.s. error may be described as the radius of a circle, which symmetrically drawn on the fix distribution, includes approximately 68% of the plots. The circles are drawn such that the master and slave stations are on the periphery of the circle. For a given chain the accuracy contours are modified according to such factors as the length of the baselines of the master/slave pairs and the angle between them. Accuracy contours for the S.W.British (1B) chain are shown in figure 3.11. It can be seen from this diagram that the contours are for full daylight coverage; for conditions other than full daylight the contours of figure 3.12 should be used in conjunction with Table 3.6 and figure 3.13 to give the predicted accuracy contours according to the time of day and the season.

3.11 Decca charts

Official navigational charts of marine areas overprinted with the Decca LOPs are produced by various governmental authorities. Latticed marine charts and plotting sheets are also available from fishing cartographers and the Decca company but these are *not* navigation charts.

The Decca charts issued by the British Hydrographer are kept up to date through Notices to Mariners and are sold corrected to the date of issue marked thereon and should afterwards be kept up to date in accordance with Notices to Mariners. On Admiralty charts the chart number is usually prefixed by the letter 'L', the letter 'D' and the chain number in brackets i.e. L(D1)2454 is the lattice chart for the Decca chain 1B covered by Admiralty chart 2454. The full designation, such as Decca chain 1B/MP (S.W.British) is

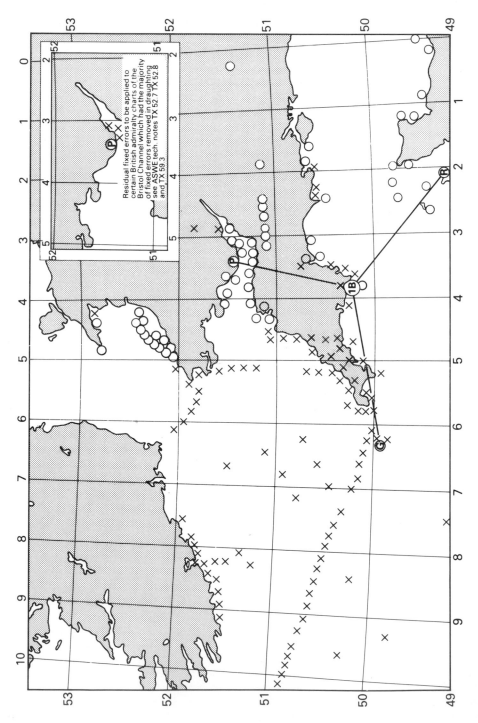

Residual fixed errors to be applied to certain British admiralty charts of the Bristol Channel which had the majority of fixed errors removed in draughting see ASWE tech. notes TX 52.7 TX 52.8 and TX 59.3.

Fig. 3.10 The Decca Navigator system – S.W. British chain (1B) Red pattern fixed error corrections. The error corrections differ according to the master/slave pair selected. The crosses represent values (in hundredths of a lane unit on the actual chart) to be added and the empty circles represent values to be subtracted

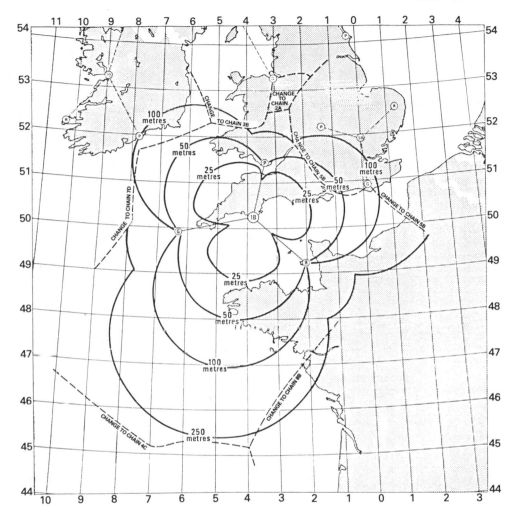

THE DECCA NAVIGATOR SYSTEM – S.W. BRITISH CHAIN (1B)

FULL DAYLIGHT COVERAGE AND ACCURACY

Fig. 3.11 The Decca Navigator System – S.W. British Chain (1B) Full daylight coverage and accuracy. The full line contours enclose areas in which *Fix Repeatability* errors will not exceed the distances shown on 68% of occasions during *Full Daylight* conditions of time

printed along the left-hand bottom border of the chart. The designation MP indicates that the chain employs multipulse transmissions.

Charts are available which are overprinted with two chains i.e. dual-chain fixing charts; the frequency channels of the Decca chains concerned are shown along the bottom border of such charts.

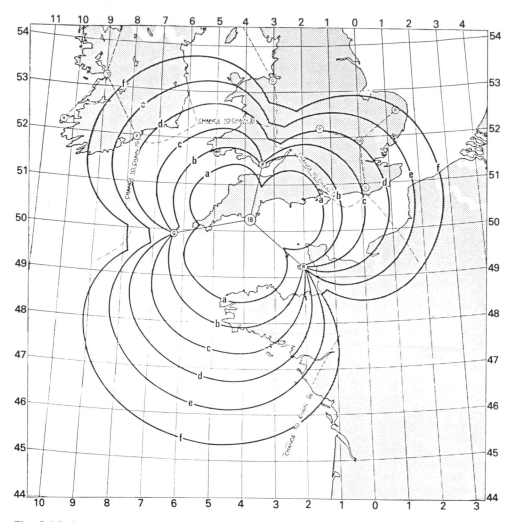

Fig. 3.12 The Decca Navigator System – S.W. British Chain (1B) Predicted coverage and accuracy diagram (68% probability level) for times other than 'full daylight'.

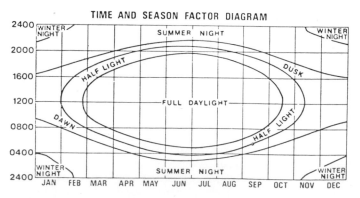

Fig 3.13 Time and season factor diagram

Table 3.6 Random fixing errors at sea level in nautical miles, 68% probability level. This information should be used in conjunction with figures 3.12 and 3.13

Decca period	a	b	c	Contour d	e	f
Half light	<0.10	<0.10	<0.10	0.13	0.25	0.50
Dawn/dusk	<0.10	<0.10	0.13	0.25	0.50	1.00
Summer night	<0.10	0.13	0.25	0.50	1.00	2.00
Winter night	0.10	0.18	0.37	0.75	1.50	3.00

3.12 Position fixing

To obtain a position fix it is normal practice to choose whichever two of the three LOPs give the best angle of cut at the vessel's position. As stated previously the relevant chain data sheet shows the best pair of lines to use in different parts of the coverage and details of Decca charts are also given in these data sheets. Figure 3.14 shows Decca lattice colours to be used for obtaining the best fix and the best position line in different parts of the operational area. Inside the inner circle drawn around the chain, the choice of colour will be obvious from inspection of the chart in use; elsewhere, the coverage is divided into sections (shown by full-line radial 'spokes') between which different pairs of colours are used for fixing. Similarly, broken-line spokes delineate areas in which different single colours give the best position line. The decometer can give a reading down to one-hundredth of a lane but the charts are usually only marked with whole number position lines so that the user has to interpolate between the printed lines in order to find the actual position line corresponding to the decometer reading.

The angle at which LOPs for two master/slave pairs intersect each other is a very important factor in determining fix error. Consider a vessel at position P where the red decometer reads C6.4 and the green decometer reads E35.7 (figure 3.15).

Suppose that because of sky wave reception the readings may be in error by 0.1 lane, then it follows that: the actual red reading lies between C6.3 and C6.5 the actual green reading lies between E35.6 and E35.8. Thus there is a diamond shaped region between these limits in which the vessel's position may be found (see figure 3.16).

Where the intersection of the two LOPs is almost at right-angles, as in the central part of the Decca pattern, the area of the 'diamond' is reduced and becomes almost square (see figure 3.17). At long distances from the transmitter stations however, the pattern becomes long and narrow (see figure 3.18). Thus at these positions the accuracy across the direction of the lattice (CD) is very good while along the lattice lines (AB) it is very poor.

This possible source of fix error may be minimized by taking advantage of the improved angle of cut that can be obtained by taking one position line from each of two adjacent chains. This method relies on the effectiveness of the multipulse mode of lane identification which allows the correct lane number to be immediately determined when switching to the second chain. Thus the method lends itself more to day than to night operation since it involves long-range working and the range limit at night tends to be set by sky wave interference. Figure 3.19 shows the effect of inter-chain fixing with the resulting improved accuracy contours.

3.13 Mark 21 receiver

The Mk. 21 is a solid-state receiver housed in a case suitable for bulkhead, deckhead or table mounting.

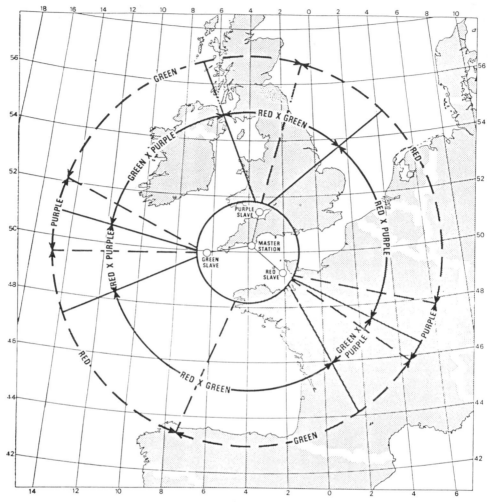

Fig. 3.14 The Decca Navigator System – S.W. British Chain (1B) Diagram showing Decca Lattice Colours to be used for obtaining the best fix and the best position line in different parts of the operational area

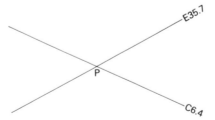

Fig. 3.15 Position P is found by the intersection of two specified LOPs

High selectivity is obtained by the use of 'flywheel' oscillators which generate noise-free replicas of the incoming signals and this allows satisfactory operation under high atmospheric and electrical interference conditions. Power consumption on a.c. is 15 W and on d.o. is 25 W. The antenna can be a simple insulated wire (the standard Decca type)

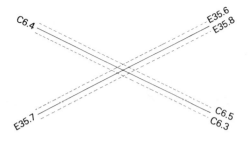

Fig. 3.16 The possible spread in lane reading accuracy caused by skywave reception

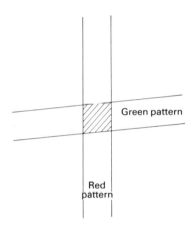

Fig. 3.17 The central part of the Decca pattern

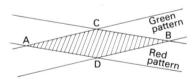

Fig. 3.18 The Decca pattern at great distances from the transmitters

or a fibreglass whip which is connected to the receiver via an antenna filter unit.

Figure 3.20 shows the front panel of the receiver. As can be seen there are three decometers, identified from left to right as red, green and purple, and the LI indicator. A control panel is below and is accessed by opening the cover. The controls available are as follows:

Chain switch

There are two switches, one controlling the chain number and marked 0–10, the other controlling the chain letter and marked A–F. Turning the respective controls to select a particular chain causes the receiver to be tuned to that chain.

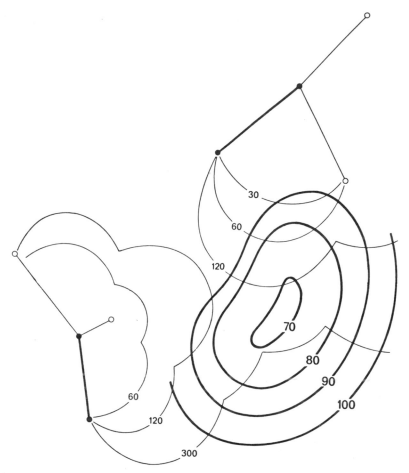

Fig. 3.19 Example of improvement in accuracy gained by two-chain fixing. The contour values are in metres (68% probability, p.02 lane SD) and refer to the full daylight condition. The two baselines used, and the resulting contours, are shown as thick lines

Function switch

This switch has five settings:

Off   Disconnects receiver from the power supply.

Lock 1   Assists the locking of the receiver to the incoming signals. A discriminator forces the flywheel oscillator to assume gradually the frequency and phase of the incoming signal i.e. 'locking'. This setting should only be used when first switching 'on'.

Ref.   The equipment itself should introduce no phase shift. Any phase shift in the receiver (drift) can be eliminated by setting the decometer pointers to zero by using their own zero control. This action may be required during the first hour of operation or when changing chains. When the receiver is switched to this setting the antenna is disconnected and the signals supplied by a special oscillator.

Lock 2   This setting ensures that the receiver re-locks as quickly as possible, after referencing, to the incoming signals.

Op   The setting for normal operation.

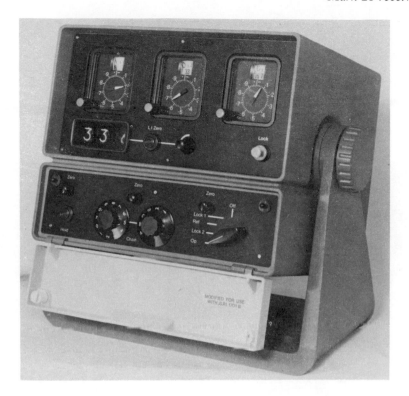

Fig. 3.20 Front view of a Mk. 21 receiver with its front cover removed

Lock indicator lamp

This lamp illuminates steadily when the receiver has locked to the master signal, except for a flicker at each LI reading. The lamp gives an indication as to signal/noise conditions and is brightest when such conditions are good. Flickering increases with the noise level. The lamp may be dimmed by turning its amber cover.

Hold push button

Pressing this button causes the decometer pointers to stop rotating and sets them at a nominal reading of 12.5 centilanes. This is maintained as long as the button remains pressed. The lane and zone pointers will also stop rotating since they are mechanically coupled to the centilane pointers. This control is useful when carrying out an inter-chain fix since it prevents loss of the stored lane and zone information as a result of the rapid rotation of the centilane pointers. The button should also be depressed for a short time when switching from 'Op' to 'Ref' during referencing. Also when switching on initially the button can be depressed until the lock lamp illuminates steadily.

Decometers

Each of the three decometers provides line of position information in terms of a lane fraction (centilane) pointer, lane number and zone letter. A reset knob on each meter allows the dials to be initially set by hand, after which they are automatically given via the lane pointer. Below the window in which the zone dial appears there is a dot and dash symbol. There is also a dot or dash just below each lane number in the window. When two zone letters appear in the window at the same time, the correct zone letter is that one positioned over the same symbol as that displayed under the lane number. Thus, in the decometers illustrated in figure 3.21 the readings are Red F3.29, Green J44.37 and Purple C57.32. If there are two lane numbers visible, the centilane pointer indicates the correct one to be used.

Fig. 3.21 The red, green and purple decometers of the Mk. 21 receiver, viewing from left to right

Zero controls

The three controls marked 'zero' are used for setting the respective decometer controls to zero when 'referencing'. This procedure allows the maximum instrumental accuracy to be achieved with the system. The zero controls are also electrically linked with the LI section of the receiver and the LI readout will not operate correctly unless the decometers have been correctly referenced.

LI digital readout

The LI readout on the number tubes indicates the correct lane number within a zone for each of the three sets of patterns in turn in a sequence repeated every 20 seconds. Thus when setting up the receiver, the user is able to correctly adjust each lane dial to the lane number for the vessel's position. The LI readout also provides a constant check of the satisfactory tracking of the decometers when the vessel is under way. The readout is scaled 0–23.9 for Red, 30–47.9 for Green and 50–79.9 for Purple.

LI zero pushbutton

Since, when first switching on, the LI readout will indicate a value that is not necessarily correct, it is required to zero the readout for the master LI reading in order that the values displayed for the LI sequence (master-red-green-purple at 2½ second intervals) is correct. Once the button is pressed and released the following master readings should be zero. The control should be used during night time with circumspection because of the likely skywave reception path.

LI dimming control

Adjusts the brilliance of the number tubes.

Use of LI on entering the coverage or when setting up within the coverage

The Decca instruction manual gives extremely detailed and specific instructions for all aspects of receiver operation. However, a précis is given here as an indication of the use of the LI readout:

1. Switch on and set up the receiver in the prescribed manner.

2. Plot the estimated position of the vessel on the Decca chart and from this information set the zone letter, lane number and centilane pointer for each decometer. At this stage, of course, the settings are an approximation. When the reset knob is released the centilane pointer may move away from the set reading by a few tenths of a lane. **Do not attempt to reset** as the pointer automatically takes up the correct value and swings via the *shortest* path to this value producing lane and centilane readings nearest to the ones set. For example, if the meter has been set to 11.3 and the true value is 0.9 then the needle will swing to 10.9 and not 11.9.

3. Observe the LI over several sequences and check that the correct Red, Green and Purple sequence is being obtained. This is an essential prerequisite for the following instructions.

4. Observe a group of three complete and, if possible, consecutive colour sequences, each sequence consisting of the LI reading followed by the decometer reading. These readings should be recorded and also the difference between the LI and decometer readings for each colour. The meters should not be reset but the sequence repeated at regular intervals; if the difference between the LI and decometer readings for any colour is consistent and less than half a lane then the decometer reading can be considered accurate and the decometer correctly set. Otherwise the decometers should be reset by the appropriate number of lanes.

Lane identification is also a useful check on the decometer readings at any time and whenever a log entry is made of a decometer reading, a LI reading should also be taken and logged. The decometers should not be reset, however, on the basis of a single LI reading which may differ from the decometer value, especially at night.

Operating procedures

Once again the Decca manual is specific on this point and the following is only a brief summary of the requirements.

Initial setting up
The chain controls should be set to the values of the required chain and the function switch from 'Off' to 'Lock 1'. The Lock lamp should start flashing and the decometer pointers will jitter or rotate. A large resetting adjustment may be necessary and the 'Hold' button may be depressed until the receiver has locked to the master signal to prevent the pointer rotation. The Lock lamp flashing will slow down as the receiver tunes to the master frequency and the lamp will shine steadily on final locking except for a flicker at each LI signal. Final slave locking is indicated by steady decometer pointers.

Next set the function switch to 'Ref', wait for the pointers to take up a steady reading with the Lock lamp steady, and adjust the three zero controls to set the respective pointers to zero.

Set the function switch to 'Lock 2' and wait until any flashing of the lamp or rotation of the pointers steadies.

Now set the function switch to 'Op' during the 10 second interval between LI signal sequences, as indicated by the Lock lamp and/or pointer movements.

If necessary check the master LI readings which should indicate zero within a range of readings 23.8, 23.9, 00.0, 00.1, 00.2. If successive readings are obtained outside this tolerance range then press and release the LI Zero button and check the master reading again on the next LI sequence. Note that when setting up under conditions of possible skywave reception, several LI sequences in succession should be taken and zeroing should only be undertaken if a consistent deviation is observed.

Operation during voyage
During the first hour of operation and occasionally during each day of operation, the function switch should be turned to 'Ref' and the lane pointers to zero if in error. Switching to and from 'Ref' can cause the lane pointers to rotate and thus lose the lane count. To prevent this the following procedure is recommended:
1. Press the 'Hold' button and keep it pressed.
2. Turn function switch to 'Ref'.
3. After 10 seconds release the 'Hold' button.
4. Check that the decometer zeros and adjust zero controls as necessary.
5. Press the 'Hold' button and keep it depressed.
6. Turn the function switch to 'Lock 2'.
7. When the 'Lock' lamp is steady, turn the function switch to 'Op'.
8. When correct LI is apparent, release 'Hold' button.

The previous comments about checking the master LI readings, especially in the case of possible skywave reception, should also be followed.

Changing chain
1. Transfer the vessel's position from the chart, latticed for the chain in use, to the chart latticed for the required new chain, allowing for fixed error corrections for both chains.
2. Set the chain controls to the new values.
3. When the receiver has acquired the new chain, the Lock lamp will soon illuminate steadily without the need to relinquish the 'Op' setting.
4. When Lock lamp is steady, turn function switch to 'Ref'.
5. Wait for decometer movement to stop, and set lane pointers to zero using zero controls.
6. Turn to 'Lock 2' and wait for decometers and Lock lamp to become steady.
7. Turn to 'Op' and press LI button.
8. Set all three decometers to the zone and estimated lane readings for the vessel's position. Observe the LI readout over several sequences and allowing for this reading to be correct, adjust the lane dials to the observed Red, Green and Purple LI values.

Inter-chain fixing
The reading from the second chain is obtained from the LI readout. The procedure is as follows:
1. Record the pattern readings and the LI values for the chain currently selected.
2. Depress the 'Hold' button and keep it depressed until the following sequence is completed.
3. Select required chain on chain controls (the Lock lamp will flash and then shine steadily when the receiver has acquired the new chain).
4. With the function switch at 'Op', press and release the LI zero button.

5. Check that the next master LI reading is within the tolerance values 23.8−0.02 and if not press and release the LI zero button again.

6. Read the LI readout to obtain the desired pattern reading (lane number and fraction) and confirm this reading and the master 'zero' reading on at least two successive LI sequences.

7. Restore chain selector to the values for the chain previously used. Lock lamp will flash and then shine steadily when the chain has been acquired. the 'Lock 2' setting may be used to accelerate acquisition.

8. Select 'Op' and, when the Lock lamp shines steadily, press and release the LI zero button.

9. Observe the LI readings. As soon as a correct sequence is seen, release the 'Hold' button.

10. Check decometer lane values and reset if necessary.

The technique described relies on the accuracy of the Multipulse lane identification and the range for which this system may be used varies according to daylight or night time reception and the reception conditions. The range may be 400 nautical miles during daylight and 250 nautical miles by night. In adverse conditions and in low magnetic latitudes the range at night may be reduced and in the latter case to such an extent that the use of night time inter-chain fixing may be ruled out.

Lane slip

This may occur, due to a variety of reasons, and cause an incorrect lane reading to be displayed. Suppose, for example, a simultaneous sky wave and ground wave reception occurred. Each wave would have different strengths and, because of the different paths travelled, different phases too. This may cause the centilane pointer to give a possibly incorrect reading. The sky wave reception is irregular and may change suddenly or even disappear altogether and this will obviously affect the phase of the resultant signal, causing the pointer to move suddenly to a new position. The pointer will always move along the shortest route to its new position and it follows that if the pointer had moved more than half a revolution away from its correct position, because of the effects of sky wave reception, then it will complete the revolution if the sky wave suddenly ceases. Thus the pointer will give the correct centilane reading but will indicate the wrong lane.

This possibility is, of course, rare but it highlights the need for the operator to check the decometer readings with the readout of the LI display.

Other possible causes of lane slip are:

1. Switching to 'Ref' when any of the lane pointers is close to 50 or by remaining on 'Ref' too long.

2. Breakdown of, or incorrect transmission from, a Decca station or chain, and the operator should listen to radio transmissions of Notices to Mariners which, should such an event occur, give the appropriate warning.

3.14 Mark 53 receiver

The Mark 53 Navigator is the latest Decca receiver, comprising four separate channels for the continuous reception of master and slave transmission signals. Two microprocessors are used, one dedicated to r.f. signal processing and the second to co-ordinate conversion and system management. Receiver operation is normally automatic but a manual override facility is provided.

Chain selection is achieved automatically, once the latitude and longitude of a position have been entered into the receiver memory, using stored data to select the best chain for use in the locality. Alternatively, any chain within range may be selected manually. The

Fig. 3.22   Racal Decca Mk 53G combined Decca/GPS receiver

Mk. 53 has the ability to display vessel position in latitude/longitude format to 0.01 of a minute, in Decca coordinate format to 0.01 of a Decca lane or as distance and bearing from a defined waypoint location to a resolution of 0.1 nautical mile and one degree, respectively. Up to 100 waypoint positions can be stored either as plotted waypoints or auto-waypoints; up to 19 waypoints may be programmed into a route with several routes available in either direction. Routes can be extended to form a 'string' of routes. An auto-waypoint may be established by pressing a single button (AUTO WP) which allows the position of the craft to be determined at any instant. Such auto-waypoints can be transferred to the waypoint store without re-specification of the auto-waypoint position.

Decca lines of position (LOPs) can be implemented in one of three modes.

Normal Pattern (NP)
A position is fixed from a pair of LOPs, generated by continuous single frequency transmissions from the respective stations of the chain.

Line Identification Pattern (LIP)
LIPs are derived from four frequency multipulse signals, transmitted in sequence from the chain and repeated every 20 seconds.

Two-chain (2CH) or Cross Chain
The position fix is formed from an LOP from each of two adjacent chains.

Dead reckoning can be initiated when a loss of radio signal is expected e.g. moving from coverage of one chain to another where the coverage areas do not overlap. Normally, rate of change of position, corresponding to course and speed made good is stored in memory and progressively updated by radio position fixes. In the event of an alarm condition, caused by inadequate radio signal say, computation and display of position is based on stored velocity data to overcome short periods of signal loss.

The receiver computes Course and Speed Made Good over ground on the basis of successive position fixes averaged over a known time interval.

Displays

There are two front panel displays:
Navigation   (upper display) 10mm high, 7-segment liquid crystal.
Management   (lower display) 40 character dot-matrix liquid crystal.

Navigation
Information displayed:
(a) Latitude and longitude of present position (degrees, minutes – to 0.01 minute). N, S,
E or W are indicated as appropriate by a small bar opposite letters engraved on the display
bezel. A small letter *c* precedes the latitude reading if corrections have been applied to
LOPs forming the fix.
(b) LOP1 and LOP2; two Decca position lines which form the hyperbolic fix of the present
position. Readings comprise the pattern: Red (R), Green (G), Purple (P) followed by zone
group number, zone letter, lane number and lane fraction (to 0.01 lane). A small bar
following a pattern letter indicates it is one of a preferred pair automatically selected by
the receiver to give the best fix. Three small bars preceding the LOP indicate a manually
selected pair.
(c) Speed Made Good (SMG) and Course Made Good (CMG).
(d) Bearing and distance to the next waypoint in a steering plan (rhumb line, degrees,
nautical miles).
(e) Course to steer and estimated time of arrival to next waypoint in a steering plan (rhumb
line, degrees, hours, minutes).

Management
This display is used for data entry, operating and monitoring procedures. The function
required is chosen from a list of options (in the form of indexes) shown on the display.
Selection is effected using the pushbuttons to enter the chosen prefix number.
   To examine data already held in the memory store, the Management Display
may be used. Different function displays can be selected in turn by entering the
appropriate prefix number. This can be done without the need to return to the management index.

Indicator Lamps
Green indicator lamps marked NP, LIP and 2CH show the position fixing mode in use.
In the two chain and cross chain position fix mode both NP and 2CH lamps are lit.
   Red alarm indicator lamp flashes at 2 second intervals in the event of an alarm or alert.
It is lit continuously in the Dead Reckoning (DR) mode.

Mark 53 operation

General
All functions are accessed using one of three main indexes:
POSN (P)   Position
CHAINS (C)   Chains
RxSIGs (R)   Receiver Signals
The main indexes are displayed on the Management Display by successively pressing
button marked INDEX.
   Every main index has a series of management indexes each prefixed by a number,
indicating the button to press to display the required management index.

To Inspect Index Contents

With the receiver in operation and locked to a chain, the procedure is as follows:

1. Select main index by pressing button INDEX until appropriate index appears in window.
2. Select management index required by pressing appropriately numbered button number.
3. Select function required by pressing button with number relating to required function prefix number.
4. All functions in the function display can be displayed in turn by pressing the buttons relating to the various prefix numbers, without the need to press button 0.
5. To select a subject in the management index, the main index must first be selected.
6. To return to management index from which a function has been selected and displayed, press button 0.
7. To return to the main index press button INDEX or 0.

With the exception of the Test menu, data is not lost from memory when inspecting displays.

Inputs and Outputs

Interface between receiver and peripheral equipment is by serial interface ports of which there are two or three according to the type of receiver. Type A receivers have two ports while type B receivers have an extra port intended for peripheral equipment used in continuous operation with the receiver. For such a receiver inputs include Compass & Speed Log.

Outputs include Autopilot, Remote Decameter Display, Auto Radar Plotting Aid, Printer and Video Plotter CVP 3500. Additionally outputs for the Type B receiver include Track Plotter 350T and External Alarm.

General Specification

The Mk. 53 has a nominal supply voltage of 24 V d.c. (18 V d.c. minumum to 36 V d.c. maximum) and consumes 18 watts maximum. The supply may be a.c. provided a Power supply unit type 5540PA is used. Antenna is type 80325 powered from the receiver via r.f. feeder cable, 50 metres maximum length. An internal battery, of nominal shelf life 3 years, is used to maintain the receiver memory.

4
Loran-C

LORAN is an acronym for LOng RAnge Navigation. It is an electronic system of land based transmitters broadcasting low frequency pulsed signals that enable ships and aircraft to determine their position. The system was developed at the Radiation Laboratory of the Massachusetts Institute of Technology and subsequently operated by the US Coastguard during World War II. The original system, known as Loran-A, has now been superseded by an improved version known as Loran-C. However, the basic principles of both systems are the same.

4.1 System principles

The Loran transmitter stations send out a stream of pulses at a specified rate (the pulse repetition rate, PRR or the reciprocal of the pulse repetition frequency, PRF). Assume the PRF is 25, i.e. 25 pulses are transmitted every second, and the pulse width is 40 microseconds, then the period of the pulse is 1/25 seconds or 40 000 microseconds.

Assuming that the velocity of radio waves in free space is $3 \times 10\,\mathrm{m\,s}^{-1}$, then the distance travelled by a pulse may be measured in terms of the *time* taken to travel that distance, i.e. if a pulse took 1000 microseconds to travel a certain distance then the distance is given by:

$$d = v \times t$$

where

d = distance in metres

v = velocity of radio waves in $\mathrm{m\,s}^{-1}$

t = time in seconds taken for pulse to travel d metres.

then $d = (3 \times 10^8 \times 1000 \times 10^{-6})$ metres

or $d = 300\,\mathrm{km}$

4.2 Loran lines of position (LOPs)

Consider two transmitters A and B simultaneously transmitting the same pulse stream (Figure 4.1). If we assume that the distance between the transmitters is 972 nautical miles

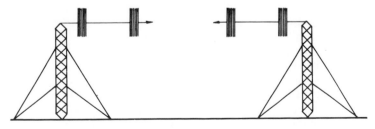

Fig. 4.1 The Loran system: two transmitters each radiating short pulses of specified length at a specified repetition interval

or 1800 km (since 1 nautical mile = 1.85 km approximately), then the time taken to cover the distance between the transmitters is 6000 microseconds. It follows that LOPs may be plotted for *difference* in arrival time of the pulses from each transmitter. In figure 4.2 a plot of all possible positions where the time difference in pulse reception is 2000 microseconds is shown.

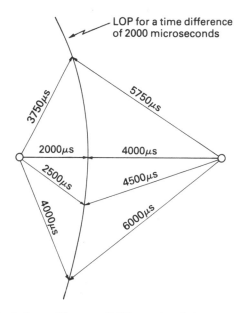

Fig. 4.2 Line of constant time difference (LOP) produced from two stations emitting pulses simultaneously

This plot is of a hyperbola with the transmitter stations as the foci. It is obvious that other hyperbolae may be plotted for other time differences and this has been done in figure 4.3 for time differences in steps of 1000 microseconds. Note that from this diagram the time difference LOPs are symmetrically disposed about the centre line i.e. there are two 2000 μs LOPs. Hence if the only information at the receiver is the time difference value then an ambiguity can occur.

The ambiguity may be avoided by causing the second station, say station B, to be triggered by the pulse received from station A. The hyperbolic LOPs for this arrangement are no different from the original arrangement but the values of time difference are different for each LOP as shown in figure 4.4. Station A in this case is known as the *Master* station while station B is known as the *Secondary* station.

This arrangement, although apparently solving the ambiguity problem, has in fact created another problem, since as figure 4.4 shows, in the region of the baseline extension for the Secondary (station B), the difference in arrival time of the two sets of pulses is smaller than the width of the actual pulse and is in fact zero on the baseline extension. Hence in these regions it would be impossible to separate the two pulses to measure the difference in arrival times.

This drawback is solved by delaying the transmission of the pulse from the Secondary for a certain period of time after the pulse from the Master has arrived. This delay period is known as a coding delay. Figure 4.5 has been drawn indicating a coding delay of 1000 microseconds. Again no two LOPs have the same time difference, eliminating possible

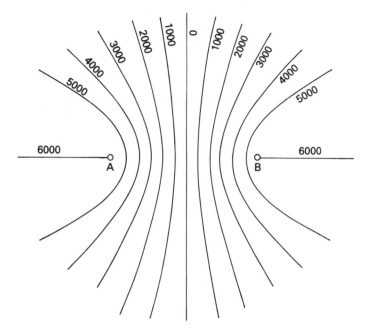

Fig. 4.3 Lines of constant time difference (LOPs) produced from two stations emitting pulses simultaneously

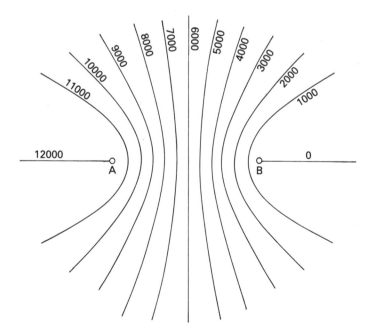

Fig. 4.4 Modification of the LOPs in figure 4.3. Station B is now allowed to transmit until triggered by a pulse from Station A

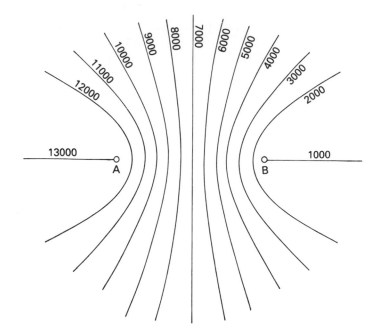

Fig. 4.5 A further modification of figure 4.3. Not only must Station B wait for a pulse to arrive from Station A but there is also a coding delay of 1000 μ s in this example, thus further altering the time difference values of each LOP

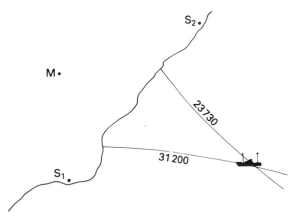

Fig. 4.6 Position fixing by using LOPs from two pairs of master/secondary stations

ambiguity, and the coding delay ensures that no area is unable to receive two distinctly separate pulses. It is important to ensure that the coding delay is kept accurately constant since any variation in this value would cause errors in received time differences giving erroneous positioning of the vessel containing the receiver.

The LOPs are overprinted on charts showing the value of time difference for each LOP. Thus using an on-board receiver which is capable of comparing the delay in reception of the pulses from the Master and Secondary stations, it is possible to plot the position of the vessel along a particular LOP (or, by interpolation between two adjacent LOPs, if the time difference obtained is not the exact value printed on the chart). All that is necessary to establish a position fix for the vessel is to establish the position along a second, intersecting, LOP (whether actual or interpolated) using another pair of transmitting stations i.e. the Master, common to all station pairs, and a second Secondary station. (Figure 4.6)

4.3 Loran-A

This system uses Master and Secondary stations separated by 200–300 nautical miles (370–550 km approx.) and transmitting in the frequency range 1850–1950 kHz. The pulses from each station are compared in the receiver using a cathode ray tube (CRT) which enables the pulses to be visually observed. The CRT (Figure 4.7) is provided with a saw tooth voltage signal which produces a horizontal deflection of the electron beam to drive the spot across the face of the tube. The pulses received from the transmitter stations are applied to the vertical deflection plates of the CRT so that they appear as vertical deflections on the trace (Figure 4.8). Measurement of the time difference T will give the time difference value (LOP) for the receiver for that particular master/secondary pair. The rate at which the time base causes the CRT spot to be deflected across the face of the tube can be controlled and if it is made equal to the pulse repetition rate of the transmitted pulses then the pulses appear to be stationary on the screen. Pulses received at any other PRF would not appear as stationary pulses but would 'drift' across the face of the tube and hence can easily be rejected by the operator.

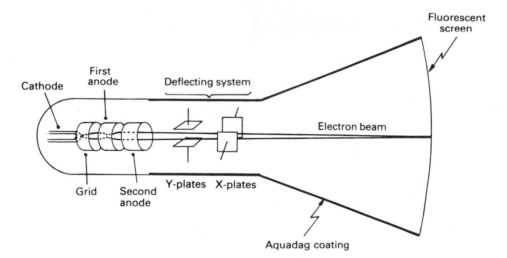

Fig. 4.7 Basic construction of a cathode ray tube. The electrons emitting from the indirectly heated cathode are excited to a high velocity by a large potential difference between the anode and the cathode. This high velocity accelerates the electron beam through the anodes to strike the screen producing a bright spot (due to the fluorescent material). The beam may be deflected to any part of the screen by applying suitable potentials to the X and Y plates. The aquadag coating, held to the same potential as the final anode, helps to maintain the electron beam velocity and provides a return path for the electrons.

A process known as envelope-matching enables the operator to superimpose the master and secondary pulses on the cathode ray tube screen; the amount of delay having to be applied to effect the lining-up of the two pulses being used to indicate which LOP the

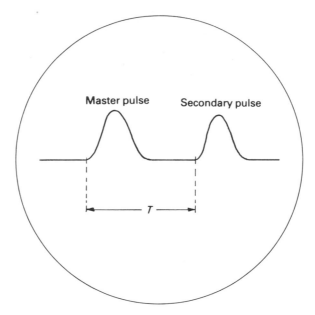

Fig. 4.8 Face of a CRT screen showing the received pulses from the master and secondary stations

vessel is on. This envelope-matching can be achieved manually or automatically according to the receiver used.

The Loran-A stations are identified by the master and secondary of a pair using the same transmitting frequency and transmitting at the same pulse repetition rate. This rate differs from the value used by other pairs in the same chain. Since a receiver is tuned to a particular frequency and pulse repetition rate, then only the pulses from that particular master/secondary pair will be shown on the CRT screen. The receiver has controls which enable selection of a pulse repetition rate as follows:

(a) A basic pulse repetition rate switch with six positions:

H	33 pulses per second
L	25 pulses per second
S	20 pulses per second
SH	16 pulses per second
SL	12 pulses per second
SS	10 pulses per second

(b) A specific pulse repetition rate switch with eight positions which vary the basic repetition rates as shown in Table 4.6.

Loran-A charts are marked to indicate for a particular station pair:

1. The channel number i.e.   1 – 1950 kHz
                              2 – 1850 kHz
                              3 – 1900 kHz

2. Basic and specific pulse repetion rates e.g. 1SL2 indicates a transmission frequency of 1950 kHz at a pulse repetition rate of 79 800 microseconds (a PRF of 10/79 800 pulses per second).

The range of the system is from 500–700 nautical miles (900–1300 km) during the day with an absolute accuracyof ½–2 nautical miles (approximately 1–4 km).

4.4 Loran-C

In the early 1970s the US Department of Transportation which, through the US Coastguard, was responsible for the Loran stations, decided that the existing coverage and accuracy provided by the Loran-A stations was below standard and the system of Loran-C, already extant in some regions of the U.S., was adopted to replace it.

The Loran-C system uses a chain of from three to five land-based transmitting stations. One station is designated the Master (M), while the other stations are designated as secondary stations Whisky (W), X-Ray (X), Yankee (Y) and Zulu (Z). See figure 4.9. All transmitters are synchronized so that signals from the secondaries have precise time interval relationships with transmissions from the Master. This is achieved by the use of atomic oscillators at the stations.

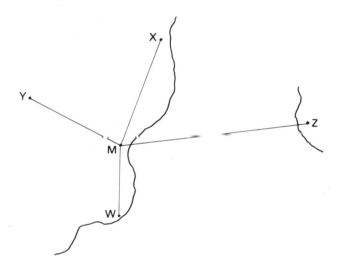

Fig. 4.9 A chain may be configured from a master and up to four secondaries

Loran-C uses a transmission frequency of 100 kHz and this lower frequency compared with Loran-A gives greater range of reception. The pulse width is 250 microseconds compared to 40 microseconds for Loran-A. The actual pulse shape is different for both systems as figure 4.10 shows. Since Loran-C achieves its greater accuracy by a process of

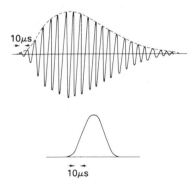

Fig. 4.10 Comparison of pulses for Loran-A (lower) and Loran-C (upper)

'cycle-matching' i.e. matching specified *cycles* of the received master and secondary pulses rather than the *envelope* as in Loran-A, the Loran-C pulse is subject to stringent specification requirements.

Each station transmits a pulse which increases rapidly in amplitude and decays at a rate depending on the particular transmitter (Figure 4.11). The standard pulse leading edge requirement is defined as

$$i(t) = 0 \qquad ; \text{ for } t < \tau$$

$$i(t) = A(t - \tau)^2 \exp\left[\frac{-2(t - \tau)}{65} \right] \sin(0.2\pi t + PC) \quad ; \quad \text{for } \tau < t < (65 + \tau)$$

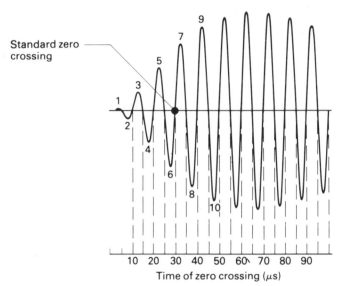

Fig. 4.11 Zero crossing times and labels for half-cycles. This figure shows a 'positive' pulse. For a 'negative' pulse the polarity changes but the labels remain the same

where $i(t)$ is the Loran-C antenna waveform
  A is the normalization constant related to the peak antenna current magnitude in amperes
  t is the time in microseconds
  τ is the envelope to cycle difference (ECD) in microseconds
  PC is the phase-code parameter, in radians, which is 0 for positive phase code and π for negative phase code

The ECD is determined as the difference in time between the actual waveform, sampled at the first eight half-cycle peaks, and the standard leading edge as defined above.

The pulse trailing edge (that portion of the pulse following the peak of the pulse, or 65 microseconds, whichever occurs first) is controlled in order to maintain spectrum requirements. At different transmitting sites, or with different transmitting equipments, the pulse trailing edge may differ significantly in appearance and characteritics. Regardless of these differences, for each pulse and for all $t > 500$ microseconds, $i(t)$ satisfies the pulse trailing edge tolerances based upon peak amplitude (A)

Category 1: $i(t) \le 0.0014 A$
Category 2: $i(t) \le 0.016 A$

There is a tolerance placed on the amplitude of half-cycles both individually and as a group (considering only the first eight half-cycles). Zero crossing times and tolerances of the first group of pulses are shown in Table 4.1 for the first pulse. The zero crossing times are measured with respect to the standard zero crossing which gives a positive going zero crossing at 30 microseconds for a positively coded pulse. ECDs in the range -2.5 to $+2.5$ microseconds are assumed.

Table 4.1 Zero crossing times (with respect to the standard zero crossing) and tolerances.

Zero Crossing (μs)	Time (μs)	Tolerance (ns) Category 1	Category 2
5	-25	± 1000	± 2000
10	-20	± 100	± 1500
15	-15	± 75	± 1000
20	-10	± 50	± 500
25	-5	± 50	± 250
30	Standard zero crossing	(Time Reference)	
35	5	± 50	± 100
40	10	± 50	± 100
45	15	± 50	± 100
50	20	± 50	± 100
55	25	± 50	± 100
60	30	± 50	$+ 100$

Beyond 60 μs the zero crossings conform to 100 kHz $\pm$ 1 kHz

Pulse groups

Each Loran-C station operates with a specified group repetition interval (GRI) which are multiples of 10 μs from 4000 μs up to 99 990 μs. The particular GRI is recognized by its GRI value divided by 10 i.e. 7980 would define a GRI of 79 800 μs.

Secondary pulse groups are transmitted with the same GRI as the master pulse group and are linked in time to the master. The delays in transmissions from secondary stations with respect to the master are selected to ensure the following criteria are met wherever signals can be received for any particular chain:
(a) Minimum time difference between any secondary and master is 10 900 μs.
(b) Minimum difference of any two time differences is 9900 μs.
(c) Maximum time difference is the Group Repetition Interval minus 9900 μs.
(d) Minimum spacing between corresponding points of the last pulse of any stations group and the first pulse of the next group in the same chain is 2900 μs, except that the minimum spacing between the master's ninth pulse and the next secondary pulse (of the same chain) may be as little as 1900 μs. This is a direct result of applying the first three criteria.

Figure 4.12 gives an indication of the constraints for emission delay.

Uniformity of pulses within a pulse group
The uniformity of pulses within a pulse group depends not only on the equipment used but whether the station is single-rated (SR) or double-rated (DR). Double-rated means that the master station is common to *two* chains and transmits on *two* different GRIs. The amplitude of the smallest pulse in the group compared with the amplitude of the largest pulse in the same group should not differ by more than the limits specified in Table 4.2.

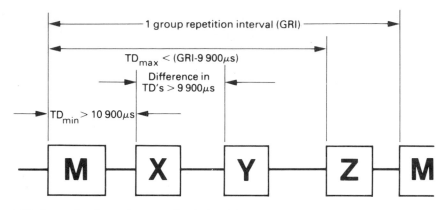

Fig. 4.12 Constraints for assignment of emission delay

Table 4.2 Pulse-to-pulse amplitude tolerance, or percent droop (D)

	Category 1	Category 2
Single Rate	5%	10%
Dual Rate	10%	20%

Table 4.3 Pulse-to-pulse ECD tolerances

	Category 1	Category 2
Single Rate	$0.5\,\mu s$	$1.0\,\mu s$
Dual Rate	$0.7\,\mu s$	$1.5\,\mu s$

Percentage droop is given by:

$$D = \left[\frac{I_{\text{pk. max}} - I_{\text{pk. min}}}{I_{\text{pk. max}}} \right] \times 100$$

where

$I_{\text{pk. max}}$ is the value of $i(t)$ at the peak of the largest pulse

$I_{\text{pk. max}}$ is the value of $i(t)$ at the peak of the smallest pulse

Pulse-to-pulse ECD tolerances

The pulse-to-pulse ECD tolerances account for the pulse-to-pulse leading edge differences and the pulse-to-pulse zero-crossing differences. The ECD of any single antenna current pulse does not differ from the average ECD of all pulses by more than the values given in Table 4.3.

Transmission of Loran-C pulses

Whereas Loran-A transmitted one pulse from the master and another from the secondary, with the two pulses compared in the receiver to obtain a time delay, the Loran-C transmitter emits a series of pulses from the master and secondary stations.

A typical transmission sequence for a Loran-C chain is shown in figure 4.13. The GRI is defined as the time interval between successive pulse groups measured from the third cycle (or zero crossover) of the first pulse of any one station in the group to the third cycle of the first pulse of the same station in the following pulse group. All stations in the chain have the same GRI, and the GRI expressed in tens of microseconds is the identifier for that chain and is called the chain "rate".

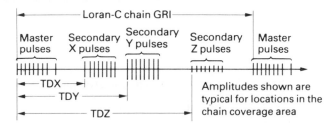

Fig. 4.13 Loran-C chain Group Repetition Interval showing the receipt of master and X, Y and Z secondaries

The master transmitter sends out a series of nine pulses while the secondaries transmit only eight pulses.

Phase coding

Each Loran-C station phase-codes the series of pulses in accordance with Table 4.4. For identification, the first group of pulses in the sequence is labelled Group A and the second group, one GRI later, is labelled Group B. A transmission sequence (the phase-code interval or PCI) comprises both Group A and Group B and the PCI sequence is thereafter repeated. The minus sign in Table 4.4 stands for a pulse that is 180° out of phase with the "normal" pulse i.e. the phase of the pulse is inverted.

Fig. 4.4 Loran-C phase codes

	Station	
Group	Master	Secondary
A	+ + − − + − + − +	+ + + + + − − +
B	+ − − + + + + −	+ − + − + + − −

Pulse-to-pulse timing tolerances

Pulses two to eight of a group are referenced in time to the first pulse of each group. The timing relationship and tolerances of the standard zero crossings of pulses two to eight with respect to pulse one standard zero crossing are shown in Table 4.5. The ninth pulse of the master transmission is spaced 2000 microseconds from the eighth pulse of the group. This pulse is used primarily as a visual aid to master group identification and not as an aid to navigation.

The use of phase coding allows automatic Loran-C receivers to distinguish between master and secondary transmissions and also assists the receiver to operate when the Loran signals are weak in the presence of noise.

Table 4.5 Pulse-to-pulse timing tolerances. *N* is the pulse number (2 through 8) of the pulses which follow the first pulse within each group. C is 0 for positively phase coded pulses; ICI ≤ 150 ns for negatively phase coded pulses. The standard zero crossing of pulse one is the time reference within each group

	Category 1	Category 2
Single Rate	(N − 1) 1000 μs ± 25 ns	(N − 1) 1000 μs ± 50 ns + C
Dual Rate	(N − 1) 1000 μs ± 50 ns	(N − 1) 1000 μs ± 100 ns + C

Blink

Blink is a repetitive on-off pattern (approximately 0.25 seconds 'on, 3.75 seconds 'off') of the first two pulses of the secondary signal which indicates that the baseline is unusable for one of the following reasons:
(a) TD out of tolerance
(b) ECD out of tolerance
(c) Improper phase code or GRI
(d) Master or secondary station operating at less than one-half of specified power output or master station off the air.

   Blink continues until the out of tolerance condition is eliminated. The ninth pulse of the master may also be blinked simultaneously but by itself master blink is not an indication of an out of tolerance condition.

   Master blink is normally only used for internal Loran-C system communication. If used, the master's ninth pulse will be blinked in accordance with the code shown in Figure 4.14.

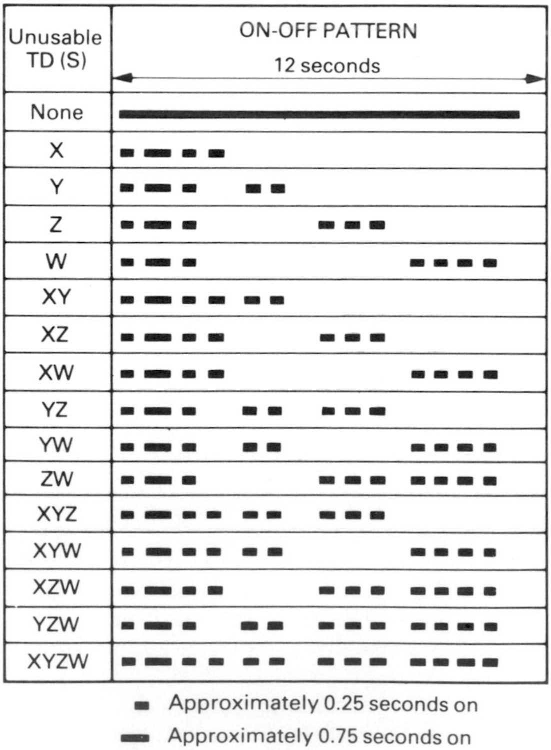

Fig. 4.14 Master ninth pulse blink codes

Table 4.6 List of Loran-C stations together with their compliance requirements

Station	Rate	Pulse trailing edge	Pulse zero crossings	Uniformity of pulses Amplitude	ECD	Timing
Iwo Jima, Japan	9970	1	2	1	2	1
Marcus Island, Japan	9970	1	2	1	2	1
Hokkaido, Japan	9970/5970	1	2	1	2	1
Gesashi, Japan	9970/5970	1	2	1	2	1
Barrigada, Guam	9970	1	2	1	2	1
Johnston IS	4990	2	2	2	2	2
Upolo PT, HI	4990	2	2	2	2	2
Kure IS, HI	4990	2	2	2	2	2
St Paul, AK	9990	2	2	2	2	2
Attu, AK	9990	2	2	2	2	2
Port Clarence, AK	9990	1	2	2	2	2
Narrow Cape, AK	9990/7960	2	2	1	2	1
Tok, AK	7960	1	1	1	1	1
Shoal Cove, AK	7960/5990	1	1	1	1	1
Williams Lake, BC	5990	2	1	1	1	1
George, WA	5990/9940	1	1	1	2	1
Port Hardy, BC*	5990	1	1	1	1	2
Fallon, NV	9940	2	1	1	1	1
Middletown, CA	9940	2	1	1	1	1
Searchlight, NV	9940	1	1	1	1	1
Malone, FL*	8970/7980	1	1	1	1	1
Grangeville, LA*	7980	1	1	1	1	1
Raymondville, TX*	7980	1	1	1	1	1
Jupiter, FL	7980	2	2	2	2	2
Carolina Beach, NC	9960/7980	1	2	1	2	2
Seneca, NY*	9960/8970	1	1	1	1	1
Caribou, ME	9960/5930	1	2	1	2	2
Nantucket, MA	9960/5930	1	2	1	2	2
Dana, IN	9960/8970	2	2	1	2	1
Baudette, MN	8970	2	2	2	2	2
Cape Race, NFLND	5930/7930	2	2	1	2	2
Fox Harbour, LABR	5930/7930	1	1	1	1	1
Angissoq, Greenland	7930/9980	2	2	1	2	2
Sandur, Iceland	9980/7970	2	1	1	1	1
Ejde, Faeroe IS.	7970/9980	2	2	1	2	2
Boe, Norway	7970	2	2	2	2	2
Sylt, Germany	7970	2	2	2	1	2
Jan Mayen, Norway	7970	2	2	2	2	2
Sellia Marina, Italy	7990	2	2	2	2	2
Lampedusa, Italy	7990	2	2	1	2	2
Kargabarun, Turkey	7990	2	2	2	2	2
Estartit, Spain	7990	2	2	2	2	2

* Stations equipped with an AN/FPN-64 solid transmitter.
Other Loran-C stations have become operational since this table was compiled.

A list of Loran-C stations together with their category status as regards pulse generation is shown in Table 4.6.

Elimination of skywave reception

Normal operation of Loran-C assumes reception by ground wave for high accuracy of position fixing. Sky waves always arrive later than ground waves although this difference

In arrival time becomes less as the distance from the transmitter increases. However, the time difference is never less than 30 μs anywhere in the Loran-C coverage area. If therefore only the first 30 μs of the Loran-C pulse is used then sky wave contamination cannot occur.

At distances greater than 1000 nautical miles (1850 km) the ground wave is likely to be unusable because it suffers more attenuation than the sky wave. Thus the sky wave may be used beyond this range but reception of sky wave signals gives lower accuracy and corrections must be applied to compensate for the difference in path travelled compared to the ground wave.

Cycle matching

The technique of matching the pulse envelope, as used in Loran-A, is also used in Loran-C. However, this is only used to give coarse position fixing. The system used to give greater accuracy is cycle-matching. With this technique the receiver has a flywheel oscillator which acquires the frequency and phase of the incoming 100 kHz master pulses. Thus the receiver has a reference frequency which is continually updated by the master pulses and has the same phase as the master signals.

The difference in phase between the flywheel oscillator and the secondary station pulses as received is measured in the receiver and displayed as a time difference down to one-tenth of a microsecond, since the period of a cycle at 100 kHz is 10 μs and the phase difference can be measured up to approximately 1/100 of a cycle.

For example, suppose a phase difference of 0.63 cycle is measured, then the phase difference in microseconds is given by $(0.63 \times 10) \mu$s = 6.3 μs.

The envelope matching method gives the phase difference in tens of thousands, thousands, hundreds and tens of micro-seconds with a tolerance of $\pm$ 4 μs while the cycle-matching gives the units and tenths of a unit. Thus if envelope matching gave a time difference of, say, 52 700 μs and cycle matching gives 4.3 μs, then the accurate value of time difference is 52 704.3 μs.

One method of automatic pulse envelope matching is to compare the received pulses from the secondary station with the pulses from the receiver flywheel oscillator after the latter have been passed through a variable time delay circuit. The delay circuit is necessary because the master pulses will always arrive first anywhere in the system (this is because the secondaries are triggered after the master transmission and there is a coding delay). If the timing of the pulses does not coincide then an error voltage is produced which adjusts a time delay until the start of the two pulses is caused to coincide. When this happens the delay voltage is reduced to zero. The value of the delay must be the same as the delay between the received master and secondary pulses and if displayed in digital form would give the coarse delay figure in microseconds.

One method of fine matching is to use the technique as illustrated in figure 4.15. The received pulse is amplified by a specific amount and shifted in phase by 180°. This new wave is algebraically added to the original wave to produce a resultant wave with a well defined minima at a time before the value where sky wave contamination can occur. The difference in time between the sampling of the master pulse and the secondary pulse is determined in the same way as for envelope matching and the result is also presented on the digital display.

An automatic method of fine matching to allow coverage on extended range utilizes cycle-matching on the *seventh* cycle of the received pulse. A mode switch allows the operator to choose third or seventh cycle-matching facility. Matching may be extended to ranges 500 nautical miles (925 km) grreater than with normal matching because of the greater amplitude of the seventh cycle. The inherent inaccuracies due to possible sky wave

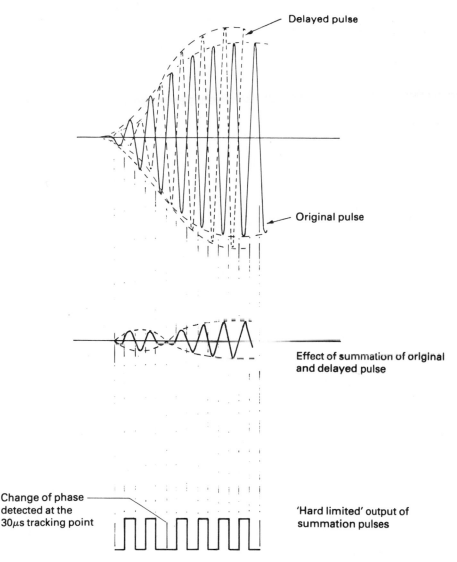

Delayed pulse

Original pulse

Effect of summation of original
and delayed pulse

Change of phase
detected at the
$30\mu s$ tracking point

'Hard limited' output of
summation pulses

Fig. 4.15 Third cycle tracking by the use of the original pulse and a pulse delayed by 5 microseconds, amplified and summed with the original pulse to give a change of phase at the standard zero crossing point

contamination must be taken into account but may be acceptable at the longer ranges involved.

4.5 Loran-C charts

Nautical charts, overprinted with Loran-C LOPs, are available from several sources. They are
(a) The US National Ocean Survey, for charts principally around the US coast,
(b) The Defence Mapping Agency, for world-wide charts,

(c) The Canadian Hydrographic Service, for charts of Canadian waters and

(d) The British Hydrographer of the Navy, for charts of British waters.

Catalogues of charts and the areas covered are available from the organizations mentioned. The charts are identified in terms of the area covered and the designations of the stations serving the area; for example, a chart serving an area in the Atlantic Ocean may require Loran-C LOPs for a master and, say, three secondary stations. In this case the stations are identified by the GRI number and the secondary designation i.e. 7990-X, 7990-Y and 7990-Z.

Not all LOPs are printed on charts. Usually LOPs separated by time intervals of 10 microseconds are used to give lines spaced at reasonable intervals. For LOPs not specified on the chart the operator must interpolate between the lines.

The National Ocean Survey first edition charts are produced with the Loran-C LOPs based on predicted coverage rather than actual field measurements. Since Loran-C signals will have to pass over land for a portion of their path to the receiver (the transmitter stations are land-based and some are considerably distant from the coast) and since the predicted coverage was based on an all sea path then an error is likely to result. The propagation velocity of a low-frequency radio signal is directly related to the conductivity of the surface over which it passes and any change in surface conductivity will affect the propagation of the signal, resulting in a phase retardation at the receiver. This land effect causes an error known as the additional secondary phase factor or additional secondary factor (ASF).

Since additional secondary phase factors can vary from one location to another, there will be points on the chart where there are differences, although usually small, between the actual additional phase factor and the average value that was used for making the chart. In such circumstances there would be a large difference between the Loran-C readings measured and the location on the chart where these readings would be plotted. It is expected that, when necessary, future chart editions will remedy this situation by using varying values for additional phase factors on a chart rather than just a single reading.

Loran-C correction tables are available for those charts that have not been corrected for ASF errors. These tables contain a complete chain and a table section is prepared for each master—secondary pair in that chain. The ASF corrections can be either positive or negative; negative values are indicated by a negative sign preceding the number, the positive values have no sign. The ASF correction tables are intended primarily for the situation where the Loran-C time differences are converted electronically to geographic coordinates. To use the tables the position of the vessel must first be determined to the nearest five minutes of arc in longitude and latitude and the relevant page of the table referred to, to find the value of the correction. The ASF correction is added algebraically to the time difference for the Loran-C pair.

Consider the following example. Loran-C receiver dial readings are 12 153.31 microseconds and 44 451.83 microseconds for pairs 9960-W and 9960-Y respectively. From these readings the computer determines a position of 44°15.1′ N latitude and 67°25.4′ W longitude. Entering the page index of Section W with the latitude and longitude nearest to the computed position of the vessel, the page number containing the derived geographics is found to be 17W (see Table 4.7). Entering page 17W the correction at 44°15′ N and 67°25′ W is + 1.5 microseconds. On page 17Y (Table 4.8), at the same position the correction is + 2.7 microseconds.

The ASF corrections would be applied to the dial readings as follows:

W TD	12 153.31	Y TD	44 451.83
ASF correction	+ 1.5	ASF correction	+ 2.7
Corrected TD	12 154.81	Corrected TD	44 454.53

Table 4.7 Extract from Loran-C correction tables. (Reproduced by courtesy of the Defense Mappling Agency Hydrographic/Topographic Center)

		9960-W												17W
		LONGITUDE WEST												
		68° 0'	55	50	45	40	35	30	25	20	15	10	5	67° 0'
45°	0'													
	55													
	50				LAND									
	45													2.0
	40												1.7	1.6
	35									1.7	1.7	1.6	1.6	1.6
	30							1.7	1.6	1.6	1.6	1.5	1.5	1.5
	25					1.6	1.5	1.5	1.6	1.6	1.6	1.5	1.5	1.5
	20	1.6	1.5	1.6	1.6	1.5	1.4	1.5	1.5	1.5	1.5	1.5	1.5	1.5
	15	1.6	1.5	1.5	1.5	1.5	1.5	1.5	(1.5)	1.5	1.5	1.5	1.4	1.4
	10	1.5	1.4	1.5	1.5	1.4	1.4	1.4	1.4	1.4	1.4	1.4	1.4	1.3
L	5	1.4	1.4	1.5	1.4	1.4	1.4	1.4	1.3	1.3	1.3	1.3	1.3	
A 44°	0'	1.3	1.3	1.3	1.3	1.3	1.3	1.3	1.2	1.3	1.3			
T														
I	55	1.3	1.3	1.2	1.3	1.3	1.3	1.3	1.3	1.2				
T	50	1.3	1.3	1.3	1.3	1.3	1.3	1.3						
U	45	1.3	1.3	1.2	1.3	1.3	1.3							
D	40	1.2	1.2	1.3	1.3	1.3								
E	35	1.3	1.2	1.3										
	30	1.3	1.3	1.3										
	25	1.2	1.3	1.3						OUTSIDE CCZ				
	20	1.2	1.3	1.3	1.3									
N	15	1.2	1.3	1.3	1.3	1.3								
O	10	1.2	1.2	1.3	1.3	1.3								
R	5	1.2	1.2	1.2	1.3	1.3	1.3							
T 43°	0'	1.2	1.2	1.2	1.2	1.3	1.3	1.3						
H														
	55	1.2	1.2	1.2	1.2	1.3	1.3	1.3						
	50	1.2	1.2	1.2	1.2	1,2	1.3	1.3	1.3					
	45	1.2	1.2	1.2	1.2	1.2	1.2	1.3	1.3	1.3				
	40	1.2	1.2	1.2	1.2	1.2	1.2	1.3	1.3	1.3	1.3			
	35	1.2	1.2	1.2	1.2	1.2	1.2	1.3	1.3	1.3	1.3			
	30	1.3	1.2	1.2	1.2	1.2	1.2	1.2	1.2	1.3	1.3			
	25	1.2	1.2	1.2	1.2	1.2	1.3	1.3	1.3	1.2	1.3	1.3	1.3	1.3
	20	1.2	1.2	1.2	1.2	1.2	1.2	1.2	1.3	1.2	1.2	1.2	1.2	1.3
	15	1.2	1.2	1.2	1.2	1.2	1.2	1.2	1.2	1.2	1.2	1.3	1.2
	10	1.2	1.2	1.2	1.2	1.2	1.2	1.2	1.3	1.2	1.2	1.2	1.3	1.2
	5	1.2	1.2	1.2	1.2	1.2	1.2	1.2	1.2	1.2	1.2	1.2	1.2	1.2
42°	0'	1.2	1.2	1.2	1.2	1.2	1.2	1.2	1.2	1.2	1.2	1.2	1.2	1.2

The corrected dial readings are used to re-compute a new latitude and longitude for the Loran-C fix. The new position is: 44°15.4′ N latitude and 67°26.4′ W longitude.

The Loran-C correction tables for a particular chain may be obtained from the US Defense Mapping Agency in the LCPUB221 series.

RASMUSON LIBRARY
UNIVERSITY OF ALASKA-FAIRBANKS

Table 4.8 Extract from Loran-C correction tables. (Reproduced by courtesy of the Defense Mappling Agency Hydrographic/Topographic Center)

		9960-Y												17Y
						LONGITUDE WEST								
		68°0'	55	50	45	40	35	30	25	20	15	10	5	67°0'
45°	0°													
	55													
	50													
	45				LAND									3.4
	40												3.1	3.0
	35									3.0	3.1	3.0	2.9	2.9
	30							2.9	2.9	2.9	2.9	2.8	2.8	2.8
	25					2.7	2.8	2.8	2.8	2.8	2.8	2.8	2.7	2.7
	20	2.8	2.7	2.7	2.7	2.7	2.7	2.7	2.8	2.7	2.7	2.6	2.7	2.6
	15	2.7	2.6	2.6	2.7	2.8	2.7	2.7	(2.7)	2.7	2.6	2.6	2.6	2.6
	10	2.7	2.6	2.6	2.7	2.7	2.6	2.6	2.5	2.5	2.6	2.6	2.6	2.6
L · 5	5	2.6	2.6	2.6	2.6	2.5	2.5	2.4	2.4	2.4	2.5	2.5	2.5	
A · 44°	0'	2.5	2.5	2.5	2.5	2.4	2.4	2.4	2.3	2.4	2.4			
T	55	2.4	2.4	2.4	2.4	2.4	2.4	2.4	2.4	2.4				
I	50	2.4	2.4	2.4	2.4	2.4	2.4	2.4						
T	45	2.4	2.4	2.3	2.4	2.4	2.4							
U	40	2.3	2.3	2.3	2.4	2.4								
D	35	2.4	2.4	2.4										
E	30	2.4	2.4	2.4										
	25	2.4	2.4	2.4						OUTSIDE CCZ				
	20	2.4	2.4	2.4	2.4									
N	15	2.4	2.4	2.4	2.4	2.4								
O	10	2.4	2.4	2.4	2.4	2.4								
R	5	2.4	2.4	2.4	2.4	2.4	2.4							
T · 43°	0'	2.4	2.4	2.4	2.4	2.4	2.4	2.4						
H	55	2.4	2.4	2.4	2.4	2.4	2.4	2.4						
	50	2.4	2.4	2.4	2.4	2.4	2.4	2.4	2.4					
	45	2.4	2.4	2.4	2.4	2.4	2.4	2.4	2.4	2.4				
	40	2.4	2.4	2.4	2.4	2.4	2.4	2.4	2.4	2.4	2.4			
	35	2.5	2.4	2.4	2.4	2.4	2.4	2.4	2.4	2.4	2.4			
	30	2.5	2.5	2.4	2.4	2.4	2.4	2.4	2.4	2.4	2.4			
	25	2.4	2.4	2.4	2.4	2.4	2.4	2.4	2.4	2.4	2.4	2.4	2.4	2.5
	20	2.4	2.4	2.4	2.4	2.4	2.4	2.4	2.4	2.4	2.4	2.4	2.4	2.4
	15	2.4	2.4	2.4	2.4	2.4	2.4	2.4	2.4	2.4	2.4	2.4	2.4	2.4
	10	2.4	2.3	2.4	2.4	2.4	2.4	2.4	2.4	2.4	2.4	2.4	2.4	2.4
	5	2.4	2.3	2.4	2.4	2.4	2.4	2.4	2.4	2.4	2.4	2.4	2.4	2.4
42°	0'	2.4	2.3	2.3	2.4	2.3	2.4	2.4	2.4	2.4	2.4	2.4	2.4	2.4

4.6 Loran-C lattice tables

Loran-C lattice tables provide the coordinates necessary for the construction of straight line representations of segments of the hyperbolic LOPs. Except when the user of the Loran-C system is within 20 nautical miles (37 km) of a transmitting station, the straight line segment joining any two tabulated points can be used without appreciable error. For information about lattice table availability, the DMA catalogue of nautical charts (Publication 221, Loran-C Table) should be consulted. This publication is a series of lattice tables, there being a separate table for each secondary station of a chain.

Each table is identified by the publication number (221) and its pertinent suffix, for example Pub. 221(2016) is for the pair 5990-Y of the Canadian West Coast chain. These tables are *not* compensated for ASF so care should be taken to compensate for at least one calibration correction.

Points on hyperbolae separated by a time difference of 10 microseconds are tabulated in the lattice tables at intervals of whole degrees of latitude or longitude except in those areas close to a transmitting station. In such areas, points are tabulated at intervals of whole degrees or quarters of degrees, depending on the amount of curvature of the line. A separate column is given for each tabulated reading at intervals of 10 microseconds, with an extra labelled column which gives the change in longitude (or latitude) to 0.01' for a 1 microsecond change in the time difference reading.

Tabulated readings are for ground waves; sky wave readings should be corrected to give an equivalent ground wave reading before entering the tables.

A ground wave reading is designated T_G, and a sky wave reading T_S. If a ground wave is matched with a sky wave, the reading is labelled T_{GS} if the ground wave is from the master station and T_{SG} if the ground wave is from the secondary station.

The lattice table is entered with the ground wave reading in microseconds and the latitude or longitude. Two points may thus be determined, one each side of the dead reckoning position, and the straight line connecting them is an approximation of a small segment of the LOP.

Since the tables are in columns at 10 microsecond intervals, interpolation is usually required. The lattice table is entered with the tabulated time difference (T) nearest the ground wave reading. The lattitude or longitude extracted are then corrected by the amounts of the products of ($T_G - T$) and Δ, the change in latitude or longitude for a 1 microsecond change in T.

Although this publication is not intended to be a guide to navigation, the following example on the use of the lattice tables is included since the tables form an important adjunct to the Loran-C system.

Example

The 15.30h position of a vessel is latitude 48°35'N, longitude 30°17'W. The vessel is on a 70° course, speed 30 knots. Loran-C readings are taken as follows:

15.30h	7930-X	T_G 29 523.8
15.30h	7930-Z	T_G 48 635.7

The requirement is the 1530h Loran-C fix.

Solution

Enter the time difference tables in the T column nearest to the value of T_G and with the latitudes or longitudes closest to and on each side of the dead reckoning position.

Extract the corresponding longitudes or latitudes for these two points. Interpolate if necessary. Plot the two points thus obtained. Connect these two points with a straight line to determine a segment of a Loran line. Label each plotted line with the time and pair used. The intersection of two lines for different pairs determines a Loran fix, as shown in figure 4.16.

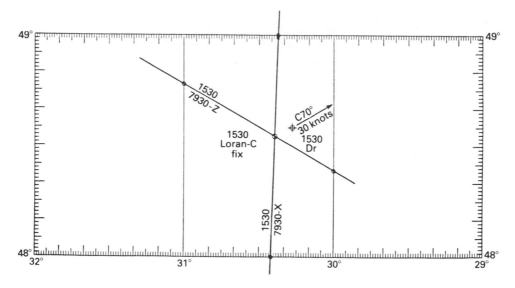

Fig. 4.16 The fix — Loran-C lines are plotted through the following positions: Latitude 48°N, longitude 30° 25.1'W; latitude 49°N, longitude 30° 22.3'W; and latitude 48° 23.4'N, longitude 30°W; latitude 48° 46.7'N, longitude 31°W. The intersection of these lines locates the 1530h Loran-C fix at latitude 48° 32.7'N, longitude 30° 23.6'W

Pair 7930-X Table GF, page 240 (see Table 4.9)

		Lat.	Tabulated Longitude	Δ	Long. Change $(T_G - T) \times (\Delta)$	Interpolated Longitude
T	29 520					
T_G	29 523.8	48°N	30°24.3'W	+ 22	$(+3.8) \times (+.22) = +0.8'$	30°25.1'W
$T_G - T$	+ 3.8	49°N	30°21.5'W	+ 21	$(+3.8) \times (+.21) = +0.8'$	30°22.3'W

Pair 7930-Z Table GR, page 197 (see Table 4.10)

		Long.	Tabulated Latitude	Δ	Lat.. Change $(T_G - T) \times (\Delta)$	Interpolated Latitude
T	48 640					
T_G	48 635.7	30°W	48°24.3'N	+ 20	$(-4.3) \times (+.20) = -0.9'$	48°23.4'N
$T_G - T$	− 4.3	31°W	48°47.5'N	+ 19	$(-4.3) \times (+.19) = -0.8'$	48°46.7'N

The fix.—Loran-C lines are plotted through the following positions: Latitude 48°N, longitude 30°25.1'W; latitude 49°N, longitude 30°22.3'W; and latitude 48°23.4'N, longitude 30°W; latitude 48°46.7'N, longitude 31°W. The intersection of these lines locates the 1530h Loran-C fix at Latitude 48°32.7'N, Longitude 30°23.6'W.

The following example serves to illustrate how the sky wave correction tables may be used. These tables also form part of Pub. 221(2016). The inclusion of this example is to show that the different propagation conditions that can exist at a particular area in the Loran C coverage need to be compensated for to give an accurate fix.

Table 4.9 Extract from Loran-C lattice tables. (Reproduced by courtesy of the Defense Mapping Agency Hydrographic/Topographic Center)

(240) GF   7930-X

T / Lat	29500	Δ	(29520)	Δ	29540	Δ	29560	Δ	29580	Δ
25 N	31 39.6W	36	31 46.8W	35	31 53.9W	35	32 01.1W	36	32 08.3W	36
26 N	31 36.1W	35	31 43.3W	35	31 50.4W	35	31 57.5W	35	32 04.5W	35
27 N	31 32.8W	34	31 39.7W	34	31 46.8W	35	31 53.8W	35	32 00.8W	34
28 N	31 29.4W	34	31 36.3W	34	31 43.2W	34	31 50.0W	34	31 57.0W	34
29 N	31 25.9W	34	31 32.8W	33	31 39.5W	33	31 46.3W	34	31 53.1W	34
30 N	31 22.4W	33	31 29.1W	33	31 35.8W	33	31 42.6W	33	31 49.3W	33
31 N	31 19.0W	32	31 25.5W	32	31 32.1W	32	31 38.7W	33	31 45.4W	33
32 N	31 15.4W	32	31 21.9W	32	31 28.4W	32	31 34.9W	32	31 41.4W	32
33 N	31 11.9W	31	31 18.2W	31	31 24.6W	31	31 31.0W	32	31 37.5W	31
34 N	31 08.3W	31	31 14.6W	31	31 20.8W	31	31 27.1W	31	31 33.4W	31
35 N	31 04.7W	30	31 10.9W	30	31 17.0W	30	31 23.2W	31	31 29.4W	30
36 N	31 01.1W	30	31 07.1W	30	31 13.1W	30	31 19.2W	30	31 25.3W	30
37 N	30 57.5W	29	31 03.4W	29	31 09.3W	29	31 15.3W	29	31 21.3W	29
38 N	30 53.8W	29	30 59.6W	28	31 05.4W	29	31 11.3W	29	31 17.2W	29
39 N	30 50.2W	28	30 55.9W	28	31 01.6W	28	31 07.2W	28	31 13.0W	28
40 N	30 46.6W	27	30 52.1W	27	30 57.6W	27	31 03.3W	28	31 08.9W	27
41 N	30 42.9W	27	30 48.4W	27	30 53.8W	27	30 59.3W	27	31 04.8W	27
42 N	30 39.3W	26	30 44.7W	26	30 50.0W	27	30 55.3W	26	31 00.7W	26
43 N	30 35.7W	26	30 41.0W	26	30 46.2W	26	30 51.4W	26	30 56.6W	26
44 N	30 32.3W	25	30 37.4W	25	30 42.5W	25	30 47.5W	25	30 52.6W	25
45 N	30 28.9W	24	30 33.9W	24	30 38.8W	24	30 43.7W	24	30 48.7W	25
46 N	30 25.7W	24	30 30.5W	23	30 35.3W	24	30 40.1W	24	30 45.0W	24
47 N	30 22.6W	23	30 27.3W	23	30 31.9W	23	30 36.6W	23	30 41.4W	23
(48 N)	30 19.7W	22	30 24.3W	22	30 28.9W	22	30 33.4W	22	30 37.9W	22
(49 N)	30 17.2W	22	30 21.5W	21	30 25.9W	22	30 30.4W	22	30 34.8W	22
T	29500		29520		29540		29560		29580	T

Example

The 2130 dead reckoning position of a vessel is latitude 48°35′N, longitude 46°45′W. The Loran-C readings are as follows:

2130	7930-X	T_S 33114.3
2130	7930-Z	T_{SG} 45632.2

Solution

The observed sky wave reading must be corrected to an equivalent ground wave reading. Since the readings are taken at night, the night-time sky wave correction table must be entered with the dead reckoning position to obtain the correction, interpolating if necessary.

If a sky wave and a ground wave are matched, the observed reading (T_{SG} or T_{GS}) must also be corrected to an equivalent ground wave reading (T_G). Ground wave to sky wave tables also exist in Pub. 221 so that where necessary such a correction can be made. To determine T_G, the correction obtained from the table must be applied to the observed T_{SG}

Table 4.10 Extract from Loran-C lattice tables. (Reproduced by courtesy of the Defense Mapping Agency Hydrographic/Topographic Center)

7930-X   GR (197)

T	48600		48620		(48640)		48660		48680		T
Lat											Long
° '	° '	Δ	° '	Δ	° '	Δ	° '	Δ	° '	Δ	° '
	47 51.8N	21	47 56.0N	21	48 00.3N	21	48 04.5N	21	48 08.7N	21	21 29 W
	48 16.2N	20	48 20.3N	20	48 24.3N	20	48 28.3N	20	48 32.3N	20	20 (30 W)
	48 39.9N	19	48 43.7N	19	48 47.5N	19	48 51.3N	19	48 55.1N	19	19 (31 W)
	49 02.7N	18	49 06.3N	18	49 09.9N	18	49 13.6N	18	49 17.2N	17	32 W
	49 29.7N	17	49 28.1N	17	49 31.5N	17	49 35.0N	17	49 38.4N	17	33 W
	49 45.9N	16	49 49.2N	16	49 52.4N	16	49 55.7N	16	49 58.9N	16	34 W
	50 06.4N	15	50 09.5N	15	50 12.5N	15	50 15.6N	15	50 18.7N	15	35 W
	50 26.1N	14	50 29.1N	14	50 32.0N	14	50 34.9N	14	50 37.8N	14	36 W
	50 45.2N	13	50 48.0N	13	50 50.8N	13	50 53.5N	13	50 56.2N	13	37 W
	51 03.6N	13	51 06.2N	13	51 08.9N	13	51 11.5N	12	51 14.0N	13	38 W
	51 21.3N	12	51 23.9N	12	51 26.3N	12	51 28.8N	12	51 31.3N	12	39 W
	51 38.5N	11	51 40.8N	11	51 43.2N	11	51 45.6N	11	51 47.9N	11	40 W
	51 55.0N	11	51 57.3N	11	51 59.6N	11	52 01.8N	10	52 04.0N	11	41 W
	52 11.1N	10	52 13.2N	10	52 15.3N	10	52 17.5N	10	52 19.6N	10	42 W
	52 26.6N	10	52 23.6N	10	52 30.6N	10	52 32.7N	10	52 34.7N	9	43 W
	52 41.5N	9	52 43.5N	9	52 45.5N	9	52 47.4N	9	52 49.3N	9	44 W
	52 56.1N	9	52 58.0N	9	52 59.8N	9	53 01.7N	9	53 03.6N	9	45 W
	53 10.2N	9	53 12.0N	9	53 13.9N	9	53 15.6N	8	53 17.4N	9	46 W
	53 23.9N	8	53 25.7N	8	53 27.4N	8	53 29.2N	8	53 31.0N	8	47 W
	53 37.2N	8	53 39.0N	8	53 40.7N	8	53 42.4N	8	53 44.1N	8	48 W
	53 50.2N	8	53 51.9N	8	53 53.6N	8	53 55.3N	8	53 57.0N	8	49 W
	54 02.8N	8	54 04.5N	8	54 06.2N	8	54 07.9N	8	54 09.6N	8	50 W
	54 15.0N	8	54 16.7N	8	54 18.4N	8	54 20.2N	8	54 21.9N	8	51 W
	54 26.9N	8	54 28.6N	8	54 30.3N	8	54 32.1N	8	54 33.8N	8	52 W
	54 38.3N	8	54 40.1N	8	54 41.9N	9	54 43.7N	8	54 45.5N	8	53 W
T	48600		48620		48640		48660		48680		T

or T_{GS} reading. After T_G is found, the remainder of the solution is the same as for the previous example.

Pair 7930-X Table GF, page LXV (Table 4.11)			Pair 7930-X Table GF, Page 328 (Table 4.13)	
T_S	33114.3		T	33120
Conventional Correction	+ 8.1		T_G	33122.4
T_G	33122.4		$T_G - T$	+ 2.4

Lat.	Tabulated Longitude	Δ	Long. Change $(T_G - T) \times (\Delta)$	Interpolated Longitude
48°N	46°59.5'W	+ 40	(+2.4) × (+.40) = +1.0'	47°00.5'W
49°N	46°20.3'W	+ 30	(+2.4) × (+.38) = +0.9'	46°21.4'W

Fig. 4.11 Extract from Loran-C skywave correction tables. (Reproduced by courtesy of the Defense Mapping Agency Hydrographic/Topographic Center).

7930-X SKYWAVE CORRECTION GF

NIGHTTIME (h = 91 km.)

Longitude–59° W to 45° W

GF	59	58	57	56	55	54	53	52	51	50	49	48	47	46	45	GF
89																89
88																88
87																87
86																86
85																85
84																84
83									0.0	0.0	0.0					83
82	0.0	0.0	0.0	0.0	0.0	0.0	0.0	0.0	0.1	0.1	0.1	0.0	0.0	0.0	0.0	82
81	0.2	0.2	0.2	0.2	0.3	0.3	0.3	0.3	0.2	0.2	0.2	0.2	0.1	0.1	0.1	81
80	0.4	0.5	0.5 ADD	0.5	0.5	0.5	0.4	0.4 ADD	0.4	0.3	0.3	0.3	0.2 ADD	0.2	0.2	80
79	0.7	0.7	0.7	0.7	0.7	0.6	0.6	0.6	0.5	0.5	0.5	0.4	0.4	0.4	0.3	79
78	1.0	1.0	1.0	0.9	0.9	0.9	0.9	0.8	0.8	0.8	0.7	0.7	0.6	0.6	0.5	78
77	1.3	1.3	1.3	1.3	1.3	1.2	1.2	1.2	1.1	1.1	1.1	1.0	1.0	0.9	0.8	77
76	1.7	1.7	1.7	1.7	1.7	1.7	1.7	1.6	1.6	1.6	1.5	1.5	1.4	1.3	1.3	76
75	2.3	2.3	2.3	2.3	2.3	2.3	2.3	2.3	2.2	2.2	2.2	2.1	2.0	2.0	1.9	75
74	2.9	3.0	3.0	3.1	3.1	3.1	3.1	3.1	3.1	3.1	3.0	3.0	2.9	2.8	2.7	74
73	3.8	3.9	4.0	4.0	4.1	4.2	4.2	4.2	4.2	4.2	4.2	4.1	4.1	4.0	3.9	73
72	4.9	5.0	5.2	5.3	5.4	5.5	5.6	5.7	5.7	5.7	5.7	5.7	5.6	5.5	5.4	72
71	6.2	6.4	6.7	6.9	7.1	7.3	7.4	7.6	7.7	7.7	7.8	7.8	7.7	7.6	7.5	71
70	7.8	8.1	8.5 ADD	8.8	9.2	9.5	9.8	10 ADD	10	10	10	10	10 ADD	10	10	70
69	9.7	10	11	11	12	12	13	13	13	14	14	14	14	14	14	69
68	12	13	14	14	15	16	17	17	18	18	19	19	19	19	19	68
67	15	16	17	18	19	20	21	22	23	24	25	25	26	26	26	67
66	17	19	20	22	24	26	27	29	31	32	33	34	35	35	35	66
65	20	22	25	27	30	32	35	38	40	43	45	47	48	49	49	65
64	23	26	29	32	36	40	44	48	53	57	61	65				64
63	26	29	33	38	42	48	54	61								63
62	28	32	36	42	48	56	64									62
61	29	33	38	45	52	61										61
60	29	33	38	45	52	62										60

DO NOT USE SKYWAVES

(Latitude North)

Fig. 4.11 *(contd.)*

SKYWAVE CORRECTION

7930-X — Longitude 59°W to 45°W — NIGHTTIME — LATITUDE NORTH

IN THIS AREA ADD

LAT	59	58	57	56	55	54	53	52	51	50	49	48	47	46	45	GF
59	27	31	36	42	50	58										59
58	25	29	33	38	44	52	60									58
57	22	25	29	33	38	44	50	57	65							57
56	19	22	25	28	32	36	40	45	50	56	61	65				56
55	16	18	21	23	26	29	32	35	39	42	45	48	50	51	51	55
54	13	15	17	19	21	23	25	27	30	32	34	35	37	37	37	54
53	11	12	14	15	17	18	20	21	23	24	26	27	27	28	28	53
52	9.0	10	11	12	13	14	15	17	18	19	19	20	21	21	21	52
51	7.3	8.0	8.8	9.6	10	11	12	13	14	14	15	15	16	16	16	51
50	5.8	6.4	7.0	7.6	8.2	8.8	9.4	10	11	11	11	12	12	12	12	50
49	4.6	5.0	5.5	5.9	6.4	6.8	7.3	7.7	8.1	8.4	8.7	9.0	(9.1)	9.2	9.3	(49)
48	3.6	3.9	4.3	4.6	5.0	5.3	5.6	5.9	6.2	6.5	6.7	6.9	(7.0)	7.0	7.1	(48)
47	2.8	3.1	3.3	3.6	3.8	4.1	4.3	4.6	4.8	4.9	5.1	5.2	5.3	5.4	5.4	47
46	2.2	2.4	2.6	2.7	2.9	3.1	3.3	3.5	3.6	3.8	3.9	4.0	4.0	4.1	4.1	46
45	1.6	1.8	1.9	2.1	2.2	2.4	2.5	2.6	2.7	2.8	2.9	3.0	3.0	3.1	3.1	45
44	1.2	1.3	1.5	1.6	1.7	1.8	1.9	2.0	2.1	2.1	2.2	2.3	2.3	2.3	2.3	44
43	0.9	1.0	1.1	1.2	1.2	1.3	1.4	1.5	1.5	1.6	1.6	1.7	1.7	1.7	1.7	43
42	0.6	0.7	0.8	0.8	0.9	0.9	1.0	1.1	1.1	1.2	1.2	1.2	1.2	1.2	1.3	42
41	0.4	0.4	0.5	0.5	0.6	0.6	0.7	0.7	0.8	0.8	0.8	0.8	0.9	0.9	0.9	41
40	0.1	0.2	0.2	0.3	0.3	0.4	0.4	0.5	0.5	0.5	0.5	0.6	0.6	0.6	0.6	40
39	0.0	0.0	0.0	0.1	0.1	0.1	0.2	0.2	0.2	0.3	0.3	0.3	0.3	0.3	0.3	39
38				0.0	0.0	0.0	0.0	0.0	0.0	0.0	0.1	0.1	0.1	0.1	0.1	38
37											0.0	0.0	0.0	0.0	0.0	37
36																36
35																35
34																34
33																33
32																32
31																31
30																30

Table 4.12 Extract from Loran-C skywave correction tables. (Reproduced by courtesy of the Defense Mapping Agency Hydrographic/Topographic Center.)

7930-Z GROUNDWAVE TO SKYWAVE CORRECTION GR

NIGHTTIME (h = 91 km.)
Groundwave from Slave (R) to First-hop skywave from Master (G)

Longitude 59° W to 45° W

		59	58	57	56	55	54	53	52	51	50	49	48	47	46	45		
	69																69	
	68																68	
	67																67	
	66																66	
	65																65	
	64																64	
	63																63	
	62																62	
	61																61	
	60																60	
	59																59	
	58																58	
	57																57	
	56																56	
	55																55	
			ADD															
	54	68	69	71	73												54	
	53	65	66	68	69	71	72										53	
	52	63	64	65	66	67	68	70	71	72	73						52	
	51	61	62	63	64	65	65	66	67	68	68	69	69	70	70	70	51	
L	50	60	60	61	62	62	63	63	64	65	65	66	66	66	66	66	50	L
A						ADD					ADD							A
T	49	59	59	60	60	60	61	61	62	62	63	63	63	63	63	63	49	T
I	48	58	58	58	59	59	59	60	60	60	61	61	61	61	61	61	48	I
T	47	57	57	57	58	58	58	58	59	59	59	59	59	59	59	59	47	T
U	46	56	56	57	57	57	57	57	58	58	58	58	58	58	58	58	46	U
D	45	56	56	56	56	56	56	57	57	57	57	57	57	57	57	57	45	D
E			ADD						ADD						ADD			E
	44	55	55	56	56	56	56	56	56	56	56	56	56	56	56	56	44	
	43	55	55	55	55	55	55	55	56	56	56	56	56	56	56	56	43	
	42	55	55	55	55	55	55	55	55	55	55	55	55	55	55	55	42	
	41	54	55	55	55	55	55	55	55	55	55	55	55	55	55	55	41	
	40	54	54	54	54	54	54	55	55	55	55	55	55	55			40	
						ADD												
	39			54	54	54	54	54	54	54	54						39	
N	38																38	N
O	37																37	O
R	36																36	R
T	35																35	T
H																		H
	34																34	
	33																33	
	32																32	
	31																31	
	30																30	
		59	58	57	56	55	54	53	52	51	50	49	48	47	46	45		

Longitude—59° W to 45° W

Groundwave from slave (R) to First-hop Skywave from Master (G)
NIGHTTIME

Pair 7930-Z   Table GR, Page XLVII (Table 4.12)   Pair 7930-Z   Table GR, page 97 (Table 4.14)

T_{SG}	45632.2	T	45700
Special Correction	+ 62	T_G	45694.2
T_G	45694.2	$T_G - T$	− 5.8

Long	Tabulated Latitude	Δ	Lat. Change $(T_G - T) \times (\Delta)$	Interpolated Latitude
46°W	48°10.9′N	+ 13	$(-5.8) \times (+.13) = -0.8′$	48°10.1′N
47°2	48°41.8′N	+ 11	$(-5.8) \times (+.11) = -0.6′$	48°41.2′N

The fix.—Following the procedure for plotting loran lines as shown in the previous example on p. 98, the 21.30 h Loran-C fix is Latitude 48°31.3′N, Longitude 46°40.2′W.

Table 4.13 Extract from Loran-C lattice tables. (Reproduced by courtesy of the Defense Mapping Agency Hydrographic/Topographic Center)

7930-Z												GR (97)
T (45700)		45720		45740		45760		45780		T		
Lat										Long		
° ′	° ′	Δ	° ′	Δ	° ′	Δ	° ′	Δ	° ′	Δ	° ′	
	46 57.7N	16	47 01.0N	16	47 04.3N	15	47 07.6N	15	47 10.8N	16	44 W	
	47 36.2N	14	47 39.2N	14	47 42.1N	14	47 45.0N	14	47 47.8N	14	45 W	
	48 10.9N	13	48 13.6N	13	48 16.2N	12	48 18.7N	12	48 21.3N	12	46 W	
	48 41.8N	11	48 44.2N	11	48 46.5N	11	48 48.8N	11	48 51.1N	11	47 W	
	49 08.9N	10	49 11.0N	10	49 13.1N	10	49 15.2N	10	49 17.2N	10	48 W	
	49 32.1N	9	49 34.0N	9	49 36.0N	9	49 37.9N	9	49 39.8N	9	49 W	
	49 37.3N	9	49 39.2N	9	49 41.1N	9	49 43.0N	9	49 44.9N	9	49 15W	
	49 42.3N	9	49 44.2N	9	49 46.0N	9	49 47.9N	9	49 49.8N	9	49 30W	
	49 47.0N	9	49 48.9N	9	49 50.8N	9	49 52.6N	8	49 54.4N	9	49 45W	
	49 51.6N	8	49 53.4N	9	49 55.2N	9	49 57.1N	9	49 58.8N	8	50 W	
	49 56.0N	8	49 57.7N	8	49 59.4N	8	50 01.3N	9	50 03.1N	8	50 15W	
	50 00.0N	8	50 01.7N	8	50 03.5N	8	50 05.3N	8	50 07.0N	8	50 30W	
	50 03.9N	8	50 06.6N	8	50 07.4N	8	50 09.1N	8	50 10.9N	8	50 45W	
	50 07.6N	8	50 09.3N	8	50 11.0N	8	50 12.7N	8	50 14.5N	8	51 W	
	50 11.0N	8	50 12.7N	8	50 14.4N	8	50 16.1N	8	50 17.9N	8	51 15W	
	50 14.3N	8	50 15.9N	8	50 17.7N	8	50 19.4N	8	50 21.1N	8	51 30W	
	50 17.4N	8	50 19.0N	8	50 20.7N	8	50 22.4N	8	50 24.1N	8	51 45W	
	50 20.2N	8	50 21.9N	8	50 23.6N	8	50 25.2N	8	50 26.9N	8	52 W	
	50 22.8N	8	50 24.5N	8	50 26.2N	8	50 27.9N	8	50 29.5N	8	52 15W	
	50 25.3N	8	50 27.0N	8	50 28.7N	8	50 30.4N	8	50 32.0N	8	52 30W	

4.7 Position fixing using the Loran-C System

For a particular location covered by more than one Loran-C chain, the operator should select the best chain available, and where possible, select a chain that can be used throughout the voyage so that the receiver can "lock on" to the signal and "track" throughout the trip.

Having selected a chain, it is necessary to select secondary stations which give the best fix. There may be a choice of more than two master-secondary station pairs and it is

Table 4.14 Extract from Loran-C lattice tables. (Reproduced by courtesy of the Defense Mapping Agency Hydrographic/Topographic Center)

(328) GF   7930-X

T	33100	Δ	(33120)	Δ	33140	Δ	33160	Δ	33180	Δ	T
Lat	° '	°	° '	°	° '	°	° '	°	° '	°	Long ° '
34 N	54 29.0W	56	54 40.5W	57	54 51.9W	57	55 03.5W	58	55 15.1W	58	
35 N	54 01.1W	55	54 12.3W	56	54 23.6W	56	54 35.0W	57	54 46.5W	57	
36 N	53 32.6W	54	53 43.5W	55	53 54.7W	55	54 05.8W	56	54 17.2W	56	
37 N	53 03.4W	53	53 14.1W	54	53 25.1W	54	53 36.0W	55	53 47.2W	55	
38 N	52 33.4W	52	52 44.1W	53	52 54.8W	53	53 05.6W	54	53 16.5W	54	
39 N	52 02.9W	51	52 13.3W	52	52 23.8W	52	52 34.3W	53	52 45.0W	53	
40 N	51 31.5W	50	51 41.7W	51	51 52.0W	51	52 02.4W	51	52 12.8W	52	
41 N	50 59.5W	49	51 09.4W	49	51 19.5W	50	51 29.5W	50	51 39.8W	51	
42 N	50 26.5W	48	50 36.3W	48	50 46.0W	49	50 56.0W	49	51 05.9W	50	
43 N	49 52.8W	47	50 02.3W	47	50 11.8W	47	50 21.5W	48	50 31.2W	48	
44 N	49 18.3W	45	49 27.5W	46	49 36.7W	46	49 46.1W	47	49 55.6W	47	
45 N	48 42.9W	44	48 51.8W	44	49 00.8W	45	49 09.9W	45	49 19.1W	46	
46 N	48 06.6W	43	48 15.2W	43	48 23.9W	43	48 32.8W	44	48 41.6W	44	
47 N	47 29.5W	41	47 37.8W	41	47 46.2W	42	47 54.7W	42	48 03.3W	42	
48 N	46 51.5W	39	46 59.5W	40	47 07.7W	40	47 15.8W	40	47 21.1W	41	
49 N	46 12.9W	38	46 20.5W	38	46 28.3W	38	46 36.1W	39	46 44.0W	39	
50 N	45 33.6W	36	45 40.9W	36	45 48.3W	37	45 55.7W	37	46 03.3W	37	
51 N	44 53.0W	34	45 00.8W	34	45 07.7W	35	45 14.8W	35	45 21.9W	35	
52 N	44 13.9W	32	44 20.5W	32	44 27.0W	33	44 33.7W	33	44 40.4W	33	
53 N	43 34.2W	30	43 40.4W	30	43 46.5W	30	43 52.8W	31	43 59.0W	31	

essential to choose those two pairs which give the most accurate fix. Consider figure 4.17 which shows LOPs for two master-secondary stations, the lines shown for a particular pair being separated by 10 microseconds. The distance between the 'Y' lines is 1 nautical mile (1.85 km), while the distance between the 'X' lines is 2 nautical miles (3.7 km)

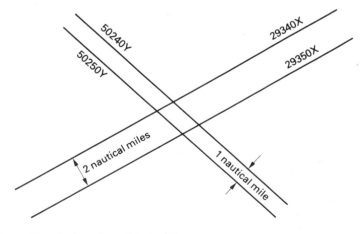

Fig. 4.17 Loran-C gradients and crossing angles

Assuming an error in the Loran reading of ± 0.01 microsecond,, then the error in terms of distance is ± 0.01 nautical miles (18.5 km) for the 'Y' lines and ± 0.02 nautical miles (37.5 m) for the 'X' lines.

Consider now figure 4.18 with much larger gradients for both sets of lines. In this case the order of error, assuming an accuracy of ± 0.1 microsecond as before, is ± 166.5 m for the Z lines and ± 222.0 m for the W lines. Given gradients as shown in these examples, the X and Y secondaries would be chosen in preference to the W and Z secondaries.

Ideally two LOPs that cross at right angles should always be used since this would give the greatest accuracy. Since this is not always possible to achieve, then LOPs that intersect as close as possible to 90° such as shown in figure 4.17 should be used, subject of course to suitable values of gradient.

The area in the region of the baseline extension of a master–secondary pair should never be used since, as figure 4.19 shows, the gradients near these lines become very large, giving rise to potentially very large errors. Baseline extensions are always indicated on the charts.

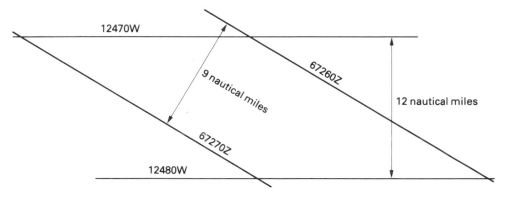

Fig. 4.18 Loran-C gradients and crossing angles

4.8 Loran-C coverage

Diagrams are available which show the predicted ground wave coverage for each chain. Briefly the coverage diagrams are generated as follows:

(a) Geometrix-fix-accuracy limits

Each of two LOPs in chain is assigned a TD standard deviation of 0.1 microseconds. The geometric-fix-accuracy is assigned a value of 1500 feet, $2d_{RMS}$ where d_{RMS} is the radial or root mean square error. Using these constraints a contour is generated within the chain area representing the geometric-fix-accuracy limits.

(b) Range limits

Predicted atmospheric noise and cross-rate Loran-C interference is compared with estimated Loran-C signal strength for each Loran-C transmitting station to obtain an expected 1:3 SNR (signal to noise ratio) range limits for each transmitted signal.

(c) The predicted Loran-C coverage for each chain is the result of combining the geometric-fix-accuracy limits and predicted SNR range limits. Where the geometric-fix-accuracy limits extend beyond the range limits, the range limits are used on the coverage diagrams and vice-versa.

Coverage diagrams for selected chains are shown in figures 4.20 and 4.21, together with data sheets for those chains.

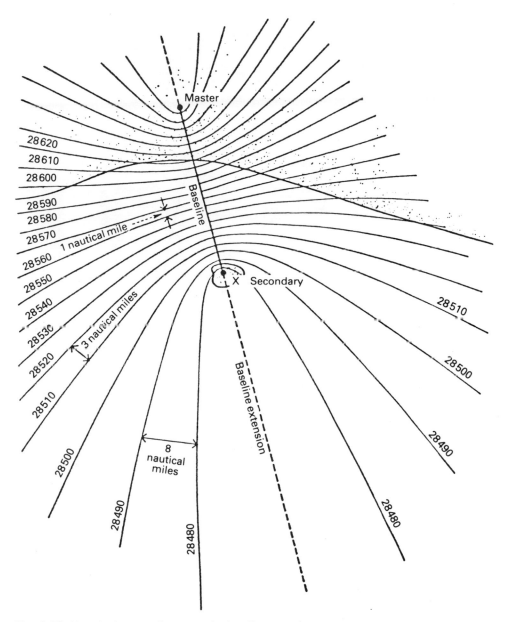

Fig. 4.19 Note the large gradients near the baseline extension

The function of the monitor and control stations specified in these data sheets and coverage diagrams is to ensure that certain specified parameters, such as phase time difference TD, for each chain are sampled and maintained at the correct levels.

Clarinet Pilgrim (CP) and Clarinet Pilgrim with TTY2 is a system used, at specified stations, where certain pulses in each group are subject to pulse position modulation of ± 1 microsecond to provide backup administrative and control signals.

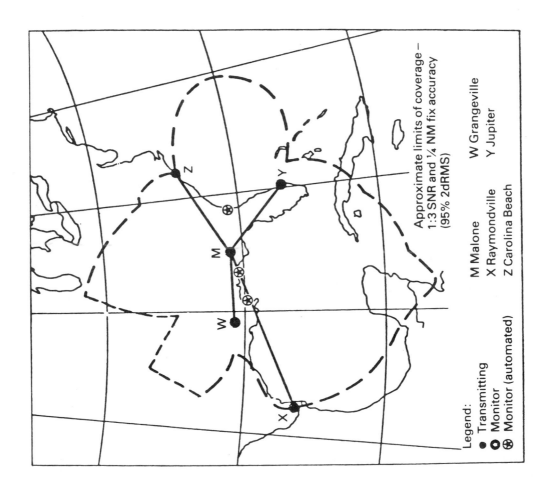

Approximate limits of coverage –
1:3 SNR and ¼ NM fix accuracy
(95% 2dRMS)

M Malone   W Grangeville
X Raymondville   Y Jupiter
Z Carolina Beach

Legend:
● Transmitting
◐ Monitor
⊕ Monitor (automated)

Station	Function	Coordinates	Coding delay/base-line depth	Radiated power (kW)	Remarks
Malone, FL	Master	30 59 38.7N 85 10 09.3W		800	Control for W,X,Y and Z. Dual-rated to great lakes chain
Grangeville, LA	Whisky	30 43 33.0 N 90 49 43.6 W	11000/ 1809.54	800	
Raymond-ville, TX	Xray	26 31 55.0 N 97 50 00.1 W	23000/ 4443.38	400	
Jupiter, FL	Yankee	27 01 58.5 N 80 06 53.5 W	43000/ 2201.88	275	
Carolina Beach, NC	Zulu	34 03 46.0 N 77 54 46.8 W	59000/ 2542.72	550	
Mayport, FL	Monitor	30 22 58.9 N 81 25 13.1 W			Unmanned receiver site
Eglin, FL	Monitor	30 35 05.3 N 86 36 54.4 W			Unmanned receiver site
New Orleans, LA	Monitor	29 49 17.3 N 90 01 44.2 W			Unmanned receiver site

Fig. 4.20 Loran-C data sheet and coverage diagram. South-east U.S. Chain

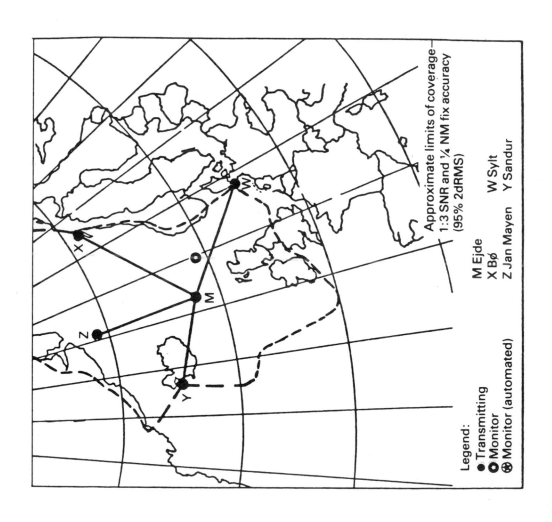

Station	Function	Coordinates	Coding delay/base-line depth	Radiated power (kW)	Remarks
Ejde, Faero Is. Denmark	Master	62 17 59.7 N 07 04 26.7 W		325	Host nation manned, dual-rated to North Atlantic chain
Bø, Norway	Xray	68 38 06.2 N 15 27 47.0 E	11000/ 4048.10	165	Host nation manned
Sylt, Germany	Whisky	54 48 29.8 N 08 17 36.3 E	26000/ 4065.64	523	
Sandur, Iceland	Yankee	64 54 26.6 N 23 55 21.8 W	46000/ 2944.53	1500	Host nation manned, dual-rated to North Atlantic chain
Jan Mayen, Norway	Zulu	70 54 52.6 N 08 43 58.7 W	60000/ 3216.3	165	Host nation manned
Shetland Is., U.K.	Monitor/ control	60 26 25.3 N 01 18 05.7 W			Control for X.W.Y and Z

Fig. 4.21 Loran-C data sheet and coverage diagram. Norwegian sea, chain

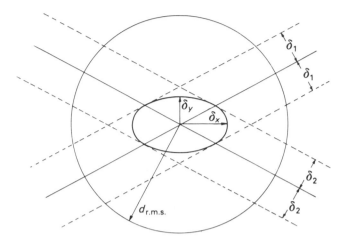

Fig. 4.22 The error ellipse

Radial or root mean square error, d_{RMS}, is defined as the radius of the error circle produced from the square root of the sum of the square of the sigma error components along the major and minor axes of a probability ellipse, see figure 4.22.

The ellipse is produced by virtue of the deviation expected along each LOP as indicated by δ_1 and δ_2 in figure 4.22, and varies according to the gradient and angle of cut of the LOPs at that point.

$1\,d_{RMS}$ is defined as the radius of a circle obtained when $\delta_x = 1$ and δ_y varies from 0 to 1.

$2\,d_{RMS}$ is defined as the radius of a circle obtained when $\delta_x = 2$ and δ_y varies from 0 to 2.

The relationship between δ_1, δ_2 and δ_x, δ_y and the probability values associated with $1\,d_{RMS}$ or $2\,d_{RMS}$ values are beyond the scope of this book but may be obtained from standard reference books.

As far as the accuracy of Loran-C coverage is concerned the coverage diagram (figure 4.20) shows that for ground wave reception areas the fix probability is 95% ($2\,d_{RMS}$) at 1500 feet with a standard deviation of 0.1 microsecond and 1/3 SNR.

Sky wave reception will extend the coverage area but accuracy cannot be guaranteed.

Actual Loran-C geometry contours for selected chains are shown in figures 4.23 and 4.24.

For the Loran-C system the absolute accuracy, i.e. the ability to determine the true geographic position (latitude and longitude), is claimed to be from 0.1 to 0.25 nautical mile (185 to 463 metres) depending on the position of the receiver within the coverage area.

Repeatable accuracy is the measure of the ability to return to a previously plotted position time and time again by using Loran-C readings for that position as a reference. For Loran-C the repeatable accuracy is claimed to be from 0.008 to 0.05 nautical mile (15 to 90 metres).

The complete Loran-C coverage is shown in figure 4.25.

Changes and additions to the Loran-C coverage occur from time to time. Modifications to the Loran-C coverage of the Canadian East Coast by the addition of a new station at Fox Harbour, Labrador, Canada was completed early in 1984. This resulted in chain modifications as follows:

1. Canadian East Coast Chain (CEC), GRI 5930. This added the new station at Fox Harbour as Zulu secondary. Monitor stations are at Cape Elizabeth, Maine, USA and Prince Edward Island, Newfoundland, Canada.

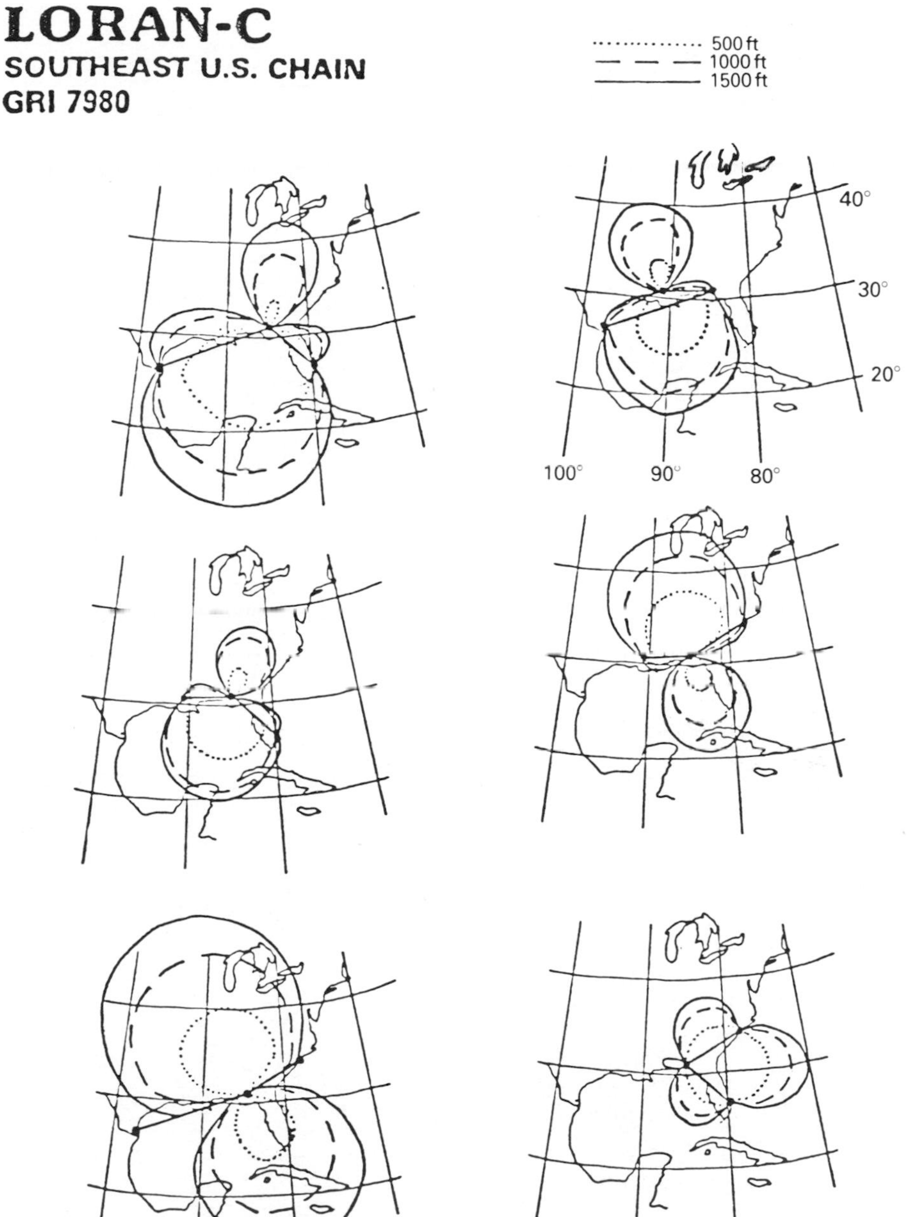

LORAN-C
SOUTHEAST U.S. CHAIN
GRI 7980

Fig. 4.23 Loran-C geometry contours. South-east U.S. Chain $2d_{r.m.s}$ fix accuracy; $\delta = 0.1\,\mu s$
Note: These contours are based on geometry only and do not include range limits

2. Labrador Sea Chain (LABSEA), GRI 7930. This chain was formed using the Fox Harbour station as Master and the stations at Cape Race, Newfoundland, Canada and at Angissoq, Greenland as secondaries. Monitor station is at St. Anthony, Newfoundland, Canada.

LORAN-C
NORWEGIAN SEA CHAIN
GRI 7970

.... 500 ft
— — — 1000 ft
————— 1500 ft

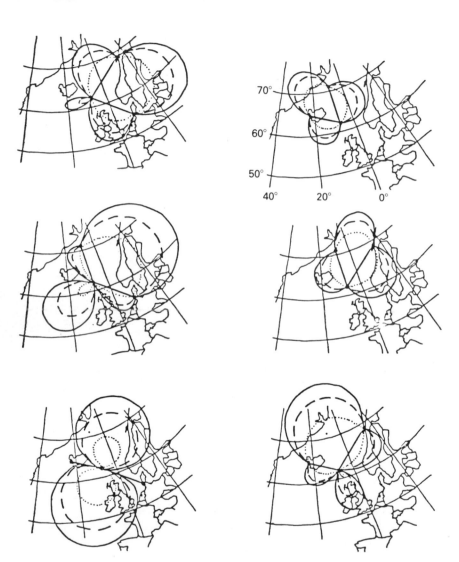

Fig. 4.24 Loran-C geometry contours. Norwegian sea chain.
$2d_{r.m.s}$ accuracy; $\delta = 0.1\,\mu s$
Note: These contours are based on geometry only and do not include range limits

3. Icelandic chain, GRI 9980. The North Atlantic Chain (NORLANT), GRI 7930 has been reconfigured to GRI 9980 with the Master station at Sandur, Iceland. The stations at Angissoq, Greenland and Edje, Faroe Island are the secondaries. Monitor station is at Keflavik, Iceland.

The changes extend the coverage area to include the area from the eastern Grand Banks up to the Hamilton Banks and complete the coverage in the mouth of the Saint Lawrence River. The extended coverage is shown in figure 4.25b.

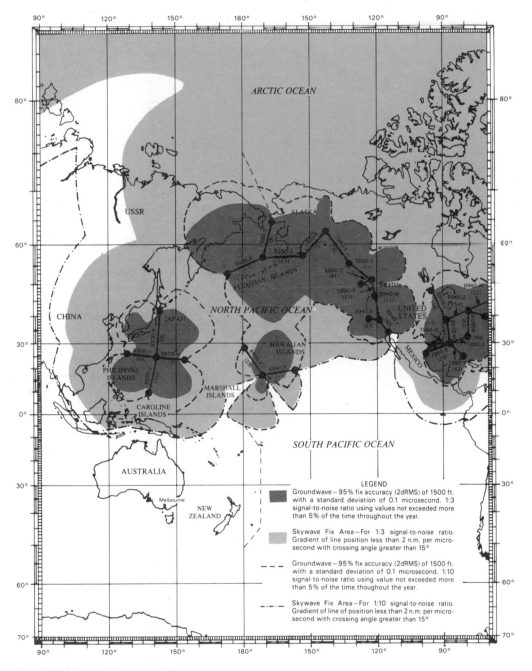

Fig. 2.5(a) Loran-C coverage diagram

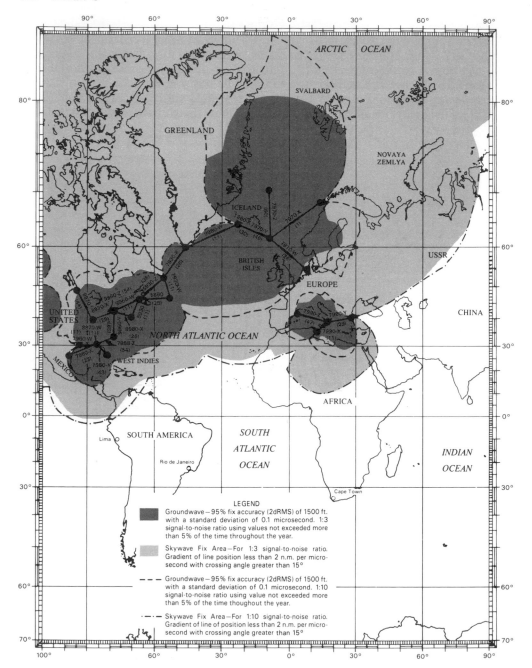

Fig. 4.25(b)   Loran-C coverage diagram

Also two new chains were made operational in 1984 in Saudi Arabia:
1. Northern Saudi Arabian Chain, GRI 8990, with a Master station at Afif and secondaries at Salwa, Ar Ruqi, Ash Shaykh Humayd, Al Lith and Al Muwassam.
2. Southern Saudi Arabian Chain, GRI 7170, with a Master station at Al Khamasin and secondaries at Salwa, Afif, Al Lith and Al Muwassam.
Details regarding chain coverage are not shown in figure 4.25b nor are they shown in

Table 4.6. Additionally a feasibility study is under way to establish compatibility between the Loran-C system and the Soviet Chayka system in use in the eastern and western USSR. Details have been released recently.

Mariners should consult relevant local Notice to Mariners whereby official notification of changes to the Loran-C system should be found.

4.9 Loran-C receivers

A Loran-C receiver which is capable of measuring position with the claimed accuracy for the system should possess the following characteristics:

(a) It acquires the Loran-C signals automatically, without the use of an oscilloscope.

(b) It identifies master and secondary ground-wave pulses automatically, and accomplishes cycle-matching on all eight pulses for each master–secondary pair used.

(c) It tracks the signals automatically once acquisition has been achieved.

(d) It displays two time-difference readings, to a precision of at least one tenth of a microsecond.

(e) It has notch filters, adjusted by the manufacturer if required, to minimize the effects of radio frequency interference in the area in which the buyer expects to operate.

Some Loran-C receivers do not possess all the automatic features mentioned. These so-called "manual acquisition" receivers still depend on the use of an oscilloscope to acquire signals. A receiver of this type is not always usable over the full range of Loran-C coverage since this has boundaries where the strength of the Loran-C signal may be only one third that of the noise level. To obtain the signal reliably on an oscilloscope, the signal strength generally must be equal to or greater than the noise level. This sort of signal strength would only usually be obtained at points nearer the transmitter station than the outer coverage area.

The simplest Loran-C receiver is used almost exactly like a Loran-A receiver. The operator matches the master and secondary envelopes on the oscilloscope and reads the time difference from a scale of some kind. Generally, the accuracy obtained with a receiver of this type is no better, at best, than that obtainable from a Loran-A receiver. It may be worse in fact, because the Loran-A pulse is better suited for this type of operation than the Loran-C pulse.

Some Loran-C receivers allow the operator to match *cycles* within the master and secondary pulses by superimposing individual cycles on the oscilloscope. The individual cycles within the Loran-C pulse appear many times and to obtain a correct time difference measurement, corresponding cycles within the master and secondary pulses must be matched i.e. if the third cycle in the master pulse is to be used, then the third cycle in the secondary pulse must be matched to it. The accuracy obtained with this type of receiver is much higher than can be obtained with just envelope matching, as long as the correct cycles are matched as previously specified. It may be difficult to identify the specific cycle being used in each pulse because of the presence of noise or sky waves. Since individual cycles are 10 microseconds apart, errors which are multiples of 10 microseconds may be introduced quite easily and unknowingly into measurements made with this type of receiver.

The most sophisticated type of "manual acquisition" Loran-C receiver requires only the initial acquisition and alignment of signals on the oscilloscope by the operator. The receiver then identifies and matches cycles within all eight pulses automatically. This type of receiver is capable of accuracies comparable to those possible with fully automatic receivers, provided that the operator is able to identify and align the signals initially under the signal and noise conditions at his location.

Fully automatic receivers operate without the need for an oscilloscope and can automatically acquire and track the master and secondary stations and present the

Fig. 4.26 Koden Electronics LR-707 Loran-C receiver

information regarding the vessel's position as either a pair of time difference readings or an actual position in terms of latitude and longitude.

A typical automatic receiver is illustrated in figure 4.26. This is the Koden Electronics LR-707 receiver. Details of the functions offered by this receiver and its operation are described in the following paragraphs.

Station selection

Switches S1 and S2 control the two time displays. When the receiver is first initialized (see p. 125) display 2 will be rolling i.e. displaying various secondary time differences in an ascending sequence. The roll frequency is once every three seconds. When the required secondary time difference appears on display 2, pressing switch 2 will retain that output. If it is required to change the chosen secondary, pressing S2 again will restore the roll action. S1 serves the same function as S2 except that it controls display 1. An exception to the functions performed by the two switches is that if display 1 is adjusted for roll, display 1 will indicate all time differences including that being shown by display 2. With S1 adjusted for non-roll, S2 will indicate a time difference reading other than that indicated on display 1 i.e. it will skip that time difference. As a result of this feature, when only two secondaries are acquired (or available) and S1 adjusted for non-roll, S2 will also appear to be adjusted for non-roll.

The S1 display is also used to indicate certain alarm functions and to supply technical data.

Function switch

When initializing the receiver the function switch must be set to SEL. After the *settling alarms* have been extinguished, the function switch should be placed in NORM position to inhibit cycle selection of all stations and to enable certain functions of + /MEMO and − /RECALL (see under the appropriate heading for a description of these functions).

Setting the function switch in either S1, M or S2 position allows the time difference of the selected station to be manipulated using the + /MEMO and − /RECALL controls.

The cycle selection process is inhibited for all other stations except the selected station. With the function switch set to SEL, the cycle selection process is activated for all stations. In addition, the + /MEMO and − /RECALL buttons will jump all stations by 10 microseconds depending on the button chosen and the number of times it is pressed. If the control is left in this position, the readings should return to correct values provided propagation conditions are normal and the + /MEMO and − /RECALL buttons have not been pressed excessively which would cause the tracking point to move off the pulse. Simultaneously pressing + /MEMO and − /RECALL will initialize the receiver.

+ /MEMO   With the function switch in TEST and + /MEMO pressed, the display will indicate the oscillator offset frequency. Pressing the button again will restore the normal technical information to the display.

With the function switch set to SEL, the tracking points of all stations will shift by + 10 microseconds each time the button is pressed.

With the function switch in NORM, pressing the + /MEMO buttom will 'freeze' the display and place all acquired time differences into memory. Pressing + /MEMO again will restore the display to time difference readings.

With the function switch in S1, pressing the + /MEMO button will cause the tracking point of the station appearing on display 1 to move + 10 microseconds.

With the function switch set to M, pressing the + /MEMO button will cause the tracking point of the master station to move by + 10 microseconds, causing S1 and S2 display to indicate 10 microseconds lower.

− /RECALL   With the function switch set to NORM, pressing the − /RECALL button will recall and display all time differences previously entered into the memory. Pressing the button again will restore display to the normal tracking mode.

NOTCH FILTERS   These controls are used to eliminate interference that is sinusoidal. When not in use, two should be tuned fully clockwise and two fully anticlockwise or improper operation may result (see page 123).

TUNE CONTROL   Used in conjunction with the tune meter to locate inteference.

TUNE (NOISE) METER   Together with TUNE CONTROL this meter will locate interference. It does not indicate signal strength of the Loran-C signal.

SIGNAL TO NOISE ALARMS   When lit, these indicate a possible problem with the associated station. When operating at great distances from the station or under adverse weather conditions, these alarms may light from time to time. Simultaneous flashing of all three alarms indicates that the RECALL control has been activated.

SETTLING ALARMS   These indicate that the associated station is settled and is ready for tracking. Simultaneous flashing of all three alarms indicates that the + /MEMO control has been activated.

DIMMER CONTROL   This controls the intensity of both displays and all six l.e.d. alarms.

CHAIN SELECTOR   This must be utilized prior to initializing the receiver to select the required Loran-C chain. To determine the setting of the required GRI number, reference should be made to the appropriate Loran-C chart for the area of operation. Only the first three digits of the chain identification need be set since the last (fourth) digit is always zero.

POWER ON/OFF   This controls the power to the receiver. It is the only switch that should be used to energize or de-energize the receiver since the use of an external switch could damage the receiver.

Normal operation

The chain selector should be set for the chain of the area in which the vessel is operating. Next set the function switch to SEL and detune the notch filters by setting two completely clockwise and two completely anticlockwise. Ensure also that the dimmer switch is set fully clockwise.

Switch the power switch to ON; after about four seconds both displays will sequentially indicate all secondaries acquired. When the required time difference appears on the display, select the wanted secondaries by pressing display control S1 and S2. Wait until the settling alarms are no longer alight and then set the function switch to NORM.

The unit has now acquired the wanted signals and will track those signals.

Use of the notch filters

Rotate TUNE CONTROL and check for signal interference. When TUNE CONTROL is in the 'six-o'clock' position, it indicates the centre of the Loran frequency and the tune meter should indicate a reasonably large deflection. When rotated either side of the centre position, the tune meter should indicate a smaller deflection. Any 'bouncing' or increased deflection of the meter indicates the presence of noise.

Noise may be eliminated by using the notch filters which are highly tuned circuits and can sharply reduce the signal level of any frequency if the filters are tuned to that frequency. Thus if TUNE CONTROL finds any interfering signals in the frequency range of the Loran signals, the notch filter controls may be adjusted to eliminate that interference. The technique to be used is described as follows:

(a) Turn all notch filter knobs fully clockwise.
(b) Set the TUNE CONTROL knob to its centre ('six o'clock') position and note the deflection on the tune meter which is an indication of the Loran signal.
(c) Turn the TUNE CONTROL knob slowly anticlockwise and note the abrupt deflection on the tune meter; a similar effect should be found if the knob is rotated slowly clockwise. See figure 4.27a.
(d) Set the TUNE CONTROL knob to the point where the meter deflection is greatest in the anticlockwise direction.
(e) Reset notch filter knob N1 to the centre position and slowly rotate it anticlockwise until the meter deflection is minimized.
(f) Check that the meter deflection for the interference signal is less than the Loran signal and if not, repeat steps (d) and (e) above using the notch filter N2.
(g) Reset the TUNE CONTROL knob to its centre position and slowly rotate clockwise until the interference frequency below the Loran centre frequency is found.
(h) Reset notch filter knob N3 to its centre position and slowly rotate clockwise until the meter deflection is minimized.

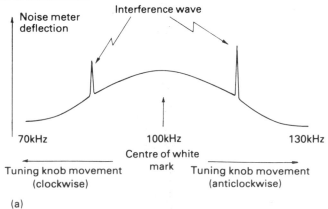

Fig. 4.27(a) Possible interference levels prior to adjustment of the tuning controls

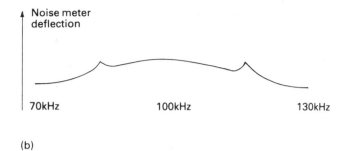

(b)

Fig. 4.27(b) Possible interference levels after adjustment of the tuning control. The interference level should always be set to less than the level of the Loran signal

(i) Use the notch filter N4, by turning it clockwise from its centre position, if the use of notch filter N3 has not reduced the interference signal level below that of the wanted Loran signal.

(j) Repeat step (c) and note that the levels of the interference signals are reduced below the level of the Loran signal above and below the Loran centre frequency. See figure 4.27b.

Receiver alarm indications

The various alarms that are possible with this receiver as an aid to the operator are as follows:

(a) Secondary blink
This is indicated when the third and fourth digit of either display is flashing. During the blink alarm, only the time difference reading of the secondary station at fault will flash. This station should not therefore be used for position fixing. The blink alarm will not automatically reset itself. When two or more secondaries are flashing, it is usually an indication of problems with the master station and all time difference readings should be used with extreme caution.

(b) Test alarm
When the function switch is set to TEST, the second digit of both displays will flash once every three seconds.

(c) Memo alarm
When the display is 'frozen' by activating the + /MEMO button, all three settling alarms will flash once every three seconds.

(d) Recall alarm
When the − /RECALL control has been activated, all three signal to noise alarms will flash once every three seconds.

(e) Function switch alarm
If the function switch was in any position other than SEL when power was applied to the receiver, the number 9 will appear in the window of each display. To correct, the receiver should be turned OFF and the function switch to SEL before restoring the supply.

(f) Signal to noise alarms
When lit, the signal to noise alarms indicate a poor signal to noise ratio. If the alarm is lit for 50% or more of the time, the tracking capabilities on the problem station will be

severely impaired or, in some cases, impossible to track. This alarm should be ignored during the settling process.

(g) *Settling alarm*

This alarm will light any time the cycle selection circuit is not satisfied with a decision. Since propagation conditions are variable, the settling alarm may light even though the displayed time difference reading is correct. with the function switch in the NORM position, no 10 microsecond jump will occur even though a jump is indicated by the settling alarm. If the function switch is in the SEL position, a jump will occur automatically.

To cancel any alarm function, first turn the function switch to TEST and then back to NORM. IF the receiver detects that the alarm condition still exists, the alarm will, after a short delay, become active again.

Other functions of the display

When the function switch is moved to TEST, both displays will automatically indicate the number 8 in each position, allowing the operator to check that all display segments are operating correctly. In addition the cycle selection alarms and the signal to noise alarms will light. This type of display will remain for three seconds, then the following information becomes available:

The first two digits of each display indicate the station under observation. The first two digits correspond to the first two numbers of the respective time differences (99 indicates the master). The second digit will flash, indicating a non-tracking condition for the displays:

The third digit of the time difference indicates the signal condition at the beginning of the pulse.

The fourth digit indicates the signal condition at the tracking point of the pulse.

The fifth digit indicates the signal condition at the crest of the pulse. In each of these cases '0' is the lowest value and '9' is the highest value.

The sixth digit indicates the mode of the receiver, with 4 being the final and tracking mode.

When the + /MEMO button is pressed, the oscillator offset frequency is displayed on a scale of − 20 to + 20, with '0' indicating no offset. Press again to reset. If zeros appear in the first to fourth digit, the frequency is low. The converse is true if no zeros appear.

Initializing procedure

The receiver is initialized in four stages. The modes can be checked by the sixth digit when the function switch is set to TEST.

Mode 1 *stage*

For those Loran signals received from a chain, the GRI of which is preset on the front panel, the received pulse is compared with an internally generated pulse. The master pulse is detected first and then the secondary pulses. The time difference values are displayed on the display panels.

Mode 2 *stage*

The detection and tracking of the zero cross point of the carrier is commenced and the tracking point is transferred to the start of the Loran signal in 10 microsecond steps until the signal becomes zero in the signal to noise detection circuit; the noise indicator lamps will then light.

This operation is performed for master and secondary stations independently.

Mode 3 *stage*

The tracking point is now transferred in the signal direction in 10 microsecond steps until the signal is detected. The noise indicator lamps should now be extinguished.

Once again the operation is performed independently for master and secondary stations.

The function of modes 2 and 3 is to ensure that the pulses for master and secondary stations are overlapped correctly i.e. pulse 1 of the master is overlapped with pulse 1 of the secondary station.

Mode 4 *stage*

At the end of mode 3 stage, the 10 microsecond step operation switches from the signal to noise detection circuit to the third wave detection circuit. The tracking point is now set to the correct tracking position, namely the point after the third wave as seen from the pulse leading edge. The set indicator lamps are then extinguished. The initialization operation is now complete.

When the function switch is set to SEL, the check operation continues and if the circuit decides the previously determined position is incorrect, the 10 microsecond step sequence is re-started and the set indicator lamps are then lit.

The indicator lamps will only be extinguished after a second setting-up routine has been performed.

Refer to the diagram of lamp lighting sequence for the initialization routine (Figure 4.28).

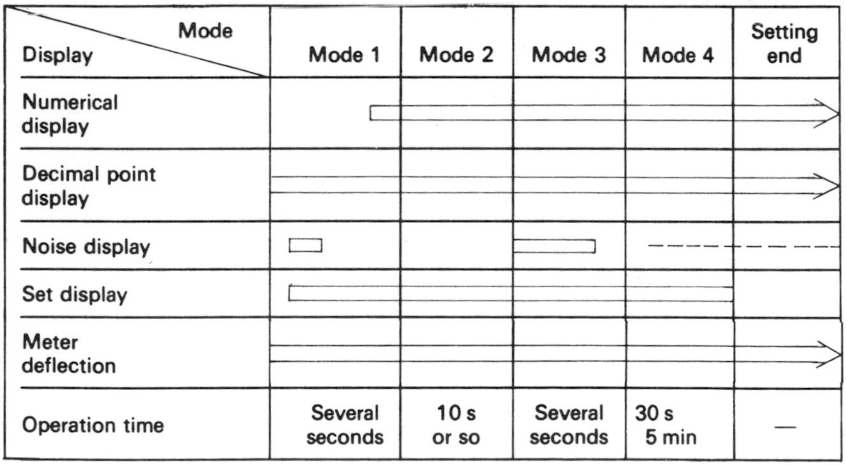

Display \ Mode	Mode 1	Mode 2	Mode 3	Mode 4	Setting end
Numerical display					
Decimal point display					
Noise display					
Set display					
Meter deflection					
Operation time	Several seconds	10 s or so	Several seconds	30 s 5 min	—

Fig. 4.28 Initialization and lighting/extinction of indicator lamps

Notes:
1. It is possible that if the signal level is lower than − 20 dB or the S/N ratio is very low, mode 1 will not proceed to the next stage, and no display appears
2. The noise indicator lamp may light during mode 4 operation or after setting ends if the S/N ratio is too low

Circuit description

This receiver uses a microprocessor and associated logic circuitry to detect and track the Loran-C 100 kHz pulse trains from master and secondary transmitter stations. The system also presents the time differences between the receipt of the master and secondary pulse trains as a direct visual display; two such time differences can be indicated which give a position fix as the point of intersection of the two time difference lines (LOPs). The microprocessor used is a Motorola 6800 equivalent. The means of detection, sampling and tracking the signals is initiated by the use of interrupt signals IRQ (interrupt request) and NMI (non-maskable interrupt).

A basic block diagram is shown in figure 4.29. The antenna coupler provides some filtering and gives some initial amplification prior to connection to the receiver block. The receiver block provides band-pass filtering and amplification. Separate circuits are provided for the CYCLE and ENVELOPE outputs with the signals hard limited to give digitized values. The band-pass filter allows for a restriction on the received signal frequencies to a range of 70 kHz to 130 kHz. The notch filter can be used to minimize the effects of noise signals within the pass-band. The logic block is shown in more detail in figure 4.30.

The incoming CYCLE signal to the logic block is fed to a sampling circuit consisting of 50 bit shift registers and a D-type flip-flop. The shift registers are integrated circuits 9C, 10C, 12C and 13C while the flip-flop is integrated circuit 8C.

The Loran signal format is 8 pulses of 100 kHz, each pulse lasting for 250 microseconds. The signal, after passing through the receiver and being hard limited, appears as digital pulses. The pulse train is clocked through the shift registers using a clock pulse duration of average value 20 microseconds so that for each pulse period of the received pulse train of 1000 microseconds there are 50 bits. These bits are shifted continuously through the registers recording the presence, or absence, of a pulse as the case may be. As an example, considering master transmissions only and with a GRI of, say, 79 300 microseconds, then after the reception of the eighth pulse (ignoring the ninth pulse for the moment) there is a time difference of (79 300 − 7250) microseconds or 72 050 microseconds before the next pulse is received. Obviously the receipt of secondary station signals will occur during this period.

Considering master signals only for the moment, the phase coding of the eight pulses has the form:

$$\text{Group A} \quad + \; + \; - \; - \; + \; - \; + \; -$$
$$\text{Group B} \quad + \; - \; - \; + \; + \; + \; + \; +$$

and the phase code interval (PCI) has the form A, B, A, B etc., for successive master transmissions.

For the receipt of a master pulse train the CPU can cause the A and B code to be latched into a D-type octal latch. The required code could be outputted and compared with a sample from each of the outputs of the 50 bit registers (and D-type flip-flop) as shown in figure 4.31.

The coincidence of sampled signal with, say, the A code results in an output signal from the quad XOR gates that is logic '0' and this, through the gate circuit shown, results in a logic '1' output from the gate circuit. The coincidence output is shaped by a monostable circuit and fed via a buffer circuit to the input of a RAM 1024 × 4 bit memory circuit. The memory circuit address 000 to 3FF (0 to 1024) is selected by the output of a binary counter. The rate of data input to the memory address locations, governed by the counter, is 100 microseconds. Since the counter has 1024 locations to access before resetting there is a total of 102 400 microseconds to be represented by the 1024 bits of the memory. The bits corresponding to GRI can be represented within the memory since no GRI exceeds 99 900 microseconds and the counter is reset every GRI.

After the memory has been loaded for 1GRI and the counter is reset, the procedure is repeated for 2GRI, 3GRI etc. The memory chip is configured as 4 rows of 1024 locations and for each address location data is latched from row 1 to row 2, row 2 to row 3, and row 3 to row 4 as new data are written into row 1. This means that row 1 is used for the latest GRI with the previous GRI latched into row 2; the GRI before that is in row 3 etc. Thus the results of four previous GRIs are held in the memory and these results are available on the output data lines as each memory is accessed. These four previous GRI outputs are checked, together with outputs of present GRI, in a coincidence gate, see figure 4.32.

The output of the coincidence AND gate arrangement is only a logic '1' if all inputs are logic '1' i.e. the data output of each address location accessed for the four rows (each of the four previous GRI) and the data for the present GRI are all identical at logic '1'.

After pulse shaping, the coincidence output is used as an input to the interrupt request (IRQ) input of the MPU chip. the receipt of an IRQ input causes the microprocessor to finish any current instruction and to move to a high order address location where the starting address of a required subroutine is stored. In this case the routine causes the MPU to read the flip-flop (IC 8C) in the sampling circuit to determine whether the master signal was detected by A or B code. This determines whether the phase coding of the secondaries should be A or B code. The code for the secondaries is as follows:

$$\text{Group A} \quad + \ + \ + \ + \ + \ - \ - \ +$$
$$\text{Group B} \quad + \ - \ + \ - \ + \ + \ - \ -$$

The interrupt subroutine causes the correct code to be latched into the phase code latch circuit (ICs 6B and 6C) ready to detect the received secondary signals which are processed in exactly the same way as described above for the master signals.

The MPU outputs the GRI pulse which resets the counter (IC 15D) ready for the next GRI input data sequence.

The coincidence output (GRI signal) is also used to latch the outputs of a continuous counter to the data bus, using D-type flip-flops (ICs 8A and 11A), and to the MPU. The timing of the IRQ pulse in relation to the Loran signal is shown in figure 4.33.

The MPU calculates the time 2 milliseconds before the first position of the Loran signal in the *next* GRI cycle to set the values of octal D-type flip flops (ICs 8B, 11B and 14B). The MPU waits until that time for an interrupt. When the values set in the D-type flip-flops coincide with the values of the continuous counter then an NMI (non-maskable interrupt) signal is sent to the MPU. See figure 4.34.

The NMI interrupt performs a similar function to that of the IRQ signal in that a jump to a subroutine is initiated. The difference is that the IRQ request will only be obeyed if the interrupt mask bit in the MPU flag register is not set; the NMI request will always be obeyed since the interrupt mask bit has no effect on NMI. On receipt of the NMI signal the MPU clears a counter (IC 3G) which masks the IRQ interrupt for about 9 milliseconds [* (read data) + 1GRI − approximately 9 ms = time about 2 ms before the position of Loran signal in the next cycle]. See figure 4.35.

The Loran signal tracking point is set by the MPU by adding 2 ms to the value obtained previously* and setting this value, via the data bus, to the octal D-type flip-flops. The MPU then waits for an interrupt which recurs after 2 ms and coincides with the reception of the first Loran pulse.

The first Loran signal pulse is sampled when the MPU outputs a CYCLE ENV pulse. See figure 4.36.

After sampling the MPU adds 1 millisecond to the previously set value of the octal D-type flip-flops and waits for another interrupt pulse. This second Loran pulse is sampled as for the first pulse.

This procedure is repeated for all the Loran pulses and the complete sequence is repeated for any secondaries that need to be tracked. Figure 4.37 should make the sequence clear.

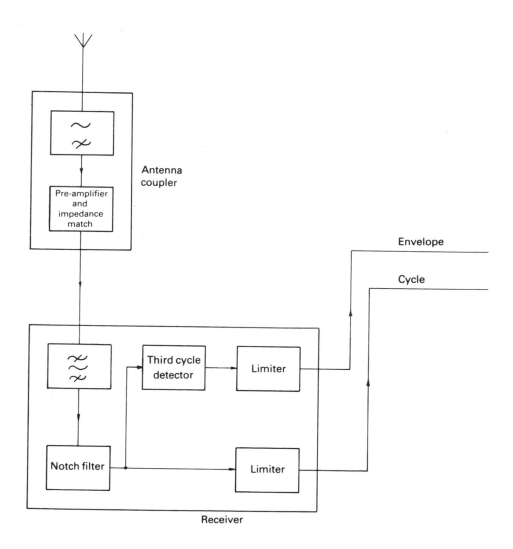

Fig. 4.29 Basic block diagram of Loran-C receiver

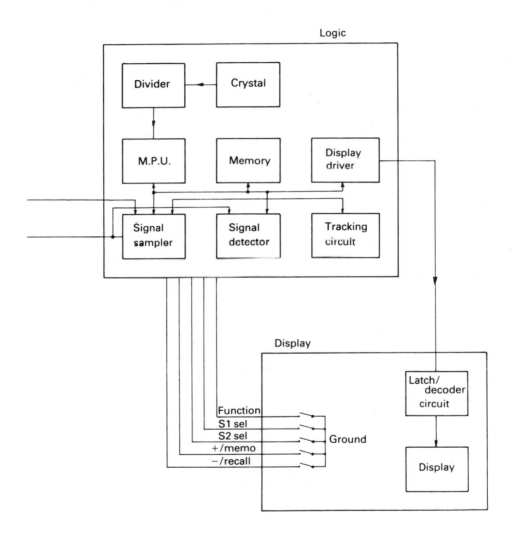

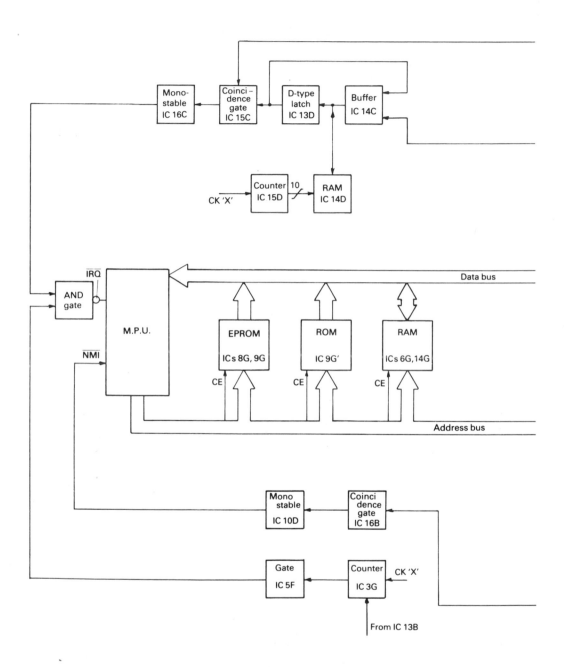

Fig. 4.30 Block diagram of logic board

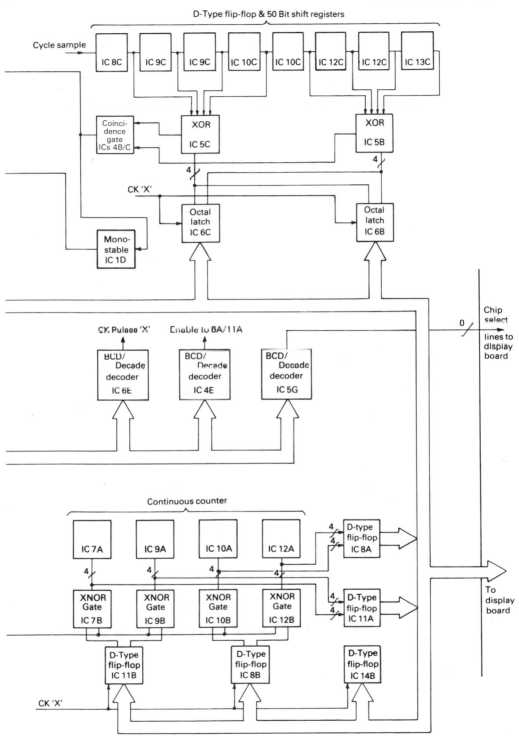

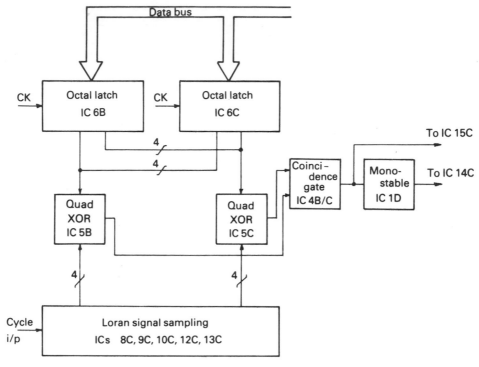

Fig. 4.31 Sampling and coincidence circuit

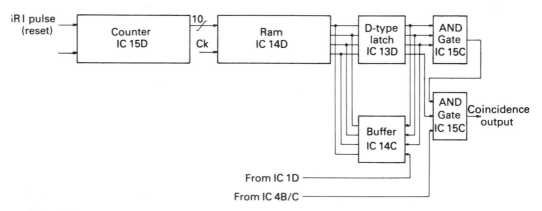

Fig. 4.32 Production of coincidence (IRQ) circuit

The display board contains two sets of six filament displays each of which is fed from a BCD to 7-segment C-MOS decoder/driver with integral latch. The six filament display elements are arranged to give the time differences between the reception of master and secondary station signals in tens of thousands, thousands, hundreds, tens, units and tenths of microseconds.

Each decoder is fed from 4 of the 8 data bus lines so that time multiplexing is employed to give a full display. Figure 4.38 shows the arrangement. Although only one set of display elements is shown, the other circuit is an exact duplicate. Each pair of decoders is enabled

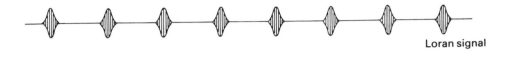

Fig. 4.33 Timing of IRQ pulse with received Loran signal

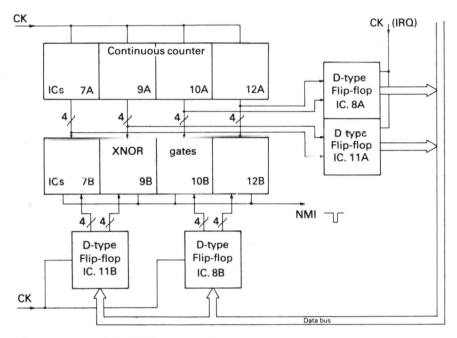

Fig. 4.34 Production of the NMI interrupt ppulse

via a chip select line which will go active low to latch data into the decoder. The chip select line is in turn fed from a BCD to decimal decoder on the logic board which operates under the control of the MPU.

Additionally the display board contains the function switch and the S1 SEL, S2 SEL, + /MEMO and − /RECALL switches. Connections when made will connect GROUND to that input on the logic board via a 44-way plug and socket arrangement which allows in addition the data line inputs and chip select lines to the display board from the logic board. Connecting an input, or combination of inputs to GROUND will, via the logic circuitry, fulfil the conditions as explained in pages 195–196 when describing receiver function. The logic circuits on the logic board concerned with the function switch inputs have not been shown in figure 4.30 in order to keep that diagram simple. As an example, however, o f the circuit action consider the case when function switch is set to S1 and the + /MEMO switch is pressed. The logic circuit concerned would cause the value set in to the D type flip-flops (ICs 8B, 11B and 14B) to change by + 10 microseconds.

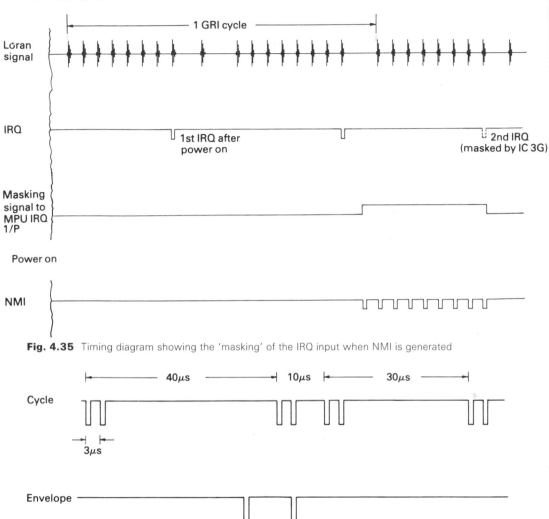

Fig. 4.35 Timing diagram showing the 'masking' of the IRQ input when NMI is generated

Fig. 4.36 Timing diagram for Loran signal sampling

Also on the display board and connected via the data bus, when chip select allows, is the information regarding the settling alarm and signal to noise alarm indication using LEDs.

The use of microprocessors for Loran-C receivers has improved the reliability of positional information and its presentation for the operator's use; the Koden Electronics LR-707 receiver is a good example of this. Koden also offer other Loran-C receivers, some with improved facilities. One of their latest, the LR-717, is shown in figure 4.39. Some of the features of this receiver are described below:

1. Easily read liquid crystal display and other indicators. The function of the display includes the following.
(a) Position display in two simultaneous LOPs or LAT/LONG mode
(b) Vessel's speed and heading
(c) Bearing to waypoint, distance and time to go

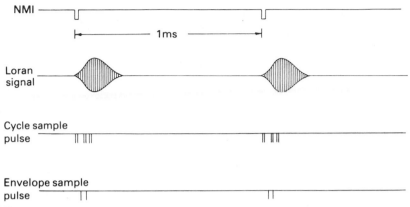

Fig. 4.37 Timing sequence for NMI pulses

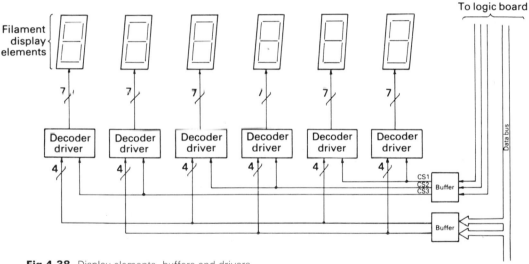

Fig 4.38 Display elements, buffers and drivers

(d) Cross track error from present course and its direction
(e) Ship's speed and heading
(f) Elapsed time
(g) Monitoring of signal conditions and oscillator accuracy
(h) blink signal alarm
2. Automatic Notch filters for noise suppression
3. Memory capacity for 50 waypoints and 8 position instant memory
4. Interfacing capabilities to Auto Pilot and Plotter
5. Keyboard for entering data as follows:
(a) Numerical keys 0/N 1/S 2/E 3/W 4 5 6 7 8 9 denote a numeric character or latitude/longitude.
(b) M/ + memorizes a waypoint or designates positive compensation or adds 10 μs to the time difference reading.
(c) R/ − recalls a waypoint or designates negative compensation or subtracts 10 μs from the time difference reading.

Fig. 4.39 Koden Electronics LR-717 Loran-C receiver

(d) S1 selects the secondary to be displayed on the upper position display. Also designates normal calculation in LAT/LONG calculation, and compensation for compass deflection.

(e) S2 selects the secondary to be displayed on the lower position display. Also designates special calculations in LAT/LONG calculations.

(f) Cl cancels the display when a numeric key entry is incorrect. Can also cancel the buzzer and elapsed timer.

(g) DIM selects brightness of the indicator lamps and indicator.

(h) ENT is used to input the waypoint and compensation values entered by the numeric keys.

6. Function switch. This has several positions, the purpose of each of which is as follows:

(a) GRI sets GRI of a required chain.

(b) M moves the master station time difference by ± 10 μs, or adds a compensation value to the master station time difference.

(c) S2 moves the time difference of secondary 2 by ± 10 μs, adds a compensation value to the time difference of secondary 2 or resets secondary 2 acquisition.

(d) S1 performs the same functions for secondary 1 as S2 performs for secondary 2.

(e) SEL is used for resetting acquisition of all the signals.

(f) WP-TD enters a waypoint in time difference.

(g) TD displays present position in time difference, or resets the buzzer or elapsed time.

(h) LAT/LONG displays present position in LAT/LONG, or resets the buzzer and elapsed time.

(i) WP-L/L sets a waypoint in LAT/LONG

(j) COMP compensates for the LAT/LONG position or for the bearing display for compass. Also converts a time difference position into a LAT/LONG position.

(k) NOTCH is for monitoring the notch filter or for manually operating the notch filter.

(l) TEST is for monitoring signal conditions or oscillator frequency deviation. Also for converting time difference into LAT/LONG

5
Omega

5.1 Introduction

Omega is a very low frequency (VLF) system using frequencies in the band 10 kHz–14 kHz. The system evolved from experiments first carried out in 1947 by Professor J. A. Pierce who, noting the long range and stability achieved with VLF radio waves for communications, suggested a hyperbolic navigation system based on phase difference techniques rather than time differences. An experimental system based on Pierce's proposals was set up by the Naval Electronics Laboratory; the system was called Radux. Pierce suggested a carrier frequency in the frequency band 40 kHz–50 kHz and to minimize the ambiguity of lines of position, sinusoidal modulation at a low frequency (200 Hz) on which the phase comparison would be carried out.

An experimental Radux system using a carrier of 40 kHz was set up in the Pacific with a baseline length of 2000 miles. The system gave accuracy figures of ± nautical miles for 90% of the time. Also, Pierce noticed that the 16 kHz emissions of GBR Rugby, received in the USA, were remarkably stable (allowing for certain variations according to the time of day and year which were entirely predictable). In 1955 a 10 kHz element was added to the LF Radux signal to give fine phase indications as a complement to the normal coarse-phase indications. The new system, called Radux–Omega, showed that the 10 kHz element (Omega) increased the accuracy of the original system to better than ± 1 nautical mile over the same range. The lane ambiguity problem still existed and multiple frequency transmissions were suggested as a solution.

The Radux element was soon dropped in favour of the Omega element because the LF element, for practical transmitter powers, had a range of only 3000 miles requiring more than 30 sites to achieve global coverage. With the Omega element at VLF, baseline lengths of up to 6000 miles were possible and global coverage obtainable with only 8 transmitter stations. Also the longer lane widths produced at VLF reduced the risk of lane slip caused by temporary signal loss.

In 1957 the VLF only system appeared and the first signals for system evaluation were radiated in 1961 using 3 transmitters. A four station system was established in 1966 and the remaining four stations have been added progressively in recent years. A coverage diagram for the Omega system is shown in figure 5.1. It should be noted that station G shown in this diagram as sited in Trinidad, is now sited in Australia. The Trinidad site was used to transmit temporarily while the Australian site, the last to be built, was under construction. The new station G began transmitting in 1981.

5.2 System principles

The principles are similar to those employed by the Decca system with the important difference that the phase comparison with Decca is achieved using a frequency multiplexing technique while Omega uses time multiplexing. The basic Omega frequency

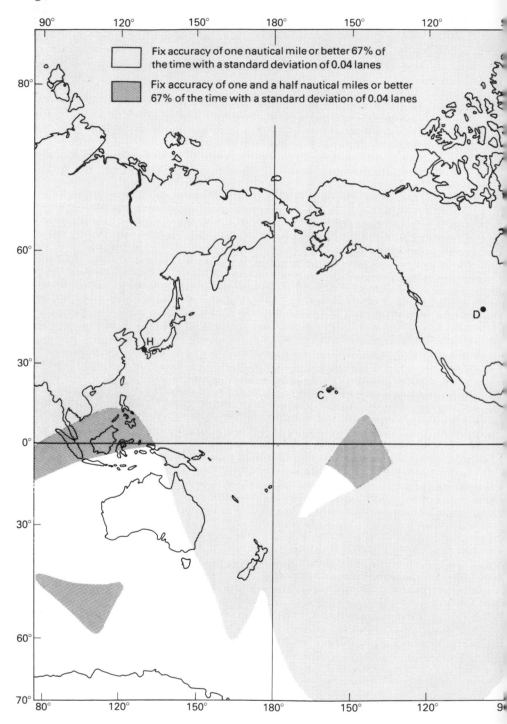

Fig. 5.1 Omega coverage

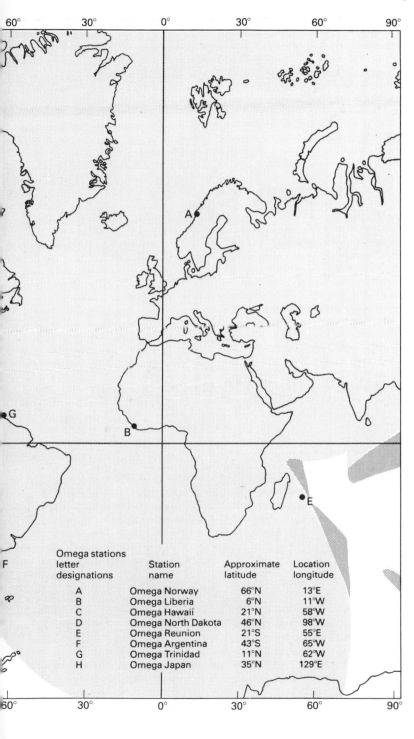

Omega stations letter designations	Station name	Approximate latitude	Location longitude
A	Omega Norway	66°N	13°E
B	Omega Liberia	6°N	11°W
C	Omega Hawaii	21°N	58°W
D	Omega North Dakota	46°N	98°W
E	Omega Reunion	21°S	55°E
F	Omega Argentina	43°S	65°W
G	Omega Trinidad	11°N	62°W
H	Omega Japan	35°N	129°E

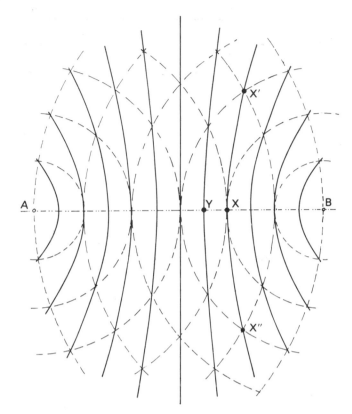

Fig. 5.2 Simplified Omega hyperbolic lattice. The hyperbolas represent lines of zero phase difference that occur every half wavelength of the transmission frequency

is 10.2 kHz with only one of the eight stations actually transmitting at any one time. Just as in the Decca system, the measured phase difference of phase-synchronized, and in this case time-shared, signals received at a particular location with respect to two transmitting stations, depends purely on the actual distances from the location to the transmitting stations. The signals are phase-synchronized at source by the use of caesium frequency standards.

Figure 5.2 shows transmitting stations A and B radiating phase-synchronized signals simultaneously. The concentric circles round each transmitter represent one wavelength at the transmitted frequency. Considering a receiver situated on the baseline (the line joining the two transmitters) at point X, then signals are received from the two transmitters in phase. If the receiver moves to point Y then the two signals are again received in phase since the receiver has moved away from station B by half a wavelength ($\lambda/2$) while it has moved towards station A by the same amount. Thus a 'lane' width occurs every half wavelength.

In theory, the phase of the signal received from each station can be compared with a locally generated reference signal having the same wavelength and phase-synchronized with the transmitter stations. Thus it is possible to indicate fractions of a wavelength in excess of an integral number of wavelengths distant from the transmitter. The receiver can, of course, be anywhere along a particular phase difference hyperbola, as indicated by points X' and X''. These hyperbolas are produced by joining all points of constant phase difference as figure 5.2 shows. Each hyperbola is known as a line of position (LOP).

Repeating measurements for another pair of transmitting stations would give a second LOP and the receiver position is established as the point of intersection of the two LOPs.

As stated earlier, the 'lane' width of the Omega system operating at 10.2 kHz is half a wavelength i.e. approximately 8 nautical miles (since λ is approximatelfy 16 nautical miles at that frequency). Since the baseline length between stations is about 5000 nautical miles, there are approximately 600 lanes between stations. The long baseline length and large number of lanes means that the divergence of the hyperbolas away from the baseline is reduced and using any pair of LOPs within the coverage area for a position fix gives an angle of cut of not less than 60°.

Measurement of phase difference in the receiver is made in intervals of one hundredth of a cycle, or 3.6° of phase difference, at 10.2 kHz, called centilanes (cels). Thus an LOP can be defined by a lane number (depending on position of the receiver with respect to the two transmitting stations) and a centilane value which determines the position within a lane.

5.3 Signal format

The problem of mutual interference between received signals from different sources at the same frequency is determined by allowing each station to transmit for approximately one second with a transmission break of 0.2 second between each transmission. The transmission break eliminates the possibility of overlapping between signals received from different stations. The signal format for all eight stations is shown in figure 5.3. Note that the transmission format lasts for 10 seconds after which it is repeated.

As can be seen from figure 5.1, the stations are designated by a letter uniquely identifying that station. Table 5.1 shows their positions.

Table 5.1 Omega stations

Station letter designation	Location	Latitude	Longitude
A	Aldra, Norway	66° 25′ N	13° 08′ E
B	Monrovia, Liberia	6° 18′ N	10° 40′ W
C	Haiku, Hawaii	21° 24′ N	157° 50′ W
D	La Moure, N. Dakota	46° 21′ N	98° 20′ W
E	La Reunion	20° 58′ S	55° 17′ E
F	Golfo Nuevo, Argentina	43° 03′ S	65° 11′ W
G	Australia	38° 29′ S	146° 56′ E
H	Tsushima, Japan	34° 37′ N	129° 27′ E

5.4 Lane identification

For an Omega receiver the lane position readout indicates the centilane value for any transmitter pair. To accurately define the actual lane, the operator must know the position of the vessel within an accuracy of 4 nautical miles on the baseline. Since Omega is a global system the receiver may be initialized in port, say, where the location of the vessel is accurately known, and the receiver relied upon to 'count' the number of lane crossings when the vessel is under way. However, lane counting capability of the receiver may not always be reliable, due possibly to equipment failure. Nevertheless, the operator can usually determine the true lane value by dead reckoning or the use of other navigational aids.

The Omega format provides facilities for resolving lane ambiguity since, as figure 5.3

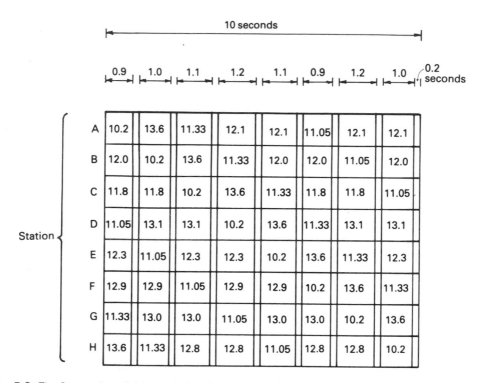

Fig. 5.3 The Omega time-division multiplexed transmission format

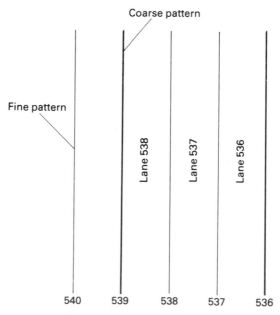

Fig. 5.4 Part of an Omega hyperbolic lattice showing 'normal' 10.2 kHz series of lanes (fine pattern) and the 3.4 kHz coarse pattern for resolving lane ambiguity

shows, each station transmits frequencies other than the 10.2 kHz value and some of these may be used to provide coarse lane fixing.

Consider the relationship between the 10.2 kHz and 13.6 kHz transmissions; the difference frequency is 3.4 kHz which is exactly one third of the value of the normal 10.2 kHz transmission. Using this value of frequency for comparison for any pair of stations would give a lane width of 24 nautical miles which is 3 times the normal value. Since all transmissions are phase synchronized, it follows that the coarse lane pattern is formed upon and coincident with *three* 10.2 kHz lanes as shown in figure 5.4. Thus the operator need now only know the vessel's position within an accuracy of 12 nautical miles on the baseline to identify the coarse lane without ambiguity. Having established the position within the coarse lane it should then be possible to determine the actual fine (10.2 kHz) lane without ambiguity.

Referring again to figure 5.4, suppose the cel reading is 50 but the operator, using the 10.2 kHz transmissions, is unsure as to whether the lane value is 536.5, 537.5 or 538.5.

Using the coarse lane which encompasses the LOPs 536 to 539, gives a centilane reading which corresponds to that lane. Thus if the coarse lane cel reading is 0.16 then the correct fine lane is 536. If the coarse lane cel reading is 0.5 then the correct fine lane is 537. If the coarse lane cel readng is 0.83 then the correct fine lane is 538.

The lane resolution process can be extended further by using even lower difference frequencies. For example, if the uncertainty in the vessel's position exceeds the 12 nautical miles possible with a difference frequency of 3.4 kHz, then a difference frequency of 1.133 kHz (one ninth of the normal 10.2 kHz value) can be achieved using the transmitted 10.2 kHz and 11.333 kHz values. This gives a coarse lane width of 72 nautical miles on the baseline allowing resolution to within 36 nautical miles. The same procedures apply as for the 13.6 kHz transmission regarding lane resolution.

The frequency of 11.05 kHz shown in the signal format is also available for resolution of lane ambiguity since the difference between this frequency and 11.333 kHz is 0.283 kHz which has a coarse lane width equal to 36 of the normal 10.2 kHz lanes. The use of this frequency for lane ambiguity resolution was intended to meet the requirements of air navigation where the high speeds of aircraft makes use of a 'wide' lane imperative. This frequency is not expected to be used for marine navigation.

The other frequencies shown in the signal format, figure 5.3, are unique to a particular station and are available to provide possible data links and control information between stations. These frequencies are not used for navigation purposes.

5.5 Omega propagational performance

The propagation of VLF electromagnetic (e.m.) waves is such that the waves tend to progress by reflection between the D-layer of the ionosphere and the earth's surface. The manner of the propagation of such waves is analogous to the propagation of an e.m. wave in a waveguide with the D-layer and the earth's surface acting as boundaries. Normally of course the frequencies propagated by reflection along the inner surface of a waveguide are very much higher than the value of the Omega signal but the dimensions of the waveguide used or those high frequencies are much smaller than the height of the lower region of the ionosphere which is typically 90 km.

As with all wave guide systems, the propagation of an e.m. wave along the guide causes interaction between incident and reflected waves to produce propagation modes. More than one mode may be produced in the waveguide at any instant and this is true of the Omega system 'waveguide'. The Omega transmissions create transverse magnetic (TM) propagation modes within the 'waveguide'. Only the first and second modes, TM_1 and TM_2, are large enough to warrant consideration.

There are parameters which define how a mode will propagate in the earth's surface-ionosphere waveguide, namely excitation factor, rate of attenuation and the velocity of propagation (phase velocity) of the mode.

Excitation factor

There is approximately the ratio of power projected into the Omega 'waveguide' to that projected into a flat waveguide with perfectly conducting boundaries. Figure 5.5 shows that the TM_2 mode is excited more than TM_1, the difference becoming larger with increasing frequency and height of the ionosphere. Note that the height of the ionosphere is shown in figure 5.5 as 70 km and 90 km. As will be discussed later, the height of the ionosphere does vary, on a diurnal basis between these two approximate values.

Attenuation

Experiment has shown that the rates of attenuation for TM_1 and TM_2 modes are as given in figure 5.6. As in normal waveguide use attenuation is quoted in dB per linear distance. The results show that the TM_2 mode is attenuated more, with distance, than is the TM_1 mode. The difference in attenuation rates is greater at 10 kHz than at 14 kHz and this is one of the reasons why 10.2 kHz is used to determine the most accurate LOPs. The rates given are average values which do not take into account the anisotropic nature of the ionosphere at VLF.

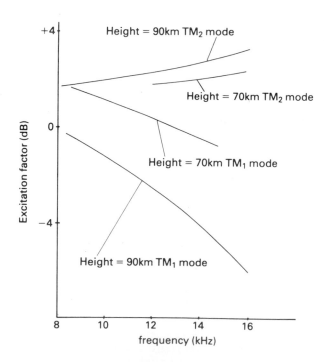

Fig. 5.5 Excitation factor against frequency for TM_1 and TM_2 mode and different values of height of the ionosphere D-layer

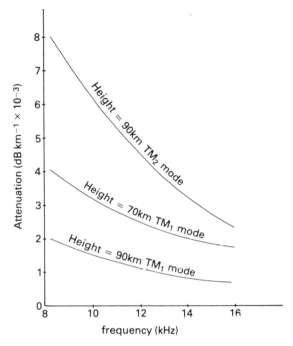

Fig. 5.6 Attenuation against frequency for TM$_1$ and TM$_2$ modes and different values of height of the ionosphere D-layer. The curve for TM$_2$ mode at a height of 70 km lies above 9 dB per 1000 km

Phase velocity

Figure 5.7 shows the phase velocity of TM$_1$ propagation. This shows that the waveguide is dispersive with velocity, being greater at 70 m than at 90 m. TM$_2$ phase velocity is not shown but is greater than that of TM$_1$.

Mutual interference between modes

Figures 5.5 and 5.6 show that the TM$_2$ mode is liable to be stronger than TM$_1$ at regions near a transmitter but that differences in attenuation rates are such that after certain distances the TM$_2$ mode can be neglected. The theoretical crossover points where TM$_1$ ≈ TM$_2$ are approximately 100 km by day and 400 km by night at 10.2 kHz, and 200 km by day and 1800 km by night at 13.6 kHz. Since all Omega measurements are based on the use of the TM$_1$ mode measurements taken with the ranges mentioned above will lead to possible errors. As the phase velocities, and hence waveguide wavelengths of the two modes are different, the effects of the mutual interference on amplitude and phase of the received signal will be cyclic with distance from the transmitter. LOPs are marked as dashed lines within 450 nautical miles of a transmitter station on Omega charts to indicate that those readings are liable to error. Figure 5.8 shows the TM$_1$ and TM$_2$ modes which exist together in regions close to the transmitters.

The effective height of the D-layer on the ionosphere has already been quoted as 90 km; however, this value is only correct for night conditions, the height falling to about 70 km during daylight hours – hence the two values of ionospheric height mentioned in figures 5.5, 5.6 and 5.7. The TM$_1$ mode phase velocity is critically dependent on the ionospheric height and increases as the height decreases, and vice versa. Obviously the phase of the

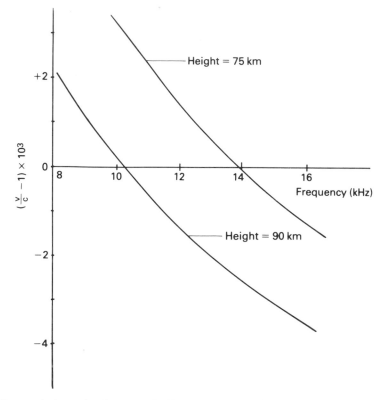

Fig. 5.7 Phase velocity against frequency for TM_1 mode only at different values of height of the ionosphere D-layer

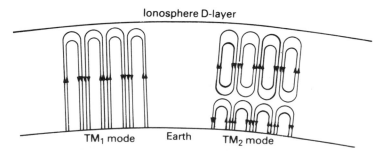

Fig. 5.8 Propagation at VLF producing TM_1 and TM_2 modes in the 'waveguide' between the earth and the D-layer of the ionosphere

signal received by a vessel will depend on the phase velocity so that changes in this velocity caused by changes in the ionospheric height will cause the received signal phase to be advanced or retarded.

Generally if a transmitter and its path to a receiver are in darkness and the sun rises first on the transmitter then the phase will decrease i.e. advance from the night value to the day value. The converse is true if the transmitter and path were initially in daylight and dusk falls initially on the transmitter

Another problem that the transition from day to night and vice versa is relatively long for east-west paths and short for north-south paths. Since one wavelength is covered by a wave in one cycle travelling at the phase velocity, the LOPs relative to the charted values will be closer together in going from day to night conditions and stretched for night to day changes.

Other effects on the propagation of the Omega signal are caused by geophysical parameters which include the magnetic field of the earth, latitude, solar activity, arctic paths and auroral zones.

1. Earth's magnetic field

It has been assumed that propagation occurs in a similar fashion in all directions. In fact this does not happen because of the effect of the earth's magnetic field on the reflecting property of the ionosphere. Attenuation is affected considerably according to direction. Typical figures for 10.2 kHz attenuation rates for TM_1 mode at low altitudes are:

$$
\begin{array}{ll}
\text{E–W} & 4.2\,\text{dB per } 1000\,\text{km} \\
\text{W–E} & 1.9\,\text{dB per } 1000\,\text{km} \\
\left.\begin{array}{l}\text{N–S} \\[2em] \text{S–N}\end{array}\right\} & 2.7\,\text{dB per } 1000\,\text{km}
\end{array}
$$

Hence at a range of about 5000 nautical miles to the west of a low altitude transmitter the signals from shorter and longer great-circle paths will be of comparable strength rendering the transmissions unusable.

TM_2 mode suffers in the same way as the TM_1 mode except that propagation to the east at night has a rate of attenuation that will cause modal interference out to about 1000 nautical miles. There will be a region where all great-circle paths intercept to give a very large but obviously unusable signal.

2. Latitude

The height of the ionosphere varies with latitude; during summer months the ionosphere height is greater over the higher latitudes than the lower latitudes.

3. Solar activity

This can take different forms as follows:

(a) Sudden ionospheric disturbances (SIDs) arise when there is a sudden large rise in X-ray emission from the sun accompanying a solar flare. The effect occurs on sunlit propagation paths and causes a phase advance; these phase changes are known as sudden phase anomalies (SPA). The onset of the disturbance is rapid, reacing a maximum effect after about 5 to 10 minutes and is followed by a slow recovery over a period of up to 60 minutes. The SID effect occurs mostly in lower latitude regions and significant SIDs could cause positional errors of up to 2 miles.

(b) Polar cap absorption. It has been found that radio waves arriving at the polar regions show rapid phase changes caused by the focusing effect of the earth's magnetic field which attracts particles released from the sun and concentrates them in the polar regions. The amount of transmission anomaly depends on how much of the transmission path actually crosses the region of the magnetic pole. A transmission path that is outside the polar region will be unaffected by PCA whereas a transmission path that is affected suffers anomalies that are random and unpredictable. It is known, however, that the effect increases during periods of high solar activity.

4. Arctic paths

Very high attenuation occurs with propagation over freshwater icecap regions. Little data is available for these regions and hence propagation corrections are only estimates. In particular, rapid attenuation of the Omega signal with position occurs as one passes into the shadow of the Greenland icecap.

5. Auroral zones

Paths which intercept the auroral zones surrounding the south and north geomagnetic poles affect the phase of Omega signals. These effects are believed to arise from electron precipitation in the higher regions of the ionosphere which serves as a source of ionization for the D-layer. The effect occurs in a circular band between 60° and 80° north and south geomagnetic latitude and causes a decrease in phase i.e. a phase advance with respect to nominal values.

5.6 Omega skywave correction tables

The US Defense Mapping Agency Hydrographic/Topographic Center produces a series of charts overprinted with Omega LOPs for certain transmitter pairs. To avoid the confusion that could arise by printing all LOPs for all relevant transmitter pairs on one chart, it is usual to print only every third LOP. The LOPs shown are in fact those which are concident with 10.2 kHz and 13.6 kHz i.e. the 3.4 kHz LOP.

Some British charts are available with overprinted LOPs and a list of such charts is available from the Hydrographer to the Navy, Taunton, Somerset. Figure 5.9 is an example of an Omega chart.

The printed LOPs are the result of a computation based on nominal conditions of propagation and earth conductivity. Since as has already been discussed, propagation conditions are liable to continual change, phase corrections have to be applied and are available for all Omega coverage areas published for each station. The US Defence Mapping Agency Office of Distribution Services, Washington D.C. publishes tables of corrections and a list of such tables is available from that agency.

Figure 5.10 shows Omega table areas and the correction tables for a particular area of a specified station can be obtained. The tables are available in the publication 224 series and are identified by that number followed by a pertinent suffix, which comprises three digits, followed by letter C. A final letter indicates the station. For example OMPUB224106CA is Omega publication (224) for frequency of 10.2 kHz (1), table area Greenland (06), correction tables, as against lattice tables (C) and pertinent station, in this case Norway (A).

Tables are available for a frequency of 3.4 kHz in which case the digit is '2', or 13.6 kHz in which case the digit is '3'. For example, OMPUB224306A is a table for the same area, and station, as before but printed for a transmission frequency of 13.6 kHz.

Propagation corrects are tabulated for each grid point of a grid constructed for 4° intervals for latitudes between 0° and 45°. The longitude interval is increased to 6° for latitudes between 45° and 60°, and to 8° for latitudes between 60° and 80°. Also propagation corrections for the north and south polar areas between 70° and 90° are tabulated at intervals of 4° of latitude and 20° of longitude. Each set of corrections is arranged as a matrix with Greenwich Mean Time (GMT) horizontally and semi-monthly periods vertically.

The values are extracted from the tables in units of centicycles (cecs) i.e. 1% of a cycle. However, the difference in cecs of the phase readings of a station pair is numerically equal to the percentage value of the lane defining the LOP so that the difference in cecs is numerically equal to the number of cels defining the LOP within the lane.

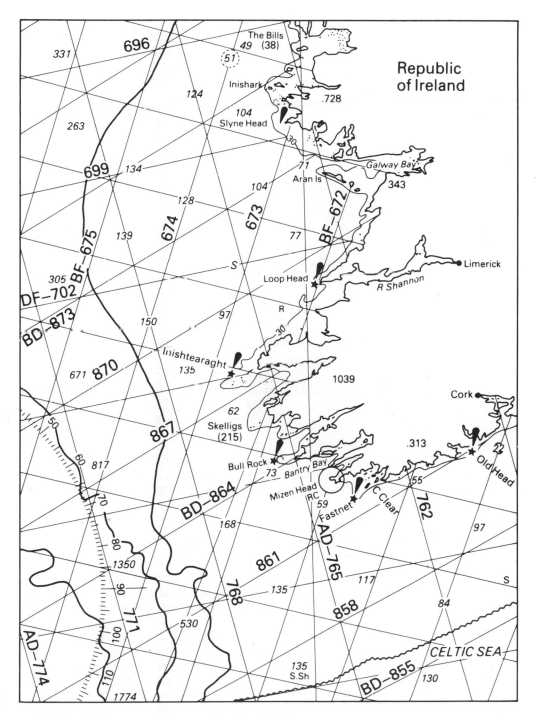

Fig. 5.9 Section of Omega plotting chart. Reproduced from British Admiralty Chart No. 1125 with the sanction of the Controller of Her Britannic Majesty's Stationery Office and of the Hydrographer of the Royal Navy.

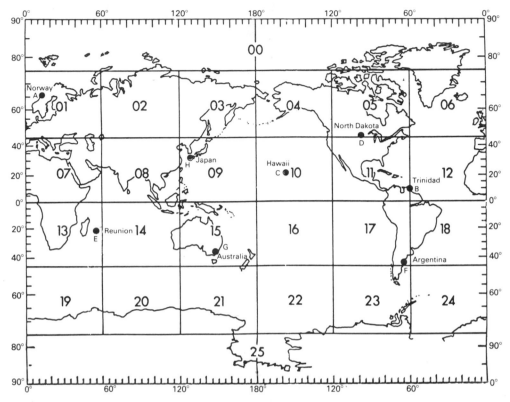

Fig. 5.10 Omega table areas and positions of Omega stations. The 'B' station is now sited at Monrovia, Liberia

To obtain the propagation correction for a station pair, the correction for each station is determined and the value of the resultant obtained by subtracting one reading from the other. For example, for a particular value of latitude and longitude and semi-monthly period,

GMT	Station D	Station H	Hyperbola D-H
09.00	− 98	− 27	− 98 − (− 27) = − 71

Note that the alphabetical order of the stations determines which order the subtraction takes place i.e. the higher order station (D in the example above) is the minuend while the station that follows alphabetically (station H in the example above) is the subtrahend. This is true for all stations.

If a multi-frequency receiver capable of tracking both 10.2 kHz and 13.6 kHz is being used then the correction tables for both frequencies may be used to give corrected 3.4 kHz readings. Consider the example: The 0700Z Dead Reckoning (DR) position of a vessel on 20 January is latitude 51° 26′ N longitude 167° 32′ W. Omega lane count has been lost but the 0700Z phase readings for station pair A-C are 0.19 cecs for 10.2 kHz and 0.99 cecs for 13.6 kHz. What is the correct 0700Z 10.2 kHz Omega lane?

The dead reckoning position is plotted on an Omega chart to identify the 3.4 kHz 'coarse' lane which, in this case, is bounded by the 10.2 kHz LOPs AC-1017 and AC-1020. Both 10.2 kHz and 13.6 kHz Omega Propagation Correction tables are used to determine the derived 3.4 kHz phase reading. This value is the percentage of the distance from LOP AC-1017 towards LOP AC-1020 (see Table 5.2 for table excerpts for stations A and C).

PPC for Station A (13.6 kHz) − 1.42
PPC for Station C (13.6 kHz) − 0.89
PPC for Station A (10.2 kHz) − 0.54
PPC for Station C (10.2 kHz) − 0.45

Corrected 13.6 kHz reading = 0.99 + (− 1.42) − (− 0.89) = 0.46
Corrected 10.2 kHz reading = 0.19 + (− 0.54) − (− 0.45) = 0.10
Corrected 3.4 kHz reading = 0.46 − 0.10   = 0.36

Plotting 36% of the 3.4 kHz coarse lane identifies the correct 10.2 kHz A-C lane as 1018. The PPC corrected 10.2 kHz reading (0.10) when combined with the resolved lane (1018) yields the LOP as AC − 1018.10.

Figure 5.11 shows the area covered by a table of Omega propagation corrections. The corrections for a given coverage area are arranged in order of increasing west longitude and increasing north latitude. The numbers in the small sections refer to the page numbers of the table for which the corrections are tabulated.

Table 5.3 shows an extract from the propagation correction tables.

Interpolation

The Omega fix will ordinarily be available 24 hours a day. However, the navigator should bear in mind certain facts regarding the system and prevailing propagation conditions when making a fix.

1. Diurnal
It may be entirely sunlit (day), entirely dark or there may be transitions from one state to another along a propagation path.

For long paths night may be only a few hours whilst for arctic paths during the summer months there may be no night at all. Stability of propagaation varies according to time of day and expecially at transitions between night and day.

To determine what interpolation procedures to follow, the navigator should examine the propagation conditions affecting his measurements. For example at 36°N 12°;w at 231940Z Jan it will be dark. However, the propagation path to the location from North Dakota and Hawaii transmitters will be almost completely sunlit and C-D LOP measurements would reflect daytime propagation conditions.

The general propagation conditions affecting a station measurement may be discerned by examining the propagation correction tables. The path will ordinarily be dark for several hours and so the tabulated corrections will be constant for a long period. The centre of this period will normally be the centre of the night. The effective centre of the propagation day can be estimated by adding about 12 hours. For example at 36° N 12° W the data in Table 5.4 may be observed.

2. Night
Since the corrections are constant at night, no interpolation is required.

3. Day
Since propagation conditions vary slowly during the day, linear interpolation may be used.

Table 5.2 Excerpts from Omega Propagation Correction Tables for stations A and C (Reproduced by courtesy of the Defense Mapping Agency Hydrographic/Topographic Center)

LOCATION STATION A — 52 0 N 168 0 M Norway

13.6 KHZ OMEGA PROPAGATION CORRECTIONS IN UNITS OF CECS

DATE	00	01	02	03	04	05	06	07	08	09	10	11	12	13	14	15	16	17	18	19	20	21	22	23	24
1–15 JAN	-119	-124	-127	-132	-137	-140	-142	-142	-141	-138	-135	-130	-136	-133	-138	-140	-142	-143	-143	-135	-124	-120	-117	-121	-119
16–31 JAN	-116	-121	-124	-129	-134	-138	-141	-139	-139	-135	-129	-131	-135	-137	-139	-140	-142	-142	-143	-131	-121	-116	-117	-118	-116
1–14 FEB	-118	-114	-119	-124	-130	-135	-140	-137	-132	-127	-126	-126	-131	-134	-135	-137	-139	-139	-139	-120	-115	-111	-116	-114	-118
15–29 FEB	-117	-117	-119	-120	-125	-131	-130	-126	-114	-123	-123	-128	-130	-130	-131	-133	-135	-138	-120	-110	-101	-106	-115	-117	-117
1–15 MAR	-114	-114	-115	-116	-112	-116	-107	-115	-126	-128	-123	-128	-124	-128	-128	-133	-130	-121	-93	-106	-115	-109	-110	-110	-110
16–31 MAR	-110	-110	-110	-103	-102	-100	-109	-107	-111	-121	-123	-123	-124	-124	-119	-115	-113	-121	-96	-99	-101	-103	-104	-105	-105
1–15 APR	-105	-105	-105	-96	-95	-96	-106	-111	-115	-115	-117	-119	-120	-119	-115	-105	-90	-92	-96	-99	-101	-103	-104	-105	-105
16–30 APR	-101	-101	-99	-95	-94	-96	-98	-107	-108	-107	-111	-115	-116	-116	-113	-105	-90	-97	-98	-97	-98	-98	-97	-101	-101
1–15 MAY	-97	-97	-96	-95	-96	-95	-95	-101	-108	-104	-110	-112	-113	-112	-107	-94	-92	-93	-95	-96	-96	-95	-96	-97	-97
16–31 MAY	-95	-94	-94	-93	-94	-94	-94	-96	-104	-106	-109	-109	-109	-99	-95	-91	-91	-93	-94	-95	-95	-95	-95	-95	-95
1–15 JUN	-93	-93	-93	-93	-93	-93	-94	-95	-101	-103	-105	-107	-107	-106	-102	-93	-93	-94	-93	-93	-93	-94	-93	-94	-93
16–30 JUN	-93	-92	-92	-93	-93	-93	-94	-94	-100	-104	-105	-107	-108	-107	-101	-92	-91	-94	-94	-93	-93	-94	-93	-94	-94
1–15 JUL	-95	-94	-94	-93	-93	-94	-95	-96	-99	-106	-110	-107	-108	-109	-99	-95	-91	-94	-94	-95	-95	-94	-94	-93	-95
16–31 JUL	-98	-97	-97	-95	-94	-95	-98	-99	-109	-107	-112	-113	-113	-110	-96	-90	-90	-94	-95	-100	-100	-96	-97	-97	-98
1–15 AUG	-102	-101	-100	-96	-96	-98	-106	-108	-113	-116	-118	-115	-116	-116	-109	-105	-96	-92	-98	-102	-104	-105	-106	-101	-102
16–31 AUG	-106	-106	-105	-103	-98	-103	-112	-117	-120	-122	-123	-120	-120	-114	-109	-92	-96	-91	-96	-100	-102	-104	-105	-106	-106
1–15 SEP	-110	-110	-110	-114	-113	-108	-112	-120	-128	-128	-124	-124	-124	-119	-121	-110	-93	-93	-97	-108	-109	-109	-110	-110	-110
16–30 SEP	-114	-114	-114	-116	-113	-116	-130	-127	-128	-128	-128	-128	-128	-129	-119	-124	-128	-110	-93	-104	-116	-115	-115	-115	-114
1–15 OCT	-118	-118	-119	-122	-129	-134	-141	-135	-116	-124	-129	-131	-131	-132	-133	-135	-138	-115	-111	-104	-112	-111	-111	-115	-118
16–31 OCT	-119	-121	-123	-128	-134	-133	-141	-135	-132	-126	-128	-133	-132	-133	-136	-141	-141	-142	-132	-117	-114	-113	-114	-115	-119
1–15 NOV	-119	-119	-123	-123	-128	-133	-141	-133	-128	-128	-128	-128	-133	-136	-140	-142	-142	-132	-114	-114	-113	-116	-115	-115	-119
16–30 NOV	-116	-122	-126	-132	-136	-140	-142	-142	-138	-133	-130	-131	-136	-138	-141	-141	-143	-143	-141	-125	-119	-116	-119	-120	-116
1–15 DEC	-118	-124	-128	-133	-138	-141	-142	-143	-143	-137	-133	-133	-139	-139	-141	-142	-143	-143	-143	-123	-119	-115	-118	-120	-118
16–31 DEC	-118	-124	-128	-133	-138	-141	-142	-143	-142	-139	-136	-136	-134	-138	-140	-142	-143	-143	-143	-135	-126	-120	-121	-118	-118

LOCATION STATION C — 52 0 N 168 0 W HAWAII

13.6 KHZ OMEGA PROPAGATION CORRECTIONS IN UNITS OF CECS

DATE	00	01	02	03	04	05	06	07	08	09	10	11	12	13	14	15	16	17	18	19	20	21	22	23	24
1–15 JAN	-53	-54	-55	-58	-74	-81	-87	-89	-90	-91	-91	-91	-91	-91	-91	-91	-91	-85	-54	-47	-52	-54	-53	-53	-53
16–31 JAN	-53	-54	-55	-57	-69	-81	-87	-89	-90	-90	-91	-91	-91	-91	-91	-91	-91	-85	-52	-47	-52	-54	-53	-53	-53
1–14 FEB	-52	-53	-54	-55	-62	-82	-87	-89	-90	-90	-91	-91	-91	-91	-91	-91	-91	-81	-46	-49	-53	-53	-52	-52	-52
15–29 FEB	-52	-52	-53	-56	-56	-80	-84	-88	-89	-90	-91	-91	-91	-91	-91	-91	-91	-69	-40	-51	-53	-53	-53	-52	-52
1–15 MAR	-51	-51	-52	-54	-56	-75	-82	-87	-89	-90	-91	-91	-91	-91	-91	-91	-69	-53	-45	-52	-53	-52	-51	-51	-51
16–31 MAR	-50	-51	-52	-53	-55	-69	-80	-86	-89	-90	-90	-91	-91	-91	-91	-66	-44	-41	-49	-54	-53	-52	-51	-51	-50
1–15 APR	-50	-51	-52	-53	-54	-64	-77	-84	-88	-89	-90	-91	-91	-91	-91	-44	-42	-46	-51	-54	-53	-51	-50	-50	-50
16–30 APR	-50	-50	-51	-53	-54	-59	-74	-83	-85	-88	-89	-90	-91	-91	-83	-42	-42	-49	-54	-54	-53	-51	-50	-49	-50
1–15 MAY	-49	-50	-51	-53	-54	-57	-71	-81	-85	-87	-89	-90	-91	-91	-73	-50	-42	-50	-54	-53	-52	-51	-50	-49	-49
16–31 MAY	-49	-50	-51	-52	-54	-56	-67	-78	-84	-87	-88	-90	-91	-89	-68	-50	-42	-50	-54	-52	-51	-50	-50	-49	-49
1–15 JUN	-49	-50	-51	-52	-54	-56	-67	-78	-85	-86	-88	-90	-91	-90	-72	-49	-43	-47	-54	-53	-51	-50	-50	-49	-49
16–30 JUN	-49	-50	-51	-52	-54	-57	-69	-80	-84	-88	-89	-90	-91	-91	-80	-49	-46	-45	-53	-53	-51	-50	-51	-50	-49
1–15 JUL	-50	-50	-51	-53	-55	-60	-72	-82	-86	-88	-90	-90	-91	-91	-88	-52	-48	-47	-54	-54	-52	-50	-51	-50	-50
16–31 JUL	-49	-50	-51	-52	-53	-57	-67	-80	-85	-89	-89	-90	-91	-91	-91	-64	-42	-45	-52	-53	-52	-50	-50	-49	-49
1–15 AUG	-49	-50	-51	-53	-55	-60	-69	-80	-84	-89	-90	-90	-91	-91	-80	-48	-43	-47	-54	-53	-52	-50	-50	-50	-49
16–31 AUG	-50	-51	-52	-53	-54	-66	-81	-85	-87	-90	-90	-91	-91	-91	-88	-43	-46	-42	-52	-53	-52	-50	-50	-49	-50
1–15 SEP	-51	-51	-52	-54	-55	-75	-83	-87	-89	-91	-91	-91	-91	-91	-91	-82	-91	-39	-41	-54	-54	-53	-51	-51	-51
16–30 SEP	-52	-52	-53	-54	-56	-81	-86	-89	-90	-91	-91	-91	-91	-91	-91	-89	-91	-62	-45	-51	-54	-53	-52	-52	-52
1–15 OCT	-53	-53	-54	-55	-66	-81	-86	-89	-90	-91	-91	-91	-91	-91	-91	-90	-91	-70	-49	-54	-54	-53	-53	-53	-53
16–31 OCT	-52	-52	-53	-54	-68	-81	-86	-89	-90	-91	-91	-91	-91	-91	-91	-91	-91	-77	-48	-53	-53	-53	-52	-52	-52
1–15 NOV	-53	-54	-55	-56	-76	-83	-87	-90	-90	-91	-91	-91	-91	-91	-91	-91	-91	-70	-49	-48	-54	-54	-53	-53	-53
16–30 NOV	-53	-54	-55	-58	-78	-84	-88	-89	-90	-91	-91	-91	-91	-91	-91	-91	-91	-51	-48	-48	-53	-54	-52	-52	-53
1–15 DEC	-54	-54	-55	-60	-78	-84	-88	-90	-90	-91	-91	-91	-91	-91	-91	-91	-91	-70	-51	-48	-54	-54	-53	-53	-54
16–31 DEC	-54	-54	-55	-60	-77	-84	-89	-89	-90	-91	-91	-91	-91	-91	-91	-91	-91	-82	-54	-48	-52	-51	-51	-53	-54

Table 5.2 (*contd.*)

10.2 KHZ OMEGA PROPAGATION CORRECTIONS IN UNITS OF CECS

LOCATION STATION A   52.0 N   168.0 M NORWAY

GMT

DATE	00	01	02	03	04	05	06	07	08	09	10	11	12	13	14	15	16	17	18	19	20	21	22	23	24
1–15 JAN	-35	-40	-43	-47	-50	-53	-54	-54	-53	-50	-48	-44	-49	-46	-50	-53	-54	-54	-53	-48	-37	-35	-33	-36	-35
16–31 JAN	-32	-37	-41	-45	-48	-51	-53	-54	-51	-47	-48	-44	-49	-51	-52	-53	-54	-54	-53	-65	-35	-31	-33	-33	-32
1–14 FEB	-33	-30	-35	-37	-41	-49	-52	-49	-29	-41	-38	-41	-48	-48	-49	-53	-52	-51	-51	-54	-30	-27	-31	-29	-33
15–29 FEB	-31	-32	-34	-37	-42	-46	-44	-39	-29	-37	-38	-45	-45	-47	-47	-48	-50	-51	-34	-25	-18	-22	-29	-31	-31
1–15 MAR	-28	-25	-29	-32	-31	-34	-25	-32	-38	-44	-38	-42	-45	-43	-43	-45	-46	-37	-11	-27	-31	-31	-25	-29	-28
16–31 MAR	-24	-23	-25	-19	-21	-21	-30	-36	-38	-31	-38	-42	-43	-38	-39	-39	-31	-14	-15	-20	-27	-25	-24	-24	-24
1–15 APR	-20	-20	-20	-12	-13	-15	-29	-28	-29	-31	-32	-33	-38	-34	-33	-30	-13	-9	-21	-20	-19	-19	-19	-20	-20
16–30 APR	-16	-15	-14	-11	-13	-15	-17	-24	-29	-26	-28	-29	-30	-31	-28	-11	-8	-13	-15	-10	-13	-15	-15	-15	-16
1–15 MAY	-12	-12	-12	-11	-9	-8	-10	-17	-24	-23	-25	-27	-27	-26	-23	-11	-8	-9	-8	-10	-13	-11	-11	-11	-12
16–31 MAY	-9	-9	-9	-8	-6	-6	-8	-12	-19	-22	-23	-23	-24	-24	-15	-12	-8	-7	-6	-5	-6	-9	-9	-10	-9
1–15 JUN	-8	-7	-7	-6	-5	-5	-6	-9	-16	-19	-21	-22	-22	-21	-18	-11	-9	-7	-5	-5	-8	-8	-8	-7	-8
16–30 JUN	-8	-7	-7	-6	-6	-5	-7	-9	-16	-19	-21	-22	-22	-21	-17	-10	-8	-7	-6	-6	-6	-9	-9	-10	-8
1–15 JUL	-9	-8	-8	-7	-7	-6	-7	-11	-18	-22	-25	-26	-24	-24	-15	-13	-8	-8	-9	-9	-14	-11	-11	-12	-12
16–31 JUL	-12	-12	-12	-11	-10	-13	-10	-15	-25	-24	-25	-26	-27	-25	-25	-13	-8	-10	-17	-15	-20	-20	-21	-16	-16
1–15 AUG	-16	-16	-15	-11	-13	-15	-18	-24	-28	-27	-28	-30	-30	-29	-24	-15	-14	-14	-21	-22	-24	-20	-20	-20	-21
16–31 AUG	-21	-20	-20	-12	-18	-21	-30	-29	-30	-32	-33	-34	-34	-34	-29	-28	-21	-21	-21	-21	-27	-25	-25	-21	-21
1–15 SEP	-25	-24	-25	-20	-23	-27	-32	-37	-38	-38	-38	-38	-38	-39	-37	-37	-28	-27	-21	-22	-31	-29	-30	-30	-28
16–30 SEP	-28	-29	-30	-34	-32	-27	-25	-37	-43	-40	-43	-43	-43	-43	-45	-49	-44	-51	-30	-26	-37	-30	-29	-29	-28
1–15 OCT	-32	-33	-40	-40	-45	-48	-43	-41	-48	-46	-44	-46	-46	-47	-48	-49	-51	-51	-45	-39	-20	-27	-26	-30	-32
16–31 OCT	-34	-37	-45	-47	-48	-51	-54	-54	-50	-50	-44	-47	-47	-50	-50	-53	-53	-54	-53	-39	-33	-29	-30	-31	-34
1–15 NOV	-32	-38	-40	-47	-50	-53	-54	-54	-54	-46	-44	-42	-49	-52	-52	-53	-54	-54	-55	-37	-33	-32	-34	-30	-32
16–30 NOV	-35	-40	-44	-47	-51	-53	-54	-54	-50	-50	-48	-46	-50	-53	-53	-54	-54	-55	-55	-45	-37	-35	-34	-36	-35
1–15 DEC	-35	-40	-44	-48	-51	-53	-54	-54	-54	-51	-48	-48	-52	-51	-53	-54	-54	-55	-55	-48	-39	-35	-36	-36	-35
16–31 DEC	-35	-40	-44	-48	-51	-53	-54	-54	-54	-51	-48	-48	-47	-51	-53	-54	-55	-55	-55	-48	-39	-35	-36	-36	-35

10.2 KHZ OMEGA PROPAGATION CORRECTIONS IN UNITS OF CECS

LOCATION STATION C   52.0 N   168.0 M HAWAII

GMT

DATE	00	01	02	03	04	05	06	07	08	09	10	11	12	13	14	15	16	17	18	19	20	21	22	23	24
1–15 JAN	-8	-9	-11	-19	-33	-40	-44	-45	-46	-46	-46	-46	-46	-46	-46	-46	-46	-41	-14	-7	-10	-10	-9	-8	-8
16–31 JAN	-8	-8	-10	-17	-29	-39	-43	-45	-46	-46	-46	-46	-46	-46	-46	-46	-46	-41	-12	-8	-10	-9	-8	-8	-8
1–14 FEB	-7	-7	-9	-12	-24	-39	-43	-45	-46	-46	-46	-45	-46	-46	-46	-46	-46	-47	-6	-7	-10	-8	-7	-7	-7
15–29 FEB	-6	-6	-8	-10	-20	-37	-41	-44	-45	-46	-46	-45	-45	-46	-46	-46	-46	-27	-1	-9	-9	-7	-6	-5	-6
1–15 MAR	-5	-6	-7	-9	-17	-33	-40	-43	-45	-46	-46	-45	-45	-45	-46	-46	-46	-12	-4	-10	-7	-6	-5	-5	-5
16–31 MAR	-4	-5	-6	-8	-15	-29	-39	-42	-44	-46	-46	-46	-46	-46	-46	-46	-46	-2	-7	-9	-7	-5	-4	-4	-4
1–15 APR	-4	-4	-6	-8	-12	-25	-38	-41	-45	-46	-46	-46	-46	-45	-46	-46	-46	-1	-11	-8	-6	-5	-4	-4	-4
16–30 APR	-3	-4	-5	-7	-10	-19	-35	-40	-43	-45	-46	-46	-46	-46	-46	-40	-4	-6	-10	-8	-5	-4	-3	-3	-3
1–15 MAY	-3	-4	-4	-7	-9	-17	-33	-39	-42	-44	-46	-46	-46	-46	-46	-30	-3	-9	-9	-8	-5	-4	-3	-3	-3
16–31 MAY	-3	-4	-4	-5	-8	-15	-30	-37	-42	-44	-46	-46	-46	-44	-44	-26	-3	-8	-9	-8	-5	-4	-3	-3	-3
1–15 JUN	-3	-4	-5	-7	-8	-15	-28	-36	-41	-44	-45	-46	-46	-46	-44	-26	-4	-8	-8	-7	-5	-4	-4	-3	-3
16–30 JUN	-3	-4	-5	-7	-9	-15	-27	-36	-42	-44	-45	-46	-46	-46	-44	-26	-4	-7	-9	-8	-6	-5	-4	-4	-3
1–15 JUL	-3	-4	-5	-7	-9	-18	-28	-38	-42	-44	-45	-46	-46	-46	-44	-36	-8	-5	-9	-9	-6	-5	-4	-4	-3
16–31 JUL	-4	-4	-6	-8	-10	-21	-31	-41	-44	-46	-46	-46	-46	-46	-46	-38	-11	-2	-11	-8	-6	-5	-4	-4	-4
1–15 AUG	-4	-5	-6	-10	-13	-23	-35	-42	-45	-46	-46	-46	-46	-46	-46	-44	-22	-0	-10	-9	-6	-5	-4	-4	-4
16–31 AUG	-4	-5	-7	-11	-18	-26	-37	-44	-46	-46	-46	-46	-46	-46	-46	-46	-44	-2	-8	-7	-7	-6	-5	-5	-4
1–15 SEP	-5	-6	-7	-13	-22	-33	-39	-44	-46	-46	-46	-46	-46	-46	-46	-46	-46	-10	-7	-10	-8	-6	-5	-6	-5
16–30 SEP	-6	-6	-8	-15	-28	-38	-40	-45	-46	-46	-46	-46	-46	-46	-46	-46	-46	-21	-4	-10	-9	-7	-6	-6	-6
1–15 OCT	-6	-7	-9	-18	-35	-39	-43	-44	-46	-46	-46	-46	-46	-46	-46	-46	-46	-28	-6	-8	-10	-8	-7	-7	-6
16–31 OCT	-7	-8	-10	-22	-36	-40	-44	-44	-46	-46	-46	-46	-46	-46	-46	-46	-46	-34	-11	-8	-9	-8	-7	-7	-7
1–15 NOV	-8	-9	-12	-22	-36	-41	-44	-45	-46	-46	-46	-46	-46	-46	-46	-46	-46	-38	-13	-7	-10	-8	-8	-8	-8
16–30 NOV	-8	-9	-13	-23	-36	-41	-44	-45	-46	-46	-46	-46	-46	-46	-46	-46	-46	-38	-13	-7	-10	-9	-8	-8	-8
1–15 DEC	-8	-9	-13	-22	-35	-41	-44	-45	-46	-46	-46	-46	-46	-46	-46	-46	-46	-38	-13	-7	-10	-8	-8	-8	-8

Table 5.3 Excerpt from Omega Propagation Correction Tables. (Reproduced by courtesy of the Defense Mapping Agency Hydrographic/Topographic Center)

LOCATION: 16.0 N 40.0 W
STATION A: NORWAY

OMEGA PROPAGATION CORRECTIONS FOR 10.2 KHZ

GMT

DATE	00	01	02	03	04	05	06	07	08	09	10	11	12	13	14	15	16	17	18	19	20	21	22	23	24
1–15 JAN	−71	−71	−71	−71	−71	−71	−71	−71	−71	−14	−5	−2	−1	0	1	0	−3	−12	−24	−40	−61	−71	−71	−71	−71
16–31 JAN	−71	−71	−71	−71	−71	−71	−71	−71	−68	−11	−6	−3	−1	0	1	0	−1	−8	−20	−36	−57	−71	−71	−71	−71
1–14 FEB	−71	−71	−71	−71	−71	−71	−71	−71	−59	−11	−8	−4	−2	0	0	0	−2	−5	−16	−31	−52	−71	−71	−71	−71
15–28 FEB	−71	−71	−71	−71	−71	−71	−71	−67	−44	−10	−6	−3	0	−1	2	1	0	−3	−9	−24	−45	−71	−71	−71	−71
1–15 MAR	−71	−71	−71	−71	−71	−71	−70	−59	−32	−8	−4	−1	1	3	3	3	1	−2	−5	−17	−39	−70	−71	−71	−71
16–31 MAR	−71	−71	−71	−71	−71	−71	−64	−48	−18	−6	−3	2	3	5	5	4	2	0	−4	−9	−29	−67	−71	−71	−71
1–15 APR	−71	−71	−71	−71	−71	−66	−55	−37	−10	−5	−1	4	5	6	6	6	4	1	−3	−7	−16	−60	−71	−71	−71
16–30 APR	−71	−71	−71	−71	−68	−62	−59	−47	−28	−7	−3	2	6	7	6	6	5	2	−2	−6	−9	−41	−71	−71	−71
1–15 MAY	−71	−71	−71	−71	−62	−53	−41	−22	−6	1	4	5	8	8	7	6	3	−1	−5	−9	−16	−70	−71	−71	−71
16–31 MAY	−71	−71	−71	−69	−65	−59	−47	−37	−18	−5	2	5	8	8	8	8	6	4	0	−4	−8	−12	−62	−71	−71
1–15 JUN	−69	−69	−69	−65	−62	−53	−49	−34	−16	−4	3	6	8	9	9	8	6	4	1	−3	−7	−11	−50	−71	−71
16–30 JUN	−68	−68	−66	−61	−61	−55	−47	−34	−16	−5	3	6	8	9	9	8	7	4	1	−3	−7	−10	−45	−71	−71
1–15 JUL	−69	−69	−69	−65	−58	−48	−35	−20	1	4	6	8	9	10	10	9	7	5	3	0	−2	−5	−43	−66	−69
16–31 JUL	−71	−71	−71	−65	−63	−53	−40	−25	1	3	5	7	9	10	10	9	7	5	3	2	0	−5	−38	−65	−71
1–15 AUG	−71	−71	−71	−69	−63	−53	−40	−20	1	3	5	8	9	10	10	9	8	6	4	2	0	−5	−57	−70	−71
16–31 AUG	−71	−71	−71	−71	−68	−59	−45	−25	0	2	5	7	8	9	9	8	7	5	3	1	−1	−13	−65	−71	−71
1–15 SEP	−71	−71	−71	−71	−71	−65	−52	−32	−3	2	4	6	7	8	8	7	6	4	1	0	−13	−34	−65	−71	−71
16–30 SEP	−71	−71	−71	−71	−71	−70	−59	−39	−7	1	3	5	7	7	7	7	5	3	1	−6	−33	−65	−71	−71	−71
1–15 OCT	−71	−71	−71	−71	−71	−71	−67	−48	−15	0	2	4	6	6	6	6	4	1	−2	−19	−48	−71	−71	−71	−71
16–31 OCT	−71	−71	−71	−71	−71	−71	−71	−59	−33	0	2	4	5	5	5	5	3	1	−11	−38	−59	−71	−71	−71	−71
1–15 NOV	−71	−71	−71	−71	−71	−71	−71	−69	−57	−2	1	3	4	4	4	4	2	−5	−19	−38	−65	−71	−71	−71	−71
16–30 NOV	−71	−71	−71	−71	−71	−71	−71	−71	−69	−3	0	2	3	3	3	3	0	−10	−24	−42	−67	−71	−71	−71	−71
1–15 DEC	−71	−71	−71	−71	−71	−71	−71	−71	−71	−3	0	1	2	3	3	2	−2	−12	−25	−43	−67	−71	−71	−71	−71
16–31 DEC	−71	−71	−71	−71	−71	−71	−71	−71	−71	−7	−2	−1	1	2	2	1	−3	−13	−26	−43	−65	−71	−71	−71	−71

Table 5.3 (*contd.*)

OMEGA PROPAGATION CORRECTIONS FOR 10.2 KHZ

LOCATION: 16.0 N 40.0 W
STATION A: NORWAY

DATE	00	01	02	03	04	05	06	07	08	09	10	11	12	13	14	15	16	17	18	19	20	21	22	23	24
1–15 JAN	−63	−79	−94	−109	−121	−122	−122	−122	−122	−122	−111	−96	−81	−65	−49	−31	−11	1	2	2	1	−3	−25	−45	−63
16–31 JAN	−60	−77	−92	−107	−120	−122	−122	−122	−122	−122	−122	−97	−81	−66	−49	−31	−11	0	2	2	1	−2	−22	−42	−60
1–14 FEB	−58	−74	−90	−104	−118	−122	−122	−122	−122	−122	−111	−96	−81	−65	−48	−30	−11	−1	1	1	0	−3	−20	−40	−58
15–28 FEB	−54	−71	−87	−102	−116	−122	−122	−122	−122	−122	−108	−93	−77	−61	−44	−26	−6	−1	3	4	2	−1	−15	−36	−54
1–15 MAR	−51	−68	−84	−99	−114	−122	−122	−122	−122	−121	−105	−89	−73	−56	−39	−21	−2	3	5	6	4	0	−12	−32	−51
16–31 MAR	−48	−65	−81	−97	−112	−122	−122	−122	−122	−118	−101	−85	−68	−51	−33	−15	1	5	7	8	6	2	−9	−29	−48
1–15 APR	−44	−61	−78	−94	−110	−122	−122	−122	−122	−114	−96	−79	−62	−44	−27	−8	4	7	9	9	7	4	−7	−26	−44
16–30 APR	−41	−58	−75	−91	−108	−122	−122	−122	−122	−110	−91	−74	−57	−39	−22	−3	5	9	11	11	9	5	−4	−23	−41
1–15 MAY	−39	−55	−72	−88	−105	−121	−122	−122	−122	−106	−87	−70	−52	−35	−18	0	6	10	12	11	9	6	−2	−21	−39
16–31 MAY	−36	−53	−69	−85	−102	−120	−122	−122	−122	−103	−84	−67	−49	−32	−15	2	7	10	12	12	10	7	1	−16	−36
1–15 JUN	−34	−50	−66	−83	−99	−118	−122	−122	−121	−102	−83	−65	−48	−31	−14	2	7	10	12	12	10	7	1	−16	−34
16–30 JUN	−32	−49	−65	−81	−98	−116	−122	−122	−121	−102	−83	−66	−48	−31	−14	2	7	11	12	12	11	7	2	−15	−32
1–15 JUL	−26	−42	−59	−76	−94	−115	−122	−122	−121	−101	−80	−61	−44	−27	−9	7	11	13	14	14	13	11	8	−8	−26
16–31 JUL	−27	−44	−61	−78	−96	−116	−122	−122	−122	−104	−83	−64	−46	−29	−12	6	11	13	14	14	13	11	8	−9	−27
1–15 AUG	−30	−47	−64	−82	−100	−119	−122	−122	−122	−107	−86	−68	−50	−32	−15	4	10	13	14	14	13	11	6	−12	−30
16–31 AUG	−34	−52	−69	−86	−104	−121	−122	−122	−122	−110	−89	−71	−53	−35	−17	1	10	13	13	13	12	9	3	−17	−34
1–15 SEP	−40	−58	−75	−92	−110	−122	−122	−122	−122	−112	−92	−74	−56	−38	−20	−1	9	11	12	12	11	9	−2	−22	−40
16–30 SEP	−46	−64	−81	−98	−115	−122	−122	−122	−122	−113	−94	−76	−59	−41	−23	−4	8	10	11	11	10	7	−8	−28	−46
1–15 OCT	−52	−69	−86	−103	−120	−122	−122	−122	−122	−114	−96	−79	−62	−44	−26	−7	7	9	10	10	8	6	−14	−34	−52
16–31 OCT	−57	−74	−91	−107	−121	−122	−122	−122	−122	−116	−99	−82	−65	−48	−30	−10	6	8	9	8	7	3	−19	−39	−57
1–15 NOV	−62	−79	−95	−110	−122	−122	−122	−122	−122	−118	−101	−85	−69	−52	−34	−15	4	7	7	7	6	−1	−24	−44	−62
16–30 NOV	−64	−81	−97	−112	−122	−122	−122	−122	−122	−120	−104	−88	−72	−55	−38	−19	2	5	6	6	5	−3	−27	−46	−64
1–15 DEC	−65	−81	−97	−112	−122	−122	−122	−122	−122	−121	−107	−91	−75	−59	−42	−23	−2	5	6	5	4	−3	−27	−47	−65
16–31 DEC	−65	−81	−96	−111	−122	−122	−122	−122	−122	−122	−109	−94	−79	−63	−46	−28	−7	3	4	4	3	−3	−27	−47	−65

GMT

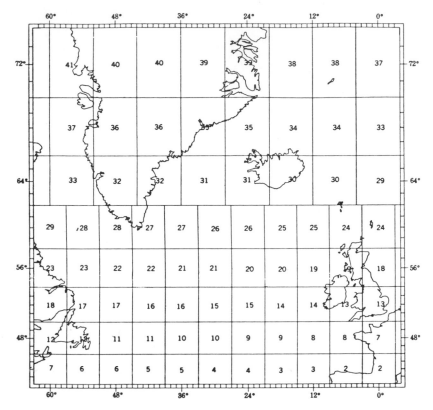

Fig. 5.11 Propagation Correction Table Page Index for Area 06 (Greenland). Corrections for a particular quadrangle can be located in this table by referring to the page numbers in this page index. (Reproduced by courtesy of the Defense Mapping Agency Hydrographic/Topographic Center)

4. Transition

Normally linear interpolation is adequate. Occasionally, however, greater accuracy may be obtained by more elaborate techniques. Consider, for example, the Norway (A) table for 16°N 40°W for 10 January.

GMT	07.00	08.00	09.00	10.00	11.00	12.00	13.00	14.00	15.00
PPC	− 0.71	− 0.71	− 0.14	− 0.05	− 0.02	− 0.01	− 0.00	− 0.01	− 0.00

The corrections in cecs are plotted in figure 5.12 as a function of time using linear interpolation. Notice that there is a large rapid change between 0800Z and 0900Z. This is due to the fact that the sun rises at close to the same universal time in northern Norway as at 16°N 40°W. Thus propagation changes over most of the 2300 nautical miles path from station A to 16°N 40°W are seen to occur quickly about 0830Z. It would appear that a propagation correction during this period would be relatively uncertain since using this station, errors in position of several miles may be expected. It would therefore be prudent to avoid making a fix during this time using this station. Alternatively a fix may be established using another station, from which the propagation path does not experience such a transition at that time.

Table 5.4 Centre of night

Station	Centre of night	Approx. centre of day
Norway (A)	0100Z	1300Z
Liberia (B)	0100Z	1300Z
Hawaii (C)	0600Z	1800Z
North Dakota (D)	0400Z	1600Z
La Reunion (E)	2200Z	1000Z
Argentina (F)	0200Z	1400Z
Australia (G)	0800Z	2000Z
Japan (H)	0800Z	2000Z

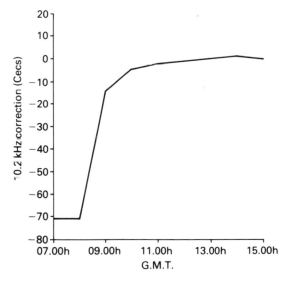

Fig. 5.12 Correction graph plotted for a particular station, location and time of year to indicate sudden transitions which otherwise might not be as noticeable when reading directly from the tables. A station should not be used for corrections during transition periods since the values would be unreliable

5.7 Lattice tables

The lattice table (Omega charting coordinate table) is the counterpart to the Omega chart and, again, is available in the 224 publication series. The table may be used to construct Omega charts of any locality within a coverage area. Each table area will have at least four parts, each part containing the charting coordinates for a single Omega station pair combination.

The tables are computed for hyperbolic lanes at a frequency of 10.2 kHz. Because all Omega frequencies are integral multiples of a common base frequency (1.133 kHz), these tables can also be used for other Omega frequencies since every third 10.2 kHz LOP is also a 3.4 kHz LOP and every fourth 13.6 kHz LOP is also a 3.4 kHz LOP.

The numbering of lanes for a station pair increases in the direction away from the station of the pair, the designation of which occurs first alphabetically. The 10.2 kHz lane which is the centreline hyperbola (perpendicular bisector of the baseline) is always given the value 900. A fictitious minimum lane count is inserted in the lattice computations to provide the 10.2 kHz lane count of 900 lanes on the centreline hyperbola.

In a similar manner to that of the Propagation Correction Tables, the lattice table is identified by the publication number (224), a digit which identifies the frequency ('l' for 10.2 kHz), two digits which identify the coverage area, followed by the station pair letters. For example:

Publication 224 (106) A–D refers to area 06 (Greenland) using a frequency of 10.2 kHz for station pair A–D (Norway–North Dakota).

Arrangement of tables

There is a separate table for each station pair. The columns are headed by lane values corresponding to Omega readings (see Table 5.5). In most cases the reading is tabulated at

Table 5.5 Except from Omega Plotting Tables (Reproduced by courtesy of the Defense Mapping Agency Hydrographic/Topographic Center)

23

T Lat		A-D 825			A-D 826			A-D 827			A-D 828			A-D 829			T Long
° '		°	'	Δ	°	'	Δ	°	'	Δ	°	'	Δ	°	'	Δ	° '
45	N	25	03.1W	163	25	19.4W	163	25	35.7W	162	25	51.9W	161	26	08.1W	161	
46	N	25	26.3W	163	25	42.6W	163	25	58.9W	162	26	15.1W	162	26	31.3W	162	
47	N	25	49.8W	163	26	06.1W	162	26	22.3W	162	26	38.6W	162	26	54.9W	162	
48	N	26	13.5W	163	26	29.9W	163	26	46.3W	163	27	02.5W	162	27	18.8W	162	
49	N	26	37.6W	163	26	54.0W	163	27	10.4W	163	27	26.7W	163	27	41.1W	162	
50	N	27	02.1W	164	27	18.5W	164	27	34.9W	163	27	51.3W	163	28	07.6W	163	
51	N	27	26.8W	165	27	43.3W	165	27	59.8W	164	28	16.2W	164	28	32.6W	164	
52	N	27	51.8W	165	28	08.4W	165	28	24.9W	165	28	41.4W	165	28	57.9W	165	
53	N	28	17.1W	165	28	33.7W	166	28	50.4W	166	29	07.1W	165	29	23.6W	165	
54	N	28	42.8W	167	28	59.6W	167	29	16.2W	166	29	32.9W	166	29	49.6W	166	
55	N	29	08.7W	168	29	25.6W	168	29	42.4W	168	29	59.2W	168	30	16.0W	168	
56	N	29	34.9W	170	29	51.8W	169	30	08.8W	169	30	25.8W	169	30	42.7W	169	
57	N	30	01.3W	172	30	18.5W	171	30	35.6W	170	30	52.7W	171	31	09.8W	171	
58	N	30	27.9W	173	30	45.2W	173	31	02.5W	173	31	19.9W	173	31	37.2W	173	
59	N	30	54.8W	174	31	12.3W	175	31	29.9W	176	31	47.5W	175	32	05.0W	174	
60	N	31	21.9W	178	31	39.6W	177	31	57.4W	177	32	15.2W	178	32	33.1W	177	
61	N	31	49.0W	180	32	07.1W	181	32	25.3W	180	32	43.3W	180	33	01.3W	180	
62	N	32	16.3W	184	32	34.8W	184	32	53.3W	184	33	11.6W	183	33	33.0W	184	
63	N	32	43.8W	188	33	02.6W	187	33	21.4W	187	33	40.1W	188	33	59.0W	188	
64	N	33	11.3W	192	33	30.4W	191	33	49.6W	192	34	08.9W	193	34	28.2W	192	
65	N	33	38.7W	196	33	58.3W	197	34	18.1W	197	34	37.9W	197	34	57.6W	196	
66	N	34	06.1W	202	34	26.3W	202	34	46.7W	203	35	07.1W	203	35	27.3W	202	
67	N	34	33.5W	208	34	54.3W	209	35	15.4W	210	35	36.4W	209	35	57.3W	208	
68	N	35	00.7W	216	35	22.4W	217	35	44.2W	216	36	05.8W	216	36	27.4W	217	
69	N	35	27.8W	225	35	50.4W	226	36	13.0W	225	36	35.W	224	36	57.9W	225	
70	N	35	54.9W	234	36	18.3W	233	36	41.7W	235	37	05.3W	236	37	29.0W	235	
71	N	36	21.4W	245	36	46.1W	247	37	10.8W	246	37	35.4W	245	37	59.9W	246	
72	N	36	48.0W	259	37	14.0W	258	37	39.8W	258	38	05.6W	259	38	31.6W	260	
73	N	37	14.3W	273	37	41.6W	272	38	08.8W	273	38	36.3W	275	39	03.9W	274	
74	N	37	40.1W	290	38	09.2W	291	38	38.4W	291	39	07.6W	290	39	36.6W	290	
75	N	38	05.9W	308	38	36.7W	310	39	08.0W	312	39	39.2W	311	40	10.2W	311	
T		A-D 825			A-D 826			A-D 827			A-D 828			A-D 829			T

intervals of one lane. Lane values corresponding to the baseline extension are so marked.

Since Omega lines of position from each pair of stations fan out in all directions, it is sometimes necessary to tabulate the latitude at which the lines intersect meridians; at other times it is necessary to tabulate the longitudes at which lines intersect parallels. The tables are always arranged so that the latitude appears to the left of the accompanying longitude.

For the entire area of coverage, points are listed at intervals of one degree of latitude or longitude from the equator to 60° of latitude, north and south. From 60° latitude to 80° latitude the interval is one degree of latitude or two degrees of longitude, from 80° to 90° latitude the interval of listing is one degree of latitude or five degrees of longitude.

Close to transmitting stations where the lines curve sharply, extra points are added at intervals of 15 minutes of arc. The spacing of the points is such that the navigator may safely use a straight line between any two adjacent points. Within twenty miles of a transmitting station, the curvature of the lines is excessive and the use of straight line segments liable to introduce appreciable error.

Interpolation

Not all the corrected receiver readings (T_G) are tabulated. However a desired Omega line can always be found by interpolation. The rate of change of latitude or longitude per lane is given in the column immediately following each tabulated point. Since the spread of hyperbolic lines is not necessarily linear and Δ is only an average rate of change for a two-lane band (assumed true at the tabulated point of the middle hyperbola) then interpolation must always be done from the nearest tabulated lane value T.

Multiply the difference ($TG - T$) by Δ and add this algebraically to the tabulated value of latitude or longitude given in the column under T. Note that either Δ or ($T - T$) may be negative.

As the baseline extensions are approached, the interpolation factor changes so greatly between tabulated points that accurate interpolation is not possible. Values of Δ have been omitted in these regions.

The use of Omega lattice tables and Propagation Correction Tables are explained in the following example:

The 0400Z DR position of a vessel on 5 February is latitude 56° 20′ N, longitude 81° 25′ W. The vessel is on course (C) 345°, speed 25 knots. Omega readings taken are as follows:

$$0400Z \quad \text{Pair A–C} \quad T_S\,813.02, \quad \text{Pair C–D} \quad T_S\,1090.41$$

To find the 0400Z Omega fix, the appropriate propagation correction (PPC) must be applied to the observed reading (T_S) to obtain the corrected reading (T_G). Enter the Propagation Correction tables for the pertinent stations with the DR position and select the PPC for the closest geographic intersection to the vessel's DR position for the time and date. Obtain the combined PPC for two stations of a pair as shown earlier and apply the correction to the observed T_S to determine T_G. Enter the Charting Coordinate table in the T column nearest the value of T_G and with latitudes or longitudes closest to and on each side of the DR position. Extract the corresponding longitudes or latitudes for these two points, interpolating if necessary. Plot the two points thus obtained and connect these two points with a straight line to determine a segment of Omega line. Each plotted line should be labelled with the time and pair used. The intersection of the two lines for different pairs gives the Omega fix (see figure 5.13).

PPC table excerpts for Stations A and C,
[see Tables 5.5(a) and (b)]

PPC for Station A	− .57
PPC for Station C	− .69
PPC for Pair A−C = (− .57) − (− .69)	+ .12

Pair A−C table excerpt,
(see Table 5.7)

T_S	813.02
PPC for Pair A−C	+ .12
T_G	813.14
T	813.00
$T_G − T$	+ .14

Lat.	Tabulated Longitude	Δ
56°N	81°00.3′W	+ 17.8
57°N	81°53.0′W	+ 18.1

Longitude Change $(T_G − T) \times Δ$	Interpolated Longitude
(+ .14) × (+ 17.8) = + 2.49′	81°02.8′W
(+ .14) × (+ 18.1) = + 2.53′	81°55.5′W

PPC table excerpts for Stations C and D.
[see Tables 5.6(a) and (b)]

PPC for Station C	− .69
PPC for Station D	− .32
PPC for Pair C−D = (− .69) − .32)	
	− .37

Pair C−D table excerpt
(see Table 5.7)

T_S	1090.41
PPC for Pair C−D	− .37
T_G	1090.04
T	1090.00
$T_G − T$	+ .04

Long.	Tabulated Latitude	Δ
81°W	56°33.6′N	− 25.6
82°W	56°22.9′N	− 25.3

Latitude Change $(T_G − T) \times Δ$	Interpolated Latitude
(+ .04) × (− 25.6) = − 1.02′	56°32.6′N
(+ .04) × (− 25.3) = − 1.01′	56°21.9′N

The fix.—Omega lines are plotted through the following positions: latitude 56°N, longitude 81°02.8′W; latitude 57°N, longitude 81°55.5′W; and latitude 56°32.6′N, longitude 81°W; latitude 56°21.9′N, longitude 82°W. The intersection of these two lines is the Omega fix at Latitude 56°27.9′N, Longitude 81°27.2′W.

5.8 Accuracy

Under normal conditions the sources of error that could influence an Omega fix are as follows:

(a) Propagation
It has been found that the diurnal LOP variation is of the order of tens of cels. However,

Table 5.6(a) Excerpt from Omega Propagation Correction Tables. (Reproduced by courtesy of the Defense Mapping Agency Hydrographic/Topographic Center)

LOCATION: 60.0 N 78.0 W
STATION A: NORWAY

GMT

DATE	00	01	02	03	04	05	06	07	08	09	10	11	12	13	14	15	16	17	18	19	20	21	22	23	24
1–15 JAN	−52	−54	−53	−54	−55	−55	−54	−54	−54	−47	−44	−42	−40	−21	−16	−25	−36	−38	−39	−41	−46	−48	−51	−49	−52
16–31 JAN	−46	−45	−48	−45	−49	−49	−49	−49	−44	−39	−38	−34	−31	−14	−11	−19	−27	−31	−36	−37	−43	−44	−45	−46	−46
1–14 FEB	−55	−60	−56	−56	−57	−57	−57	−48	−48	−43	−39	−37	−35	−30	−33	−41	−43	−38	−42	−48	−52	−56	−56	−58	−55
15–29 FEB	−50	−51	−51	−51	−51	−51	−51	−44	−37	−37	−36	−36	−31	−31	−35	−37	−33	−29	−35	−38	−41	−45	−47	−47	−50
1–15 MAR	−53	−53	−54	−54	−55	−54	−50	−42	−41	−37	−37	−32	−30	−32	−30	−34	−30	−28	−34	−38	−41	−43	−50	−49	−53
16–31 MAR	−49	−51	−54	−54	−55	−48	−40	−39	−38	−31	−31	−30	−31	−30	−26	−30	−23	−29	−34	−35	−38	−41	−44	−48	−49
1–15 APR	−51	−51	−55	−57	−46	−33	−38	−39	−37	−35	−23	−32	−30	−30	−29	−36	−31	−27	−31	−34	−35	−37	−44	−49	−51
16–30 APR	−45	−50	−50	−48	−50	−53	−47	−51	−42	−35	−28	−35	−32	−33	−30	−33	−32	−24	−26	−33	−32	−35	−38	−38	−45
1–15 MAY	−42	−46	−46	−44	−48	−56	−53	−47	−41	−41	−34	−29	−23	−23	−22	−19	−19	−25	−25	−26	−28	−28	−35	−36	−42
16–31 MAY	−37	−40	−43	−43	−43	−40	−47	−42	−37	−38	−27	−28	−24	−25	−23	−26	−26	−30	−30	−27	−27	−31	−28	−35	−37
1–15 JUN	−27	−35	−38	−36	−35	−33	−35	−37	−35	−30	−26	−24	−24	−24	−25	−24	−26	−27	−27	−25	−24	−25	−25	−26	−27
16–30 JUN	−26	−32	−36	−36	−33	−35	−33	−35	−33	−30	−26	−25	−24	−25	−24	−25	−26	−26	−27	−27	−26	−26	−25	−26	−26
1–15 JUL	−24	−28	−35	−35	−34	−34	−33	−35	−34	−30	−27	−26	−26	−24	−25	−25	−24	−25	−27	−25	−26	−26	−25	−26	−24
16–31 JUL	−29	−31	−35	−37	−39	−38	−35	−35	−34	−28	−28	−26	−25	−28	−29	−29	−29	−29	−30	−31	−27	−30	−30	−29	−29
1–15 AUG	−34	−39	−43	−44	−45	−44	−42	−39	−33	−29	−29	−29	−29	−26	−26	−26	−27	−28	−30	−31	−33	−33	−34	−34	−34
16–31 AUG	−32	−36	−41	−38	−41	−43	−40	−33	−30	−25	−24	−27	−24	−24	−25	−25	−26	−27	−29	−31	−31	−30	−32	−32	−32
1–15 SEP	−40	−46	−50	−51	−43	−33	−35	−35	−35	−30	−21	−23	−24	−26	−27	−29	−27	−29	−30	−31	−30	−32	−33	−37	−40
16–30 SEP	−45	−51	−52	−53	−50	−45	−37	−38	−39	−32	−25	−23	−23	−26	−27	−29	−30	−30	−31	−32	−33	−33	−37	−41	−45
1–15 OCT	−53	−56	−54	−51	−54	−45	−42	−42	−36	−35	−26	−19	−19	−22	−27	−31	−29	−28	−30	−32	−35	−39	−46	−49	−53
16–31 OCT	−52	−52	−54	−52	−50	−50	−45	−49	−43	−40	−33	−27	−17	−20	−29	−35	−37	−35	−43	−40	−38	−44	−46	−49	−52
1–15 NOV	−54	−56	−55	−55	−55	−55	−55	−56	−43	−40	−42	−39	−29	−21	−27	−40	−44	−45	−49	−49	−52	−53	−52	−51	−54
16–30 NOV	−52	−50	−52	−54	−53	−56	−57	−56	−54	−50	−51	−51	−46	−38	−25	−33	−42	−45	−50	−50	−50	−54	−54	−56	−54
1–15 DEC	−52	−52	−50	−52	−53	−57	−57	−58	−57	−57	−51	−51	−46	−38	−25	−30	−42	−45	−49	−48	−50	−52	−54	−55	−52
16–31 DEC	−51	−52	−52	−55	−55	−55	−53	−53	−53	−53	−48	−45	−45	−38	−30	−30	−39	−42	−49	−48	−49	−52	−51	−51	−51

Table 5.6(a) *(contd)*

LOCATION: 60.0 N   78.0 W
STATION C: HAWAII

GMT

DATE	00	01	02	03	04	05	06	07	08	09	10	11	12	13	14	15	16	17	18	19	20	21	22	23	24
1–15 JAN	−22	−31	−44	−53	−62	−68	−74	−75	−78	−76	−73	−74	−78	−77	−76	−67	−52	−15	−16	−25	−12	−6	−8	−17	−22
16–31 JAN	−23	−31	−44	−56	−69	−75	−77	−79	−82	−80	−79	−74	−81	−80	−71	−63	−50	−15	−14	−21	−6	−7	−6	−18	−23
1–14 FEB	−24	−39	−44	−57	−69	−75	−80	−82	−83	−83	−82	−80	−79	−73	−64	−55	−43	−28	−27	−18	−12	−10	−14	−18	−24
15–29 FEB	−15	−25	−35	−50	−63	−74	−77	−82	−81	−80	−79	−76	−74	−65	−54	−46	−34	−22	−18	−10	−7	−7	−7	−18	−15
1–15 MAR	−15	−25	−36	−51	−64	−75	−78	−82	−82	−83	−80	−75	−70	−60	−55	−47	−31	−21	−19	−10	−6	−6	−5	−11	−15
16–31 MAR	−16	−23	−33	−48	−62	−74	−79	−82	−83	−83	−80	−72	−65	−59	−54	−41	−25	−20	−17	−12	−7	−6	−4	−8	−16
1–15 APR	−11	−17	−24	−36	−56	−73	−77	−79	−80	−80	−77	−67	−57	−54	−47	−36	−17	−21	−14	−8	−6	−4	−5	−5	−11
16–30 APR	−11	−15	−24	−53	−71	−80	−81	−84	−80	−77	−64	−60	−54	−47	−44	−30	−17	−20	−14	−8	−6	−5	−8	−8	−7
1–15 MAY	−7	−14	−19	−28	−44	−60	−71	−76	−80	−80	−76	−64	−60	−54	−44	−30	−17	−21	−6	−4	−0	−5	−8	−8	−11
16–31 MAY	−5	−10	−16	−23	−39	−61	−68	−73	−76	−68	−62	−62	−59	−52	−42	−27	−21	−13	−5	−4	−3	−1	−0	−2	−7
1–15 JUN	−7	−5	−11	−19	−32	−53	−68	−74	−73	−59	−67	−62	−57	−47	−38	−27	−15	−10	−6	−4	−3	−2	−4	−3	−5
16–30 JUN	−3	−2	−9	−16	−29	−52	−68	−72	−79	−77	−68	−61	−52	−44	−33	−22	−10	−9	−5	−4	−1	−0	−3	−3	−7
1–15 JUL	−5	−3	−8	−16	−29	−50	−67	−75	−77	−78	−74	−62	−54	−32	−24	−21	−7	−9	−6	−4	−2	−2	−3	−4	−3
16–31 JUL	−8	−5	−16	−24	−35	−50	−70	−77	−76	−77	−63	−60	−56	−46	−34	−24	−9	−8	−7	−4	−4	−3	−3	−6	−5
1–15 AUG	−9	−14	−22	−27	−41	−56	−73	−79	−80	−76	−68	−66	−60	−54	−39	−29	−12	−11	−12	−9	−8	−5	−6	−6	−8
16–31 AUG	−11	−18	−24	−33	−49	−65	−77	−81	−83	−79	−76	−71	−65	−57	−48	−34	−10	−13	−12	−10	−7	−7	−8	−6	−9
1–15 SEP	−11	−22	−26	−37	−53	−71	−81	−84	−87	−88	−85	−77	−70	−63	−51	−35	−12	−12	−12	−9	−6	−5	−8	−8	−11
16–30 SEP	−13	−25	−31	−45	−61	−77	−85	−88	−89	−89	−89	−84	−75	−65	−54	−39	−15	−11	−11	−9	−7	−6	−10	−9	−13
1–15 OCT	−19	−24	−33	−51	−68	−78	−84	−87	−88	−88	−86	−85	−79	−68	−58	−42	−18	−11	−10	−8	−7	−6	−9	−12	−19
16–31 OCT	−16	−26	−38	−55	−69	−78	−82	−85	−86	−87	−84	−83	−72	−61	−45	−17	−9	−9	−10	−7	−5	−8	−9	−12	−16
1–15 NOV	−22	−32	−44	−60	−72	−81	−82	−81	−81	−83	−83	−81	−79	−72	−61	−45	−29	−15	−15	−16	−11	−9	−11	−19	−22
16–30 NOV	−31	−39	−50	−66	−76	−82	−83	−81	−83	−83	−80	−83	−84	−81	−74	−66	−52	−18	−24	−22	−21	−21	−21	−25	−31
1–15 DEC	−31	−45	−55	−64	−75	−76	−79	−78	−78	−76	−73	−74	−74	−74	−72	−68	−57	−20	−23	−22	−17	−17	−19	−23	−31
16–31 DEC	−30	−41	−52	−62	−71	−76	−80	−80	−80	−80	−78	−78	−78	−75	−73	−67	−60	−21	−23	−24	−18	−19	−20	−23	−30

Table 5.6(b) Excerpt from Omega Propagation Correction Tables. (Reproduced by courtesy of the Defense Mapping Agency Hydrographic/Topographic Center)

LOCATION: 60.0 N 78.0 W
STATION D: NORTH DAKOTA

GMT

DATE	00	01	02	03	04	05	06	07	08	09	10	11	12	13	14	15	16	17	18	19	20	21	22	23	24
1–15 JAN	−30	−31	−32	−32	−32	−32	−32	−32	−32	−32	−32	−32	−32	−32	−16	−16	−16	−16	−15	−15	−16	−19	−24	−28	−30
16–31 JAN	−30	−31	−32	−32	−32	−32	−32	−32	−32	−32	−32	−32	−32	−30	−15	−14	−16	−14	−13	−13	−14	−18	−22	−27	−30
1–14 FEB	−29	−31	−31	−32	−32	−32	−32	−32	−32	−32	−32	−32	−32	−23	−14	−15	−14	−12	−12	−12	−13	−15	−19	−25	−29
15–29 FEB	−28	−30	−31	−32	−32	−32	−32	−32	−32	−32	−32	−30	−16	−14	−15	−13	−12	−11	−12	−12	−13	−16	−22	−28
1–15 MAR	−26	−30	−31	−32	−32	−32	−32	−32	−32	−32	−32	−23	−14	−14	−13	−12	−11	−11	−11	−12	−13	−14	−19	−26
16–31 MAR	−23	−29	−30	−31	−32	−32	−32	−32	−32	−32	−29	−15	−13	−13	−12	−11	−10	−10	−10	−11	−12	−13	−16	−23
1–15 APR	−19	−27	−30	−31	−32	−32	−32	−32	−32	−31	−21	−13	−13	−12	−11	−10	−10	−10	−10	−11	−11	−12	−13	−19
16–30 APR	−17	−23	−28	−30	−31	−32	−32	−32	−32	−25	−15	−14	−13	−12	−11	−10	−10	−10	−10	−10	−11	−12	−13	−17
1–15 MAY	−15	−20	−27	−30	−31	−32	−32	−32	−29	−20	−14	−13	−12	−11	−11	−10	−9	−9	−9	−10	−10	−11	−12	−15
16–31 MAY	−13	−18	−25	−28	−30	−31	−32	−32	−27	−16	−14	−12	−12	−11	−10	−10	−9	−9	−9	−9	−10	−11	−11	−13
1–15 JUN	−12	−16	−22	−27	−29	−31	−32	−32	−30	−22	−16	−14	−13	−12	−11	−10	−10	−9	−9	−9	−9	−10	−11	−12
16–30 JUN	−12	−16	−22	−27	−30	−31	−32	−32	−30	−24	−15	−13	−12	−11	−11	−10	−10	−9	−9	−9	−10	−10	−11	−12
1–15 JUL	−12	−17	−23	−28	−30	−31	−32	−32	−31	−23	−17	−14	−13	−12	−11	−10	−10	−10	−9	−9	−10	−10	−11	−12
16–31 JUL	−12	−17	−24	−28	−30	−31	−32	−32	−31	−27	−18	−14	−13	−12	−11	−11	−10	−10	−9	−10	−11	−11	−11	−12
1–15 AUG	−14	−19	−27	−29	−31	−32	−32	−32	−32	−30	−22	−14	−13	−12	−11	−11	−10	−10	−9	−10	−10	−12	−12	−14
16–31 AUG	−16	−23	−28	−30	−31	−32	−32	−32	−32	−31	−27	−16	−13	−12	−12	−11	−11	−10	−10	−11	−11	−12	−14	−16
1–15 SEP	−20	−27	−30	−31	−32	−32	−32	−32	−32	−32	−31	−20	−14	−13	−13	−12	−11	−11	−11	−12	−13	−14	−18	−20
16–30 SEP	−25	−29	−31	−31	−32	−32	−32	−32	−32	−32	−32	−27	−15	−13	−13	−12	−12	−11	−11	−12	−13	−16	−22	−25
1–15 OCT	−28	−30	−31	−32	−32	−32	−32	−32	−32	−32	−32	−25	−17	−14	−14	−13	−12	−11	−11	−12	−14	−16	−22	−28
16–31 OCT	−29	−31	−31	−32	−32	−32	−32	−32	−32	−32	−32	−27	−14	−14	−14	−14	−12	−11	−12	−12	−14	−20	−26	−29
1–15 NOV	−30	−31	−32	−32	−32	−32	−32	−32	−32	−32	−32	−32	−16	−16	−15	−15	−14	−13	−13	−14	−16	−18	−23	−26	−30
16–30 NOV	−30	−31	−32	−32	−32	−32	−32	−32	−32	−32	−32	−32	−23	−15	−15	−15	−16	−15	−14	−16	−19	−23	−25	−28	−30
1–15 DEC	−31	−31	−32	−32	−32	−32	−32	−32	−32	−32	−32	−32	−29	−20	−16	−14	−17	−17	−15	−15	−17	−21	−25	−29	−31
16–31 DEC	−31	−31	−32	−32	−32	−32	−32	−32	−32	−32	−32	−32	−32	−32	−16	−16	−17	−16	−15	−16	−18	−21	−25	−29	−31

Table 5.7 Except from Omega lattice tables (Reproduced by courtesy of the Defense Mapping Agency Hydrographic/Topographic Center)

(20)

Lat		A−C 810			A−C 811			A−C 812			A−C 813			A−C 814		Long
° '	°	'	Δ	°	'	Δ	°	'	Δ	°	'	Δ	°	'	Δ	° '
45 N	72	29.5W	148	72	44.4W	148	72	59.3W	148	73	14.0W	147	73	28.8W	148	
46 N	73	05.0W	150	73	20.1W	149	73	35.0W	149	73	50.0W	149	74	05.0W	150	
47 N	73	41.5W	152	73	56.7W	152	74	11.9W	151	74	27.0W	151	74	42.2W	151	
48 N	74	18.9W	154	74	34.3W	154	74	49.7W	153	75	05.1W	154	75	20.5W	154	
49 N	74	57.5W	156	75	13.1W	155	75	28.7W	156	75	44.3W	156	76	00.0W	156	
50 N	75	37.2W	159	75	53.1W	158	76	08.9W	158	76	24.8W	158	76	40.7W	159	
51 N	76	18.3W	161	76	34.4W	161	76	50.5W	160	77	06.6W	161	77	22.8W	161	
52 N	77	00.7W	164	77	17.2W	163	77	33.5W	163	77	49.9W	164	78	06.3W	164	
53 N	77	44.7W	166	78	01.4W	166	78	18.0W	166	78	34.8W	167	78	51.5W	167	
54 N	78	30.3W	170	78	47.4W	170	79	04.3W	169	79	21.3W	170	79	38.4W	170	
55 N	79	17.8W	173	79	35.1W	173	79	52.4W	173	80	09.8W	173	80	27.2W	173	
56 N	80	07.2W	177	80	24.9W	176	80	42.5W	177	81	00.3W	178	81	18.1W	177	
57 N	80	58.7W	181	81	16.9W	181	81	35.0W	180	81	53.0W	181	82	11.3W	182	
58 N	81	52.7W	185	82	11.2W	185	82	29.8W	185	82	48.3W	186	83	07.0W	186	
59 N	82	49.2W	190	83	08.3W	190	83	27.3W	190	83	46.3W	190	84	05.5W	191	
60 N	83	48.7W	195	84	08.2W	195	84	27.7W	195	84	47.4W	196	85	07.1W	196	
61 N	84	51.4W	201	85	11.5W	201	85	31.7W	201	85	51.9W	201	86	12.1W	202	
62 N	85	57.6W	207	86	18.4W	207	86	39.2W	207	87	00.0W	208	87	20.9W	209	
63 N	87	08.0W	214	87	29.5W	214	87	50.9W	215	88	12.5W	216	88	34.1W	216	
64 N	88	22.8W	222	88	45.1W	223	89	07.5W	223	89	29.8W	223	89	52.1W	223	
65 N	89	43.0W	231	90	06.1W	231	90	29.2W	231	90	52.5W	232	91	15.7W	233	
66 N	91	09.0W	240	91	33.1W	240	91	57.2W	241	92	21.4W	242	92	45.7W	243	
67 N	92	41.8W	251	93	06.9W	252	93	32.2W	253	93	57.6W	253	94	23.0W	254	
68 N	94	22.5W	264	94	48.9W	264	95	15.5W	265	95	42.1W	266	96	08.9W	267	
69 N	96	12.5W	278	96	40.4W	279	97	08.4W	280	97	36.6W	281	98	04.8W	283	

(29)

T Lat	C-D (1090) Δ	C-D 1091	Δ	C-D 1092	Δ	C-D 1093	Δ	C-D 1094	Δ	T Long
55 31.6N	−237	55 07.6N	−242	54 43.0N	−248	54 17.8N	−255	53 51.9N	−263	86 W
55 45.8N	−241	55 21.4N	−247	54 56.3N	−253	54 30.7N	−260	54 04.2N	−269	85 W
55 59.0N	−245	55 34.2N	−251	55 08.8N	−258	54 42.6N	−265	54 15.6N	−275	84 W
56 11.4N	−249	55 46.2N	−255	55 20.3N	−262	54 53.7N	−270	54 26.2N	−280	83 W
56 22.9N	−253	55 57.3N	−259	55 31.0N	−266	55 03.9N	−275	54 35.9N	−285	82 W
56 33.6N	−256	56 07.6N	−263	55 40.9N	−271	55 13.4N	−280	54 44.9N	−291	81 W
56 43.5N	−260	56 17.2N	−267	55 50.1N	−275	55 22.1N	−284	54 53.1N	−296	80 W
56 52.7N	−263	56 26.0N	−271	55 58.5N	−279	55 30.0N	−289	55 00.5N	−301	79 W
57 01.2N	−267	56 34.1N	−275	56 06.2N	−283	55 37.3N	−294	55 07.3N	−306	78 W
57 09.0N	−270	56 41.5N	−278	56 13.2N	−288	55 43.9N	−298	55 13.4N	−311	77 W
57 16.1N	−274	56 48.2N	−282	56 19.5N	−292	55 49.8N	−303	55 18.9N	−316	76 W
57 22.5N	−277	56 54.3N	−286	56 25.2N	−296	55 53.1N	−307	55 23.7N	−321	75 W
57 28.3N	−281	56 59.8N	−290	56 30.3N	−300	55 59.7N	−312	55 27.8N	−325	74 W
57 33.5N	−284	57 04.6N	−293	56 34.7N	−304	56 03.7N	−316	55 31.4N	−330	73 W
57 38.1N	−288	57 08.8N	−297	56 38.5N	−308	56 07.1N	−321	55 34.3N	−335	72 W
57 42.1N	−291	57 12.4N	−301	56 41.8N	−312	56 09.9N	−325	55 36.7N	−340	71 W
57 45.5N	−295	57 15.5N	−305	56 44.4N	−316	56 12.1N	−329	55 38.4N	−345	70 W
57 48.3N	−298	57 17.9N	−309	56 46.5N	−320	56 13.8N	−334	55 39.6N	−350	69 W
57 50.5N	−302	57 19.8N	−312	56 48.0N	−324	56 14.8N	−338	55 40.2N	−355	68 W
57 52.2N	−305	57 21.1N	−316	56 48.9N	−329	56 15.3N	−343	55 40.2N	−360	67 W
57 53.4N	−309	57 22.0N	−320	56 49.2N	−333	56 15.2N	−348	55 39.6N	−365	66 W
57 53.9N	−313	57 22.1N	−324	56 49.0N	−337	56 14.6N	−352	55 38.5N	−370	65 W
57 54.0N	−316	57 21.7N	−328	56 48.3N	−341	56 13.4N	−357	55 36.8N	−375	64 W

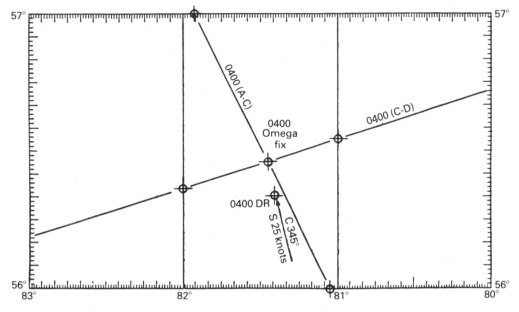

Fig. 5.13 The fix – Omega lines are plotted through the following positions: latitude 56°N, longitude 82°02.8′W; latitude 57°N, longitude 81°55.5′W; and latitude 56°32.6′N, longitude 81°W; latitude 56°21.9′N, longitude 82°W. The intersection of these two lines is the Omega fix at latitude 56°27.9′N, longitude 81°27.2′W.

this can be reduced by the use of correction tables to give, on average, a standard deviation of ± 5 cels by day. At night and at sunrise or sunset the effect is approximately doubled. These errors take into account the correlation between the two propagation paths used to produce an LOP.

(b) Transmitters
Transmitter stability is of the order of standard deviation (SD) of ± cel at the receiver. The combination of these uncorrelated errors at each transmitter gives an error of SD = ± 1.4 cels.

(c) Receiver
The receiver phase comparison is usually accurate to an SD = ± 1 cel.

(d) Lane Expansion
At distances well removed from the baseline the spacing between LOPs increases by a factor of about 1.6.

By combining the effects of the above errors, it can be shown that in general, daytime accuracy is of the order of ± 0.75 nautical miles.

By night the propagation errors tend to predominate to give an approximate fix error of ± 1.5 nautical miles. This value might be improved if *all* the transmission path is in darkness; values tend to be worse during the transition periods between day and night and vice versa.

5.9 Omega transmitters

As discussed earlier, all Omega transmitters are phase-synchronized using caesium frequency standards. These standards ensure that the phase difference between antenna currents remains stable within 1 part in 10^{10} and even then any deviations which may occur can be corrected. Omega transmissions are synchronized not only to maintain a constant phase relationship, but to produce frequencies in accordance with what is known as Universal Time (UT2) which is an international time standard.

Universal time is a particular case of the measure known as mean solar time which, on the Greenwich meridian, is measured in days of 24 mean solar hours beginning with 00.00 h at midnight. Universal time is determined by the average rate of the apparent daily movement of the sun relative to the the Greenwich meridian and when measured by astronomical observations is denoted as UT0.

However, because of the non-uniformity of the earth's rotation, corrections must be applied to UT0. Correcting for the effect of the earth's axis continuously moving with respect to the earth's crust gives UT1 (which is the same as Greenwich Mean Time used in celestial navigation). The corrections to be applied are very small. Correcting for the variation in speed of the earth's rotation due to phenomena such as tides and wind gives UT2; again the corrections to be applied are small i.e. ± 30 milliseconds in the speed of rotation.

As regards atomic time, the frequency of the caesium beam atomic clock was found by experiments conducted in the late 1950s to be 9 192 631 770 cycles per second of the caesium resonance. In 1967 the atomic second was defined as the duration of 9 192 631 770 periods of the radiation corresponding to the transition between two hyperfine levels of the ground state of the caesium 133-atom. UT2 and A1, the atomic time scale established by the US Naval Observatory, were identical in the beginning of January 1958.

Coordinated Universal Time (UTC) was introduced in 1961 by the US Naval Observatory and Royal Observatory at Greenwich whereby master oscillations, calibrated in terms of the caesium standard, were corrected simultaneously at all transmitting stations by applying a frequency offset to the oscillator so that the rate defined by the timing pulses was in general agreement with UT2.

Transmitting antennae consist, typically, of a central mast radiator of height 350 to 450 metres, top loaded with radials of 650 metres length, the distant ends of which are themselves supported by 100 metre masts. Typical antenna voltage is 150 kV with efficiency up to 20%; a radiated power level of 10 kW is normal, with about 50 kW power output from the transmitter.

The antenna systems are large and expensive to maintain. The wires must be capable of withstanding high winds or ice loading if such a location permits such a phenomenon. In certain sites, such as Norway and Hawaii, advantage has been taken of the local terrain and transmitting antenna have been sited between convenient mountain tops.

The antenna is fed via helix house which switches between the preset transmission frequencies in rapid succession with time intervals of 0.2 seconds as allowed in the Omega transmission format.

5.10 Omega receivers

There are two basic requirements to be met in the design of an Omega receiver, namely:
1. Synchronizing the receiver so that the receiver's own commutator format is the same as the transmitted format. This can be done manually, by setting the phase commutator into phase agreement with the transmitted format, by reference ot UT2 which is used for the transmission format.
2. Measurement of phase difference of two signals which are never present simultaneously and whose signal strength may be less than the noise level.

With regard to synchronization some receivers have a lamp, or lamps, as visual indication that a signal is being received. There may be 8 lamps which flash in sequence timed by the locally generated format or a single lamp.

Manual synchronization can be achieved by the operator identifying one of the stations (possibly using audible signals heard via a loudspeaker or headphones) which gives a signal strength greater than the others. This signal is assumed to originate from the nearest transmitter although, due to propagation conditions for certain receiver locations, this is not always necessarily the case. Having correctly established one of the transmitter stations, the remaining seven stations can be identified and 'lined up' with the receiver internal commutator format i.e. synchronized using the flashing lamp or lamps.

Automatic synchronization 'lines up' the receiver commutator format with the Omega transmitted format without the operator needing to positively identify the nearest transmitter. One method is to 'set' the identity of the station which would produce the strongest receiver signal. The synchronizing circuits would then check the length, and signal strength, of each received signal until the required signal length and maximum amplitude are found. Thus the start of the sequence is initiated and other signals should follow in the correct order. Note that whatever station is selected as being the closest will have a signal time length equal to that of another transmitter (for example station D, N. Dakota, and station G, Australia, both have time lengths of 1.2 seconds) but one should always give a signal of greater amplitude than the other.

Another method of automatic synchronization would check the transmission length of two consecutively received signals since, although any one station will have its transmission slot length duplicated, the time slot of the next station in the sequence will not be the same value in each case . For example, station D is followed by station E, La Reunion, with a time slot of 1.1. seconds, while station G is followed by station H, Japan, with a time slot of 1.0 seconds. Thus pairs of transmissions are unique and may be identified as such.

The measurement of phase difference by the receiver is also achieved using two basic methods:

Analog
A series of phase-locked loops derives phase difference between incoming IF (intermediate frequency) signals and a reference oscillator, and then between time-sequenced pairs of these outputs.

Digital
A typical system would use the IF signal from selected stations to start and stop a counter. If the IF is chosen to be 1 kHz and the counter operates at 100 kHz then the output will be to 0.01 cycle of the IF, which represents 1 cel.

5.11 The Redifon (Rediffusion) NV1 Omega navigation receiver

This is a sensitive superheterodyne receiver fixed tuned to the 10.2 kHz Omega transmissions which are converted to 1 kHz IF signals. The station signals are identified by length in comparison to the fixed Omega commutator pulses generated in the receiver. The pulses are assigned a switch position and are used to select the most suitable pairs of station signals to give 3 LOPs. The NV1 has only one digital output display and the information regarding the three LOPs is displayed sequentially on the display, each output appearing for 10 seconds in a 30 second cycle. Any selected LOP may be displayed continuously i.e. 'held' though its LOP measurement will continue to be updated. The displayed values are numbered to correspond to LOPs on Omega charts and the receiver will track and update each readout. Propagation corrections can be inserted for each of the three chosen LOPs and stored as centilane (cel) corrections; the receiver will automatically include the correction on the displayed value.

Figure 5.14 shows the front panel arrangement for the NV1 receiver, while figure 5.15 shows the initial setting up and service controls.

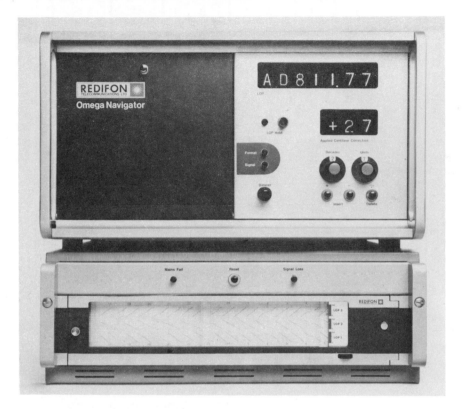

Fig. 5.14   The Redifon (Rediffusion) Omega Navigator Type NV1

Referring to figure 5.15, the controls are as follows:

1. *Initial setting up controls*
(a) <u>LOP</u> switches. Thumbwheel switches enabling the selection of any 6 of the 8 transmissions which are stored in the receiver. The selected pairs will give the requisite LOPs for those pairs.
(b) <u>Set lane</u> switches. Hundreds, tens and unit values of an initial lane count may be set using these switches prior to insertion.
(c) <u>Lane insert</u>. This push button inserts the pre-selected lane count into the receiver store and immediate display.
(d) <u>Station Synch</u> switch. A ten position switch with eight positions lettered A to H, which select the Omega transmitter to be used as the synchronizing signal and crystal lock control. The remaining two positions of the switch have service functions.
(e) <u>Auto reset</u>. A push button used for initiating the receiver automatic synchronization sequence.

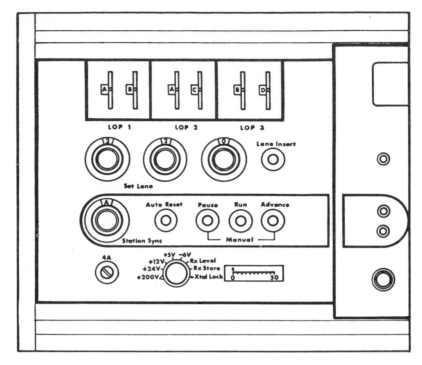

Fig. 5.15 Initial setting and service controls of the Redifon (Rediffusion) Omega Navigator Type NV1

2. *Service controls*
(a) <u>Pause.</u> This push button, while pressed, holds the format stationary.
(b) <u>Run.</u> This push button will start the format running in the absence of synchronizing station signals.
(c) <u>Advance.</u> Each operation of this push button advances the format 0.1 seconds.
(d) <u>Meter and switch.</u> The first five positions indicate adequate levels i.e.

$+ 200V$	$+ 24V$	$+ 12V$	$+ 5V$	$- 6V$
> 40	≈ 25	> 40	> 40	> 40

<u>Rx. level</u> indicates relative signal strength and aids choice of synchronization station.
<u>Rx. store</u> indicates presence of information in store.
<u>Xtal lock</u> indicates crystal locking voltage approximately 25, meter needle stationary when in lock.
Figure 5.16 shows the operating controls:
(a) <u>LOP</u> display. Seven neon display tubes reading from left to right, indicating two figures giving the station pair selected to form the LOP, three figures giving the LOP and two figures giving the centilane (cel) value. The display shows the three LOPs automatically in sequence, each being present for approximatelfy 10 seconds.
(b) <u>LOP Hold.</u> A pushbutton (or switch) which stops the LOP sequence when activated. An amber lamp indicates LOP Held state. The button/switch must be activated again to restart the sequence.
(c) <u>Applied Centilane Correction</u> display. Three neon tubes display, from left to right, delete, plus or minus followed by a two figure cel correction. The display indicates the correction added to the LOP displayed at the same time. A flashing correction display

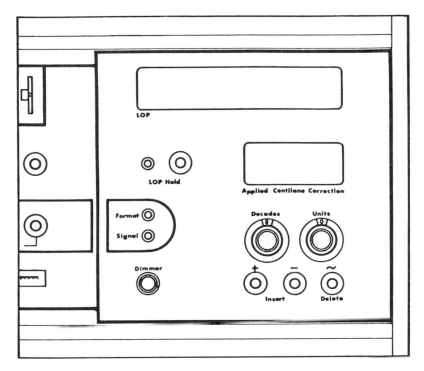

Fig. 5.16 Operating controls of the Redifon (Rediffusion) Omega Navigator Type NV1

indicates that updating has not been carried out for over an hour and figures shown may be incorrect.

(d) Centilane correction switches. <u>Decades</u> and <u>units</u> switches may be set to the required correction figure but the value is not entered until the required push button beneath is operated.

(e) <u>Insert</u> and <u>Delete.</u> These push buttons transfer or delete the figures set on the correction switches to the LOP display showing at the time.

(f) <u>Format</u> and <u>Signal</u> lamps. The format lamp will light once each for each format period and will bright up on the synch. period. The signal lamp lights once for each station received and in addition may flash if there is severe noise.

(h) <u>Dimmer.</u> Controls the brightness of the lamps and display tubes.

(h) Signal loss detector. Any loss of signal on a station selected for an LOP will cause the appropriate letter display to flash and the audible alarm in the power unit to sound.

Power unit controls
The power unit contains switches to provide the mains voltage to the unit, 24V to the receiver, internal battery in circuit etc. There is also a warble alarm which operates if there is a failure in the a.c. supply or if the signal loss detector operates.

Setting up procedure

The NV1 has the setting and service controls behind a hinged flap. Once the controls have been set up, replacement of this flap ensures that the control settings cannot be accidentally altered. The receiver is designed to be left on during the vessel's passage.

When switching on the receiver initially, the a.c. supply and RX ON switches must first be set in the power supply unit. The perspex hinged flap should then be lowered for access to the control settings.

Power supply serviceability checks
(a) Turn meter switch to + 24V position and check that the meter reads within the blue segment.
(b) Switch OFF 230V isolator to bulkhead a.c. power supply unit and confirm that warble alarm note sounds. Press alarm reset to stop alarm and confirm that NV1 meter still reads within the blue segment. The receiver is now operating from the emergency supply batteries in the power unit.
(c) Switch ON 230V isolator to the bulkhead a.c. power supply unit, and confirm that the NV1 meter still reads within the blue segment.

NV1 Serviceability checks
(a) Turn the meter switch to each position as follows and confirm that the readings are within the following limits:

Position	Approx. reading	Limits
+ 200V	40	green segment
+ 24V	24	blue segment
+ 12V	40	green segment
+ 5V	40	green segment
− 6V	40	green segment

(b) Turn the meter switch to <u>Rx. Level</u> and observe the meter readings. The meter will rise and fall once for each station received. The slight continuous movement due to noise should be ignored. At least three stations should give substantial deflection of the meter needle – this confirms that the antenna and receiver sections of the NV1 are serviceable.
(c) Set <u>Station Synch</u> switch to a strong signal in the area to be navigated.
(d) Press <u>Auto Reset</u> button (note that the receiver may have automatically synchronized itself) and after one minute observe the <u>Format</u> lamp. The lamp should light once for each of the eight segments of the Omega format. One section should bright up – this is the section matching the selected Synch station.
(e) After ten minutes from initial switch on, confirm that the signal lamp pulses are in time with the <u>Format</u> lamp, ignoring random flashes due to noise. The signal lamp flash coincident with the <u>Format</u> lamp bright up flash shows that the Synch station signal is synchronized with the format. If not repeat step (d) or use Manual Synchronization (see page 000).
(f) Turn the meter switch to <u>Xtal Lock</u> and observe the meter reading. The meter should show a steady reading midway in the blue segment during a complete 10 second format cycle. This confirms that the receiver crystal oscillator is locked in frequency to the Synch station signal.
(g) Turn the meter switch to <u>Rx Store</u> and observe the meter readings. The meter should rise to at leat 5 for each station received to confirm that these stations are being tracked. A strong station will give a much greater reading e.g. 20.
(h) Signal Loss detector. If any letter display starts to flash at the format rate, the station transmission concerned is not being received and lane slip may be occurring. The Remote alarm will indicate at random until the crystal oscillator is locked [step (f)].

Choice of Synch station

The signal strength of an Omega transmission is approximately proportional to the range hence the operator needs to compare the vessel's position with the known sites of the Omega transmitters to determine the nearest station.

The procedure is then as follows:

(a) Set the Station Synch switch to the nearest station which has the strongest signal (Rx Store reading Min 15).

(b) Wait for synchronization to be indicated. If synchronization is not achieved then depress Auto Reset a second time or choose a different station.

(c) Note that once the format is synchronized, the Synch station may be changed without losing synchronization. However, the Auto Reset button should *not* be depressed.

Note that two stations transmitting for the same duration e.g. N. Dakota and Australia, may be identified by the strength of the signal since the nearer station would have the stronger signal.

Note also that if transmissions from the Synch station fail, the receiver must immediately be reset to a different Synch station since loss of the Synch station signal could cause lane slip on any LOP using the Synch station. Periodic checks of the LOP recorder traces (see page 000) should be made for this reason.

Initial lane setting

The NV1 receiver can track as the vessel moves to give an LOP readout for selected pairs that is as accurate as the initial setting of LOP values. The first settings must be derived from Omega charts using the LOP values that correspond to the vessel's known position. The recommended procedure is:

(a) Examine the Omega charts for the area to be navigated and select three LOPs suitable for that area .

(b) Establish present position of the vessel on the Omega chart.

(c) Read off the three selected LOPs to the greatest possible accuracy and log the readings.

(d) SET the three LOP thumbwheel switches to the Omega station pairs corresponding to the LOPs chosen.

(e) Extract propagation corrections from Tables and calculate three LOP corrections and log the values.

(f) Watch the LOP display and depress HOLD LOP when LOP1 is displayed.

(g) Set applied cel correction switches to the correction figures calculated in (e) for LOP1.

(h) Depress + INSERT or − INSERT button as required.

(i) Select first three figures of LOP1 lane number on SET LANE switches.

(j) Depress LANE INSERT button.

(k) Confirm that station letters are correct and the displayed LOP figure, now including the correction, is the same as the LOP calculated from the chart. Alter SET LANE switch if necessary to correct a marginal reading.

(l) Log display reading.

(m) Depress HOLD LOP button to allow sequence to continue. Wait for LOP displayed to change and depress HOLD LOP button.

(n) Repeat procedure (g) to (o) for LOP2 and LOP3.

(o) Plot all displayed LOPs and verify the vessel's position.

(p) Set Blue Set Lane switches to 000 and Red Centilane Correction switches to 00. Set Meter switch to Rx Level.

(q) Close flap. It should not be necessary to disturb the setting en route except to change Synch station or change an LOP.

Change of station during voyage

Should it be necessary to change the Synch station during the voyage, the procedure is as follows:

Log the three LOP readings. Lower the hinged flap and set the meter switch to Rx Level. Identify the Synch station in the sequence and observe the signal strength of this station and the chosen new station. The new station should have a strong signal.

Set the Meter Switch to Xtal Lock and observe that the reading is steady midway in the blue segment before changing the Synch station, confirming that the crystal oscillator is still locked to the Present Synch station.

Set the Station synch switch to the selected new station but *do not* press the Auto Reset button unless the format is out of synchronicity. The meter reading should settle to a reading midway in the blue segment within 5 minutes.

A steady reading confirms that the crystal oscillator is now locked to the new Synch station. Confirm that the three LOP readings remain the same as before the Synch station change, allowing for vessel movement.

Should it be required to change a LOP station then the procedure is as follows:

(a) First log the three LOP figures and chart the present position. The chart should show if changing a station of an LOP pair is likely to give greater accuracy, bearing in mind the constraints of a hyperbolic system such as angle of cut, position within the coverage area etc. If a change of station is decided upon, the change should be confined to one of the three station pairs and a second change not made until the first change has been successfully completed.

(b) Read off the required new LOP from the chart as accurately as possible and log the reading.

(c) Derive centilane corrections for the new LOP.

(d) Watch the LOP display and depress LOP HOLD when the station pair to be changed is displayed.

(e) Lower the hinged flap and set the appropriate pair of thumbwheel switches to the selected new station pair.

(f) Set Applied Centilane Correction switches to propagation correction figures calculated for the new LOP and depress the + or − INSERT buttons as required.

(g) Select first three figures of lane number on SET LANE switches.

(h) Depress the LANE INSERT button and confirm that the display reads the figures inserted and that the station letters are correct.

(i) Confirm that the displayed LOP figure, including the correction, is the same as the LOP calculated from the chart. Alter the SET LANE switch if necessary to correct a marginal reading.

(j) Log and plot the display readings. Ensure that the position agrees with that found from the original LOP.

(k) Depress LOP HOLD to allow the sequence to continue.

(l) Repeat the above sequence if it is desired to change a second LOP. When LOP changes are complete, close the hinged flap.

(m) Insert station pair and lane number on the recording trace against the appropriate LOP (see figure 5.17).

LOP recorder

The NV1 is fitted with a recorder, the paper roll of which can give a continuous readout as the vessel is under way. The chart roll can last for 15 days and the recorder should be left on when the receiver itself is on.

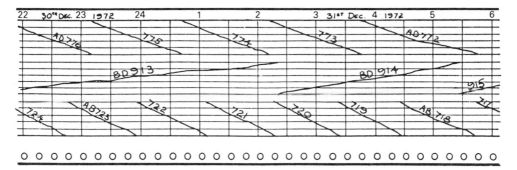

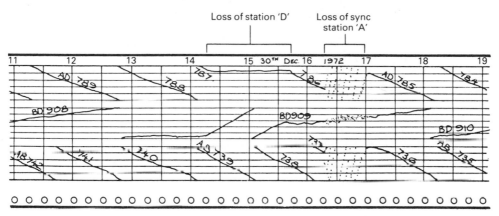

Fig. 5.17 Sample LOP record

The LOP recorder can trace three lines which are the uncorrected centilane values. The three lines should be correlated with the receiver display by observation and each labelled with its lane number each time a lane crossing occurs. See figure 5.17 for an example of an LOP record.

Manual synchronization

If Automatic Synchronization does not occur then using the following procedure will initiate manual synchronization.

(a) Press <u>Run</u> button. The format will now start cycling; the <u>Format</u> lamp will indicate each segment and bright up on selected Synch station.

(b) When <u>Format</u> lamp bright up occurs press and hold <u>Pause</u> button.

(c) Identify the selected Synch station signal by observing that the signal lamp flashes and the largest deflection of meter at <u>Rx Level</u>. Release the <u>Pause</u> button at end of the Synch station as counted using the Omega signal format.

(d) Observe both <u>Signal</u> and <u>Format</u> lamps which should bright up simultaneously. Press the <u>Advance</u> button once each cycle to advance the format 0.1 second per cycle (Touch <u>Pause</u> button if necessary to delay format).

(e) Simultaneous flashes of <u>Signal</u> and <u>Format</u> lamps indicate that the receiver is now synchronized.

Position fixing

An Omega fix is achieved by reading three sets of LOPs from the receiver and logging them for subsequent charting. The LOPs must, however, be adjusted as necessary for propagation corrections and lane slip.

Lane slip

Lane slip can be caused by loss of the signal or excessive noise, resulting either in addition or subtraction of possibly more than one number from the displayed LOP i.e. lane slip is a change in the displayed lane number not caused by a change in the position of the vessel.

If a station signal selected for an LOP ceases to be received and the Signal Loss Detector operates, the appropriate LOP store will no longer be updated. Thus the displayed value will be incorrect, giving a value larger or smaller than the true value depending on the sense of lane crossing of the course. If possible a new LOP should be selected.

If a station signal is lost that happens to be the synch signal then the receiver internal frequency reference will drift out of crystal lock and, if the synch signal is used as an LOP signal, the display could slip a number of lanes. If the synch signal is not used as an LOP signal then, although the frequency reference will still drift, the result is to cause the recording to indicate a noisy signal (blurred trace). In either case a new Synch station should be selected.

If lane slip has occurred it will show on the chart record of the LOP concerned as a discontinuity (see figure 5.17) during the fault period. After the fault period the record will return to its normal pattern. If the station signal at fault is one of those selected as an LOP station, the letter display (and loss of signal indicator) will provide a warning during the fault condition. No warning is given as a direct result of Synch station loss if the station is not used as a LOP station, but the effect may cause the alarm to operate since the LOP store information will be reduced.

Lane slip can be retrieved provided that the fault condition has ceased and that a satisfactory LOP trace is present on the recorder. To achieve this the following steps should be taken:

(a) Observe the recording. With the vessel's speed and courses nominally constant the successive lane crossing will be at a constant spacing, with a gap where lane slip occurs.

(b) Mark off onto paper sufficient crossings prior to the lane slip to cover the gap.

(c) Offer the marked paper to the gap in the recording, and check that the spacing after the gap is sensibly unchanged.

(d) Make a check mark on the recording paper for each missing LOP and write in the missing lane numbers.

Functional description of the NV1 receiver

Although this receiver was designed before the advent of microprocessors in maritime equipment, much of the technique employed for data decoding is typical of a modern microprocessor system. This equipment is still used on many vessels and the following technical description should be readily understood by merchant navy officers.

Refer to figure 5.18 which is a block diagram of the NV1 receiver. The received Omega signal format is initially preamplified before being applied to the receiver input circuits. This amplifier also provides a reasonable match between a whip (or long wire) antenna operating at VLF. A half wavelength antenna at 10 kHz would be 15 km long and therefore antenna systems of reasonable length could not be resonant at such low frequencies.

Printed circuit board 1 contains a low noise linear amplifier of wide dynamic range which provides matching with the 50 ohm coaxial downlead. Notch filters are provided to reject unwanted transmissions. It is very important that no other low frequency signals cause interference with the Omega format otherwise phase measurement will become difficult. Further filtering and amplification takes place on board 2 before the received signal is converted down to the IF of 1 kHz. A 22.4 kHz stable frequency from board 8 is divided by two and applied as 11.2 kHz, the local oscillator input to the signal mixer. The IF signal is further amplified and hard limited on board 3 to produce a pulse train of approximately 1 kHz pulses corrresponding to the received Omega format. (The IF signal is 1 kHz only when the input signal is 10.2 kHz.)

Board 6 contains a chopper filter operating from a 2 kHz stable frequency reference source, board 8. The output from this filter is the digital 1 kHz pulse train generated as a prime source from either the current incoming signal and the analogue phase store capacitors or the phase store capacitors. Due to the slow phase changes associated with the movement of marine Omega receivers the use of long time constant analogue storage smooths unwanted noise from the signal, and should the updating signal fail to arrive during a format segment, provides continuity to the display circuits. Because the time constant of the analogue storage is long, changes of phase can only occur over minutes rather than seconds, thus the effective bandwidth can be shown to be 0.07 Hz. This bandwidth represents a very high Q bandpass filter, the output of which is jitter-free to provide the necessary stability for an accurate reading out centilanes.

Narrow band filter (NBF) gate boards 11/12 operate in conjunction with board 6 to provide analogue signal storage facilities. Storage is achieved by sampling the incoming signal at known moments in time and storing as d.c. levels two values, representing the in-phase and quadrature components of the signal referenced to the master oscillator. Long term storage is achieved by using low leakage polycarbonate capacitors switched into circuit by the synchronized format as required.

Two signal outputs from board 6 carry phase informtion as d.c. levels reprresenting both in-phase and quadrature components of the Omega signal. The NBF boards each have four connections (A–D and E–H) from the format generator board 23. A logic 1 is clocked sequentially from A through H to switch the capacitors into circuit in turn to store a complete pulse train. The format generator board is clocked by a 100 kHz signal derived from the master oscillator which is phase locked with the incoming signal. The eight sequentially clocked format segment outputs are also coupled to the six thumbwheel LOP switches on the front panel which select the appropriate time scale pulses to be applied to the phase store boards 20/21/22.

For accurate phase measurement to be made the 10 MHz master oscillator, from which all clock pulses are derived, must be synchronized with one of the Omega transmitting stations. Normally the strongest station is selected for this purpose which in most cases corresponds to the nearest station. Station selection is achieved manually by operating the station select switch on the control panel as described earlier. A pulse corresponding to the selected station is applied to an AND gate on board 9 along with the received pulse train envelope (ENV). When the two inputs are coincident the selected pulse is passed to synchronize the oscillator. The master oscillator when synchronized to the Synch transmitter station achieves the stability and accuracy of that station (i.e. 1 part in 10^{12}) allowing for very accurate format reproduction over long periods measured in years rather than months. The master oscillator, along with board 8, provides all the high stability outputs used for gating and clocking purposes.

The central control board 19 forms the heart of the system to control LOP selection, lane insertion and phase store resetting. A three stage shift register is used to enable the display for each LOP sequentially, or alternatively can be held on any one selected LOP as required. The output line "LOP Select" is applied as follows:

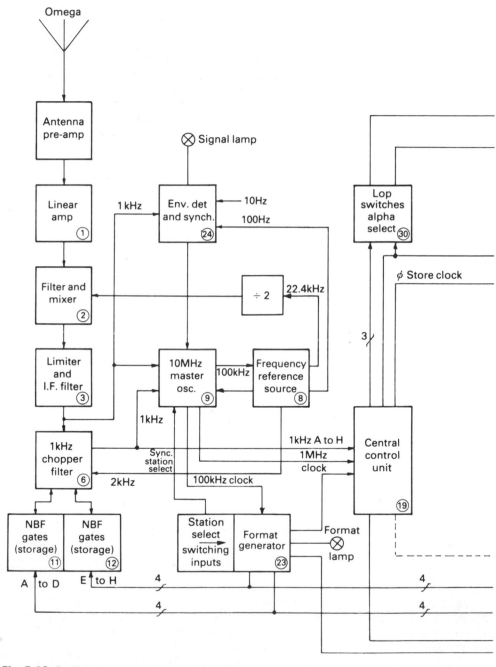

Fig. 5.18   Redifon (Redifussion) Omega NV1 Receiver

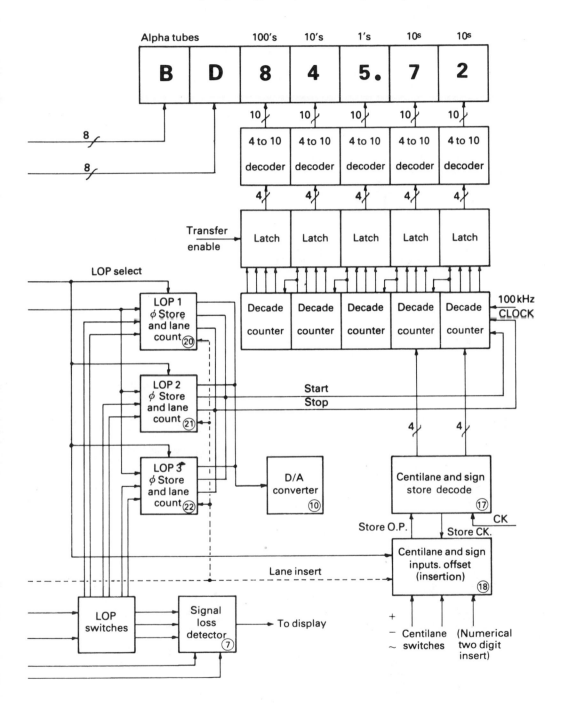

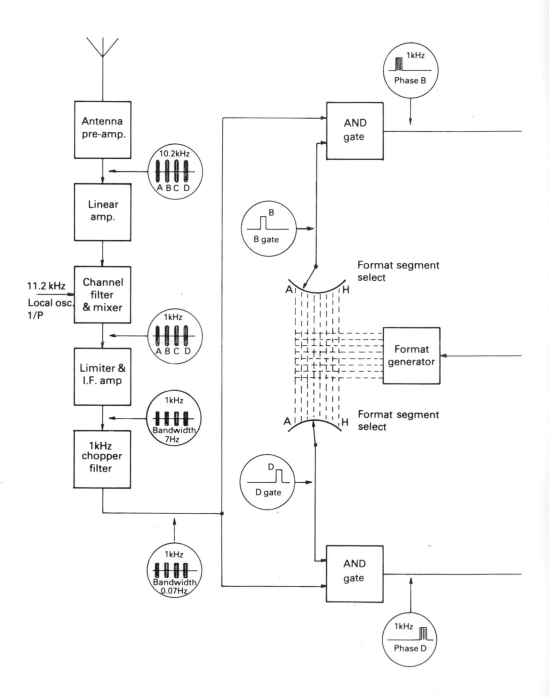

Fig. 5.19 Principle of a single LOP phase measurement (B to D phase) of the Redifon (Rediffusion) NV1 receiver

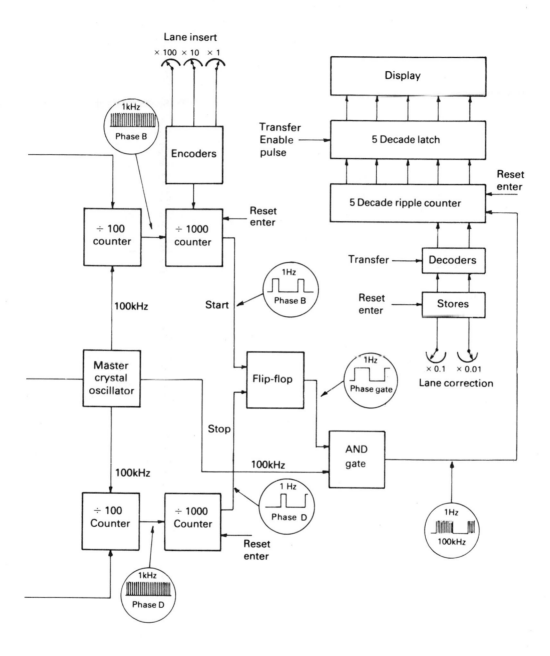

(a) Via the LOP Alpha switchin circuit to select the required station for display
(b) To LOP 1, 2 and 3 phase stores in turn in order to input the phase clock data and to output the resulting start/stop pulses to the decade counters, and
(c) to the centilane and sign store input circuits in order that the numerical and sign data may be transferred to the store decoder and clocked to the least significant two counts of the decade counter. See figure 5.19.

Boards 20/21/22, the phase store and lane count boards, are three identical units each of which stores the relative phases of two selected stations selected for an LOP and, together with the inserted lane number data produces the start/stop signals to control the LOP display decade counters. Each store has two digital decade counter circuits ($\div 100$) clocked with 100 kHz pulses. Both counters fill and reset once for every cycle of 1 kHz IF signal input whose phase is to be stored. The counters are reset by signal pulses when signals are present and therefore each reset pulse from the counter occurs simultaneously with the signal pulse. The phase of the signal is thus stored.

Two further counters, each of three decades ($\div 1000$), are used as lane counters to produce an output of one pulse per second. The start counter is reset to zero and then pre-set to any count between 000 and 999 as selected on the lane set switches. Pre-scaling the start counter in this way ensures that the output from this counter is a resultant of both signal and pre-scaled pulses. The stop counter always resets to zero. Stop/start pulses are thus produced which correspond to the phase of each of the LOPs selected. The start pulse (phase B on figure 5.19) sets the JK flip-flop to produce a logic 1 to the phase gate which enables the 100 kHz through to the 5 decade ripple counter in the display. Counting continues until the arrival of the stop pulse which causes the flip-flop to toggle and the logic 0 now applied to the phase gate inhibits further clock pulses to the counter. Binary count data now stored in the ripple counter is latched through to the display tubes by a latch enabling pulse. The 5 decade counter is now reset and the LOP select enables the second LOP phase store circuit and counting again takes place over a 10 second period for a further two selected LOPs. Centilane correction inputs are applied to pre-scale the first two decades of the ripple counter. Thus the count transferred at "stop" time is the sum of the pre-scaled offset correction and the number of 100 kHz clock pulses enabled during the start/stop period.

The station signals which are selected and fed to the LOP stores are also supplied to logic circuits in the signal loss detector, board 7. These logic circuits monitor the selected station phase stores with a timing signal from the format generator. A missing station signal causes a 0.2 second "space" signal at the format rate to lower the anode voltage on the corresponding station letter display. The station letter then flashes at the format rate to indicate loss of signal. Simultaneously a relay in the signal loss circuit closes and applies 24 volts to the remote signal loss indicator; it also causes the a.c. power supply audible alarm to sound.

5.12 Differential Omega

Differential Omega is a method for providing improved accuracy, compared to the normal system, over a relatively small area and may be useful in, say, harbour navigation.

Normal Omega systems suffer propagation effects and possible errors in diurnal correction values. These effects limit the accuracy of the system. However, due to long correlation distance of VLF transmissions then, over a certain segment of area , all users would suffer similar errors.

For differential Omega, a monitor station is established ashore at an accurately fixed location so that errors in received signals can be accurately observed. Any errors can thus be broadcast to vessels within a reasonable radius, say 200 nautical miles; see figure 5.20.

Thus the error signals received from the monitor stat ion would be used to correct the vessel'ss observed Omega readings rather than the diurnal corrections.

Tests using an experimental station in the USA have given the figure of accuracy as indicated in figurre 5.21. The minimum errors occur when two receivers are coincident and is within two cels; this error being due to noise etc. It can be seen from figure 5.21 that differential accuracy reduces very slowly with increasing range, especially by day. Differential accuracy may, however, be slightly degraded if there is a coastline between receivers and errors may be introduced by the local topography e.g. buildings and vegetation.

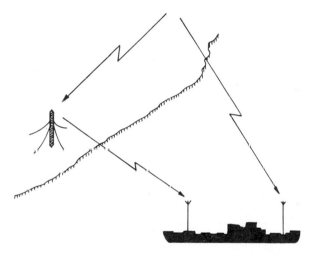

Fig. 5.20 Example of a Differential Omega system. The monitor station at a known fixed location can determine errors in the received Omega transmissions and radiate the details to vessels within range

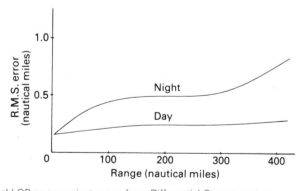

Fig. 5.21 Positional LOP error against range for a Differential Omega system

The system is still under evaluation; many details, such as the form the monitor station transmissions should take and the frequency to be used, are yet to be decided internationally. A possible block diagram representation of a Differential Omega system is shown in figure 5.22.

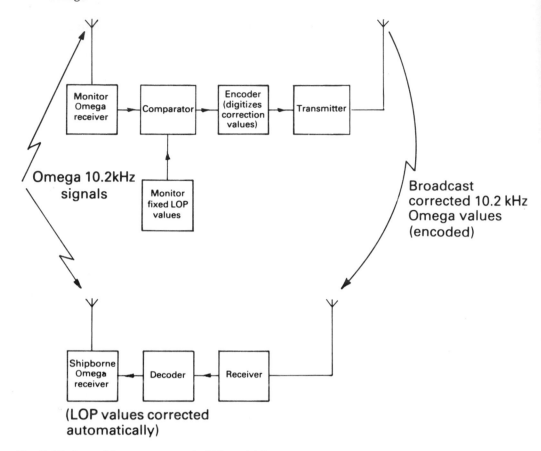

Fig. 5.22   A possible arrangement of a Differential Omega system

Application of Differential Omega

During 1981 an evaluation of Differential Omega was carried out by the US Coast Guard during a European training cruise. Two hundred data positions taken at ranges up to 500 nautical miles from a French Differential Omega station near Toulon suggested average accuracy of the Differential system was of the order of ½ nautical mile.

Also in the same year an evaluation was made in the Caribbean. For this study a Differential Omega station was installed at the Punta Tuna radiobeacon on the southeast coast of Puerto Rico. This station was the reference station. Coast Guard Cutters were fitted with Differential Omega receivers and, in the case of one of the vessels, a Transit receiver to provide reference position information was fitted. Additionally a monitor station was set up at the San Juan Coast Guard Base in Puerto Rico.

The purpose of the reference station is to collect data relating to the real time phase corrections necessary to compensate on the propagation variations local to that region and to enclode those corrections on the radiobeacon signal. Processing units at the station compute corrections for acceptable Omega station signals received and transfer the corrections to a pilot unit at the station. The pilot unit generates the 288 kHz radiobeacon frequency and modulates that carrier with a 20 Hz signal to enclode the real time corrections.

The radiobeacon transmission allows a Differential Omega coverage area within a 450 nautical mile radius of the station.

The purpose of the monitor station is twofold:

1. To provide operator access to system data.

2. To record preprocessed data which can be used to establish statistics for progressive improvement of system accuracy.

The data obtained from the monitor station and from the Coast Guard Cutters is to be analyzed by the Coast Guard to evaluate the operational characteristics of the Differential Omega system. It would appear, however, based on information gained so far that the system provides sufficient accuracy to be acceptable for operational purposes.

5.13 Range-Range mode

The range-range (or rho-rho) mode is a method of operation whereby the times for the signal to travel to the receiver from each transmitter are measured rather than their differences. For this mode of operation it is essential to have a stable time reference within the receiver. The range is calculated from the difference in known time of transmission and the measured time of arrival of the signal at the receiver. The operator's time reference must be synchronized initially with the time standard of the transmitter. Each time measurement (range measurement) provides a circular LOP (see figure 5.2).

The gradient (spacing between adjacent LOPs) increases with distance from the transmitting stations for hyperbolic mode while the gradient for the ranging mode is constant (providing propagation velocity is constant). Also the angle of cut between LOPs is improved in the ranging mode in those areas where the angle of cut between LOPs is improved in the ranging mode in those areas where the angle of cut for the hyperbolic mode may deteriorate. Thus ranging mode offers significant advantages over the hyperbolic mode in extending the coverage area. The disadvantages include the need for the on-board timing reference and the inability of the system to compensate for unpredictable propagation conditions.

6
Navigation by satellite

6.1 Introduction

Of the previous hyperbolic navigation systems discussed only the low frequency system Omega can truly be called a worldwide positioning system. Global coverage of both Decca and Loran is limited by the lack of transmitting stations in certain areas. Even the relatively reliable Omega system suffers from errors due to diurnal changes of the earth's atmosphere. However, with the use of special charts and skilled operators, the system has provided mariners with reliable position information for many years.

It was inevitable that, with the steady increase in both the payload capacity and the power of modern rockets, a global navigation system based on the use of satellites would become a reality. The space age is acknowledged to have begun in the early 1950s when the USSR surprised the world by launching a man made satellite into close orbit. Although a very small satellite by present day standards, 'Sputnik' had on board a radio transmitter the frequency of which exhibited a pronounced Doppler shift when received at a fixed point on the surface of the world. The Doppler effect was produced by the orbital velocity of the satellite as it approached and receded from the receiving antenna. American scientists quickly saw that the effect could be exploited to create a truly accurate global positioning system using a number of orbiting satellites.

In 1964 the US Navy Astronautics Department began a launch programme aimed at continuously maintaining in orbit six satellites to be used by American nuclear submarines for navigation throughout the international waters of the world. The operation was very expensive and was not at the time made available to merchant shipping. Early in 1967 by presidential order the US Navy permitted the system to be used freely by vessels of all nationalities. This action was to bring maritime navigation into the space age. The main dawback to the newly opened system was the high price of the computer hardwear required to decode the complex satellite data. With the emergence of microprocessors into the marine field, the cost and size of equipment has fallen dramatically to the point where most merchant vessels can now accommodate the sophisticated satellite navigation equipment required. Indeed the cost has fallen to such an extent that it is now economically feasible to install satellite navigation equipment in yachts and small boats.

6.2 Basic satellite theory

It is essential that a few basic facts about space technology are understood before the satellite navigation system can be discussed in detail. This explanation is mainly concerned with the basic factors relating to satellite orbits and the specific terminology used when describing such orbits.

A satellite is carried into orbit aboard a rocket capable of reaching the velocity required to enable it to overcome the earth's gravitational field. Once this has been achieved virtually any orbital altitude or plane can be accomplished by modern rocketry. The orbital plane is called the *Inclination* and is the angle produced between the eastern end of the equatorial plane and the satellite orbit. Figure 6.1 illustrates orbital inclinations of zero for the equatorial orbit, 45 degrees, and 90 degrees for a polar orbit. The final inclination desired partly determines the launching site chosen. In practice it is difficult to achieve an inclination which is less than the launching site location in latitude. A zero inclination orbit is most effectively produced from a launch pad situated on the equator. This of course is not always possible and a compromise must be made. Launch normally takes place in an easterly direction. It is possible to save fuel, and thus weight, by using the rotational speed of the earth to boost the velocity of the accelerating rocket by using an easterly launch. The necessary escape velocity required for an easterly launch at the equator is quoted as $6.89\,\mathrm{km\,s^{-1}}$, whereas for a westerly launch at the equator the figure rises to $7.82\,\mathrm{km\,s^{-1}}$. Launch velocities will also vary with latitude and the direction of the flight path.

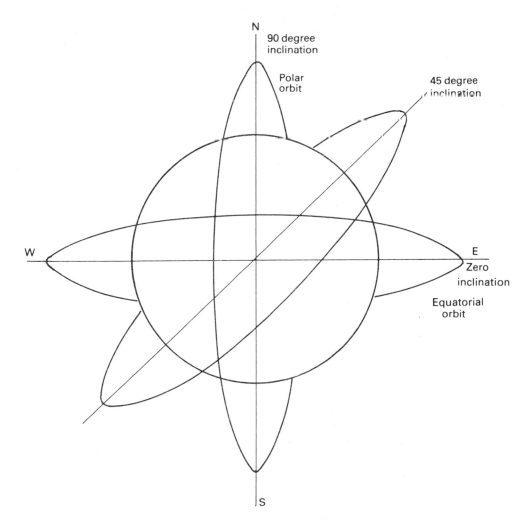

Fig. 6.1 Illustration of orbital *inclination*

Kepler's laws

An artificial orbiting satellite obeys the three laws of Kepler which were developed in the late 16th century in an attempt to explain the mysteries of the planetary orbits in our own solar system. When applied to artificial orbiting satellites the laws can be summarized as follows:
1. the orbit of an artificial satellite with respect to the earth forms an ellipse,
2. vectors dawn from the satellite orbit to the earth describe equal areas in equal times and,
3. the square of the period of the satellite orbit is equal in ration to the cube of its mean altitude above the earth's surface.

   True to Kepler, artificial earth satellites follow elliptical paths. In some cases the ellipse is large and is a requirement as the first stage of a launch to the higher geostationary orbit, but in most cases the ellipse is due to the earth not being a perfect sphere. The closest point of approach to the earth of an elliptical orbit is called the *perigee* and the furthest distance away is termed the *apogee* as illustrated in figure 6.2. When satellites are observed from the surface of the earth specific terminology must again be used. The direction vector of the satellite from the observer is called the *azimuth* and is quoted in degrees. The angle between the satellite, at any instant, and the earth's surface tangent is termed the *elevation* and again is quoted in degrees (see figure 6.3) Kepler's laws can be simplified still further if we assume the satellite orbit to be circular.

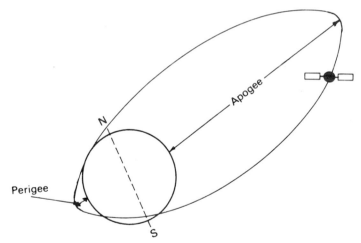

Fig. 6.2 Illustration of the terms *apogee* and *perigee*

Orbital velocity

A satellite can only remain in orbit if its velocity is great enough to overcome the pull of gravity ($9.81 \mathrm{m\,s^{-1}}$) and less than that required to escape gravity. The speed is therefore a compromise but must be absolutely precise for the orbital altitude chosen. The orbital velocity will keep the satellite in orbit for many years, the period being limited mainly by air drag slowing the speed and eventually causing the satellite to re-enter the atmosphere and burn out. The nominal orbital velocity for a satellite at any altitude can easily be calculated by using the formula:

$$V = \frac{K}{(r + a)^{1/2}} \mathrm{km\,s^{-1}}$$

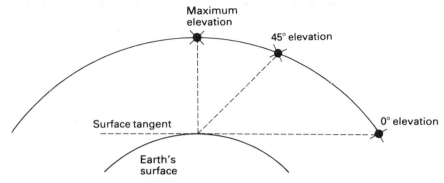

Fig. 6.3 Illustration of the changing angle of elevation. The angle reaches a maximum at the satellite's closest point of approach to the observer

where V = orbital velocity in $km\,s^{-1}$
  a = altitude of the orbit above the surface of the earth, in km
  r = the mean radius of the earth (approximately 6371 km)
  K = 630 (a constant derived from a number of parameters).
The earth is not a perfect sphere and therefore its radius will vary. However for this calculation the radius can be approximated to 6371 km. The velocity of a satellite with an altitude of 200 km would need to be:

$$V = \frac{630}{(6371 + 200)^{1/2}} = 7.77\,km\,s^{-1}$$

The velocity of a satellite with an altitude of 1075 km (a Transit satellite) would need to be:

$$V = \frac{630}{(6371 + 1075)^{1/2}} = 7.3\,km\,s^{-1}$$

Orbital paths can be transferred to a Mercator projection chart as shown in figure 6.4. The inclination must be the same in both the northern and the southern hemispheres and corresponds to latitude. The six orbits shown are for Navstar satellites with an inclination of 55 degrees. Transit satellites are in polar orbits and therefore follow longitudinal paths.

Orbital period

The time period taken for one complete orbit by a satellite can be readily calculated using the simple formula below:

$$P = K\left(\frac{r + a}{r}\right)^{3/2}\text{ minutes}$$

where P = the period of one orbit in minutes,
  a = the altitude of the orbit above the earth's surface, in km
  r = the mean radius of the earth, in km
  K = 84.49 (a constant derived from a number of parameters).
The orbital period for a satellite at an altitude of 200 km is:

$$P = 84.49\left(\frac{6371 + 200}{6371}\right)^{3/2} = 88.45\,min$$

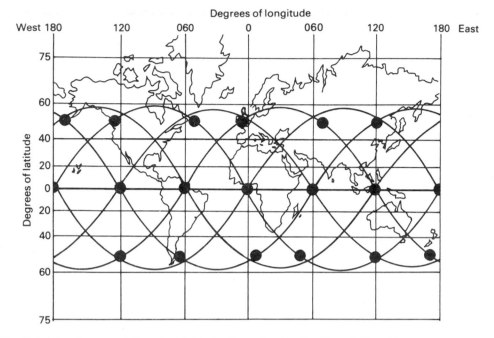

Fig. 6.4 Mercator presentation of orbital inclination paths described by satellite orbits

The orbital period for a satellite at an altitude of 1075 km is:

$$P = 84.49 \left(\frac{6371 + 1075}{6371} \right)^{3/2} = 106.8 \, \text{min}$$

The graph of figure 6.5 uses the parameters of a Transit satellite as a reference to indicate that altitude, velocity and orbital period are all interdependent.

6.3 The navy navigation satellite system (NNSS)

The present satellite navigation system uses information gathered from one or more of six satellites in low polar orbits. Of the seven satellites launched since 1967, five Transit and one Nova satellite remain in operation whilst the sixth Transit satellite is a rogue. The satellite is still in orbit and unfortunately cannot be fully switched off from the ground. In some extreme cases it can introduce errors into the system by erratic transmission. However, the conditions are rare where errors would arise due to the rogue Transit satellite. In July 1981 a new generation Nova satellite (No. 48) was launched into orbit.

Both Transit and Nova satellites are fully compatible. Transit satellites are passive in that they have no in-built jet thrusters to enable their orbits to be re-aligned. They have been launched into virtually circular polar orbits at an altitude of approximately 1075 kilometres and anticipated orbital positions at 30 degrees to each other as shown in figure 6.6. However, the ideal orbital positions have not been achieved. Furthermore the orbits are precessing at uneven rates as shown in figure 6.7, causing longer time periods between acceptable fixes than was originally intended. Orbit 'bunching' occurs because of orbital precession. The bunching effect causes long periods between fixes in some areas of the world. The 65 degrees space between satellites 30190 and 30130 is increasing and will cause even longer delays between acceptable satellite passes. Nova satellites have much more

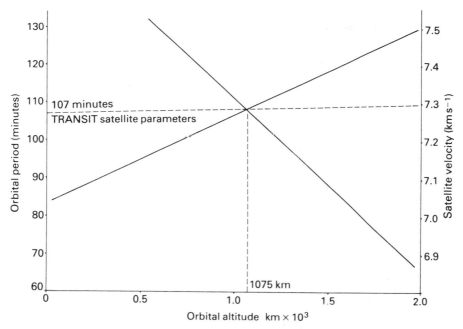

Fig. 6.5 This graph indicates that the orbital period will increase with altitude and inversely satellite velocity falls as the altitude increases

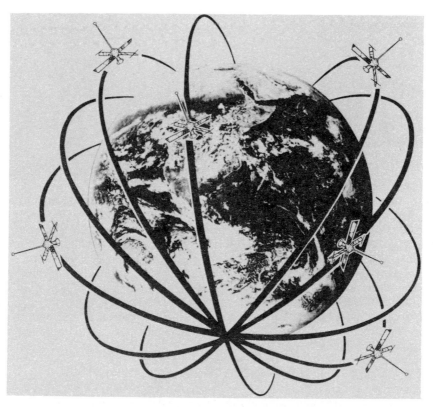

Fig. 6.6 Ideal orbital separation of satellites. Transit satellites form a 'birdcage' of circular, polar orbits about 1075 km above the earth (Courtesy of Magnavox)

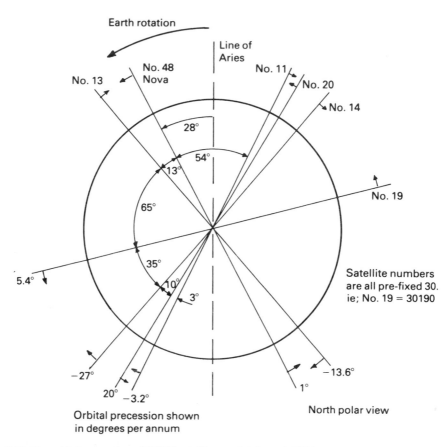

Fig. 6.7 The orbital separation of NNSS satellites on 1st August 1984

stable orbits and their introduction into the system will reduce bunching in the future.

The satellites form a 'birdcage' around the earth with the globe rotating inside it. In theory each point on the surface of the earth passes beneath each satellite twice in 24 hours. In practice, however, orbital precession negates this fact and satellite passes are fewer over some points on the globe. The satellite orbits will become bunched leading to periods approaching 10 hours between acceptable fixes. The new Nova satellite has improved the situation and therefore the pessimistic figure of 10 hours has been reduced.

The maximum time between acceptable fixes will occur at the equator diminishing to virtually continuous fixes at the poles because the satellites are in polar orbits.

A satellite velocity of $7.3\,\text{km s}^{-1}$ gives an orbital period of approximately 107 minutes. In theory one satellite will pass within sight of a surface receiver at the equator every 90 minutes but orbital precession and unacceptable passes can considerably increase this time. Satellite passes less than 10 degrees and greater than 75 degrees elevation are suspect and are therefore not accepted by the receiver.

The NNSS earthbound support system is controlled from the US Navy Astronautics Centre at Point Mugu, California. The centre controls the three other tracking stations situated at Prospect Harbour, Maine; Rosemount, Minnesota and Wahiawa, Hawaii. As shown in figure 6.8, each time a satellite passes within range of one of the tracking stations orbital data are received and passed to the main computing laboratory. The satellite's

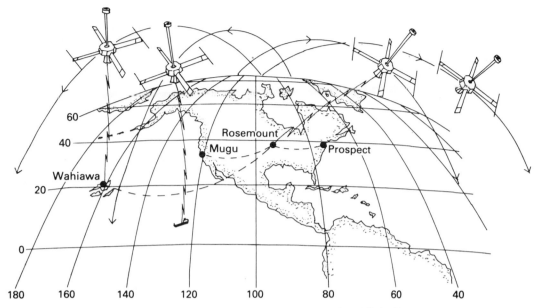

60

40

20

0

180   160   140   120   100   80   60   40

Rosemount

Mugu

Prospect

Wahiawa

Fig. 6.8 The NNSS controlled from the US Navy Astronautics Centre at Point Mugu, California

orbital data are then compared to that for its previouss interrogation and new orbital data are predicted with an accuracy of 20 metres. The new data are then re-transmitted to the satellite along with timing signals from the US Naval Observatory. Each satellite is able to store the new data until its next pass within range of a monitoring station. In figure 6.8, one satellite is being monitored via Wahiawa, Hawaii and its data returned to the Rosemount computing centre. A second satellite is programmed with new data from Rosemount whilst a third is providing navigation data for a vessel in the Pacific Ocean.

6.4 The Transit satellite

The Transit satellite (see figure 6.9) is a small compact package of electronics the contents of which are detailed in the block diagram of figure 6.10. A centrifugal stabilizing boom is attached to the outer edge of the main body in order to ensure that the lampshade transmitting antenna is always pointing earthward. The use of the boom therefore negates the need for complex tracking antenna systems aboard ship. In practice a small dipole antenna with a circular ground reflection assembly is used. The ground plane reflection assembly effectively shapes the receptive polar diagram of the antenna skyward and prevents the receiver being confused by data reflected from the earth's surface.

Each satellite draws its operating power of approximately 30 watts, from four banks of solar cells mounted on the satellite 'wings'. The power is stored in nickel–cadmium cells to enable the unit to operate continuously when on the dark side of the earth. The electronics package comprises a command receiver, a data decoder and RAM memory bank, a frequency dividing network and clock control, a highly stable 5 MHz master oscillator and two transmitters – of approximately 150 MHz respectively. The 5 MHz output from the extremely stable master oscillator (1 part in 10^{11}) is divided down to produce clock pulses for the memory system in addition to producing the two transmitted carrier frequencies. Output from the memory is used to phase modulate the carrier frequencies at a controlled rate. Thus the transmitted signals are able to provide precise

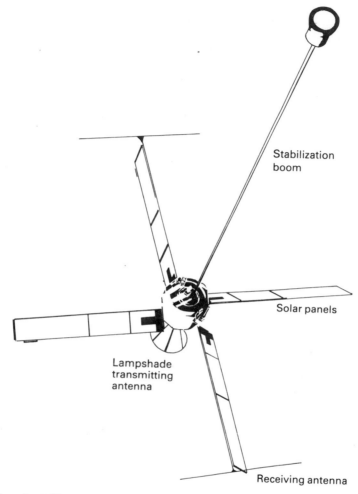

Fig. 6.9 A Transit satellite

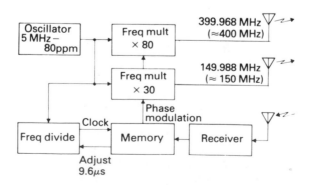

Fig. 6.10 Block diagram of a Transit satellite (Courtesy of Magnavox)

timing information in addition to data. The navigation data message is timed to begin and end at each even minute. Time correction data are stored in the memory and applied at 9.6 μs intervals. Each transmitter carrier frequency is sine and cosine phase modulated with a 60 degree duty cycle by a binary digital code as shown in figure 6.11. When the input waveform is logic 0 the phase modulator circuit is enabled causing an output sine waveform to be produced as shown. As the input goes to logic 1 modulation ceases and the output is purely carrier with no phase shift. When the input again goes to logic 0 the phase modulator is able to swing both − 60°, + 60° and return to the carrier. The output data are therefore twice the bit rate and are purely phase modulated. No frequency modulation occurs. Radiated power is 1.5 watts and is transmitted from a 'lampshade' type antenna in a circularly polarized mode. Phase modulation is used in order that data may be transmitted without affecting the carrier frequency which is continuously monitored by the receiver for a Doppler frequency shift. Other methods of modulation may produce carrier frequency shift which would be interpreted by the receiver as Doppler information and thus an error would be computed. The actual transmitted carrier frequencies are 399.968 MHz (400 MHz−32 kHz) and 149.988 MHz (150 MHz−12 kHz). The carrier frequency is held below that of the fundamental frequency by a fixed amount in order that the Doppler frequency shift produced will always be the same sign when compared to the fundamental frequency within the receiver. This factor simplifies the comparator circuit in the receiver. The carrier frequencies are directly derived from the master oscillator which must therefore be absolutely stable. Any variation in the frequency of the oscillator will cause a frequency shift of the transmitted carrier frequency which will ultimately produce an error in the final fix.

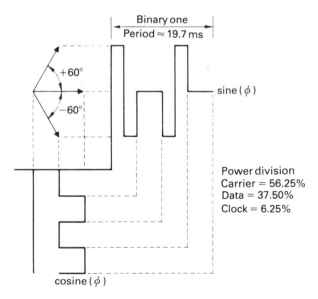

Fig. 6.11 Transit data phase modulation (Courtesy of Magnavox)

The message

The precisely timed two minute transmitted message starts and ends at each even minute. The transmitted data consits of 6103 binary bits which when decoded form 156 data words of 39 bits each and a final word of only 19 bits. The last overall 25 bits of the data

Message form a synchronization code 01111111111111111111111110 which indicates the next message is about to begin. The code is used by the receiver to synchronize data acquisition.

The first three data words provide timing information accurate to within one second. This time code is decoded and displayed on the receiver display in the 24 hour notation of G.M.T. Of the remaining data words received only one in six is used for the NNSS system data. The remainder contain classified military information which by virtue of its encoding cannot be decoded and displayed by a commercial satellite navigation receiver.

The format of the two minute transmitted message is shown in figure 6.12. Parameters defining the satellite's deviations from the elliptical orbit are contained in the first eight words of column 6.

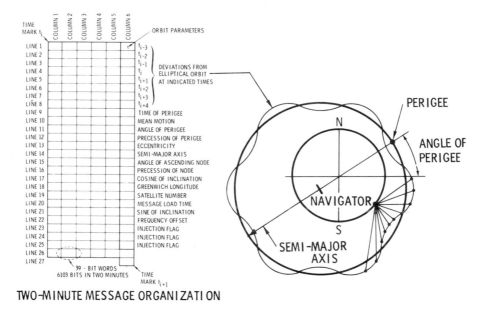

TWO-MINUTE MESSAGE ORGANIZATION

Fig. 6.12 Format of a two minute transmitted message (Courtesy of Magnavox)

Line one to line eight of the received message contain ephemeral parameters which relate to the satellite's deviation from the elliptical orbit at precise times. Lines nine to twenty-two of column 6 contain satellite data relating to orbital fixed parameters. Lines twenty-two to twenty-five indicate that the satellite is receiving data and is therefore not available. Columns one to five are military encoded and are not used for navigation data.

Figure 6.13 illustrates typical message parameters and their interpretation. The table on the right illustrates how the variable orbit parameters are decoded. The Q number provides the timing for each variable parameter word. The number 07 indicates that this action applies at seven 2 minute intervals past each half hour. This is the reason why it is necessary to initialize a Transit receiver to within 14 minutes of G.M.T. If the input was to exceed 14 minutes, the receiver would synchronize on the next period.

The fix

The accuracy of the final position fix is dependent upon interpretation of the following parameters:

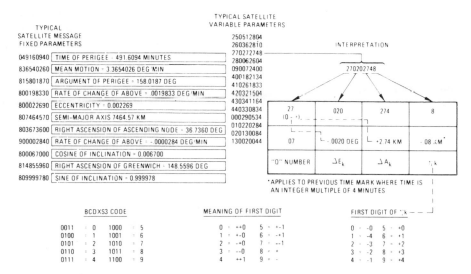

TYPICAL SATELLITE MESSAGE FIXED PARAMETERS

049160940	TIME OF PERIGEE - 491.6094 MINUTES
836540260	MEAN MOTION = 3.3654026 DEG MIN
815801870	ARGUMENT OF PERIGEE = 158.0187 DEG
800198330	RATE OF CHANGE OF ABOVE = .0019833 DEG/MIN
800022690	ECCENTRICITY = 0.002269
807464570	SEMI-MAJOR AXIS 7464.57 KM
803673600	RIGHT ASCENSION OF ASCENDING NODE = 36.7360 DEG
900002840	RATE OF CHANGE OF ABOVE = - .0000284 DEG/MIN
800067000	COSINE OF INCLINATION = 0.006700
814855960	RIGHT ASCENSION OF GREENWICH = 148.5596 DEG
809999780	SINE OF INCLINATION = 0.999978

TYPICAL SATELLITE VARIABLE PARAMETERS

250512804
260362810
270272748
280062604
090072400
400182134
410261833
420321504
430341164
440330834
000290534
010220284
020130084
130020044

INTERPRETATION

270202748

27 (0 · +).	020	274	8
07	- .0020 DEG	+2.74 KM	- .08 KM
"O" NUMBER	ΔE_k	ΔA_k	$\dot{r}_k$

*APPLIES TO PREVIOUS TIME MARK WHERE TIME IS AN INTEGER MULTIPLE OF 4 MINUTES

BCD XS3 CODE			MEANING OF FIRST DIGIT			FIRST DIGIT OF $\dot r_k$		
0011 = 0	1000 = 5		0 = ++0	5 = +-1		0 = -0	5 = +0	
0100 = 1	1001 = 6		1 = +-0	6 = -+1		1 = -4	6 = +1	
0101 = 2	1010 = 7		2 = -+0	7 = --1		2 = -3	7 = +2	
0110 = 3	1011 = 8		3 = --0	8 = +		3 = -2	8 = +3	
0111 = 4	1100 = 9		4 = ++1	9 = -		4 = -1	9 = +4	

Fig. 6.13 Interpretation of the Transit message parameters (Courtesy of Magnavox)

(a) the difference frequency caused by the Doppler effect (*Fg–Fr*),

(b) the slant range change measurement after precise timing periods,

(c) the speed of the vessel,

(d) the vessel's heading,

(e) the dead reckoning position held in memory,

(f) set and drift parameters, and

(g) the time (G.M.T.)

The vessel's speed and course information is directly interfaced with the satellite receiver from suitable compass and speed log apparatus and requires no further explanation at this stage. Set and drift figures can be entered manually as they become apparent to the navigator, or alternatively they may be calculated within the receiver. The time (G.M.T.) is directly decoded from the satellite data message.

The received carrier will vary in frequency above or below the fundamental frequency 399.968 MHz, by an amount depending upon the relative motion of the satellite and its angle of elevation with respect to the receiving antenna. In fact the carrier transmitted frequency remains constant but the wavelength is changed causing more or less hertz to be received in the same time period. A change of wavelength in a given time period produces an apparent change of frequency (see Appendix 2, p. 000)

For an accepted pass up to eight Doppler counts, each of 23 seconds, will be decoded during three or more precise two minute timing periods. A high elevation pass can produce up to 8 two minute timing periods. Therefore it is possible for the receiver to decode Doppler counts and slant range changes in excess of sixty during one satellite pass. Basically more data decoded leads to a better position fix.

The 23 second timing period, used by modern satellite navigation receivers for Doppler frequency shift data recover, corresponds exactly to the start of each new fifth line of the data message and has been chosen for convenience. The bit rate of the incoming data determines the start of each new line of 36 bits correponding to 4.6 seconds in length.

A satellite can remain 'in view' of the receiving antenna for periods approaching 18 minutes at the highest angle of elevation acceptable. Obviously the higher the satellite swings above the horizon the longer the antenna is able to receive the space wave. At the start and finish of each two minute period of the transmission a measurement of the slant range change with respect to the receiver is made. From information decoded by the receiver a slant range change curve can be plotted for each satellite pass as illustrated in figure 6.14. The three Doppler frequency shift curves shown in figure 6.15 correspond to satellite passes with elevations of 15,45 and 75 degrees with respect to a stationary receiver. It is important to note that the observed Doppler frequency shift is greatest for the highest elevation pass, reducing to zero as the CPA is reached. The gradient (or rate of change of f_R) of the Doppler curve as it passes through zero ($f_t = f_R$) is an indication of satellite elevation. The steeper the gradient, at the CPA, the smaller is the difference in longitude between satellite orbit and observer. The gradient, therefore, indicates a difference in longitude whereas the CPA defines the receiver latitude.

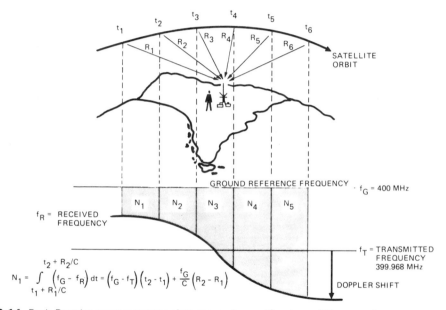

Fig. 6.14 Each Doppler count measures slant range change (Courtesy of Magnavox)

Calculation of the slant range change

Figure 6.16 illustrates two of the fixed timing periods of one satellite. The two periods correspond to three slant range changes. In this case the vessel is assumed to be stationary. All calculations which take place in the microprocessor are under the command of a dedicated program held in ROM and consequently cannot be changed. However, the following section provides a basic understanding of the complicated mathematics involved. The received frequency f_R consists of the transmitted carrier frequency f_t and a Doppler shift approaching $\pm 8\,\text{kHz}$. The reference frequency f_G is generated by a highly accurate oscillator, within the receiver logic circuitry, for comparison with the received frequency. It is an essential requirement of the system that the two oscillators, one in the satellite and the other in the receiver, remain stable otherwise an inherent error will be introduced into the final calculation.

The received frequency f_R is compared with the locally generated frequency f_G and any difference produced ($f_G - f_R$) will be a measure of the Doppler shift due to satellite motion plus the original 32 kHz offset from the 400 MHz carrier frequency. It is then a simple matter to remove the 32 kHz offset to leave the pure, or 'raw', Doppler shift for further

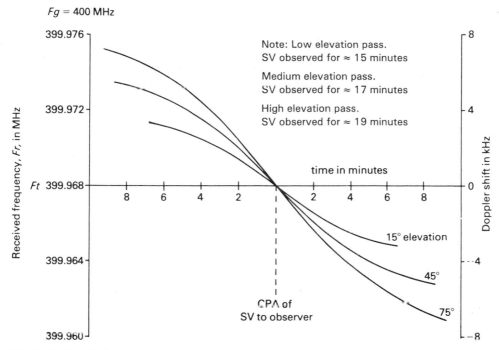

Fig. 6.15 Doppler frequency shift curves for three satellites (space vehicles (SV)) with different elevations to a fixed point

processing. The slant range is calculated at the start and finish of each two minute period in order to determine the distance between the satellite and the receiver. The velocity of radio waves must be known. Under normal refractive index conditions the speed of radio waves is that of light, $3 \times 10^8\,\mathrm{m\,s}^{-1}$.

The slant range change curve for a satellite pass for the time period $t_2 - t_1$ can be shown as:

$$N_1 = \int_{t_1 + R_1/C}^{t_2 + R_2/C} (f_G - f_R)\mathrm{d}t$$

where $f_G - f_R$ = the Doppler frequency shift and the frequency offset 32 kHz (for the 400 MHz carrier),

R_2/C = the slant range measurement at the end of the 23 seconds timing period,
R_1/C = the slant range measurement at the start of the 23 seconds timing period, and
t_2 and t_1 = timing marks.

The equation can be simplified still further to provide a clearer indication of the slant range change calculation.

$$N_1 = (f_G - f_t)(t_2 - t_1) + \frac{f_G}{C}(R_2 - R_1)$$

where $f_G - f_t$ = a fixed difference in frequency (32 kHz for the 400 MHz fundamental),
$t_2 - t_1$ = a fixed timing period of 23 seconds,
f_G/C = the wavelength of the transmitted frequency. Approximately 0.75 metres at 400 MHz − 32 kHz.

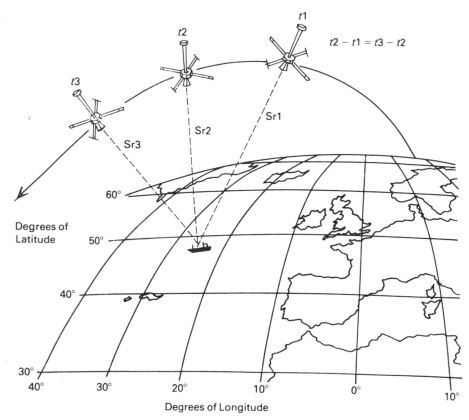

Fig. 6.16   An illustration of slant range changes from one satellite

The slant range change therefore is the difference $R_2 - R_1$ for a fixed timing period.

The use of modern technology has improved receiver design to the point where the slant range variation is calculated many times during a two minute data transmission period.

The navigation fix determination can be basically explained without the need for mathematical formulae with reference to figure 6.17.

Each satellite orbit is by definition longitudinal. The satellite is a moving transmitter the position of which can be fixed by careful calculation of the Doppler shift frequency. Thus at precisely fixed time periods the position of the satellite along its orbit can be determined. If each satellite pass is considered to be the foci of a hyperboloid then, as shown in figure 6.17, two known satellite positions form the foci of two hyperboloids. The baseline between position 1 and position 2 is approximately 975 km (satellite velocity 7.3 km s^{-1}) therefore hyperbolas representing range differences between position 1 and position 2 will be produced. The intersection of two hyperbolas will fix the receiver's position on the surface of the globe. There will be more than one point of intersection and the microprocessor determines which is the correct point. The distance between the points of intersection is very large, therefore the estimated position fed into the equipment at switch on need only be accurate to within 3 degrees of latitude or longitude.

In addition to the received information the final position accuracy will depend upon course and speed information derived from the vessel's sensors. This is normally done by interfacing suitable equipment with the receiver. Alternatively the data can be entered via the keypad.

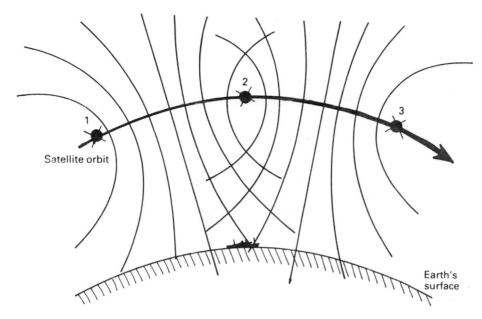

Fig 6 17 Hyporbolic representation of a satellite fix

At the start of each voyage the navigator must feed into the microprocessor an approximate position, the vessel's expected course and speed and the time in G.M.T. accurate to within 14 minutes. Upon leaving port the microprocessor calculates the position by dead reckoning using the information applied and the inputs from the speed and heading sensors. After the first acceptable satellite pass the calculated position is compared with the dead reckoning position and a new estimate made. Each successive satellite pass produces information in order that the stored position may be updated and improved. It is this iterative action of calculation and comparison which eventually leads the microprocessor to deduce the vessel's position. Obviously without the vessel's course and speed parameters the position will be wrong and in practice it is errors from these two inputs which produce the largest error in the final fix.

6.5 Errors

The NNSS system is unquestionably the most accurate global position fixing network available for use by merchant shipping. However, like all systems it is prone to errors.

The list below represents the error factors which cause fix errors in a stationary receiver. The total fix error due to the combined effect of these factors is unlikely to exceed 50 metres.

(a) Incorrectly estimated forces acting on the satellite orbit (air drag and external pressure forces) during the calculation period. (Fix error 15–25 m)

(b) Geodetic prediction errors when calculating the satellite orbital parameters. (Fix error 10–20 m)

(c) Uncertainties in the receiver altitude. (Fix error 10 m)

(d) Orbital ephemeris rounding error. (The last digit in the ephemeris data is rounded. (Fix error 5 m)

(e) Electronic apparatus errors. (Receiver clock error etc). (Fix error 5 m)

(f) Uncorrected propagation effects both ionospheric and tropospheric. (Fix error 5 m)

The error figures quoted are somewhat optimistic. Even so the maximum combined error due to these factors is unlikely to exceed 50 metres. In practice errors caused by the factors listed are reduced even further by careful design of the receiving equipment. There are however other error sources which can produce greater errors in the final navigation fix. These error sources must now be discussed.

Refraction errors

The natural phenomenon of refraction is evident whenever a radio wave passes from one medium into another of a different refractive index. This principle when applied to the ionosphere is well documented and communication engineers make use of the phenomenon to achieve worldwide communication. The radio transmissions from satellites must, by the very nature of their orbits, pass through the ionosphere on their way earthward as shown in figure 6.18. As the radio wave enters the ionosphere its wavelength will be changed slightly due to the interaction between free ions and electrons. The change in wavelength will be viewed by the receiver Doppler decoder as a change in frequency. The change will produce a corresponding error Doppler count which in turn produces an error in the final fix. The extent of the error thus produced will depend upon the extent of the radiation to which the ionospheric layers are submitted. Wavelength 'stretching' is greatest at low satellite elevations, producing the effect of apparent orbit curvature. This distortion will cause the slant range to be wrong. The wavelength increase is approximately proportional to the square of the transmitted frequency. Two frequencies are used therefore to enable the receiver to compensate for this error. The density of the ionized layers is directly related to radiation from the sun and can be simplified into the factors listed below:

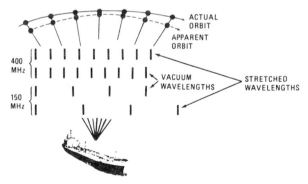

Fig. 6.18 Ionospheric refraction stretches signal wavelength causing greater apparent orbit curvature (Courtesy of Magnavox)

(a) Diurnal changes. Radiation will be greatest during the hours of daylight.

(b) The eleven year sun spot cycle. The ionosphere suffers considerable turbulence during the heavy radiation periods of the cycle.

(c) The elevation of the satellite. The error will be maximum at low elevations and will decrease as the satellite elevation increases.

Factor (a) is of course a constant and can therefore be virtually eliminated. Factor (b) is well documented and again its effect can almost be eliminated. The worst effect caused by factor (c) is nullifed by the ability of the receiver to reject low elevation satellite passes. In an overall attempt to lessen even further the effect of the ionosphere, the satellite transmits two carrier frequencies, each of which will be refracted to a different degree. The microprocessor is able to measure the frequency shift of each carrier and ultimately is able to partially compensate for refraction errors. Figures 6.19(a) and (b) are actual single and dual channel receiver refraction plots which illustrate that the error can be effectively halved by the use of a good quality dual channel receiver.

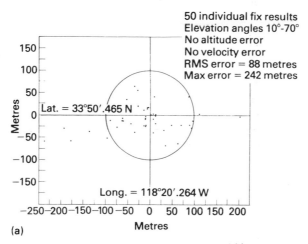

(a)

Fig. 6.19(a) Typical single channel position fix results (Courtesy of Magnavox)

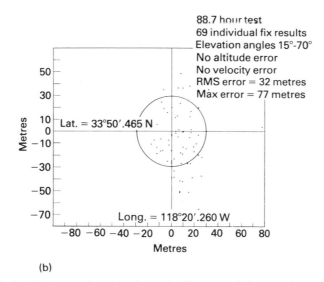

(b)

Fig. 6.19(b) Typical dual-channel position fix results (Courtesy of Magnavox)

A second propagation error is caused by the troposphere, which extends to approximatelfy 12 km above the surface of the earth. Like the ionosphere, the troposphere will again cause the transmitted wave to be refracted thus introducing a system error. Unfortunately error due to tropospheric refraction cannot be compensated for within the receiver. However, tropospheric refraction increases rapidly at low satellite elevation passes. This fact has caused manufacturers to develop equipment which will attenuate the information gathered from all passes below 10 degrees elevation. Figure 6.20 illustrates that range error increases rapidly for low elevation satellite passes.

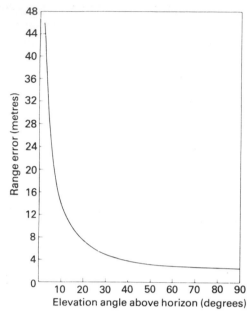

Fig. 6.20 Typical range measurement error due to tropospheric refraction (Magnavox)

Error due to the earth's gravity field influence on the satellite orbit

The accuracy of the final fix is highly dependent upon the accuracy of the satellite orbit. Any factor which changes the slant range will cause an error in the navigation fix. Unfortunately satellites deviate from their orbits under the influence of a number of external forces. One such influence is air drag which causes the satellite to have a bumpy ride instead of describing a perfect ellipse. Fortunately at the altitude of a Transit satellite orbit the atmosphere is extremely thin so the small error caused by this effect is virtually constant and can therefore be neglected. The new generation of Nova satellites has an inbuilt disturbance compensation system (DISCOS) to eliminate the effect of atmospheric drag and maintain orbital accuracy for longer periods.

Other small constant influences which can be neglected are those caused by other solar bodies. The sun's and moon's gravitation pull will cause orbit distortion, but the final error is likely to be less than 2 metres.

The greatest effect on the satellite orbit is that of the earth's gravitational field which is by no means as uniform as had once been thought. The accuracy of the navigation fix is dependent upon the accurate measurement of the slant range change, thus it is vitally important that irregularities of the satellite orbit due to magnetic field variation are taken into account. Since the early 1960s American scientists have been noting the Doppler effects produced by all the satellites under their control. From the data received they have been able to construct a true map of the earth's magnetic field. Such a map is called a Geoidal Chart. The Transit satellite system currently uses the the Geoidal Chart produced for the World Geodetic System of 1972 abbreviated to WGS72 for reference. Dimensions quoted on the chart are metres of mean sea level above the reference spheroid. The reference spheroid assumes that the earth is almost a perfect sphere approximating to sea level. Figure 6.21 shows the geoidal chart WGS72. The geoidal height may be above or below the reference spheroid by an amount determined by the earth's topography. The

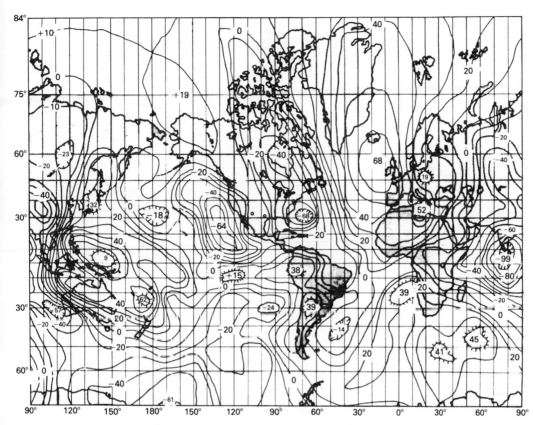

Fig. 6.21 Geoidal height chart obtained from a model of the earth's gravity field. The dimensions are metres of mean sea level above the reference spheroid (Courtesy of Magnavox)

figures quoted for the altitude of satellite orbits refer to the height above the reference spheroid to which should be added a correction factor taken from the geoidal chart. Figure 6.22 illustrates the difference between the spheroid and the geoid. If no geoidal correction factor is applied to the microprocessor during calculation, errors approaching 100 metres may result. The geodetic corrections can be derived from the geoidal chart and entered manually or as in the case of most modern equipments the information is held in memory and is applied automatically.

Antenna height and altitude errors

The vessel's antenna height above the geoid must also be known if errors are to be avoided. The error caused by an omission of this figure will be much smaller than that due to geodetic altitude error and can easily be eliminated because the antenna height is a known constant. Figure 6.23 illustrates that altitude data error produces a longitudinal fix error in the final calculation. For a given range calculation (Rx) and an antenna height, X to X_1, the actual longitudinal position indicated will be in error by a figure factor determined by the angle of elevation of the space vehicle (SV). As the elevation angle increases for a given SV the longitudinal error will increase.

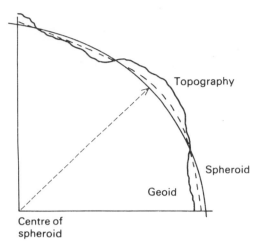

Fig. 6.22 An example of the difference between spheroidal and geoidal height

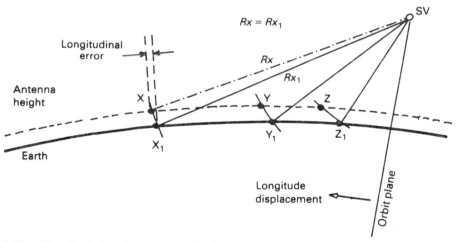

Fig. 6.23 Effect of altitude estimate on position fix

Satellite interaction or blocking

If two satellites are above the horizon at the same time it is possible that the accuracy of the navigation fix can be affected by interaction between the two satellites. Satellite blocking will occur if the receiver has locked onto the first satellite and commenced calculation when a second satellite, with a lower elevation than the first, rises. There will be a point at which the received frequency from each satellite will be the same. When this happens the receiver will be confused by the second signal and erroneous information will cause an error in the navigation calculation. Modern receivers are programmed to reject satellite passes of low elevation once the calculation has commenced.

Velocity error (see figures 6.24, 6.25 and 6.26)

The Navy Navigation Satellite System is undoubtedly the most accurate worldwide position fixing system in use today. However, its accuracy is affected by a number of external forces as has already been discussed. The largest external force, producing the greatest accuracy error is that of moving the receiver during a satellite pass when calculation has been started. In the maritime case the receiver is constantly on the move and it is this factor which can produce the largest navigational fix error in the entire system.

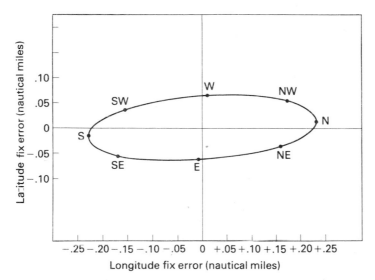

Fig. 6.24 Effect of a one-knot velocity error on the position fix from a 31° satellite pass. The direction of the velocity error is noted beside each of the 8 fix results. The satellite was east of the receiver and heading north (Courtesy of Magnavox)

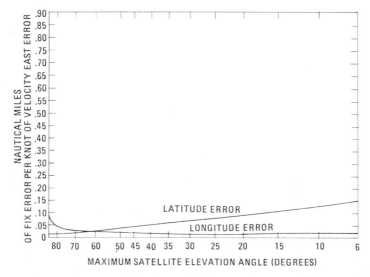

Fig. 6.25 Sensitivity of satellite fix to a one-knot velocity east estimate error (Courtesy of Magnavox)

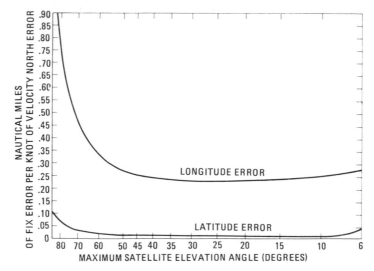

Fig. 6.26 Sensitivity of satellite fix to a one knot velocity north estimate error (Courtesy of Magnavox)

To eliminate this error an accurate assessment of the vessel's course and speed must be applied to the microprocessor during the navigation calculation period. Also, as the equipment fixes the vessel's position by dead reckoning between satellite passes, the inputs derived from speed and heading sensors must be continuous. Such information is normally interfaced directly from a suitable repeating compass and speed log. Unfortunately many of the older type speed logs measure the vessel's speed in the fore and aft line only and take no account of sideways motion. It is important therefore that a Doppler speed log indicating both fore and aft and port and starboard speeds be installed when a satellite navigation receiver is fitted to a ship.

As an example of how velocity error can affect the navigation fix consider a vessel steaming at 20 knots with a receiver locked onto a prime satellite pass for approximately 18 minutes. If no input from speed sensors is applied to the equipment the following errors could result. During a single two minute transmission sequence the error could be 0.66 nautical mile. For the full 18 minute pass the error would increase to 5.9 nautical miles. The figures quoted are a maximum and will depend upon the vessel's heading in addition to the wind velocity and drift rate. The error will also be cumulative because the vessel uses the speed information on two axes in addition to the heading information to calculate the dead reckoning position between acceptable passes.

The largest fix errors produced by a velocity error will be longitudinal because of the longitudinal orbits of Transit satellites. The gradient (or rate of change of frequency) of the Doppler curve as it passes through the CPA, is an indication of satellite elevation. If the vessel is moving parallel to the orbit and in the same direction as the satellite, the Doppler count will be less (by a factor of the ship's speed) and consequently the gradient of the Doppler curve will change. An *apparent* change of elevation occurs which produces an error in longitude. The error is greatest when the vessel is steaming north or south decreasing for easterly or westerly courses. The fix error will increase with an increasing vessel speed error. Figures 6.25 and 6.26 show that the fix error will change for different satellite angles of elevation. The largest of the longitudinal errors produced is that for a high elevation satellite pass. In practice data received from passes above 70 degrees elevation are attenuated by the receiver and thus the error from this source is minimized. The small latitude errors produced are due to the satellite orbits not being truly longitudinal. The earth is, of course, rotation beneath the longitudinal orbit, thus the orbit will have a westerly component relative to the observer.

User advantages and disadvantages when compared to the hyperbolic systems

Advantages
(a) No special charts are required when plotting the navigation fix.
(b) The fix position is displayed in latitude and longitude and therefore no corrections need be applied.
(c) Once the equipment has been purchased the use of the system is free of charge. (The Decca system requires payment of an annual rental charge.)
(d) The system provides accurate fixes at any point on the globe at any time of day or night.
(e) Accuracy is generally better than the other systems.

Disadvantages
(a) The interval between fixes may be long. A maximum of 2.4 hours has been quoted but in practice delays exceeding 12 hours have been recorded. Refer to figure 6.27.
(b) Delays between fixes are greatest near the equator falling to almost zero at the poles.

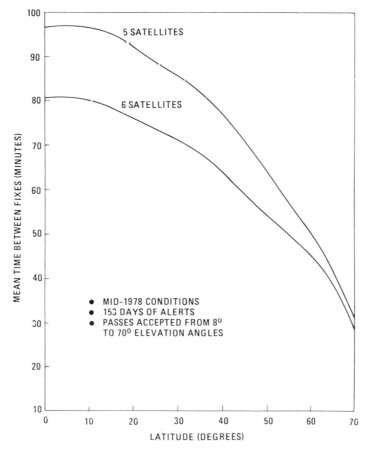

Fig. 6.27 Mean time between fixes which would occur with and without NOVA during mid-1982 (Courtesy of Magnavox)

6.6 Microprocessor controlled satellite navigation receiver

Most modern satellite navigation receivers (see figure 6.28) provide similar functions although the receiver packaging varies somewhat. Figure 6.29 is the basic functional block diagram of the Magnavox MX 1102 single channel (400 MHz) receiver. Overall system operation is controled by a Z80 central processing unit. The apparatus is interfaced directly with speed and heading equipment, although the data could be entered directly through the keypad.

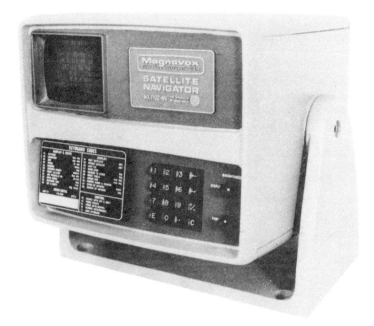

Fig. 6.28 Magnavox satellite navigator MX 1102

An output is provided, from the apparatus, to feed an external warning circuit in order that the operator may be alerted under the following conditions:
(a) If the equipment fails part of its self test function
(b) Overheating
(c) Anomalous information from the speed or heading input
(d) Loss of power. The equipment contains internal nickel–cadmium cells which will provide sufficient power to maintain operation of the equipment for up to 10 minutes if the external supply should fail. The batteries are automatically recharged when the external supply is re-connected.

The C.R.T. displays the various functions explained at the end of this section. Output data can also be interfaced with a printer to provide a "hard copy" of the displayed navigation information.

Figure 6.30 illustrates the system in more detail. It should be noted that no provision has been made for many basic logic functions. It is therefore intended to be a simple view of the complex system only.

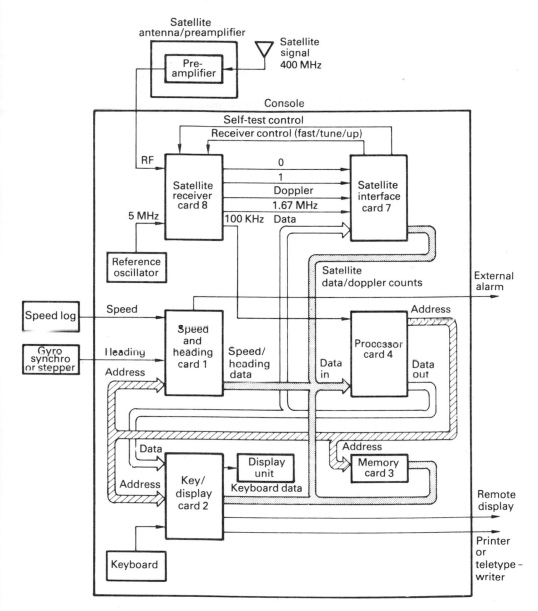

Fig. 6.29 Basic block diagram of the Magnavox MX 1102 satellite navigation receiver

Description

The 399.968 MHz received signal (*Fr*) is pre-amplified before being processed by the superhet receiver to produce a final intermediate frequency of 32 kHz. This is the quiescent IF which will be 32 kHz only when the Doppler frequency shift is zero (the satellite's closest point of approach). However, the quiescent IF will be carrying phase modulated orbital data. With the satellite approaching or receding from the receiver the intermediate frequency will change above or below the quiescent value by up to ± 8 kHz. The digital

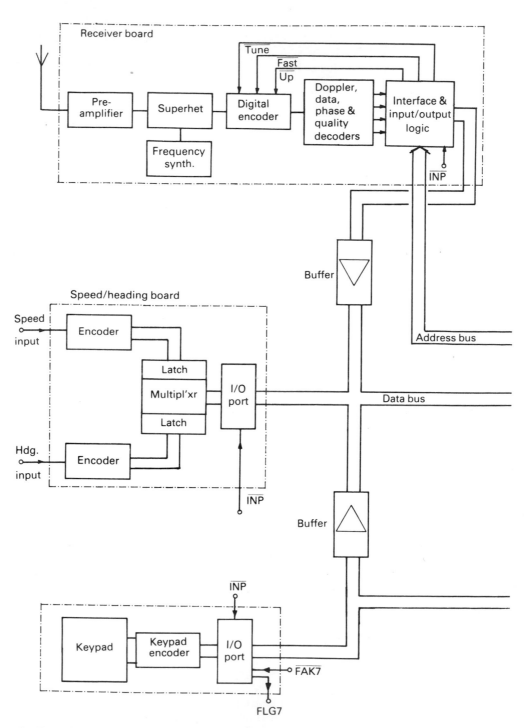

Fig. 6.30 Basic block diagram of the Magnavox satellite navigation receiver MX 1102. (Note: No provision has The diagram is only intended to be a simple overall view of the system)

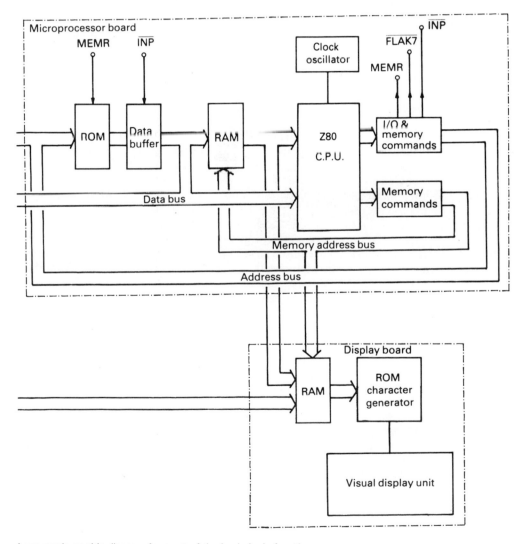

been made on this diagram for most of the basic logic functions.

encoder, under the command of the three lines $\overline{\text{UP}}$, $\overline{\text{FAST}}$ and $\overline{\text{TUNE}}$ (the bar indicates signals active when low) produces the outputs:

(a) Reconstructed or RAW Doppler shift frequency.

(b) A "Q" waveform of 64 kHz (doublet waveform) with a duty cycle varying with the phase shift of the incoming phase modulated data.

(c) The "I" waveform with a duty cycle dependent upon the quality of the incoming data. This data is then connected to four separate decoders which convert the incoming Doppler and satellite data to useful numerical values for determining the Doppler count, the data count, signal value count and a phase error count. The four logic counts thus produced are read onto the microprocessor data bus by command of the central processing unit. The CPU addresses the receiver interface four times, whilst holding the $\overline{\text{INP}}$ line low, to read the four logic data counts. A memory location in the Random Access Memory is selected by the CPU via the memory address bus in order that the data may be stored.

The keypad encoder produces a unique 8 bit data stream for each key pressed. The data word, thus commanded by the navigator, is held in the Input/Output Port (I/O port) whilst a flag (FLG7) is set on the microprocessor board indicating that data are available. An interrupt sequence follows where both the $\overline{\text{INP}}$ (input − active low) and the FLAK7 (flag acknowledge − active low) lines go to logic 0 enabling the keypad data to be read onto the data bus. These data, applied to the CPU, produce a memory command which determines the location, in the random access memory (RAM), where the data will be stored.

Both speed and heading data, from the external sensors, are digitally encoded in the interface board which also contains the necessary logic for the input/output commands. The two inputs are then multiplexed to produce eight bits of data to the I/O port buffer. The I/O port is enabled from the CPU at precise 10 millisecond intervals by causing the INP line to go low. Speed and heading datta are now located in the RAM at a location determined by the memory address from the CPU. Thus all the necessary data for a navigation calculation is held in the RAM at locations known to the CPU.

The navigation calculation program is held in Read Only Memory (ROM) which is addressed from the CPU to feed the required algorithm into locations in the RAM in order that it may be called upon as required during the calculation operation. Output from the ROM is enabled by the MEMR (Memory Read) line going high and the $\overline{\text{INP}}$ line to the data buffer going low for predetermined periods.

The CPU addresses the RAM to command the transfer of the 8 bit data words, resulting from the calculation, into the RAM on the display board. This 256 word 8 bit RAM stores 240 eight bit data words which comprise one full display of 240 characters (10 lines of 24 characters each). Each data word is applied to the ROM character generator which in turn produces the character for display. The display board also contains the necessary logic circuitry to meet the requirements of timebase, synchronization and blanking of the C.R.T. display.

Simplified self test facility

At switch on, and at regular intervals throughout the operating period, most microprocessor controlled satellite naviation equipment operate a self test program. If a failed circuit is detected the equipment will warn the navigator that the system requires attention.

Figure 6.31 illustrates that the Magnavox MX 1102 goes one step further and indicates the actual circuit card to be faulty.

Self test sequence

(*a*) *ROM memory card* 3. All memory locations are connected together and checked against a known result. Any discrepancy produces an ERR3 on the display.

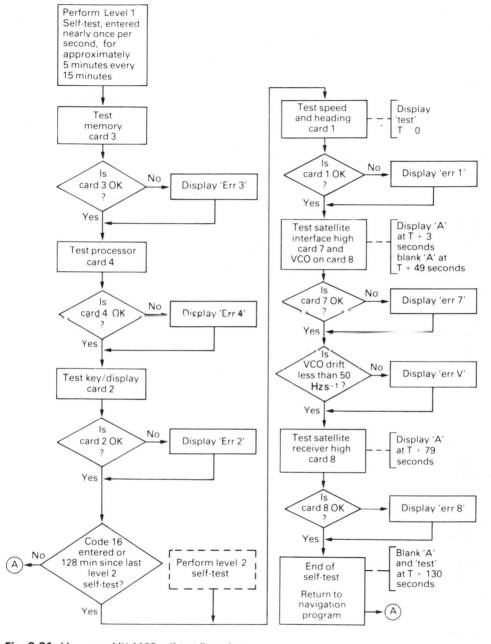

Fig. 6.31 Magnavox MX 1102 self-test flow chart

(*b*) *Processor card* 4. The microprocessor is tested by executing all of its normal functions. RAM memory testing is achieved by operating a 1's complement pattern.

(*c*) Key/display card 2. The RAM is tested by operating a 1's complement pattern as before. The ROM will display all the characters available.

(*d*) *Speed/heading card* 1.   The F & A speed circuitry is tested using the in-built self test logic. The logic pulse counter in each case is tested for toggling correctly. The P & S reading is tested for being in the correct state.

(*e*) *Satellite interface card* 7.   The card has an in-built self test logic circuit controlled by a 4 bit data stream from the microprocessor. The self test produces logic outputs to check the four decoders. Output of the decoders is then checked.

(*f*) *Satellite receiver card* 8.   Once again the card has in-built self test circuitry controlled from the processor. Initially the d.c. supply to the pre-amplifier is disconnected. Alternating doublet signals are generated on 34.7 kHz at the 32 kHz self test input. Processor decoding of this information determines whether a successful or failed test indication is to be displayed. The VCO on this card is tested by permitting the oscillator to drift. If the frequency after 46 seconds has exceeded a drift rate of $50\,\text{Hz}\,\text{s}^{-1}$, ERR V is displayed.

(*g*) *Power supplies.*   A power failure signal ($\overline{\text{FLAG6}}$) is applied to the processor card 4. If the external power fails $\overline{\text{FLAG6}}$ goes low instructing the CPU to display the word "power" to warm the operator that the apparatus is running from the internal batteries. During the self test operation the notation "test" appears on the display. Navigation information is still displayed to ensure continuous operation of the system as shown in figure 6.32. If an error is located during the self test, the navigation display remains and the notation ERR appears on the screen followed by a digit identifying the probable defective circuit.

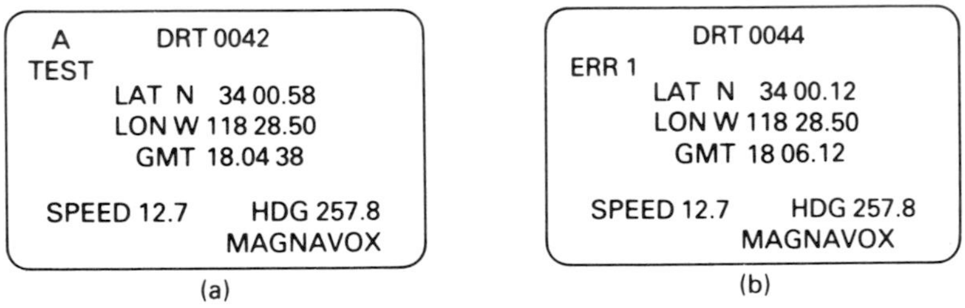

```
 A        DRT 0042
TEST
          LAT N  34 00.58
          LON W 118 28.50
          GMT 18.04 38

SPEED 12.7      HDG 257.8
                MAGNAVOX
```
(a)

```
          DRT 0044
ERR 1
          LAT N  34 00.12
          LON W 118 28.50
          GMT 18 06.12

SPEED 12.7      HDG 257.8
                MAGNAVOX
```
(b)

Fig. 6.32(a) Undergoing self-test
(b) Indication of malfunction

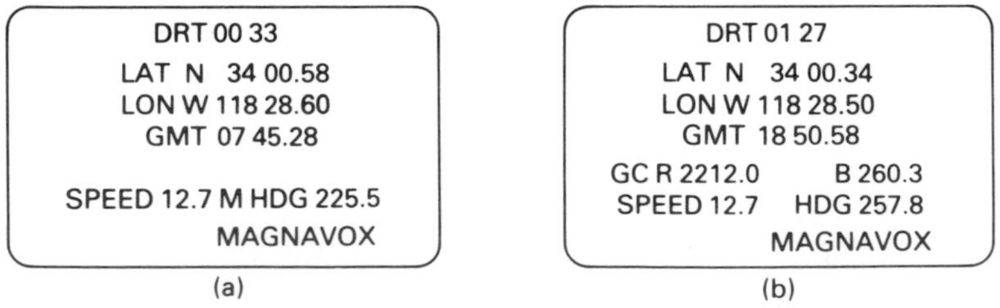

```
          DRT 00 33
          LAT N  34 00.58
          LON W 118 28.60
          GMT 07 45.28

SPEED 12.7 M HDG 225.5
                MAGNAVOX
```
(a)

```
          DRT 01 27
          LAT N  34 00.34
          LON W 118 28.50
          GMT 18 50.58
          GC R 2212.0      B 260.3
SPEED 12.7      HDG 257.8
                MAGNAVOX
```
(b)

Fig. 6.33(a) Basic navigation display
(b) Great circle range and bearing

6.7 Using a satellite navigation receiver

Satellite navigation equipment is probably the easiest to use of all the forms of navigation apparatus available. Once programmed and running the equipment requires no further attention.

Operation–Magnavox 1102

When leaving port the equipment requires the following inputs:
(a) an approximate position in latitude and longitude to within 3 degrees,
(b) the approximate time to within 14 minutes G.M.T. and
(c) the ship's course and speed.
Normally gyrocompass and Doppler speed log data will be interfaced directly with the apparatus which requires no further input via the keypad.

The microprocessor will continue to compute the vessel's position by dead reckoning. The basic navigation display (figure 6.33a) provides a readout of the dead reckoning position, course, speed and time information plus the time lapsed since the last satellite fix. After the first satellite pass, the dead reckoning position held in the microprocessor memory is updated to the new improved position. The lat/long position is accurate to within 0.1 nautical mile and the time (G.M.T.) to within 1 second. See figure 6.33b. Between satellite passes the equipment will again compute the vessel's position by dead reckoning. As the displays on figure 6.34 indicate, the navigator may select Great Circle or Rhumb Line courses; distance and course to be steered to any selected destination or way point. The dead reckoning position is dependent upon an accurate knowledge of the effect of set or drift on the vessel's course. The sat-nav receiver is capable of automatically calculating these effects. The display on figure 6.34b then provides the course to be steered to compensate for these factors. Improved microprocessor programming and increased memory capability means that the apparatus can now predict the time of the next usable satellite pass. The result is that the equipment is able to reject passes above and

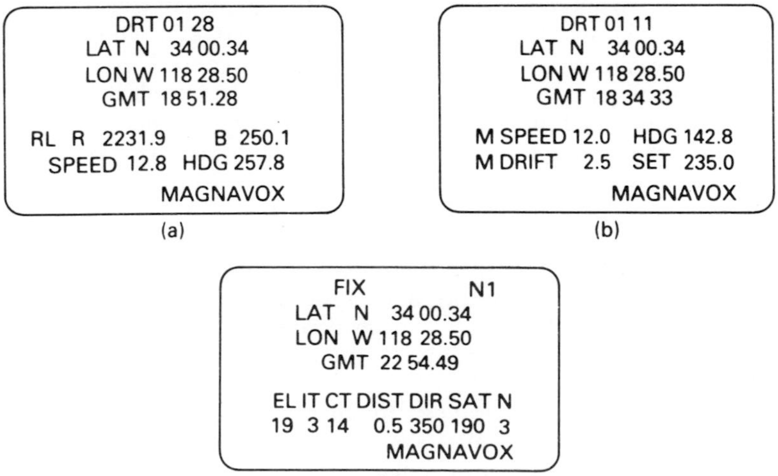

```
      DRT 01 28                          DRT 01 11
     LAT N   34 00.34                   LAT N   34 00.34
     LON W 118 28.50                    LON W 118 28.50
     GMT  18 51.28                      GMT  18 34 33

  RL  R  2231.9      B  250.1        M SPEED 12.0   HDG 142.8
     SPEED 12.8  HDG 257.8           M DRIFT   2.5   SET 235.0

           MAGNAVOX                           MAGNAVOX
```

(a)   (b)

```
          FIX            N1
       LAT  N   34 00.34
       LON  W 118 28.50
       GMT  22 54.49

    EL IT CT DIST DIR SAT N
    19  3 14   0.5 350 190  3
              MAGNAVOX
```

(c)

Fig. 6.34(a) Rhumb line range and bearing
       (b) Display of set and drift
       (c) Display of last fix

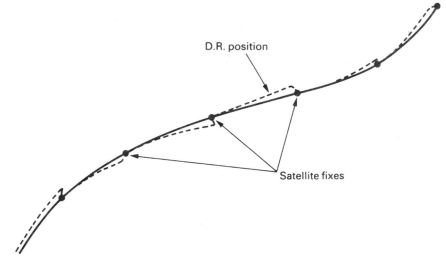

D.R. position

Satellite fixes

Fig. 6.35   Dead reckoning error is corrected by each satellite position fix update (Courtesy of Magnavox)

below the acceptable limits of elevation. Figure 6.35 illustrates a typical vessel course corrected at each acceptable satellite pass.

6.8 Racal/Decca's DS4 satellite navigator (figure 6.36)

This satellite navigator is representative of a number of modern low cost compact receivers which owe their size and economy to advances in microtechnology and the microprocessor. Obviously the processor strictly controls the whole system operation but because of its versatility it is also able to perform many of the mundane tasks of a human navigator such as the calculation of tracks to be followed between selected waypoints.

A standard 8 bit Z80 microprocessor is utilized for system control. Data is interfaced via four access ports one of which is a clock timer control (CTC). Those readers who are familiar with Z80 architecture will fully understand all the control functions illustrated in the overall system diagram of figure 6.37. However, the technical description which follows has been simplified in an attempt to give readers an understanding of system operation without the need to refer to microprocessor technology in depth. Many of the Z80 control functions are not mentioned but are listed in Appendix 3.

Once the equipment has been switched on, the operator feeds the following data into RAM via the keypad multiplexer and PIO2: a) the date, b) geoidal zone, c) antenna height, d) the approximate position in latitude and longitude (to within 60 nautical miles), e) the time in G.M.T. (to within 14 minutes), and f) speed/hearing data. These data may be interfaced directly from suitable sensors, via the peripheral board and PIO3. Information entered via the keypad in this way, is also de-multiplexed to drive the fluorescent alpha numeric display.

Immediately the equipment has been initialized, the Z80 processor continuously calculates and displays the vessel's position by dead reckoning from the input speed/heading data plus any tide or drift data. Simultaneously a varying d.c. output, via PIO1, is applied to a VCO (voltage controlled oscillator) in the sine/cosine demodulator circuitry. Output frequency of the VCO causes a variation of the reference input frequency to the slne demodulator and in this way a satellite frequency search is initiated. This is

Fig. 6.36 The Decca DS4 satellite navigation receiver

necessary because the received frequency will vary as the satellite moves in relation to the receiver. Before a satellite rises above the horizon the received Doppler shifted frequency cannot be known but will lie in the range 10 to 26 kHz, as the second IF, depending upon the orbital elevation eventually reached by the satellite.

Once a 'satellite-like' signal has been detected, the output of the sine democulator is applied to a d.c. envelope detector where it is compared with a threshold voltage (V_t). If the detected envelope voltage is above the threshold, a d.c. is produced which, (a) causes the 'satellite l.e.d.' to illuminate, and (b) is fed back to the VCO to control the reference frequency of both the sine and cosine demodulators and therefore lock the demodulator reference voltage to the incoming Doppler variation frequency. Each demodulator is switched with antiphase signals (derived from two D type flip flops) generated from this oscillator which runs at four times the Doppler tracking frequency. Output of the VCO is therefore 128 kHz for zero shift and varies between 60 and 180 kHz when searching. Another signal derived from the sine demodulator is applied to a PLL (phase locked loop) which produces a further three outputs, (a) a d.c. to illuminate the 'lock l.e.d.', (b) a d.c. lock voltage level coupled to the microprocessor to indicate that synch lock has been achieved and frequency search can be terminated, and (c) the detected 'doublet' data signal. Once lock has been achieved, the cosine demodulator produces a 10 ms bit rate data output which along with the doublet signal is used, by the processor, to retrieve the encoded binary data. One simple data retrieval method is shown in figure 6.38. Orbital and satellite data are applied, via PIO1, during an interrupt operation, to memory addresses in RAM determined by the extensive program held in PROM.

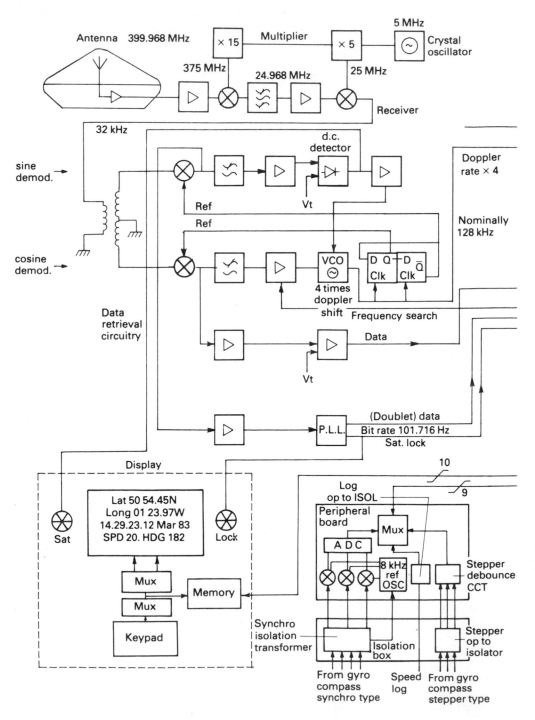

Fig. 6.37 Overall system diagram of Racal/Decca DS4 Sat-Nav receiver

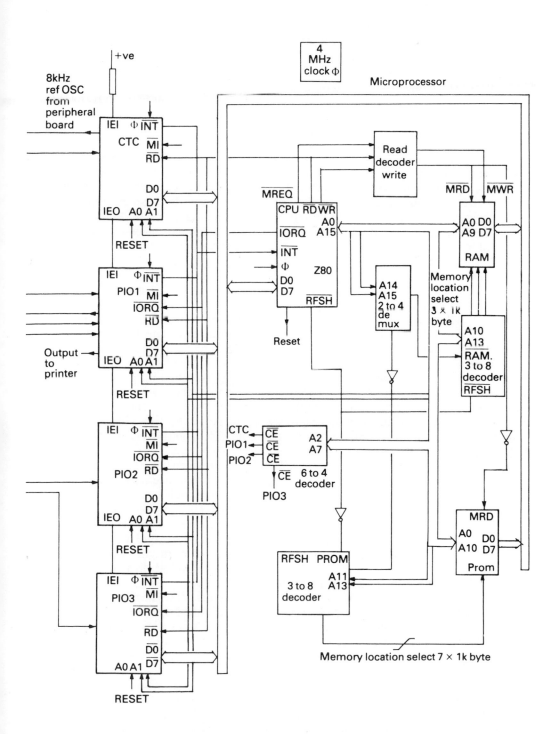

Z80 peripheral interface devices operate within an interrupt protocol of nested priority called "the daisy chain" which requests an interrupt of the main program when data are available for transfer. The CTC and the three PIOs are interconnected by the line IEI/IEO (interrupt enable input/output). A positive five volt logic level is applied to the IEI line of the CTC chip which has the highest priority order in the daisy chain. IEO lines are all connected to IEI inputs within the chain thus when no interrupt is requested all IEI/IEO pins are high. If an interrupt sequence has been requested, for instance by PIO1, its IEO line goes low and this port cannot now be interrupted by a lower order priority port (PIO2 or PIO3). It can however be interrupted by the CTC which is counting the Doppler shifted frequency during a satellite lock period.

Doppler shift counting takes place in one of the counters in the CTC which is operated as an event counter timer. The chip contains four independent counters (see figure 6.39) although only two are used for frequency shift counting. Each counter can be loaded with a pre-determined value. Thereafter application of clock pulses from an external source causes the pre-scaled count value to decrement. Each input clock pulse decrements the counter by unity from the stored value. When the counter contents reach zero a signal is generated to interrupt the main program. It is possible therefore to set up one counter of the CTC to generate precisely defined interrupt cycles. The period of interrupt cycles thus produced depends upon the initial pre-scale value fed to the counter and the frequency of the reference input source which in the case of the DS4 is 8 kHz from the peripheral board coupled to counter 0. A 5 ms counting period is derived from this clock input (0.125 ms × 40) to counter 0 to produce an interrupt period during which time the processor reads the data count (Doppler shift) held in counter 1. The output four times Doppler shift frequency from the VCO is used to clock counter 1 in the CTC. In this way the CTC is able to produce a precise count of the Doppler shifted frequency and thus the processor can determine the satellite's position along its orbit and measure slant range changes from various positions. The process of data retrieval and storage continues until the satellite drops below the horizon. At that instant, the "satellite" and "lock" l.e.d.s extinguish and the lock signal to the microprocessor reverts to its quiescent logic level. This action once again initiates the signal search line to the VCO and the receiver once again searches for a satellite signal.

The processor now goes into the "compute" mode during which time the central control unit uses the stored satellite, orbital and Doppler data to produce an estimate of the vessel's position. An extremely complex mathematical program is necessary to produce an estimated position in this way and consequently the process may take in excess of five minutes to complete. The estimate produced is then compared to the dead reckoning position held in memory and an accurate position is produced by extrapolation. If the final position is acceptable (within pre-determined limits) and other criteria such as Doppler count symmetry, signal quality and satellite elevation are satisfied then the calculated position updates the memory and is displayed.

If, however, the calculated position does not satisfy any one of the checking parameters, the coordinates are "dumped" and the alphanumeric readout displays the wors "BAD FIX". If the processor considers that either the latitude *or* longitude data derived from a high or low elevation satellite pass is acceptable, the words "HI FIX" or "LOW FIX" are displayed giving the operator the ability to accept, via keyboard commands, either coordinate.

Keyboard commands are interfaced via the multiplexer and keyboard memory, to PIO2 on the computer board. This port operates a third priority interrupt sequence in the daisy chain when a keyboard command is initiated. Multiplexed keyboard data is held in memory on the display board until latched through when PIO2 is enabled. Speed log and gyro inputs are multiplexed and processed on the peripheral board to provide the logic

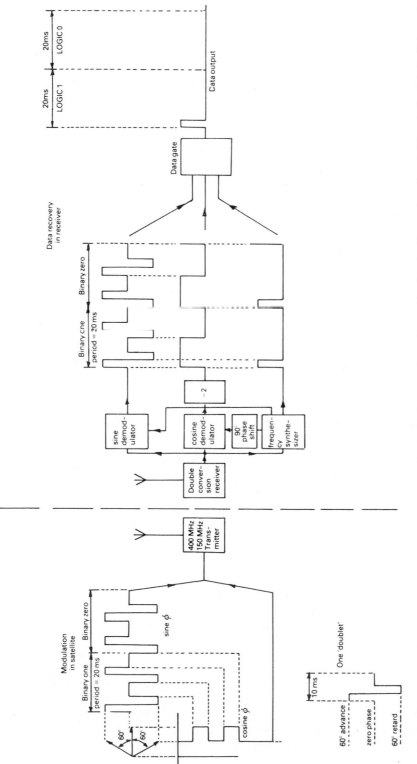

Fig. 6.38 An illustration of one possible simple method of satllite orbital data retrieval. Notes: The first doublet section of each 20 ms logic period will determine the output logic state of the data gate. The data gate will produce an output only when the three inputs are coincident (logic 1). The frequency synthesizer is frequency locked to the receiver. Output from the synthesizer to the two demodulators will be at the IF frequency (usually 32 kHz with no Doppler shift present). Doppler frequency shift retrieval and decoding is not shown.

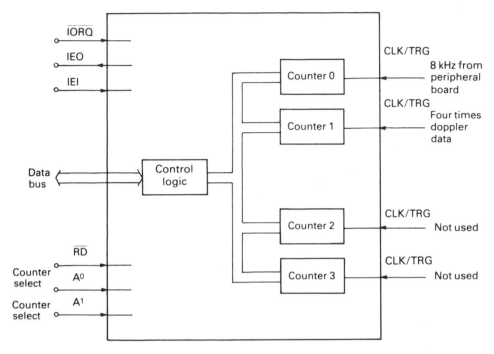

Fig. 6.39 Basic internal connections of the Z80 clock timer control chip

level pulses required for interfacing with the computer board via PIO3 with the lowest priority interrupt in the daisy chain.

Multiple keyboard commands are also available to request the following data :

Display 1   Display and enter heading, speed and printer status.

Display 2   Display entry: Data, zone, antenna height, log pulse rate, drift, set and magnetic error.

Display 3   Data entry Lat/Long, time, speed and heading.

Display 4   Waypoints: Up to ten waypoints can be nominated and stored. Display shows waypoint number, bearing (RL or GC), distance, course to steer and waypoint position.

Display 5   Dead reckoning display: Elapsed time (dead reckoning), distance and course from last satellite fix.

Display 6   Selective Update: Used when H/L pass is indicated for the operator to update coordinates as required.

Display 7   Computed set and drift. Average tidal set and drift figures are computed from comparison of two successive satellite fixes. May be entered to modify dead reckoning calculation.

Display 8   Next 100 satellite alerts: Any received satellite identifies its own predicted times of rise, maximum predicted elevation and direction from a fixed point.

A text sequence may be initiated by pressing "display 0 enter enter". The Z80 is able to test its own functions, memory locations and display under this command. Any sector which fails a test will produce a display readout of the faulty circuit area i.e. memory fail. Additionally three engineer test functions have been made available.

Display 13   Provides the following satellite data:

```
ENGINEERS TEST 1
D 33 B  101.7 CK
L  17 H   42    4
        M − 0.0
```

D   Doppler frequency to which the set is tuned at a precise moment. (These figures indicate Doppler frequency shift in kHz, although they are derived from the VCO Doppler frequency output which is four times the actual Doppler frequency shift.)

B   Bit rate frequency of the received transmission. Should be 101.7 when locked to a satellite.

LCK or NLK. Indicates lock/no lock conditions.

L   Lowest Doppler frequency achieved over observation period. (These figures indicate Doppler frequency shift in kHz, although they are derived from the VCO Doppler frequency output which is four times the actual Doppler frequency shift.)

H   Highest Doppler frequency achieved over observation period. (These figures indicate Doppler frequency shift in kHz, although they are derived from the VCO Doppler frequency output which is four times the actual Doppler frequency shift.)
     (Number following this corresponds to the minutes display from the real time clock.)

M   Indicates quality of satellite calculation. The smaller the number the better the calculation.

Display 14   Display of received data. Uninterpretable bits are replaced by an asterisk.

```
ENGINEERS TEST 2
110100111001001010
*11**01011*0*11*10
```

Display 15   Only operative with 1:1 synchro compass input.

```
ENGINEERS TEST 3
A  O  B  O  C  O
       HOOOC
```

The zeros after A, B, C are replaced by computer readings for the three gyro phases.

6.9 Global positioning system (Navstar)

The Navy Navigation Satellite System (NNSS), using Transit and Nova satellites, will provide highly accurate position fixes for the world's commercial shipping for the foreseeable future. However, in an attempt to achieve the ultimate system, the US Navy and Air Force, under the direction of a joint services program, are actively involved in the development of a completely new satellite navigation system known as GPS or Navstar. Currently the GPS is in its final phase of development and already there are a number of operational space vehicles (SVs) in orbit providing highly accurate position fixes. The cost of the GPS scheme is rapidly escalating and consequently the system has suffered some downgrading, basically by reducing the intended number of SVs from 24 to 18. The timetable for launching GPS SVs suffered a considerable setback in January 1986 with the tragic loss of the space shuttle *Challenger* and her crew. In an effort to try and reduce the two year delay which ensued and limit further delay unmanned Delta launch vehicles are now being used to launch GPS SVs. It is hoped that the system will by 1991 provide 3D fixes and total global coverage. Figure 6.40 shows predicted GPS SV availability up to 1991. It should, however, be remembered that this graph predicts a launch timetable which could again suffer from delay.

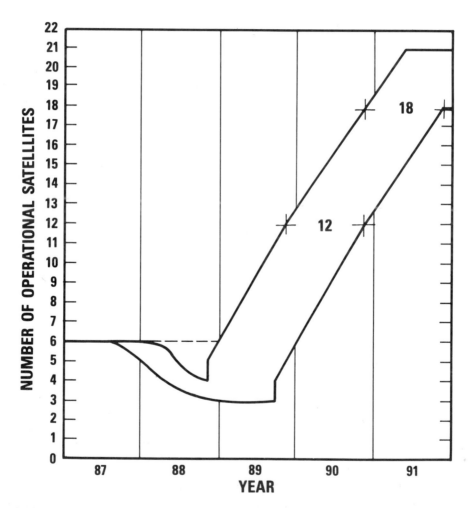

Fig. 6.40   Predicted GPS satellite availability (Courtesy of Magnavox)

At the time of writing there are six healthy SVs in orbit. Each SV possesses an on-board atomic frequency standard. The graph in figure 6.40 predicts that up to two of these SVs will fail in some way and that four healthy SVs will survive into 1991. These will provide a 2D fix which is satisfactory for many applications but not where altitude and speed are required. If everything progresses to plan 3D fixing should be achieved towards the end of 1990. It is however more realistic to assume that the right hand curve will prove to be more accurate than the one on the left.

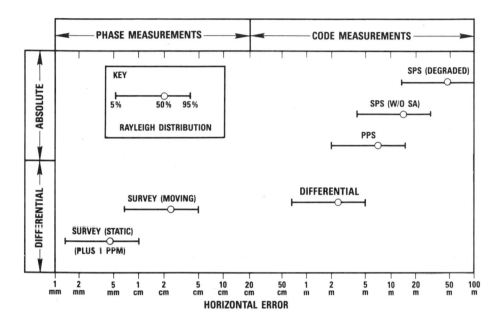

Fig. 6.41 Levels of GPS accuracy (Courtesy of Magnavox)

At this point one should consider the accuracy of the GPS system during its initializing period. As shown in Figure 6.41 there are six basic levels of accuracy available and each will be explained.

The logarithmic x scale shows horizontal position error from one millimetre to 100 metres, and each of the bars represents one of the six accuracy categories. Each bar commences at the 5% point and terminates at the 95% point of a standard cumulative radial error probability curve (Rayleigh distribution curve) and the circle marks the 50% point. This means that 5% of the results should be better than the left-most point, 95% should be better than the right-most point and half should be better and half worse than the 50% point. There are also two vertical, phase and code measurements and two horizontal, differential and absolute zones indicated. There are four applications using GPS codes to obtain a navigation fix shown in the code measurements area whilst there are two applications using resolved carrier phase measurements for a navigation fix in the phase measurements area. The three uppermost bars show absolute navigation accuracy whilst the other three indicate the use of differential techniques. The bar marked PPS (Precise Positioning Service) indicates the accuracy which may be achieved using a dual frequency P code receiver. Above this is a bar indicating SPS (Standard Positioning Service) which is representative of current receivers using only the L1 frequency and the C/A code for a fix. In future the US Department of Defense (DoD) will reduce the accuracy of GPS by offsetting orbital parameter and SV clocks. The degraded SPS achievable accuracy is shown as the uppermost bar in the diagram.

After system degradation has taken place, to be known as Selective Access (SA), it is likely that many GPS receivers will use differential techniques to improve fix accuracy. Differential techniques are explained at the end of this chapter when the Magnavox MX8400 GPS receiving system is considered. The bottom half of figure 6.41 shows three bars which indicate possible accuracies achieved by the use of differential techniques. It should be noted that differential accuracy is only possible for a range of a few hundred kilometres from a ground transmitting station.

The two bars indicating survey receivers show the optimum accuracy. The equipment used to achieve this uses phase measurement of the L1 carrier frequency in addition to code measurement. Receivers are very complex and tend to be rather expensive for standard navigational use.

System overview

The final total of eighteen SVs will be launched into six 12 hour orbital planes each containing three satellites. Each SV is attitude stabilized to within 1 metre by the action of four reaction wheels. Hydrazine thrusters enable orbital position to be maintained by providing precision re-alignment of the SV as required. The 12 hour orbital period is in sidereal time not solar time. This means that each SV noon position will shift each day. The shift is caused because a sidereal day is four minutes shorter than a solar day. Each SV in any one orbit is affected equally hence satllite spacing per orbit remains constant. The six orbits are at an altitude of approximately 19 650 km and each orbit has an inclination of 55°. See figure 6.40. Orbital altitude and inclination have been chosen to that SV telemetry can be controlled by earth stations situated in U.S. territory. This orbital configuration, encompassing eighteen SVs, ensures that at least four SVs, with an

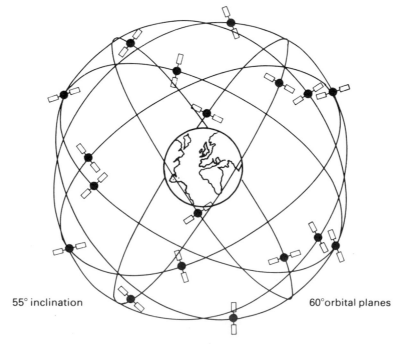

Fig. 6.42 GPS satellite coverage. When the system is fully operational there will be three satellites in each of six orbital planes

elevation greater than 9.5°, will be in view of the receiving antenna at any point on the earth's surface at any time. When one considers the problems of rapidly increasing range error caused by the troposphere at low SV elevations, 9.5° has been found to be the minimum elevation for an acceptable satellite pass with a simple antenna system.

The GPS is controlled from Vandenberg US Air Force Base in California. It is from Vandenberg that the SV telemetry and upload functions are commanded. In addition there are four monitor stations situated at Vandenberg, Hawaii, Guam and Elmendorf in Alaska. SV orbital parameters are constantly monitored by one or more of the ground tracking stations which pass the measured data to the Master Control Station (MCS) at Vandenberg. From these figures the MCS predicts future orbital data which are fed to the Upload Stations (ULS). Data are transmitted to each SV from the ULS, to be held in RAM in the SV, and sequentially transmitted as a Data Frame to receiving stations.

Transmitted data and modulation codes

Navigation data are transmitted from the SV on two frequencies in the L band: L1, 1575.42 MHz (19 cm) and L2, 1227.60 MHz (24.5 cm). Both carriers are derived from the SV clock frequency 10.23 MHz.

$$L1 = 154 \times 10.23 = 1575.42 \, \text{MHz}$$
$$L2 = 120 \times 10.23 = 1227.60 \, \text{MHz}$$

In practice the SV clock is slightly offset to a frequency of 10.229 999 995 45 MHz to allow for the effects of relativity. SV clock accuracy is maintained at better than one part in 10^{12} per day. Dual frequency transmission from the SV ensures that dual channel receivers are able to correct for signal delay (range error) caused by the ionosphere. Ionosopheric delays are proportional to $1/f^2$ hence dual frequency transmission provides additional corrective data for the receiver.

Two pseudo-random noise codes (PRN codes) are utilized for data transmission. The C/A code (coarse and acquire) is transmitted on the L1 carrier only, wereas the P code (precision) is transmitted on both the L1 and L2 frequencies. Phase quadrature modulation is used because the L1 frequency is carrying both C/A and P codes. The data transmission bit rate is 50 bits per second.

The P code, operating at 10.23 Megabits per second, is produced as the modulo 2 sum of two 24 bit registers, in the SV, termed X1 and X2. This combination produces a PRN code of 2^{48-1} steps equating to a complete code cycle (before code repetition occurs) of approximately 267 days. Each SV employs a unique and exclusive 7 day long phase segment of this code. At midnight on each Saturday, GPS time, the X1 and X2 code generators are reset to their initial state (epoch) to re-initiate the 7 day phase segment at another point along the 267 day PRN code cycle.

A code encryption is employed because a commercial receiver is unable to access the operational part of this code without prior knowledge of its starting point and how far it has run into the 7 day segment. It has yet to be decided whether commercial users will be permitted access to the P code, and thus obtain accuracies of better than 10 metres, or if the code will be available only to U.S. and NATO military forces. For any Navstar receiver to be able to access the P code it is necessary to have knowledge of the code encryption system used and initially to acquire the simpler C/A code. Commercial receivers will provide an acceptable navigation fix by acquiring the C/A code only. The C/A code is a PRN code stream operating at 1.023 Megabits per second and is generated by a 10 bit register. C/A code epoch is achieved each 1 ms period and consequently the code is readily acquired by the receiver. Each SV transmits a unique C/A code which is matched by the locally generated C/A code in the receiver.

Data

Data format structure

Subframe			Six second Subframe 10 × 30 bit word
01	TLM	HOW	Data block 1: Clock correction
02	TLM	HOW	Data block 2: Ephemeris
03	TLM	HOW	Data block 3: Ephemeris cont.
04	TLM	HOW	Data block 4: Messages
05	TLM	HOW	Data block 5: Almanac. 25 frames required for full almanac.

One Data frame is 1500 bits and takes 30 seconds to complete at the bit rate of 50 bits per second. Navigationdata are contained in five subframes each of six seconds duration and containing 30 bit words as shown above. Each subframe commences with a 14 bit TLM word (telemetry) containing SV status and diagnostic data. This is followed by a 17 bit handover word (HOW). HOW word data enable a receiver, which has knowledge of the code encryption, to acquire the P code. Data subframe block 1 contains frequency standard corrective data enabling clock correction to be made in the receiver. Data blocks 2 and 3 hold SV orbit ephemeris data. The two blocks contain such data as orbit eccentricity variations and Keplerian parameters. Message block 4 passes alphanumeric data to the user and will only be used when the ULS has a need to pass specific messages. Block 5 is an extensive almanac which includes data on SV health and identity codes.

A summary of the data contained in the 30 second data frame is listed here.
(a) SV orbital ephemeris
(b) SV clock error data
(c) Sidereal correction figures
(d) Almanac of all SVs
(e) Polar wander data (Earth axis wander)
(f) SV performance status
(g) Time of last data inject
(h) Data to enable P code acquisition (HOW)
(i) Telemetry data (TLM)
(j) SV number
(k) Specific messages as required (i.e. an indication that the SV is off station and should not be used)
(l) Receiver clock correction data
Data are modulated onto the L1 signal carrier, along with P and C/A codes, with both in phase and quadrature components as shown in figure 6.43.

P code amplitude is − 3 dB down on the C/A code signal strength, thus the slower clear and acquire code provides a better signal to noise ratio at the antenna. This makes the C/A code easier to access. The frequency spectrum produced by both P and C/A codes on the L1 carrier is shown in figure 6.44. Relative bandwidths for both codes are also indicated.

It should be remembered that data modulation at 50 bits per second produces a bandwidth of 100 Hz which cannot be illustrated on this scale. Signal bandwidth, code matching and data stripping are further explained in the GPS receiver pages at the end of this chapter.

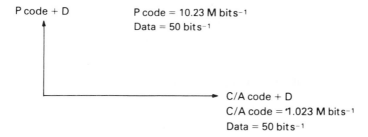

P code + D   P code = 10.23 M bits⁻¹

Data = 50 bits⁻¹

C/A code + D

C/A code = 1.023 M bits⁻¹

Data = 50 bits⁻¹

Fig. 6.43 Vector relationship of quadrature modulated signals

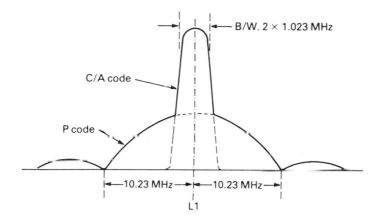

Fig. 6.44 Bandwidth/power distribution diagram for the P and C/A codes plus data

Satellite frequency stability

Satellite frequency stability is of vast importance when a system such as Navstar relies upon the accurate measurement of range for its operation. Stability is not easy to maintain in an electronic unit which is subjected to constantly varying ambient temperatures. The SV is travelling through a hostile environment where temperatures can vary by as much as 30° centigrade. In addition, at the high altitudes of any SV, there is little protection from the radiation of the sun. For these reasons the clock oscillators in SVs are under constant scrutiny.

The NNSS Transit/Nova satellites use quartz controlled clock oscillators which provide short term stability of 10^{-11} with a 24 hour change less than 10^{-9}. The first SVs to provide navigation capability, by the calculation of the range between satellite and receiver, were called Timation satellites. They were launched into orbits at an altitude of 805 kilometres with inclinations of 70°. First generation Timation SVs transmitted one UHF frequency only. This was produced from a quartz clock oscillator with a stability of 1 part in 10^{-11} per day. Timation 2 satellites had the same oscillator stability and transmitted both VHF and UHF carriers in an attempt to overcome delay errors caused by the ionosphere.

In 1973 the US Navy and the US Air force combined their efforts to produce what is now known as the GPS or Navstar system. The first test satellites launched in the new program were called Navigation Technology Satellites (NTS). NTS1 was launched in 1974. It carries a new frequency standard unit formed by a quartz oscillator locked to an atomic resonance line of rubidium. The technology utilized in rubidium and caesium clock oscillators is beyond the scope of this book. However, it should be noted that using this type of oscillator NTS1 was able to produce the two transmission signals (UHF and L band) to an accuracy of 1 part in 10^{-12} per day. Caesium/quartz units offer greater frequency stability and in 1975 the second generation of NTS vehicles was launched into orbit. NTS2 carries a caesium frequency standard unit from which are produced three carrier frequencies (SHF, L1 and L2) with an accuracy of 1 part in 10^{13} per day. These satellites are still being tested by the armed forces. Caesium clocks however, require regular updating from the ground and in an effort to improve stability and maintain it for extended periods, clock units utilizing hydrogen maser technology are being considered.

The clock oscillators of present Navstar SVs are caesium/quartz with rubidium/quartz back-up units.

The fix

Unlike the NNSS system the GPS position fix is achieved by the precise measurement of the distance between the satellite and the receiver at an instant in time. For a three dimensional fix three or four satellites would be needed depending upon the quality of the receiving equipment. An earthbound station, such as a ship, requires only two dimensional position fixing which can easily be achieved by receiving data from three satellites only. To measure the precise distance between the transmitter and the receiver requires highly accurate time clocks in both vehicles. The satellite clock is monitored from the ground and is corrected by atomic standard time. It is accepted therefore, that the satellite clock, which is used to generate the transmission frequencies, is accurate and the receiver clock may be in error.

For this reason range measurements are called false or "pseudo-ranges", and must be corrected within the receiver microprocessor. The pseudo-range measurement for a receiver with an imprecise clock is given as:

$$PsR = Rt + C\Delta td + C(\Delta tu - \Delta ts)$$

where range figures are in metres and time in seconds,

PsR = pseudo-range between satellite and receiver,

Rt = true range,

C = speed of light $(3 \times 10^8 \, \mathrm{m\,s^{-1}})$,

Δts = satellite clock error from GPS time,

Δtu = receiver clock error from GPS time, and

Δtd = propagational delays due to both the ionosphere and the troposphere.

The GPS receiver calculates the pseudo-range time taken for the transmission by measuring the phase shift of the P code and comparing it with a locally generated code in the microprocessor. Figure 6.45 illustrates that the pseudo-ranges calculated for three satellites will not converge at a specific point unless the receiver clock error is corrected.

The ship's position is solved with reference to Cartesian coordinates as shown in figure 6.46 with reference to three celestial "fixed" points (SVs).

System errors

The total error produced by a combination of the error producing factors is very slight. A position fix in four dimensions (latitude, longitude, altitude and velocity) for military users can be as good as 5 metres. However, for commercial users in the future, the system is to be downgraded to an accuracy of approximately 100 metres (95% probability). The

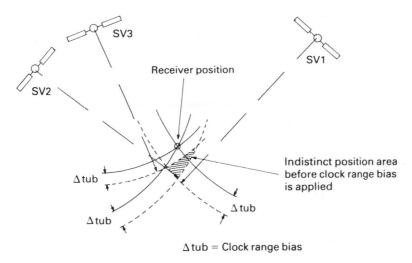

Fig. 6.45 Determination of the receiver position by applying clock range bias in the receiver

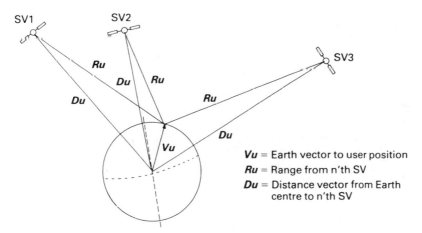

Vu = Earth vector to user position
Ru = Range from n'th SV
Du = Distance vector from Earth centre to n'th SV

Fig. 6.46 Determination of user position

error inducing factors can be simplified to three main sources assuming that the receiving equipment has been carefully designed.

Satellite clock error

Although the latest generation of satellites carry a highly accurate clock oscillator it is still necessary to re-adjust the clock from the ground support network. Each SV clock may deviate by up to 1 millisecond over a seven day period. This in turn will cause a range error to arise. SV clocks are rapidly being improved by the use of new technology and the fix error produced by the latest SV clock error is very small. Unfortunately this error is indistinguishable from ephemeris errors (small changes in orbital altitude) and the combined fix error produced will not exceed 2 metres.

Ionospheric and tropospheric delay

As the two transmitted signals pass through the ionosphere a speed reduction caused by a refraction of the radiowave occurs. The overall delay thus caused is virtually inversely proportional to the square of the frequency. Two frequencies are transmitted in order that the delay may be calculated by a comparison of the two and an error correction figure is applied to the final calculation. As with NNSS, errors due to the troposphere are independent of frequency and cannot be compensated for. Atmospheric delay produces the greatest fix error. A dual channel high quality receiver will produce position errors of approximately 5 metres due to ionospheric delay whereas a lesser quality single channel receiver could have errors in excess of 20 metres because of this effect.

Multipath error
This error results from the reception of the same SV data from more than one source. A major contributor to this error is the reflected wave from an object close to the receiving antenna. Each receiver position is unique and therefore the error is not constant. Final fix errors in the region 3 to 5 metres can be produced by this effect.

Another commonly referred error is that produced by the effects of relativity. This error is effectively cancelled in the GPS but it is briefly described below.

Relativity error   Einstein stated that time is copressed by the mass of the Earth. Time on the surface of the globe is compressed by $1.4 \times 10^{-9} \, \mathrm{m\,s^{-2}}$ compared to time in free space. It is evident that as one travels further away from the earth's surface towards free space the compression of time is of less significance. At the altitude of a Navstar SV time compression is calculated to be $0.4 \times 10^{-9} \, \mathrm{m\,s^{-2}}$. An effective rate range time error of 1 ns therefore exists between time of the SV and that at the receiver. At the accepted propagation velocity of radiowaves $300 \times 10^{6} \, \mathrm{m\,s^{-1}}$, a one nanosecond time error corresponds to a range error of 0.3 metres. Additionally a second time error is produced by time compression caused as the SV moves at $26.61 \, \mathrm{km\,s^{-1}}$ through space. To compensate for all relativity errors the SV clock oscillator frequency is slightly offset. By the time that the radio wave arrives at the receiving antenna the effects of relativity will have been cancelled and the pseudo-range can be more accurately calculated.

These are by no means the only factors which affect the accuracy of the GPS system but they are often referred to in various papers on this subject.

6.10 Navstar user equipment

Currently the GPS is still under development and is not likely to be released to commercial users for some time. Consequently Navstar user equipment (see figure 6.47) is in the development stage with most prospective manufacturers naturally reluctant to disclose specific circuit detail. It is, however, likely that the design of commercial Navstar user equipment will follow predictable lines.

When the GPS is released for commercial use it is probable that the C/A code only will be made available to non-military users. Accurate reliable navigation fixes can be made by acquiring this code only from the L1 carrier thus simplifying receiver design. To further reduce user equipment cost the receiver front end will sequentially track up to four SVs. The description of the simplified Navstar receiver which follows has been produced around the following factors:
(a) Compactness
(b) Economy
(c) Acquire C/A code only
(d) Receive L1 carrier frequency only
(e) Use a single RF channel sequenced between up to four SVs

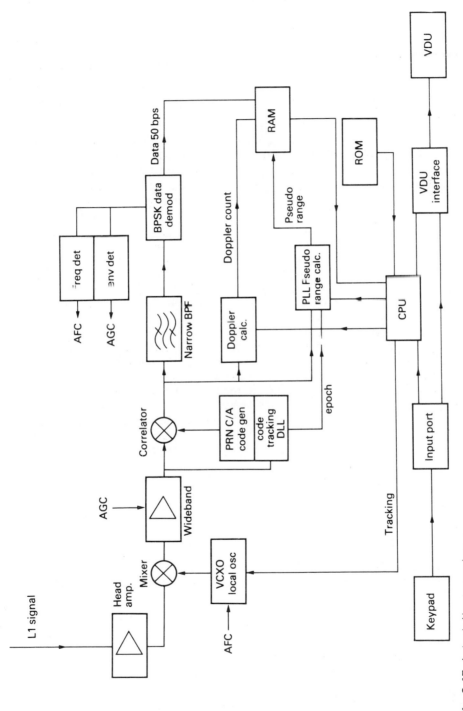

Fig. 6.47 A simple Navstar receiver

The compact above decks unit contains an isotropic antenna with ground plane radial reflectors, a low noise pre-amplifier and filters. Circularly polarized radio waves from the SV, are received by the isotropic antenna whilst the radial reflectors reduce the problem of multipath errors caused by earth surface reflected signals. The head unit should be mounted in such a way that the antenna has a clear view of the whole area in azimuth from the zenith to the horizon.

Input to the superhet receiver is therefore the amplified SV signal at 1575.42 MHz, plus slight Doppler shift, but possessing a very poor signal to noise ratio. The single signal mixer down-converts the L1 carrier to an intermediate frequency. Frequency conversion is determined by the VCXO local oscillator which is under the control of both the CPU and a signal derived AFC. CPU input to the VCXO enables initial SV tracking to be achieved whereas the d.c. AFC produced from the received signal maintains this lock. A wideband IF amplifier is used to permit reception of the 20.46 MHz bandwidth P code enabling future modification of the receiver to be made if required. Output from this amplifier is coupled to a correlator along with the locally generated PRN C/A code. It is essential that the receiver tracks the received signal precisely despite the fact that it is at an amplitude which is hardly above the locally generated noise level. To achieve tracking the received signal is applied to a Delay Lock Loop (DLL) code tracking circuit which is able to synchronize the locally generated PRN code, by means of the EPOCH datum point, with the received code to produce the reconstituted code to the narrow bandpass filter. The DLL is able to shift the local PRN code so that it is early or late (ahead or behind) when compared to the received code. A punctual (P) line output to the correlator is active only when the two codes are in synchronism. PRN codes are described in more detail at the end of this chapter.

Output of the correlator is the autocorrelation function of the input and local PRN C/A codes. Bandwidth of the narrow band bandpass filter is 100 Hz to pass data only to the BPSK data demodulator where code stripping occurs. The auto correlated C/A code is also used for both Doppler and pseudo-range measurement. The PLL used for pseudo-range measurement has a clock input from the CPU to enable clock correction and an EPOCH input each millisecond for alignment.

All receiver functions are controlled by a microprocessor with keypad and VDU display. The use of a microprocessor ensures economy of design. In this simplified description most of the control lines have been simplified by clarity.

Receiver operating sequence

01 Initialize
02 Search for satellite
03 Identify L1 carrier
04 Acquire L1 C/A code
05 Track L1 C/A code
06 Strip data
07 Measure pseudo-range
08 Measure Doppler frequency shift
09 Store data
10 Commence next SV search – repeat steps 03 to 09
11 Commence next SV search – repeat steps 03 to 09
12 Commence next SV search – repeat steps 03 to 09
13 Compute navigation position
14 Display data

Autocorrelation of random waveforms

The main function of the correlator in this receiver is to determine the presence of the received PRN code which is severely affected by noise. Correlation is a complex subject. This brief description attempts to simplify the concept of code matching using correlation techniques. Both the C/A and P codes are 'chain codes' or 'pseudo random binary sequence' (PRBS) codes which are actually periodic signals. Within each period the code possesses a number of random noise like qualities and hence is often called a 'pseudo random noise code' (PRN code). The PRN binary sequence shown assumes that the code has a period of fifteen samples i.e. it repeats every fifteen bits. The Navstar P code has a period of 267 days and the C/A code a period of one millisecond. It is obvious therefore that the PRN code can possess any period.

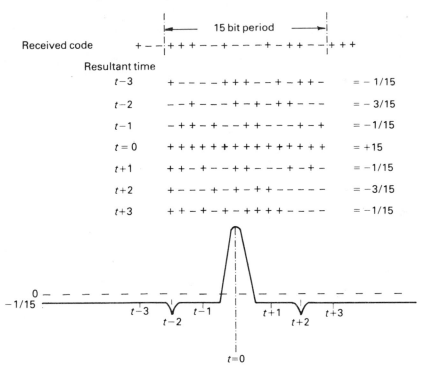

Fig. 6.48 Autocorrelation function

To establish the autocorrelation function both the received C/A code and the locally generated C/A code are applied to the correlator. Consider the local code to be shifted three stages ahead or behind (early or late) the received code by a time period (t) known as parametric time. Obtain the product of the two codes by adding each received bit with the locally generated bit shifted in time, as shown in figure 6.49.

The product is achieved by adding bits of data $(+1) + (+1) = +1, (-1) + (-1) = +1, (+1) + (-1) = -1, (-1) + (+1) = -1$. The average value of the products thus produced is $-1/15$. If the local code is now shifted one bit to the right and the products again noted it will be found that the average value of the products is $-3/15$. When the two codes are in synchronicity the product of all bits is $+1$. Therefore the average value of the products is also $+1$. This is the only time per code period when all the code products are $+1$. The peak thus produced is called the autocorrelation function and enables the

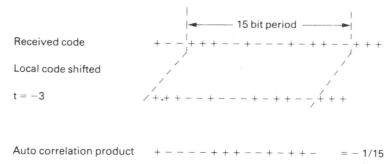

Received code

Local code shifted

t = −3

Auto correlation product   + − − − − + + + − − + − + + −   = − 1/15

Fig. 6.49 Autocorrelation product

received code to be identified, even in the presence of noise which is essentially an amplitude variation.

The PRB sequence is periodic therefore the autocorrelation function is periodic and repeats at the rate of the original signal. It is possible to determine the period of the received code by noting the periodicity of the peaks produced in parametric time. Thus the C/A code can be acquired even when it is severely affected by noise. The autocorrelation function peak also indicates the power density spectrum of the received code signal. A signal with a wide bandwidth (the P code) produces a sharper narrower correlation spike whereas a wide correlation spike indicates a narrow bandwidth signal (C/A code). Obviously the width of the correlation spike is inversely proportional to the bandwidth of the received signal code.

The user equipment just described demonstrates many of the principles of GPS reception. However, equipment manufacturers will have their own ideas about how a GPS

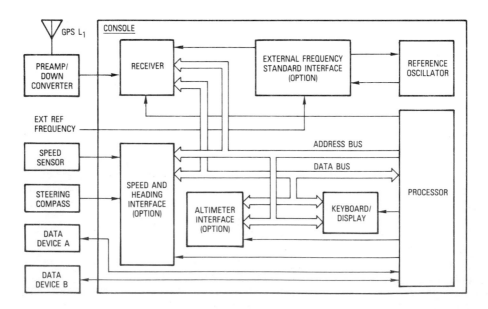

Fig. 6.50 MX5400 functional diagram

receiver should be configured. Magnavox, arguably the leader in this market, have produced the system shown below.

As is to be expected the microprocessor plays a huge part in GPS equipment design. The MX5400 is a two channel C/A code receiver for marine, land and low dynamic airborne applications. Two receiver channels are provided in order to make the system versatile. The first channel sequentially tracks the best of four SVs while the second channel updates almanac and ephemeris data as required. The second channel also acquires new SVs as they appear. This means that there is no interruption to navigation as long as there are sufficient SVs visible. The processor is also used for basic navigation functions which may be commanded from the keypad. In addition the MX5400 has been provided with two bi-directional data ports. These ports are able to accept inputs from a Transit satellite navigator or Loran-C system in order to provide continuous navigation during the establishment period of GPS.

As has been discussed, system accuracy is of utmost importance. This receiver is capable of the following accuracy during the experimental stage of GPS and before Selective Access is imposed. For a static receiver, better than 10 metres RMS (3D) or 12 metres RMS (2D). For navigation use, with interfaced speed and heading data, better than 15 metres RMS (3D) or 8 metres RMS (2D). It should be noted that accuracies are dependent upon precise time and phase measurements. This receiver is able to be fitted with an atomic frequency standard which with a 5 MHz reference signal applied will produce better than 4 parts in 10^{16} per month accuracy from a rubidium or caesium frequency standard.

Fig. 6.51 Magnavox MX5400 receiver

Differential GPS

The advantages of differential systems have been known for many years and indeed the Omega hyperbolic system utilized differential navigation to some extent.

When the GPS network of SVs is declared fully operational it is the intention of the US government to degrade the system for civilian users to 50 metres RMS navigation fix accuracy. This is due to happen when the block 2 SVs are operational. Differential GPS will significantly improve the fix accuracy under these conditions. However, the differential system requires a suitably modified receiver to receive data from a GPS ground reference station such as the Magnavox MX4818.

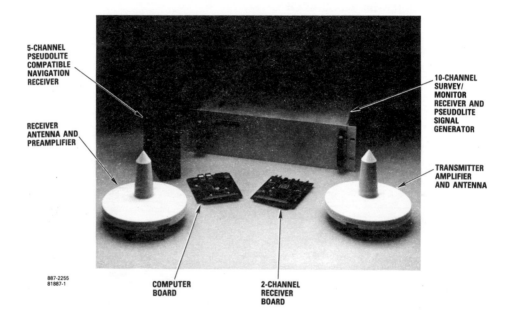

Fig. 6.52 Differential GPS and Pseudolite Components (Courtesy of Magnavox)

The MX4818 is a 12 channel, L1 frequency C/A code receiver. The receiving antenna is positioned over a known geographical point and the coordinates entered into the unit. The system then continuously tracks all visible GPS SVs and computes differential corrections to be transmitted to receivers in the area. It is also capable of taking pseudo-range and carrier phase measurements. These data, along with frequency and orbital parameter errors, are transmitted to a suitably equipped GPS receiver and are compared with data received directly from the GPS SVs. For a suitably equipped receiver, accuracies of about 5 metres RMS are possible even after Selective Access has been imposed.

7
Integrated navigation systems

7.1 Introduction

With the emergence of high power microprocessors in the maritime field, it was inevitable that one, or more, such devices would ultimately form the basis of a fully integrated ship control system. Automated control systems have for some time been available to enable one watchkeeping officer to enjoy overall control of a vessel's propulsion system and cargo spaces. A modern integrated control system has at its heart a digital processing unit which is interfaced with multiple sensors. Each sensor is capable of maintaining continuous 'watch' on a critical ship control parameter. Variation from a pre-set characteristic, or total failure of the critical parameter causes the digital processor to warn the watchkeeping officer, or ultimately take appropriate automatic action to rectify the fault.

Recent advances in electronic navigation apparatus circuitry have provided suitable sensor outputs which are ideal for integrating into one master navigation unit. However, maritime equipment manufacturers are exhibiting some caution when considering the overall philosophy of a totally integrated navigation/control system. Perhaps the reluctance to produce such expensive systems without confirmed sales orders is understandable. It is not uncommon to find a dedicated microprocessor controlling a partial integrated navigation system on board modern vessels, but it is very rare indeed to find a totally integrated system, even on the most sophisticated vessels.

Currently a number of companies are working towards the ultimate integrated navigation control system. This chapter deals with the concepts of modern and possible future systems. Specific systems are included where it has been possible to penetrate the veil of secrecy which surrounds new equipment.

7.2 Concepts of integrated navigation

For safe and economical navigation and manoeuvring an integrated navigation system requires the input of data from the following sensors:

(a) Heading sensor. Synchronous or stepping pulses from a gyroscopic compass. In many modern systems the master microprocessor is capable of automatically correcting the errors induced in the system by latitude and velocity errors acting on the gyrocompass.

(b) Velocity sensor. A pulsed input from a suitable dual-axis speed log. Sophisticated systems may have data inputs from two speed logs to overcome the error introduced by the difference in measuring speed "over the ground" and speed "through the water".

(c) Sea water temperature and salinity sensors. Analog outputs from the two sensors are converted to digital code to provide data to enable the processor to apply correction figures to compensate for the variation in speed of acoustic energy due to these parameters.

(d) Pitch and roll sensor. The output of an electronic inclinometer may be used to compensate for changes in the indicated speed due to pitch and roll of the vessel.

(e) Depth sensor. A digital output from an echo sounder may be displayed on the VDU.

(f) Satellite Navigation Receiver. Output of either a single or dual channel receiver is used to up-date the dead reckoning position.

(g) Omega/Loran-C Receiver. Although Loran-C is slightly more accurate, the Omega system is preferred because of its worldwide coverage.

(h) Decca, or other local navigation system. Decca would be preferred in those areas covered by the system.

(i) Radio direction finder. An RDF is interfaced with the unit because it is uniquely able to obtain bearings from virtually any transmitting station.

(j) Radar. Processed data from both 3 cm and 10 cm (S and X band) anti-collision radars is of paramount importance for the safe passage of a vessel.

(k) Auto Pilot. Output of an adaptive auto pilot system is interfaced for either information or total vessel control. The rudder movement indicator will also form part of the display.

In addition to these sensors a complex integrated navigation system would also include the following:
(l) A VDU with sufficient memory to permit its use by the navigator for shipboard operations
(m) An anemometer
(n) A barometer
(o) Engine and fuel sensors
(p) Cargo sensors
(q) Various alarm systems
(r) Display of weather forecasts and warnings received via satellite
(s) Automatic reports to navigators received via satellite
(t) Display of current port information on demand via satellite.

The growth towards a total integrated navigation system is following a predictable format as follows:

A position fixing system with additional facilities for computing navigational parameters such as waypoints
A modern microprocessor based satellite navigation receiver, with both gyro and log interfaces, falls into this category. Limited facilities are available to enable the device to be used for navigation calculations. This type of apparatus is limited by the possible long time span between acceptable fixes.

A position fixing system as previously described plus data from a hyperbolic system
This apparatus is the first true attempt at integration. Both satellite navigation and Omega (or Loran-C) data are under the control of a central microprocessor. Gyro and speed log data are also interfaced to enable the equipment to navigate by dead reckoning between fixes.

The previous system plus additional memory and a full keyboard
Additional microprocessor memory could be utilized for voyage calculations, or loading

and stability calculations, if this type of integrated unit were to be fitted with an ASCII keyboard and the operator trained in the BASIC computer language.

The previous system plus an ARPA interface
Data extracted from a radar system can be displayed on a VDU and either automatically or manually acted upon to prevent dangerous situations occurring. The navigator is able to operate "trial manoeuvres" as part of a limited system programming operation.

The total system
The system is under the ultimate control of a new generation of multibyte microprocessors and is described at the end of this chapter.

At the time of writing, the most popular system is that of satellite navigation (sat-nav) plus Omega with interfaces from a gyrocompass and speed log. The Magnavox MX1105 as illustrated in figure 7.1 is typical of the apparatus available in this category.

Fig. 7.1(a) Magnavox MX1105 satellite/Omega Navigator

7.3 Satellite navigation plus Omega integration

Both sat-nav and Omega suffer from deficiencies. Although the NNSS is undoubtedly accurate it does suffer from long delays between fixes because of satellite orbital bunching. Under some conditions these delays may be in excess of 10 hours, which when taken in isolation appear to be of little consequence. However, when one considers that between acceptable satellite fixes the apparatus is predicting the vessel's position by dead reckoning alone, 10 hours can lead to a considerable off course deviation. A large deviation from the required course means that safety is put at risk, and expensive fuel oil must be used to correct the error.

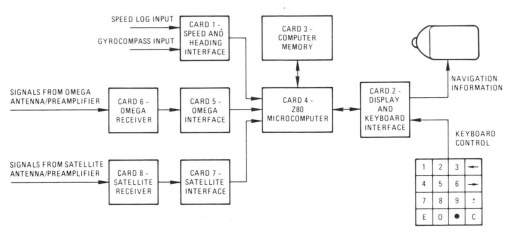

Fig. 7.1(b) Overall system diagram of the Magnavox 1105

Omega is a navigation system that provides virtually continuous worldwide position fixes at any time. Additionally the Omega system, when received by a microprocessor based unit, is able to detemine the receiver's velocity. This is possible because the Omega transmission format enables fixes to be taken at the rapid rate of six per minute. Using the data obtained from these sequential fixes the microprocessor is able to compute a rate of change of position which can be translated to the velocity of the vessel.

Unfortunately, accuracy of the Omega system varies with the geographical position of the receiver and with diurnal changes. Taken as an average, the true Omega accuracy figures fall short of the published predicted figures. Responsibility for the maintenance and monitoring of Omega lies with the US Coast Guard. Figures published by that body state that Omega has a predicted accuracy for a stationary receiver of 1.7 km r.m.s. (root mean square) during the day and 3.45 km r.m.s. at night. These are average figures formed on a worldwide basis. Errors can however, be as great as 10 km for a receiver which is moving. The sat-nav/Omega integrated receiver system has been developed to use the two systems whilst reducing the overall fix error. The Magnavox MX1105, the block diagram of which is shown in figure 7.2, is composed of five main sections, a sat-nav receiver, an Omega receiver, speed/heading interfaces, a microprocessor and a display unit. Section one, called Navigator 1, is a complete single channel (400 HMz) satellite navigation receiver. This unit, along with the microprocessor and display operates as previously described for the MX1102. Navigator 2 is the name given to the Omega receiving section which may act purely in this mode or, as is normally the case, be integrated with the NNSS receiver. This section also utilizes the vessel's speed and heading data, which are summed with Omega derived set and drift correction data, to plot the ship's position between satllite fixes. When used purely in the Omega mode, Navigator 2 is able to produce the highest accuracy Omega position fixes. The section contains the 10.2, 11.33 and 13.6 kHz receivers and a remote microprocessing unit where the Omega signal is processed before being applied to the main processor as required. Signal processing is done under the command of a Zilog Z80 CPU, the calulation algorithm for which is held in 4K words of ROM. The algorithm used is an improved version of that used by the US Coast Guard for their production of Omega accuracy predictions. Consequently the MX1105 is able to improve Omega fix accuracy. Fix data is held in RAM before being applied to the first in/first out (FIFO) buffer which is necessary to communicate the phase measurement data

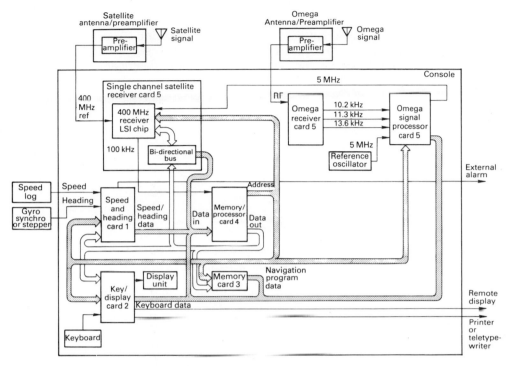

Fig. 7.2 A simplified overall functional block diagram of Magnavox MX1105

to the central processor card when commanded by the maaster microprocessor. The main unit contains sufficient memory capability to maintain simultaneous operation of both NAV1 and NAV2 units. Data from each section can be selected by the navigator and examples of each display are shown in figure 7.3.

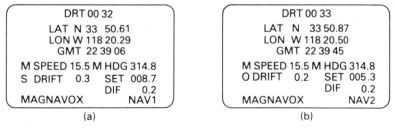

| DRT 00 32 |
| LAT N 33 50.61 |
| LON W 118 20.29 |
| GMT 22 39 06 |
| M SPEED 15.5 M HDG 314.8 |
| S DRIFT 0.3 SET 008.7 |
| DIF 0.2 |
| MAGNAVOX NAV1 |

(a)

| DRT 00 33 |
| LAT N 33 50.87 |
| LON W 118 20.50 |
| GMT 22 39 45 |
| M SPEED 15.5 M HDG 314.8 |
| O DRIFT 0.2 SET 005.3 |
| DIF 0.2 |
| MAGNAVOX NAV2 |

(b)

Fig. 7.3(a) Navigator 1 display
(b) Navigator 2 display

Both NAV1 and NAV2 displays illustrate the range difference (DIF) produced between the two navigation sections, in nautical miles. This is effectively a quality index of the position accuracy to enable the navigator to access the overall system accuracy. A small DIF figure indicates that the position data derived from all three systems (NNSS, Omega and dead reckoning) agree and therefore the displayed position fix is good. NAV1 and NAV2 are two of many data displays which this apparatus can provide.

Navigation operation

The equipment operates by constantly estimating the vessel's position from the data inputs of speed, heading and Omega. Omega stations are automatically selected depending upon signal quality. A direct Omega display can be selected by the navigator at any time during the operational sequence. See figure 7.4.

```
DRIFT:ON   FIX:READY
STATIONS IN USE   A .CO ..GH
RECOMMENDED       A .CO ..GH
FORCE ENABLE            . . . . . . . .
FORCE INHIBIT          . . . . . . . .
CALIBRATE              . . . .E . . .
SIGNAL LOW            .B . . .F . . .
OUT OF RANGE         .B . .E . . .
MODAL INTERFERE      .B . . .F . .
STATUS                          OO
```

Fig. 7.4 Omega status display

The master microprocessor in the equipment calculates the vessel's position by Omega at each ten second period. Successive Omega fixes are compared with successive dead reckoning fixes to produce a "rate of change" of fix error. System operation is under the control of an improved US Coast Guard Omega Phase Propagation Correction (PPC) algorithm which is maintained in ROM in the main microprocessing unit of the MX1105. The improved algorithm is the result of many years of extensive global testing during which the actual measured phase of the received Omega signals was compared with the US Coast Guard predicted phase. Differences between the two parameters lead to the creation of the PPC error correction algorithm now utilized in this equipment.

Thus the receiver provides navigation data for display by continuously estimating the vessel's position by the use of corrective figures produced from Omega fixes. An additional correction figure is produced each time an NNSS prime satellite pass occurs. The highly accurate position fix produced from satellite data can be viewed as the ultimate correction factor of such an integrated system. This method of constantly updating the vessel's estimated position enables the apparatus to substantially reduce the many errors present in the Omega system and consequently provide better fix accuracy.

To improve this still further it is possible to add a GPS receiver module as shown in figure 7.5. Where GPS coverage is available the MX1105 receiver system navigates by utilizing its two channel GPS receiver to sequentially track available SVs. Outside current GPS coverage Transit satellite fixes are provided with a continuous update from Omega. It should be remembered that the system also has inputs from speed and heading sensors and operates continuously on dead reckoning. An advantage of interfacing GPS even in its experimental stage is that GPS velocity measurements can be used to calibrate input from speed and heading sensors and thus improve accuracy still further.

7.4 Automated Bridge Systems

The final part of this chapter looks at the way in which two leading manufacturers of marine electronic systems have created automated bridge systems to satisfy the requirements of vessels into the next century.

Racal Marine Electronics Ltd have produced an Integrated Navigation System (INS) which is primarily based upon two established navigation and data processing sysems. The Marine Navigation System (MNS 2000) and Live Situation Report System (LSR) form the heart of this sysem into which numerous operational sensors input data. The MNS 2000 provides a continuous indication of essential navigation parameters whilst the LSR

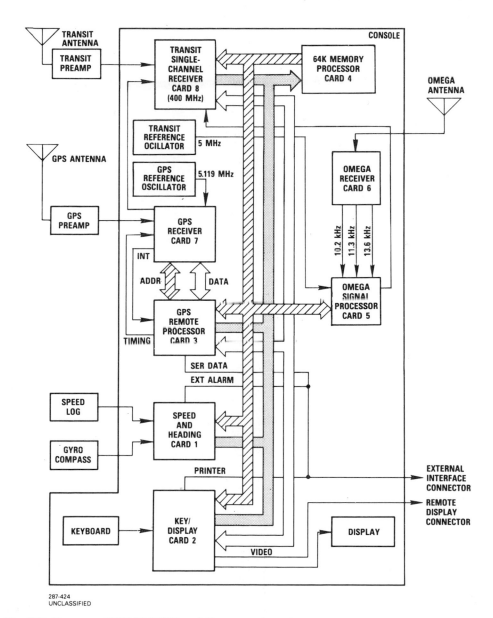

287-424
UNCLASSIFIED

Fig. 7.5 Magnavox MX1105 GPS/Transit/Omega equipment

provides an overall summary of information relevant to planning and execution of the current voyage and immediate conning of the vessel.

The reader will find the block schematic diagram figure 7.6 self-explanatory. The nucleus of the system is the LSR 4000 processor which is able to handle multiple sensor inputs whilst providing a range of displays on the cathode ray tube display unit.

The MNS 2000 is in fact a stand alone fully integrated navigation system. The standard position fixing systems (Decca, Loran-C, Omega and Transit) are all input to the MNS

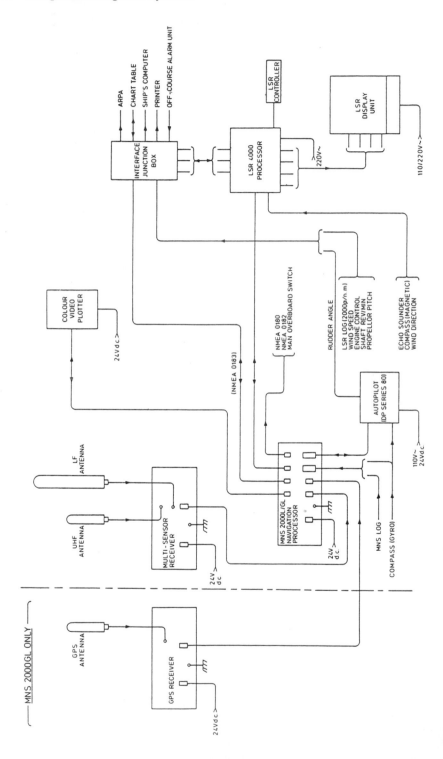

Fig. 7.6 RACAL DECCA Integrated Navigation System: schematic diagram

2000 along with GPS where fitted. The unit will choose the optimum input data and provide a position display accordingly. However, during the experimental period of GPS when data may be lost, the MNS 2000 will automatically update the GPS position by whichever of the other navigational sensors its processor has calculated will give the most accurate position. Other inputs include a Doppler log and gyrocompass to aid dead reckoning position fixing.

Fig. 7.7 Racal MNS 2000 G navigation system, with automatic selection of Decca, Loran-C, Transit, Omega and GPS

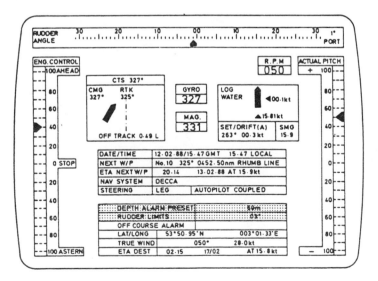

Fig. 7.8 Page 1. Full away on passage

As can be seen in figure 7.6 the LSR processor has a multitude of data inputs which enable a full bridge data system to be created. Extensive use of a C.R.T. for information display provides versatility, as can be seen in the Full Away Passsage Display, figure 7.8. However, the format of displays such as this one is very subjective and it is unlikely that two identical displays would be produced independently by two navigation officers charged with the design task. It is interesting to compare this format with that used by other manufacturers. This 14 inch colour display is able to provide three pages of data:

Page 1.   Full Away Passage (figure 7.8). This is a combination of alphanumeric and graphic displays providing data relevant to passage in open waters.

Page 2.   Ship Manoeuvring. Repeats much of Page 1 data, but provides further information for use when proceeding at slower speeds in restricted waters.

Page 3.   Voyage Plan. The plan of a voyage may be constructed by entering details of departure point, time of departure and estimated voyage speed via waypoints to final destination.

As has been stated previously, integrated navigation systems have been created because of the need to improve effectiveness and efficiency in ship operation. Because of the increasing size of ships and a reduction in manning levels there has been new thinking in bridge design and ship operations. It should be noted that the quality of the man/machine interface is of the utmost importance when considering total ship control, therefore the

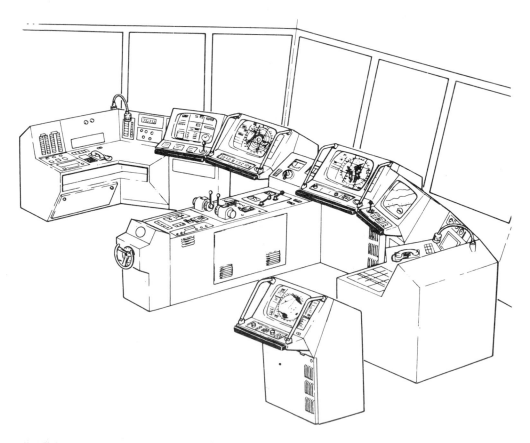

Fig. 7.9 Krupp Atlas NACOS 25 bridge layout

operator console must present, in a clear format, all data which are likely to affect the operation of the vessel. Additionally, ergonomic design of the bridge unit is essential to prevent operator fatigue.

The Krupp Atlas Elektronic NACOS 25 is a fine example of a fully integrated bridge system intended for ships operating in today's demanding maritime environment. The system has been designed to satisfy the requirements for reduced ship manning levels whilst maintaining efficiency and safety. The NACOS 25 bridge layout is shown in figure 7.9. Provision is made for two ship operators which is the minimum requirement: one watchkeeping officer controls the safe operation of the vessel whilst the other maintains watch on engine room parameters (on those ships operating with an unmanned engine room).

The system was designed with due consideration to the following parameters:

(a) Optimum integration of sub sysems
(b) Adaptation of bridge equipment to the capability of the operator
(c) Efficient man/machine interface
(d) Central display of data and information
(e) Modular design and standardization of equipment
(f) Improvement of efficiency and economy
(g) Improvement of safety
(h) The availability of an automatic adaptive steering device for ship's steering from berth to berth
(i) The flexibility of interfacing external machinery e.g. main engine data, bow and stern thruster data, and steering gear.

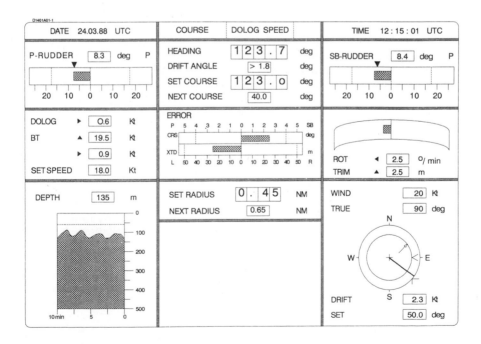

Fig. 7.10 Krupp Atlas NACOS 25 nautical information display

The functions of this fully integrated navigation and command system may be summarized as follows:
(a) Position fixing
(b) Route planning
(c) Radar navigation and collision avoidance
(d) Automatic track control
(e) Measurement of water depth
(f) Measurement of ship speed
(g) Fuel oil consumption, monitoring and control
(h) Storage of navigational data and mapping system

Figure 7.10 shows the nautical information and environment display which would be used for on-voyage navigation purposes. This display can be changed when commanded by the operator to include fuel consumption and efficiency, together with port and starboard engine shaft data. It will also provide details of engine power in kW, shaft r.p.m. and propeller pitch.

7.5 Total integration

When considering the possibilities for total integration (figure 7.11) one must not forget that in some cases the human ability to apply reasoning to a complex situation can make the difference between success and failure. Failure, in the navigation sense, could mean colossal disaster resulting in both the loss of life and the vessel. It would therefore be most unwise to completely remove from a navigator the final decision in the chain of events leading to a possible disaster. It could be argued that if all vessels were under the total control of a microprocessor decision taking navigation system no collisions could occur. Unfortunaately, very few systems, no matter how perfect they may appear to be, are totally reliable. This fact, coupled with the unnecessary cost of such equipment on some vessels makes it very unlikely that the shipping lanes of the future will be populated with fully automated vessels constantly taking action to avoid each other.

There is little doubt that modern systems will be expanded to include data drawn from other sources such as communications and engine control. The design of a total integration system will, as always, be a compromise between design parameters (limited by the available technology) and finance (limited by the ever increasing need to operate a fleet of ships efficiently). The final part of this chapter deals with a possible fully automated bridge navigation system. Much of the electronic technology required for this system has already been proved in one form or another. The system is designed in control segments which means that it can be tailor made for a situation with further "add on" units fitted as required. This dictates that the heart of the unit is a powerful new generation 24 or 32 bit microprocessor with sufficient memory capability to cover all eventualities. The master processor is connected by data highways to command each of the 8 and 16 bit remote dedicated microprocessors which carry out interface functions. The four 8 bit remote processors are provided with a VDU and keypad as a fail safe system in order that commands may be input to each section in the unlikely event of a failure of the master processor.

Each of the data sensors is interfaced with the appropriate remote processor via suitable logic gates, ports and digital encoders to produce 8 bits of data for each data bus. The remote processors execute a dedicated program, held in EPROM, to input data sequentially from each input port. However, interrupts to the main program can be initiated as required by a flag system from an input port when priority data is available. Such data takes precedence and therefore subroutines are included for the priority display of warnings, errors or critical deviations from the normal readings of monitoring sensors. Clearly the software of such a system is of critical importance for efficient and safe operation.

The navigation unit (figure 7.12)

Dual axis speed data, with reference to the sea bed, or to the flow of water past the hull, is available for display from both Doppler and electromagnetic speed logs. The master processor will command e.m. log data when operating normally in the navigation mode and displaying radar data. During the period that the remote navigation processor computes data from a prime satellite pass, speed data from the Doppler log will automatically be selected. Sea water temperature and salinity are constantly monitored. Data from these sensors is used to correct the slight depth indication errors which may arise due to changes of the two parameters. Data from the inclinometer is used to derive corrective figures to enable corrections to be made to the Doppler speed log readout.

One of the deep sea navigation systems, Omega or Loran-C, is interfaced to provide instantaneous position fixing. Omega is normally chosen because of its total coverage whereas Loran-C may be chosen by ship owners who operate their vessels in the northern hemipshere only. The hyperbolic input along with data, when available, from the satellite navigation receiver is commanded by a subroutine in the navigation microprocessor in much the same way as has previously been described. Decca has been included to enable precise navigation in those coastal waters which are covered by the system. Readout of the hyperbolic aids can be requested, by the navigator, in either LOP or latitude and longitude.

The time display, accurate to one second G.M.T., is derived from the satellite navigation transmission. Data from the radio direction finder may be displayed as a true/relative bearing on the remote navigation display, or as a vector on the master navigation PPI.

Either synchronous or stepper input from a gyrocompass is digitally encoded and displayed in three figure notation on both the navigation displays. The encoded data is also applied, via the master processor, to the navigation PPI in order to stablize the display.

The adaptive auto pilot input/output port enables data to be input for display and/or the master microprocessor to produce an output to control the helm of the vessel. This function can be overriden by the helmsman at any time.

Both 3 cm and 10 cm interswitched radar systems can be selected for display on the radar PPI. Data is extracted by the ARPA 16 bit microprocessor and is applied to the navigation PPI under the command of the central processor. Failure of the data PPI would not affect the radar PPI display and therefore vessel safe ty would be unaffected.

The engine unit

Fuel and water tank gauges are interfaced to provide data for direct display of fluid levels. Comparator data codes can be input by the operator as part of the alarm system. If the binary encoded data derived from one of the sensors matches the preselected code both visual and audible alarms are initiated. Critical engine component sensors continuously monitor such points as drive shaft bearing temperature and provide warning of impending failure. In some cases, where the failure can be averted by preventive action such as an increase in oil pressure, the engine microprocessor is able to output data via the appropriate I/O port to re-establish the correct operating conditions. The temperature of

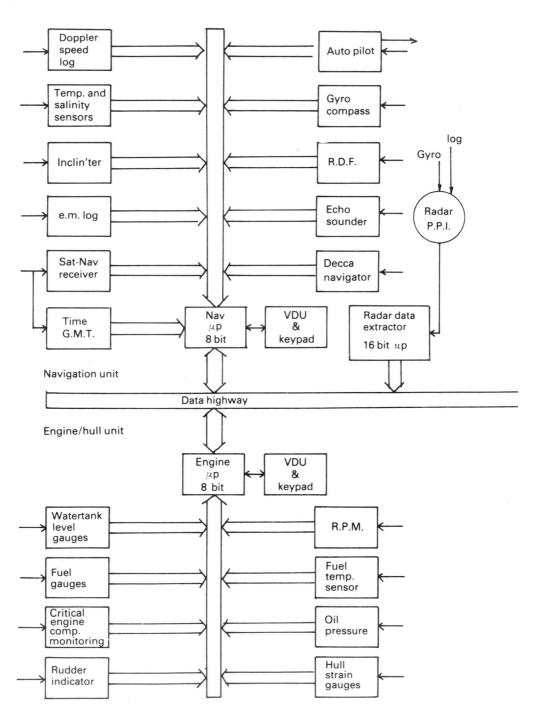

Fig. 7.11 Architecture of a complete integrated system

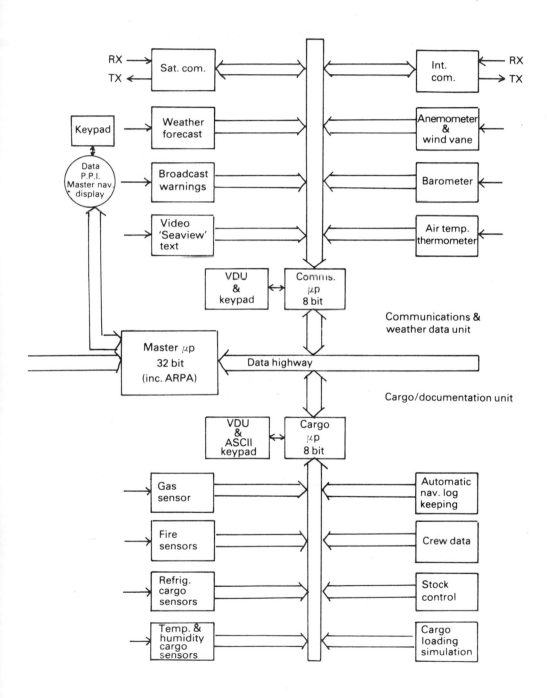

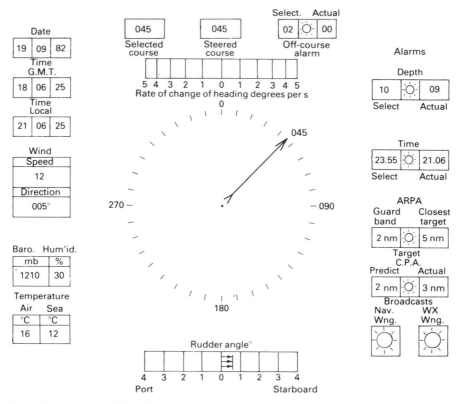

Fig. 7.12 The navigation VDU display

engine fuel oil is critical. Data from the fuel oil temperature sensor, via the I/O port, enables the temperature to be monitored and adjusted as necessary by control of the fuel oil pre-heater.

Engine shaft revolutions are input for display on the engine VDU. In addition the data is coupled to the master processor where an estimate of the vessel's speed is calculated.

Rudder movement data is input for display on the navigation VDU. Excessive rudder action causes drag which in turn leads to loss of momentum and inefficiency. Rudder movement data is integrated with engine RPM data to improve the accuracy of the vessel's displayed speed calculated in this way. Additionally rudder movement data is processed to provide corrective data which can be output via the adaptive auto pilot port to minimize excessive rudder action.

A variety of strain gauge sensors are able to monitor stress points at various points along the hull. Data from these sensors can, via a comparator, trip both audio and visual alarm systems should stress increase above preset limits.

The communications/weather unit

The satellite communication interface provides I/O data via satellite to shoreside terminals and thence internationally. The microprocessor controls transmit and receiver synthesized frequency selection in addition to selecting the system for communication (telex or voice). A standard telephone handset is provided on the operations panel. Internal communications are handled in the same way.

Output from a suitable receiver provides input data for the automatic display of weather forecasts, warnings and satellite weather pictures. Weather forecasts and warnings, normally transmitted in Morse code, are decoded by the microprocessor, which holds a suitable algorithm in ROM, for display on the VDU.

Video information, received directly via satellite, can provide the navigator with up-to-date visual displays of various items such as harbour facilities. Mari-text, a possible future system, similar in most respects to the shore based Prestel system, permits the operator to dial into a master computer and request data for any port he is likely to visit. This is of course dependent upon the requested information being available in the computer. The system could easily be extended to include official documents and chart corrections thus relieving the navigator of tiresome correction work.

Wind direction and speed are constantly checked and displayed. Drift correction figures can be derived from this input and used, via the adaptive auto pilot, to correct the vessel's drift. Air temperature and pressure data are also input for display on both the navigation and the weather VDUs.

The cargo/documentation unit

Cargo spaces are continually monitored for gas build-up and fire. Both visual and audible alarms operate in the event of any of the sensors being triggered. The visual display provides location data and the system is able to take suitable action to extinguish the fire or release unwanted gas.

Refrigerated cargo sensors continually monitor the temperature providing data for the cargo microprocessor which is able to increase or decrease the temperature within prescribed limits. Container vessels may require additional monitoring of cargo. Individual containers may be connected via an interface to the cargo unit. This facility provides both security and monitoring of ambient conditions.

The documentation half of this unit holds, in digital form, the official ship's documents. This data can be accessed, by the operator, via the ASCII keyboard which also enables the navigator to utilize the increased memory capacity to run cargo loading simulation programs. The documentation part of this unit is protected against unauthorized interrogation by a unique computer code.

Finally it must be emphasized that this concept of total integration is not a manufactured design. It is simply one possible system which, depending upon the constraints of both finance and ship manning levels, may become commonplace in the future. Only time will tell.

8
The ship's compass

8.1 The gyrocompass

At the heart of a marine gyrocompass assembly is a modern gyroscope consisting of a perfectly balanced wheel which is arranged to spin symmetrically at high speed about an axis or axle. The wheel, or rotor, spins about its own axis and by suspending the mass in a precisely designed gimbal arrangement, the unit is free to move in two planes each at right angles to the plane of spin. There are therefore three axes in which the gyroscope is free to move as illustrated in figure 8.1: a) the spin axis, b) the horizontal axis and c) the vertical axis.

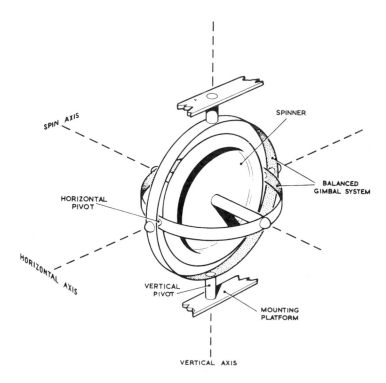

Fig. 8.1 The free gyroscope (Courtesy of S. G. Brown Ltd.)

In a "free gyroscope" none of the three freedoms is restricted in any way. Such a gyroscope is almost universally used in the construction of modern marine gyrocompass mechanisms. Two other types of gyroscope, the "constrained" and the "spring restrained" are now rarely seen.

260

In order to understand the basic operation of a free gyroscope reference must be made to some of the first principles of physics. A free gyroscope possesses two inherent properties, both of which need to be fully understood by the reader. One of these properties is gyroscopic *inertia*, a phenomenon which can be directly related to one of the basic laws of motion documented by Sir Issac Newton. Newton's first law of motion states that "a body will remain in its state of rest or uniform motion in a straight line unless a force is applied to change that state". From this law it should be noted that a spinning mass will remain in its plane of rotation unless acted upon by an external force. The spinning mass therefore offers opposition to an external force which is termed gyroscopic *inertia*. A gyroscope rotor maintains the direction of its plane of rotation unless an external force of sufficient amplitude to overcome inertia is applied to alter that direction. In addition a rapidly spinning free gyroscope will maintain its position in free space irrespective of any movement of its supporting gimbals. See figures 8.2(a) and (b).

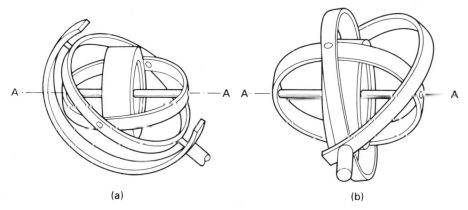

(a)   (b)

Fig. 8.2 The gyrospin axis is stabilized irrespective of any movement of the supporting gimbals (Courtesy of Sperry Ltd.)

Also from the laws of physics it is known that the linear momentum of a body in motion is the product of its mass and velocity (*mv*). In the case of a freely spinning wheel, it is more convenient to think in terms of angular momentum. The angular momentum of a particle spinning about an axis is the product of its linear momentum and the perpendicular distance of the particle from the axle.

i.e. angular momentum = $mv \times r$ where r = radius.

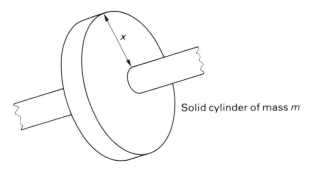

Solid cylinder of mass m

Fig. 8.3 A spinning rotor

The velocity of the spinning rotor must be converted to angular velocity, ω by dividing the linear tangential velocity, v by the radius, r. The angular momentum for any particle spinning about an axis is now:

$$m\omega r^2$$

For a spinning rotor of constant mass where all the rotating particles are the same and concentrated at the outer edge of the rotor, the angular momentum is the product of the moment of inertia (I) and the angular velocity:

$$I\omega$$

where $I = 0.5\,mr^2$

It can now be stated that gyroscopic inertia depends upon the momentum of the spinning rotor. The momentum of such a rotor depends upon three main factors:
(a) the total mass, M of the rotor (for all particles)
(b) the radius r summed as the constant K (for all the particles) where K is the radius of gyration
(c) the angular velocity ω
The angular momentum is now proportional to ωMK^2. If one or more of these factors is changed, the rotor's gyroscopic inertia will be affected. In order to maintain momentum a rotor is produced with a large mass, the majority of which is concentrated at its outer edge. Normally the rotor will have a large radius and will be spinning very fast. To spin freely the rotor must be perfectly balanced (its centre of gravity will be at the intersection of the three axes) and its mounting bearings must be as friction free as possible. Once a rotor has been constructed, both its mass and radius will remain constant. To maintain gyroscopic inertia therefore it is necessary to control the speed of the rotor accurately. This is achieved by the use of a precisely controlled servo system.

Precession

Precession is the term used to describe the movement of the axle of a gyroscope under the influence of an external force. If a force is applied to the rotor by moving one end of its axle, the gyroscope will be displaced at an angle of 90 degrees from the applied force. Assume that a force is applied to the rotor in figure 8.4 by lifting one end of its axle so that point A

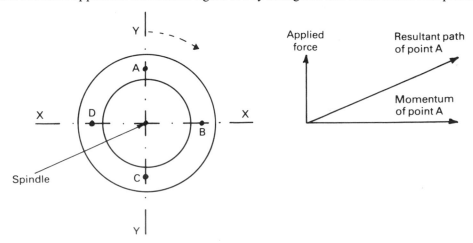

Fig. 8.4 Gyro precession shown as a vector sum of the applied force and momentum

on the rotor circumference is pushed downwards into the paper. The rotor is rapidly spinning clockwise, producing gyroscopic inertia restricting the effective force attempting to move the rotor into the paper. As the disturbing force is applied to the axle point A continues its clockwise rotation but will also move towards the paper. Point A will therefore move along a path which is the vector sum of its original gyroscopic momentum and the applied disturbing force. Point A will continue on its circular path and will move deeper into the paper. Point C undergoes a reciprocal action and moves away from the paper. The plane of rotation of the rotor, has therefore moved about the H axis although the applied force was to the V axis.

The angular rate of precession is directly proportional to the applied force and is inversely proportional to the angular momentum of the rotor. Figures 8.5(a) and (b) illustrate the rule of gyroscopic precession.

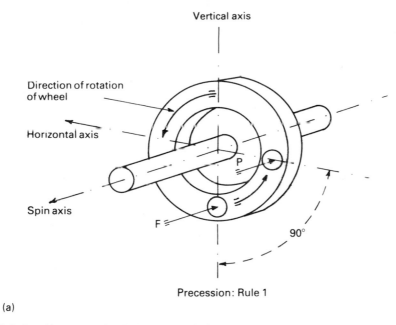

(a)

Fig. 8.5(a) Resulting precession *P* takes place at 90° in the direction of spin from the applied force *F*. This direction of the precession is the same as the applied force (Courtesy of Sperry Ltd.)

The free gyroscope in a terrestrial plane (see figure 8.6)

We will now consider these case of a free gyroscope perfectly mounted in gimbals to permit freedom of movement on the XX and YY axes. The effect of gravity is initially ignored.

It should be noted that the earth rotates from west to east at a rate of 15 degrees per hour and completes one revolution in a "sidereal day" which is equivalent to 23 hours 56 minutes 4 seconds. The effect of earth rotation beneath the gyroscope causes an *apparent* movement of the mechanism. This is because the spin axis of the free gyroscope is fixed by inertia to a celestial reference (star point) and not to a terrestrial point. If the free gyro is sitting at the north pole, with its spin axis horizontal to the earth's surface, then an apparent clockwise movement of the gyro occurs. The spin axis remains constant but as the earth rotates anticlockwise (viewed from the north pole) beneath it, the gyro *appears* to rotate clockwise at a rate of one revolution for each sidereal day. The reciprocal effect

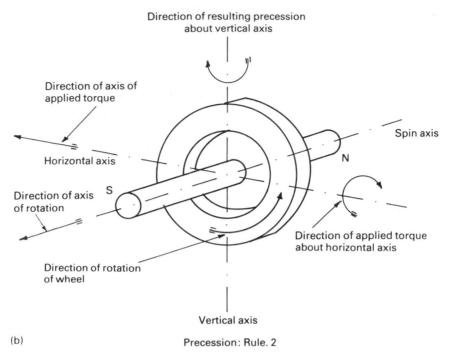

(b)   Precession: Rule. 2

Fig. 8.5(b) The direction of axis of rotation will try to align itself with the direction of the axis of applied torque (Courtesy of Sperry Ltd.)

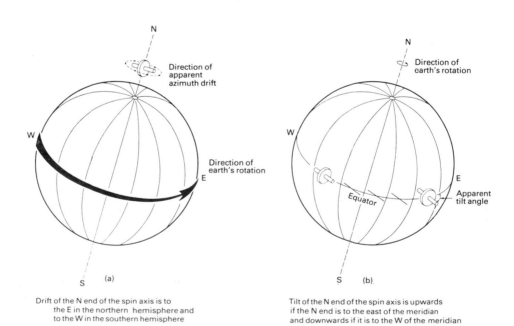

Drift of the N end of the spin axis is to
the E in the northern hemisphere and
to the W in the southern hemisphere

Tilt of the N end of the spin axis is upwards
if the N end is to the east of the meridian
and downwards if it is to the W of the meridian

Fig. 8.6(a) Effect of earth rotation on the gyro (Courtesy of S. G. Brown Ltd.)

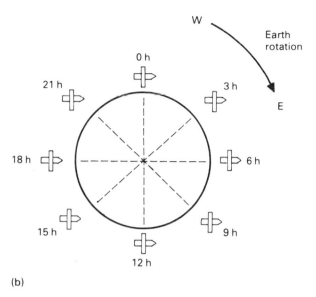

Fig. 8.6(b) View from the South Pole. The earth rotates once every 24 hours carrying the gyro with it. *Gyroscopic inertia* causes the gyro to maintain its plane of rotation with respect to the celestial reference point. However, in relation to the surface of the earth the gyro will TILT

would occur at the south pole. This phenomenon is known as *gyro drift*. *Drift* of the N end of the spin axis is to the E in the northern hemisphere and to the W in the southern hemisphere. There will be no vertical or tilting movement of the spin axis. Maximum gyro *tilt* occurs if the mechanism is placed with its spin axis horizontal to the equator. The spin axis will be stabilized in line with a star point because of inertia. As the earth rotates the eastern end of the spin axis *appears* to tilt upwards. *Tilt* of the N end of the spin axis is upwards if the N end is to the east of the meridian and downwards if it is to the W of the meridian. The gyro will appears to execute one complete revolution about the horizontal axis for each sidereal day. No drift in azimuth occurs when the gyro is directly over the equator.

The relationship between *drift* and *tilt* can be shown graphically. Figure 8.7 illustrates that gyro drift will be maximum at the poles and zero at the equator, whilst gyro tilt is the reciprocal of this. At any intermediate latitude the gyro will suffer from both drift and tilt with the magnitude of each error being proportional to the sine and cosine of the latitude respectively.

When a gyro is placed exactly with its spin axis parallel to the spin axis of the earth at any latitude, the mechanism will maintain its direction relative to the earth. There is no tilt or azimuth movement and the gyro may be considered to be meridian stabilized. As the earth rotates the gyro will experience a movement under the influence of both tilt and azimuth motion.

The rate of *tilt* motion is given as:

$$tilt = 15° \cos latitude \text{ (degrees per hour)}$$

where 15° is the hourly rate of the earth's rotation and Azimuth is the angle formed between the gyrospin axis and the earth's spin axis.

$$Azimuth\ drift = 15° \sin latitude \text{ (degrees per hour)}$$

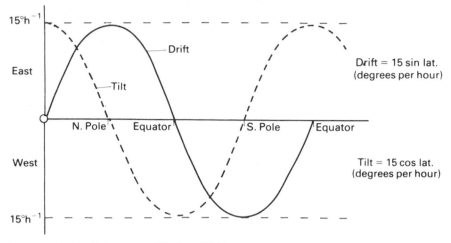

Fig. 8.7 The relationship between DRIFT and TILT

Movement over the earth's surface

The free gyroscope, as detailed so far, is of no practical use for navigation since its rotor axis is influenced by the earth's rotation and movement over the earth's surface. The stabilized gyroscopic change in position of longitude along a parallel of latitude requires a correction for the earth's rotary motion. Movement in latitude along a meridian of longitude involves rotation about an axis through the centre of the earth at right angles to its spin axis. Movement of the mechanism in any direction is simply a combination of the latitudinal and longitudinal motions. The faster the gyroscope moves the greater the rate of angular movement of the rotor axle attributable to these factors.

The controlled gyroscope

It has been stated that a free gyroscope suffers an apparent movement in both azimuth and tilt of the rotor axis depending upon its location in latitude. When fitted to a vessel the latitude is known and consequently the extent of movement in azimuth and tilt is known. It is possible therefore to calculate the necessary force required to produce a reciprocal action to correct the effect of apparent movement. A force can be applied to the gyro which will cause both azimuth and tilt precession to occur in opposition to the unwanted force caused by the gyro position of the earth. The amplitude of the reciprocal force must be exactly that of the force producing the unwanted movement, otherwise over or under correction may occur. If the negative feedback is correctly applied, the gyro will no longer seek a celestial point but will be terrestrially stabilized and will assume a fixed attitude. If the gyro is drifting in azimuth at 'N' degrees per hour in an anticlockwise direction, an upward force sufficient to cause clockwise precession at a rate of '$-N$' degrees per hour needs to be applied vertically to the appropriate end of the rotor axle. The result will be that the gyro drift is cancelled and the instrument points to a fixed point on earth. Gyro tilt movement can also be cancelled in a similar way by applying an equal and opposite force in a horizontal direction to the appropriate end of the rotor axle. Although the gyro is now stabilized to a terrestrial point it is not suitable for use as a navigating compass. The reasons for this are as follows:

(a) It is not north seeking. Since the recognized compass datum is north, this factor is the prime reason why such a gyro is not of use for navigation.

(b) It is liable to be unstable and will drift if the applied reciprocal forces are not precise.

(c) A complex system of different reciprocal forces needs to be applied due to continual changes in latitude.

(D) The mechanism is liable to drift due to precessional forces acting upon it through the friction of the gimbal bearings. This effect is not constant and is therefore difficult to compensate.

The north seeking gyro

The gyrospin axis can be made meridian seeking (maintaining the spin axis parallel to the earth's spin axis) by the use of a pendulum acting under the influence of earth gravity. The pendulum causes a force to act upon the gyro assembly which will precess under its influence. Precession, the second fundamental property of a gyroscope, enables the instrument to become north seeking. As the pendulum swings towards the centre of gravity a downward force is applied to the wheel axle, which in turn causes horizontal precession to occur. Thus gravitational force acting downward on the spinner axle causes the compass to precess horizontally to maintain the axle pointing towards true north.

The two main ways of achieving precessional action due to gravity are to make the gyro spin axis either bottom or top heavy. Bottom heavy control with a clockwise rotating gyro spinner is used by S. G. Brown Ltd in their range of compasses, whereas a top heavy system with an anticlockwise rotating spinner is favoured by Sperry Ltd. Figures 8.8(a) and (b) illustrate these two principles. In bottom heavy control, tilting upwards of the south end produces a downward force on the north end which for this direction of rotation produces a precession of the north end to the west. In top heavy control, tilting upwards of the north end of the gyro produces a downward force on the south end which for this direction of rotation produces a westerly precession of the north end. In each the system will produce the same result.

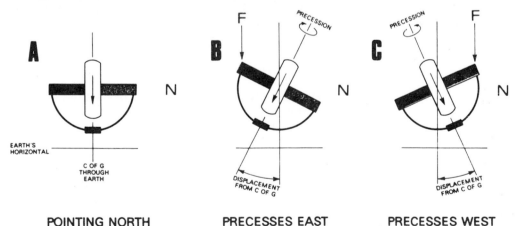

POINTING NORTH   **PRECESSES EAST**   **PRECESSES WEST**

Fig. 8.8(a) Principle of the gravity control (Courtesy of S. G. Brown Ltd.)

The S. G. Brown control system

Figure 8.8(a) illustrates the principle of precession caused by gravity acting on the bottom weighted spin axis of a gyroscope. The pendulous weight will always seek the centre of gravity and in so doing will exert a torque about the gyro horizontal axis. However, due to

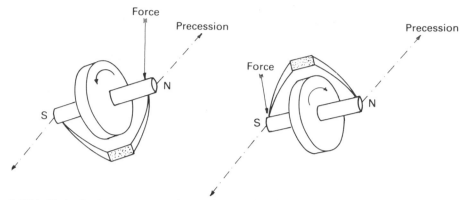

Fig. 8.8(b)   Methods of gravity control: bottom heavy principle and top heavy control

earth rotation and gyro rigidity the pendulum will cause the gravity control to move away from the centre of gravity. In the S. G. Brown gyrocompass the spinner is rotating clockwise when viewed from the south end. Precession, caused by the force exerted on the spin axis by gravity, will cause the north-east end of the spin axis to move to the east when it is below the horizontal. A reciprocal action will occur causing the north-east end of the spin axis to precess towards the west when above the horizontal. The spin axis will always appear to tilt with its north end away from the earth (up) when to the east of the meridian, and north end towards the earth (down) when to the west of the meridian because of the effect of earth rotation and gyro rigidity (see Figure 8.9). This action will cause the north end of the spin axis, of a gravity controlled undamped gyro, to describe an ellipse about the meridian. The gyro will not settle on the meridian. Figure 8.9 illustrates this action for a gyro with a clockwise rotating spinner. The ellipse produced will be anticlockwise due to the constant external influences acting upon the gyro. The extent of the ellipse will however vary depending upon the initial displacement of the gyro spin axis from the meridian and from the earth's horizontal. The term 'north seeking' is given to the undamped gravity controlled gyro mechanism because the north-east end of the spin axis describes an ellipse around the north pole and never settles. Obviously such a gyro is not suitable for use as a precise north reference compass aid.

The damped controlled gyro (*north settling*)
The ellipse described by the previous gyro mechanism possesses a constant ratio of the major and minor axes. Clearly therefore if the extent of one axis can be reduced, the length of the other axis will be reduced in proportion. Under these conditions the gyro spin axis will eventually settle both on the meridian and horizontally. If the gyro axis is influenced by a second force which exerts a damping torque about the vertical axis so as to cause the spin axis to move towards the horizontal it is obvious from figure 8.10 that the minor axis of the ellipse will be reduced. As the north end of the spin axis moves to the west of the meridian, earth rotation will cause a downward tilt of the axis. This effect and the torque (T_v) will cause the gyro axis to meet the earth's horizontal at point H, which is a considerable reduction in the ellipse major axis. As figure 8.10 clearly shows this action continues until the gyro settles in the meridian and to the surface of the earth.

The Sperry control system

Whereas the previous compass relies on a bottom weighed spin axis and a clockwise spinning rotor to produce a north settling action, the Sperry company design their gyrocompasses to be effectively top weighted and use an anticlockwise spinning rotor. Adding a weight to the top of the rotor casing produces a number of undesirable effects, as does a top heavy weight, as will be described later. The effects become pronounced when the vessel is subjected to severe movement in heavy weather. To counteract unwanted effects, an apparent top weighting of the compass is achieved by the use of mercury fluid ballistic contained in two reservoirs or pots. As shown in figure 8.11, each ballistic pot, partly filled with mercury, is mounted at the north and south sides of the rotor on the spin axis. A small bore tube connects the bases of each pot together providing a restricted path for the liquid to flow from one container to the other. The ballistic system is mounted in such a way that, when the gyro tilts, the fluid will also tilt and cause a displacement of mercury. This action produces a torque about the horizontal axis with a resulting precession in azimuth. Consider a controlled gyroscope to be at the equator with its spin axis east west as shown in figure 8.12. As the earth rotates west to east, the gyro will appear to tilt about its horizontal axis, the east end rising causing mercury to flow from pot A to pot B. The resulting unbalance of the ballistic will cause a torque about the horizontal axis. This causes precession about the vertical axis and the spin axis will move in azimuth towards the meridian. The right hand side of the gyro spin axis in figure 8.9 now moves towards the north and is referred to as the north end of the spin axis.

As has previously been described this type of gyro is north seeking only and will not settle in the meridian. The north end of the spin axis will therefore describe an ellipse as shown in figure 8.9. As the extent of the swings in azimuth and the degree of tilt are dependent upon each other, the gyro can be made to settle by the addition of an offset control force.

The gyrocompass

The apparent tilting of the gyroscope can be reduced by producing an offset controlling force which creates "anti-tilt" precession causing the unit to settle in the meridian. This is achieved by producing a force about the vertical axis to cause precession about the horizontal axis. In the Sperry gyro system the mercury ballistic controlling force is offset slightly to the east of the vertical. The point of offset attachment is carefully calculated to provide sufficient damping action to cause the gyro to settle in the meridian. A comparatively small force is required to produce the necessary anti-tilt precession for the gyrocompass to be made suitable for use as a navigation instrument.

Figure 8.10 illustrates the curve now described by the north end of the damped gyro-compass which will settle in the meridian. An alternative and more commonly used method of applying anti-tilt damping is illustrated in figure 8.13. The damping weight method provides a more readily adjustable system for applying damping. The period of gyro damping is directly related to the size of the damping force. If the weight is increased the damping percentage will be increased. The effect of alternative damping application is illustrated in figure 8.14.

Gyro damping

The amount of damping required depends upon the rate of tilt of the gyro axle and as such will be affected by latitude. As h as been shown previously, tilt is a maximum at the equator. It follows, therefore that damping should also be maximum at the equator. However, the damping period will always remain constant, at approximately 86 minutes for some gyros, despite the change of amplitude of successive swings to east and west of the gyro axle. Figure 8.15 shows a typical settling curve for a gyro with a 75 minute damping period. The time taken for one oscillation, from A1 to A3 is termed the natural period of the compass. For the SR120 this is stated to be 75 minutes for a gyro approximately initiated

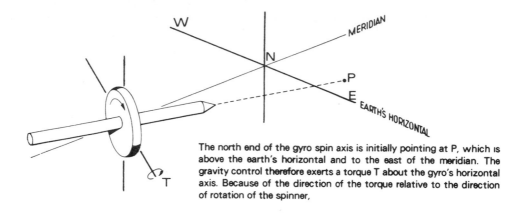

The north end of the gyro spin axis is initially pointing at P, which is above the earth's horizontal and to the east of the meridian. The gravity control therefore exerts a torque T about the gyro's horizontal axis. Because of the direction of the torque relative to the direction of rotation of the spinner,

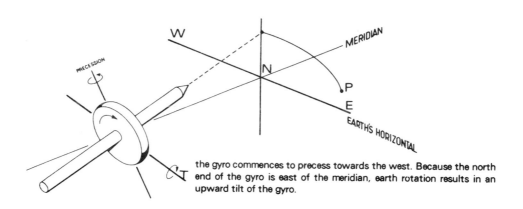

the gyro commences to precess towards the west. Because the north end of the gyro is east of the meridian, earth rotation results in an upward tilt of the gyro.

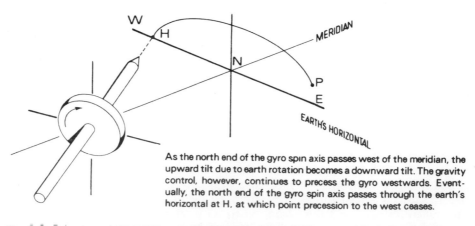

As the north end of the gyro spin axis passes west of the meridian, the upward tilt due to earth rotation becomes a downward tilt. The gravity control, however, continues to precess the gyro westwards. Eventually, the north end of the gyro spin axis passes through the earth's horizontal at H, at which point precession to the west ceases.

Fig. 8.9 Behaviour of the gravity-controlled gyro (undamped) (Courtesy of S. G. Brown Ltd.)

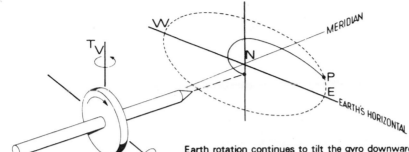

Earth rotation continues to tilt the gyro downwards, and once the gyro spin axis is below the earth's horizontal the gravity control again exerts torques T_H and T_V, but this time in an opposite direction. Torque T_H now causes precession eastwards, whilst torque T_V causes precession upwards and thus damps the downward tilt that is due to earth rotation. The resultant movement of the gyro causes the north end of the gyro spin axis to pass through the meridian at a point that reduces even more the minor axis of the ellipse.

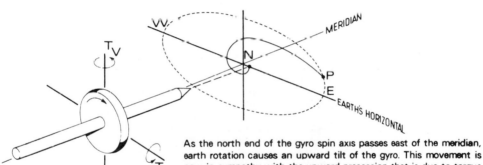

As the north end of the gyro spin axis passes east of the meridian, earth rotation causes an upward tilt of the gyro. This movement is now in sympathy with the upward precession that is due to torque T_V. The north end of the gyro spin axis thus passes through the earth's horizontal at a point that reduces even more the major axis of the ellipse.

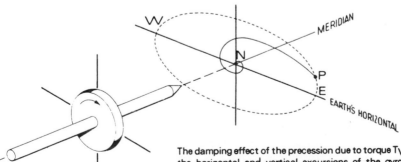

The damping effect of the precession due to torque T_V continues, with the horizontal and vertical excursions of the gyro spin axis being progressively reduced until the gyro finally settles in the meridian and horizontal to the earth's surface.

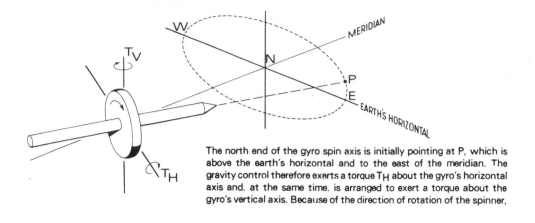

The north end of the gyro spin axis is initially pointing at P, which is above the earth's horizontal and to the east of the meridian. The gravity control therefore exerts a torque T_H about the gyro's horizontal axis and, at the same time, is arranged to exert a torque about the gyro's vertical axis. Because of the direction of rotation of the spinner,

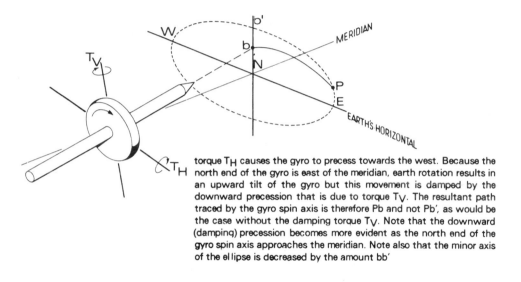

torque T_H causes the gyro to precess towards the west. Because the north end of the gyro is east of the meridian, earth rotation results in an upward tilt of the gyro but this movement is damped by the downward precession that is due to torque T_V. The resultant path traced by the gyro spin axis is therefore Pb and not Pb', as would be the case without the damping torque T_V. Note that the downward (damping) precession becomes more evident as the north end of the gyro spin axis approaches the meridian. Note also that the minor axis of the ellipse is decreased by the amount bb'

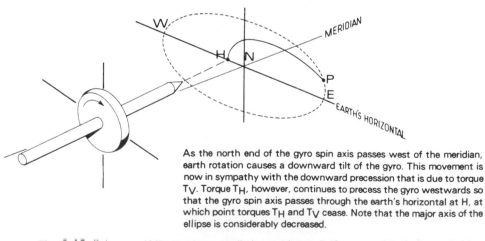

As the north end of the gyro spin axis passes west of the meridian, earth rotation causes a downward tilt of the gyro. This movement is now in sympathy with the downward precession that is due to torque T_V. Torque T_H, however, continues to precess the gyro westwards so that the gyro spin axis passes through the earth's horizontal at H, at which point torques T_H and T_V cease. Note that the major axis of the ellipse is considerably decreased.

Fig. 8.10 Behaviour of the gravity-controlled gyro (damped) (Courtesy of S. G. Brown Ltd.)

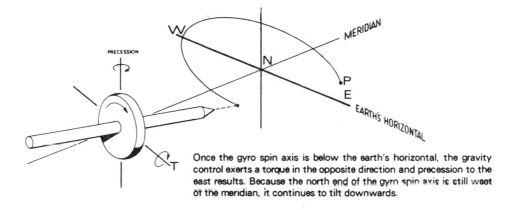

Once the gyro spin axis is below the earth's horizontal, the gravity control exerts a torque in the opposite direction and precession to the east results. Because the north end of the gyro spin axis is still west of the meridian, it continues to tilt downwards.

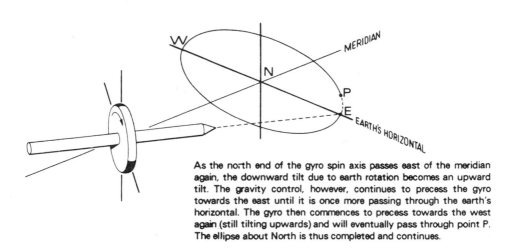

As the north end of the gyro spin axis passes east of the meridian again, the downward tilt due to earth rotation becomes an upward tilt. The gravity control, however, continues to precess the gyro towards the east until it is once more passing through the earth's horizontal. The gyro then commences to precess towards the west again (still tilting upwards) and will eventually pass through point P. The ellipse about North is thus completed and continues.

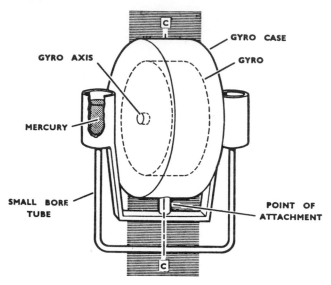

Fig. 8.11 A method of applying 'offset damping' to the gyro wheel (Courtesy of Sperry Ltd.)

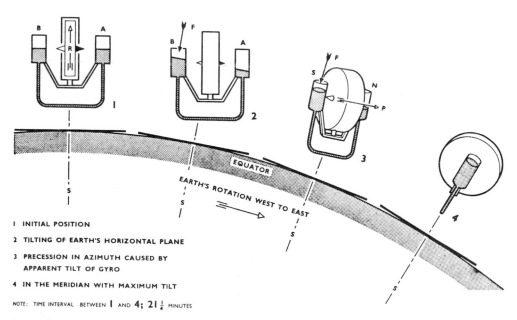

1 INITIAL POSITION

2 TILTING OF EARTH'S HORIZONTAL PLANE

3 PRECESSION IN AZIMUTH CAUSED BY
   APPARENT TILT OF GYRO

4 IN THE MERIDIAN WITH MAXIMUM TILT

NOTE: TIME INTERVAL BETWEEN 1 AND 4; $21\frac{1}{4}$ MINUTES

Fig. 8.12 A controlled gyroscope at the equator

In the meridian at a latitude of 35 degrees. From this graph the damping percentage may be easily calculated as follows:

$$\left(\frac{A2 - A3}{A1 - A2} \times 100\right)\%$$

For the SR120 this is approximately 30%.

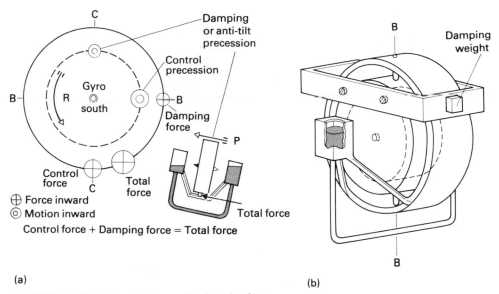

(a)   (b)

Fig. 8.13(a) Effect of control force plus damping force
     (b) An alternative method of applying offset damping (Courtesy of Sperry Ltd.)

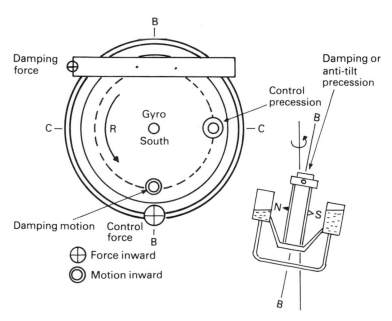

Fig. 8.14 The effect of alternative damping application

The amount of tilt remaining on a settled gyro

The settling curve traced by the north end of the gyrospin axis illustrated in figure 8.10 assumes that the gyrocompass is situated at the equator and will, therefore, not be affected by gyro tilt. It is more likely that a vessel will be at some north/south latitude and

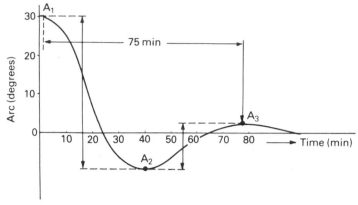

Fig. 8.15 The damping curve of the Sperry SR120

consequently drift must be taken into account. It has been stated that for a gyrocompass in northern latitudes, the gyrospin axis will drift to the east of the meridian and tilt upwards. For any fixed latitude the easterly drift is constant. Westerly precession, however, is directly proportional to the angle of tilt of the rotor axle from the horizontal, which itself is dependent upon the deviation between it and the meridian. At some point the easterly deviation of the north end of the spin axis produces an angle of tilt causing a rate of westerly precession which is equal and opposite to the easterly drift. The north end, although pointing to the east of the meridian, is now stabilized in azimuth.

As the north end moves easterly away from the meridian both the rate of change of the tilt angle and the angle itself are increasing. The increasing angle of tilt produces an increasing rate of downward damping tilt until a point is reached where the upward and downward rates of tilt cancel. The north end of the axle is above the horizontal although the rotor axle is stabilized. Figure 8.16 shows that the gyrocompass has settled, at point 0, to the east of the meridian and is tilted up. The extent of the easterly and northerly (azimuth and tilt) error in the settled position is determined by latitude. An increase in latitude causes an increase in both the easterly deviation from the meridian and the angle of tilt above the horizontal. It is necessary therefore for latitude error, as the discrepancy is called, to be corrected in a gyrocompass.

As latitude increases, the effect of earth rotation becomes progressively less and consequently tilting of the rotor axle becomes less. It follows therefore that the rate of damping precession needed to cancel the rate of tilt, also will be less.

Follow up systems

A stationary gravity controlled gyrocompass will adequately settle close to the horizontal and near to the meridian provided that it has freedom to move about the horizontal and vertical axes. However, if the gyrocompass is to be mounted on a ship, the base (phantom) ring needs to be capable of rotating through 360 degrees without introducing torque about the vertical axis.

Freedom about the vertical axis is particularly difficult to achieve without introducing torque to the system. The most common way of permitting vertical axis freedom is to mount the gyro in a vertical ring with ball bearings on the top and base plates. Obviously the weight of the unit must be borne on the lower bearing which can create considerable friction and introduce torque. A number of methods have been developed to eliminate

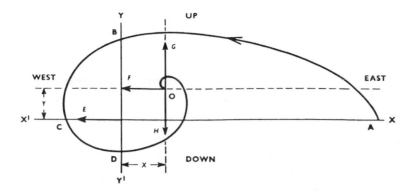

E: RATE OF WESTERLY MOVEMENT OF MERIDIAN CAUSED BY TURNTABLE MOVEMENT OF THE EARTH'S SURFACE	F: RATE OF WESTERLY PRECESSION OF THE GYRO CAUSED BY THE NORTH END HAVING TILTED UPWARDS
G: RATE OF UPWARD TILT OF NORTH END OF SPIN AXIS DUE TO GYRO SETTLING TO EAST OF MERIDIAN	H: RATE OF DOWNWARD PRECESSION OF NORTH END OF SPIN AXIS DUE TO DAMPING (ANTI-TILT) PRECESSION

Fig. 8.16 A curve showing error to the east and tilt caused by latitude of a settled gyrocompass. X is the angle away from the meridian and Y is the angle with the horizon (tilt). (Courtesy of Sperry Ltd.)

torque about the vertical axis. These include the use of high tensile torsion wires and buoyancy chambers as described for each compass later in this chapter.

8.2 Compass errors

The accuracy of a gyrocompass is of paramount importance, particularly under manoeuvring situations where the compass is interfaced with a collision avoidance radar system. An error, either existing or produced, between the actual compass reading and that presented to the radar could produce potentially catastrophic results.

Assuming that the compass has been correctly installed and aligned, the fixed compass errors briefly listed below, should have been eliminated. They are, however, worthy of a brief mention.

Fixed errors

An alignment error can be:
(a) an error existing between the indicated heading and the vessel's lubber line, or
(b) an error existing between the indicated lubber line and the fore and aft line of the vessel. Both these errors can be accurately eliminated by critically aligning the compass and the lubber line at installation.

Transmission errors
An error existing between the indicated heading on the master compass and the heading produced by any remote repeater is a transmission error. Transmission errors are kept to a minimum by the use of multispeed pulse transmission.

Variable errors

Variable compass errors can effectively be classified into two groups.
(a) Dynamic Errors which are caused by the angular motion of the vessel during heavy weather and manoeuvring.
(b) Speed/Latitude Errors which are caused by movement of the vessel across the earth's surface.
The magnitude of each error can be reduced to some extent as shown in the following text.

Dynamic errors: rolling error
The gyrocompass is made to settle on the meridian under the influence of weights, thus it will also be caused to shift due to other forms of acceleration acting upon the same weights. When a vessel rolls, the compass is swung like a pendulum causing a twisting motion which tends to move the plane of the sensitive element towards the plane of the swing. For a simple explanation of the error consider the surge of mercury caused in both the north and south reservoirs by a vessel rolling.

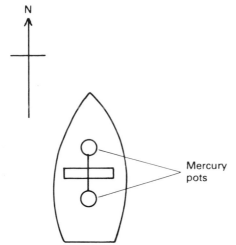

Fig. 8.17 A ship steaming due north or south produces no roll error

If the ship is steaming due north or south, no redistribution of mercury occurs due to roll and there will be no error (see figure 8.17). With a ship steaming due east or west, maximum lateral acceleration occurs in the north/south direction causing precession of the compass. However, rolls to port and starboard will be equal producing equivalent easterly and westerly precession. The resultant mean error is therefore zero, as illustrated in figure 8.18.

If the ship is on an intercardinal course the force exerted by the mercury (or pendulum) must be resolved into north/south and east/west components (see figure 8.19).

The result of the combined forces is that precession of the compass occurs under the influence of an effective anticlockwise torque. Rolling error can be dramatically reduced by damping the pendulum system. In a Sperry gyrocompass this is achieved by restricting the flow of mercury between the two pots. The damping delay introduced needs to be shorter than the damping period of the compass and much greater than the period of roll of the vessel. Both of these conditions are easily achieved. Electrically controlled compasses are roll damped by the use of a viscous fluid to damp movement of the gravity

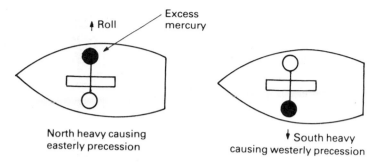

Fig. 8.18 Precession rates due to vessel rolling are equal and will cancel

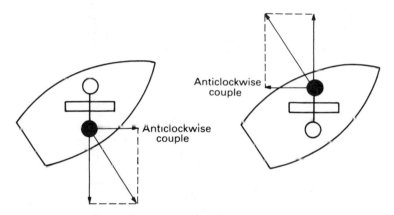

Fig. 8.19 Rolling produces an anticlockwise torque for a vessel on an intercardinal course

pendulum. Such a fluid is identified by a manufacturer's code and a viscosity number. For example, in the code number 200/20, 200 refers to the manufacturer and 20 the viscosity. A higher second number indicates a more viscous silicon fluid. One viscous fluid should never be substituted for another bearing a different code number. Additionally since roll error is caused by lateral acceleration, mounting the gyrocompass low in the vessel and as close as possible to the centre of roll will reduce the error still further.

Dynamic errors: manoeuvring (ballistic) error
The error occurs whenever the ship is subject to rapid changes of speed or heading. Because of its pendulous nature, the compass gravity control moves away from the centre of gravity whenever the vessel changes speed or alters course. Torques produced about the horizontal and vertical axis by manoeuvring, cause the gyro mechanism to precess in both azimuth and tilt. If the ship is steaming due north and rapidly reducing speed, mercury will continue to flow into the north pot, or the gravity pendulum continues to swing, making the gyro spin axis north heavy and thus causing a precession in azimuth. In figure 8.20 the decelerating vessel causes easterly precession of the compass. Alternatively if the ship increases speed the compass precesses to the west.

Latitude (damping) error
Latitude error is a constant error the magnitude of which is directly proportional to the earth's rotation at any given latitude. It is, therefore, present even when the ship is

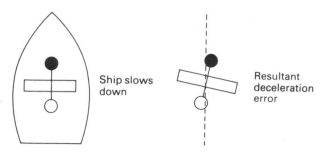

Fig. 8.20 Resultant easterly error caused by the vessel slowing down

stationary. As has been previously stated a gyrocompass will always settle close to the meridian with an error in tilt. To maintain the gyro pointing north it must be precessed at an angular rate varying with latitude. At the equator the earth's linear speed of rotation is about 900 knots and rotation from west to east causes a fixed point to effectively move at [900 $\times$ cos (latitude)] knots in an easterly direction. For any latitude (λ) the rate of earth spin is $\omega = 15°$ per hour which may be resolved into two components, one about the true vertical at a given latitude ($\omega \sin \lambda$) and the other about the north/south earth surface horizontal at a given latitude ($\omega \cos \lambda$) as illustrated in figure 8.21. The component of earth rotation about the north/south horizontal may be resolved further into two components mutually at right angles to each other. The first component is displaced $a°$ to the east of the meridian producing a rate of spin $\omega \cos \lambda \, a°$, whilst the other is $90° - a°$ to the west of north to produce a rate of spin $\omega \cos \lambda \cos a°$.

Correction for latitude error requires that a torque be applied to precess the gyro at an angular rate, varying with latitude, to cancel the error. This will be an external correction which can be either mechanical or electronic. For mechanical correction a weight on the gyro case provides the necessary torque. The weight, or "mechanical latitude rider", is made to move enabling corrections to be made for varying latitudes. Another method of mechanical correction is to move the lubber line by an amount equal to the error. This method is detailed in section 8.5. Latitude corection in the S. G. Brown Mk 1 compass is achieved by the introduction of a signal which is proportional to the sine of the vessel's latitude, to cause the gyro ball to precess in azimuth at a rate equal and opposite to the apparent drift caused by earth rotation.

Speed and course error
If a vessel makes good a northerly or southerly course, the north end of the gyro spin axis will apparently tilt up or down since the curvature of the earth causes the ship to effectively tilt bows up or down with respect to space. Consider a ship steaming due north. The north end of the spin axis tilts upwards causing a westerly precession of the compass, which will finally settle with the meridian with some error in the angle, the magnitude of which is determined by the speed of the ship. On a cardinal course due east or west, the ship will display a tilt in the east/west plane of the gyro and no tilting of the gyro axle occurs – hence no speed error is produced. The error varies, therefore, with the cosine of the ship's course. Speed/course gyrocompass error magnitude must also be affected by latitude which has previously been shown to produce an angle of tilt in the settled gyro. Hence speed/course error is sometimes referred to as L. C. S. error,

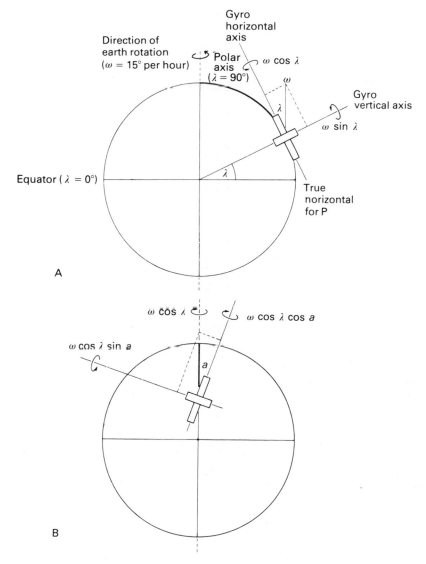

Fig. 8.21 Apparent movement of the gyro (Courtesy of S. G. Brown Ltd.)

Use of vectors in calculating errors (*see figure* 8.22)

V = ship's speed in knots $V \sin \alpha$ = Easterly component of speed

α = ship's course $v \cos \alpha$ = Northerly component of speed

angle acb = angle dcb

angle abc = angle bdc = 90 degrees

angle bac = angle cbd = θ = error

In triangle abc:

Error in degrees = angle bac = θ = $\tan^{-1} \dfrac{V \cos (\text{course})}{900 \cos (\text{latitude}) + V \sin (\text{course})}$

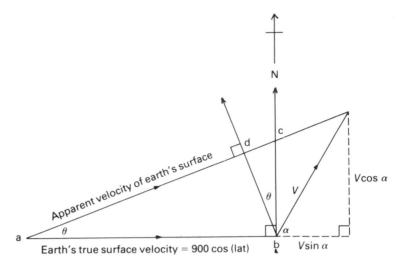

Fig. 8.22 Use of vectors in calculating errors

Obviously the ship's speed is very much less than the velocity of the earth's suface therefore:

$$\tan \theta \approx \frac{V \cos (\text{course})}{900 \cos (\text{latitude})}$$

The angle θ may be approximately expressed in degrees by multiplying both sides by sixty.

$$\text{Approximate error in degrees} = \frac{V \cos (\text{course})}{15 \cos (\text{latitude})}$$

8.3 Principle of the Sperry SR120 gyrocompass apparatus

The master compass, shown in figure 8.23, consists of two main assemblies, the stationary element and the movable element.

The stationary element

This is the main supporting frame which holds and encases the movable element. It consists of the main frame and base, together with the binnacle and mounting shock absorbers. The top of the main support frame (11) (figure 8.23) holds the slip rings, lubber line and the scale illumination circuitry, whilst the main shaft, connected to the phantom ring (12), protrudes through the supporting frame to hold the compass card visible from above.

A high quality ball bearing race supports the movable element on the base of the main support frame in order that movement in azimuth can be achieved. The base of the assembly consists of upper and lower base plates which are connected at their centre by a shaft. Rotation of the upper plate in relation to the lower plate enables mechanical latitude correction to be made. The latitude corrector (16) is provided with upper and lower latitude scales which are graduated in ten units, up to 70° north or south latitude, either side of zero. Also supported by the base plate are the azimuth servo motor and gear train, and the bearing stepper transmitter.

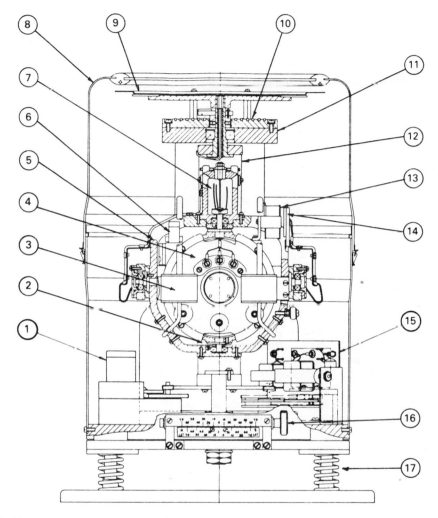

Fig. 8.23 A south elevation sectional view of the Sperry SR120 master compass (Courtesy of Sperry Ltd.)

1. Stepper transmitter
2. Support ball bearings
3. Ballistic posts
4. Rotor (encased)
5. Rotor case
6. Damping weight
7. Suspension wire
8. Cover
9. Compass card
10. Slip rings
11. Main support frame
12. Phantom ring support assembly (cutaway)
13. Follow-up primary transformer
14. Follow-up secondary transformer
15. Follow-up amplifier
16. Latitude corrector
17. Spring/shock absorber assembly

The movable element (figure 8.24)

With the exception of the phantom ring, the movable element is the sensitive element. At the heart of the unit is the gyro rotor freely spinning at approximately 12 000 r.p.m. The

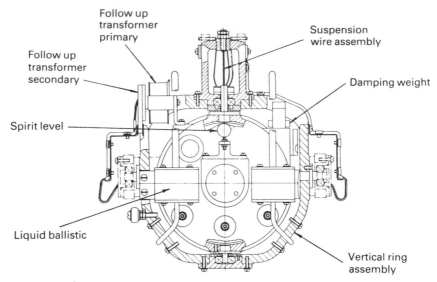

Fig. 8.24 The Sperry SR120 sensitive element (Courtesy of Sperry Ltd.)

rotor is 110 mm in diameter and 60 mm thick and forms, along with the stator windings, a three phase induction motor. Gyroscopic inertia is produced by the angular momentum of the rapidly spinning heavy rotor. Rotation is counter clockwise (counter earthwise) when viewed from the south end.

A sensitive spirit level graduated to represent 2 minutes of arc, is mounted on the north side of the rotor case. This unit indicates the tilt of the sensitive element. A damping weight is attached to the west side of the rotor case in order that oscillation of the gyro axis can be damped and thus enable the compass to point north.

The rotor case is suspended, along the vertical axis, inside the vertical ring frame by means of the suspension wire (7). This wire is a bunch of six thin stainless steel wires which are produced to be absolutely free from torsion. Their function is to support the weight of the gyro and thus remove the load from the support bearings (2).

TILT stabilization (liquid ballistic)

To enable the compass to develop a north seeking action, two ballistic pots (3) are mounted to the north and south sides of the vertical ring. Each pot possesses two reservoirs which contain the liquid 'Daifloil'. Like mercury, Daifloil has a high density. Each north/south pair of pots is connected by top and bottom pipes providing a total liquid/air sealed system which operates to produce the effect of top heaviness.

Because the vertical ring and the rotor case are coupled to each other, the ring follows the *tilt* of the gyro spin axis. Liquid in the ballistic system, when tilted, will generate a torque which is proportional to the angle of the *tilt*. The torque thus produced causes a precession in *azimuth* and starts the north seeking action of the compass. For the operation of this mechanism see the Sperry Gyro ballistic principles in the previous section of this chapter.

Azimuth stabilization (phantom ring assembly)

Gyro freedom of the north/south axis is enabled by the phantom ring and gearing. This ring is a vertical circle which supports the north/south sides of the horizontal ring (on the spin axis) by means of high precision ball bearings.

A small oil damper (6) is mounted on the south side of the sensitive element to provide gyro stabilization during the ship's pitching and rolling.

The compass card is mounted on the top of the upper phantom ring stem shaft and the lower stem shaft is connected to the support ball bearings enabling rotation of the north/south axis. The *azimuth* gearing, located at the lower end of the phantom ring, provides freedom about this axis under a torque from the *azimuth* servo motor and feedback system.

Azimuth follow-up system (figue 8.25)

This system enables the phantom ring to follow any movvement of the vertical ring. The unit senses the displacement signal produced by misalignment of the two rings, and amplifies the small signal to a power level of sufficient amplitude to drive the *azimuth* servo rotor. Movement of the *azimuth* servo rotor causes rotation, by direct coupling, of the phantom ring assembly in the required direction to keep the two rings aligned.

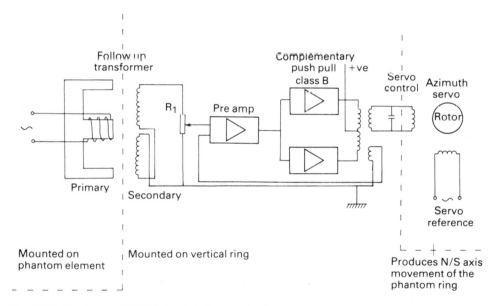

Fig. 8.25 The Sperry SR120 Azimuth follow up circuit

The sensing element of the follow-up system is a transformer which has an 'E' shaped laminated core with a single primary winding supplied with an a.c. the two secondary windings are connected, as shown in figure 8.25, to feed a pre-amplifier. With the 'E' shaped primary core in its central position, the phase of the e.m.f.s. induced in the two secondaries is such that they will cancel and the total voltage produced across R1 is the supply voltage only. This is the stable condition during which no rotation of the *azimuth* servo rotor occurs. If there is misalignment in any direction between the phantom and the vertical rings, the two e.m.f.s. induced in the two secondaries will be unbalanced and the voltage across R1 will increase or decrease accordingly. This error signal is pre-amplified and used to drive a complementary push/pull power amplfier which produces the necessary signal level, causing the *azimuth* servo to rotate in the required direction to re-align the rings and thus cancel the error signal. Negative feedback from T2 secondary to the pre-amplifier ensures stable operation of the system.

Latitude correction

Latitude correction is achieved by mechanically rotating the movable element relative to the stationary element thus producing a shift in *azimuth*. The fixed scale of the latitude adjuster (16 in figure 8.23) is secured to the stationary element with a second scale fixed to the movable element. To set the correction value, which should be within 5° of the ship's latitude, it is simply a matter of aligning the ship's latitude on the lower scale with the same indication on the upper scale of the vernier.

8.4 Sperry SR220 gyrocompass

At the heart of the gyrocompass is the gyrosphere which is contained within a unit called the sensitive element. The gyrowheel, 98 mm in diameter by 30 mm thick, forms part of a three phase squirrel cage induction motor the power leads for which form the dual purpose of suspending the gyrosphere inside the sensitive element unit as shown in figure 8.26.

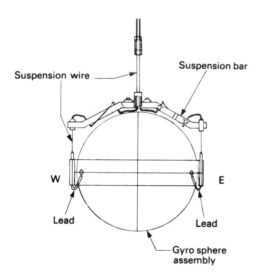

Fig. 8.26 The Sperry SR220 Gyrosphere (Courtesy of Sperry Ltd.)

Spinning at 12 000 r.p.m. the gyrowheel is typical of many current Sperry gyrowheels. However, the rotor spins clockwise when viewed from the south end of the spin axis. The significance of this is that for northerly precession to occur, the gyro must unlike all Sperry gyros before it, be effectively bottom heavy. When assembled the gyrosphere containing the gyroscope is watertight and is hung on ultrafine suspension wires from a supporting bar assembly. To obtain near neutral buoyancy (the sphere is slightly heavy to damp oscillations due to bouncing) the unit is immersed in a high viscosity silicon liquid, contained by the outer casing of the sensitive element. A viscous damping device is fitted at the base of the lower housing to reduce errors due to the vessel pitching and rolling. This device is designed to control the clearance between the gyrosphere and the hemisphere (see figure 8.27). Damping is factory adjusted by varying the clearance between the

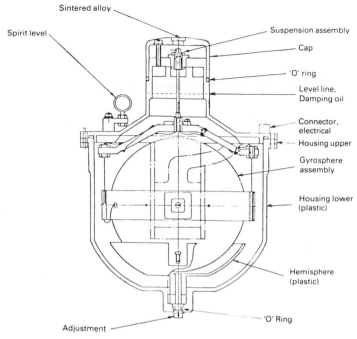

Fig. 8.27 The Sperry SR220 sensitive element (Courtesy of Sperry Ltd.)

gyrosphere and the plastic hemisphere to prevent rapid movement of the gyrosphere within the sensitive element assembly.

The entire sensitive element assembly is supported by a mounting ring which pivots about a horizontal axis in the horizontal ring. One advantage of this design is that the complete sensitive element unit may be easily replaced should servicing be necessary.

Simplified description of follow up

Figure 8.28 is a simplified diagram of the gyrosphere inside the sensitive element chamber. In practice only a few millimeters separate the sphere from the sensitive element chamber. The point of connection of the suspension wires with the gyrosphere, is deliberately made slightly above the centre line of the sphere on the east west axis. At the north south ends of the horizontal axis are mounted the primary coils of the follow up pick off transformers. With no tilt present, the sphere will be horizontal and central causing distance x to be equal to distance y producing equal amplitude outputs from the follow up transformers which will cancel. Assuming the gyrocompass is tilted up and to the east of the meridian, the gyrosphere will take up the position shown in figure 8.28. The sphere has moved closer to the south side of the chamber producing a difference in the distances x and y. The two pick off secondary coils will now produce outputs which are no longer in balance. Difference signals thus produced are directly proportional to both azimuth and tilt error.

Each pick off transformer is formed by a primary mounted on the gyrosphere and secondary pick off coils mounted on the sensitive element assembly. The primary coils provide a magnetic field, from the 110 V a.c. supply used for the gyrowheel rotor, which couples with the secondary to produce e.m.f.s. depending upon the relationship between the two coils. Figure 8.29 illustrates that the secondary coils are wound in such a way that

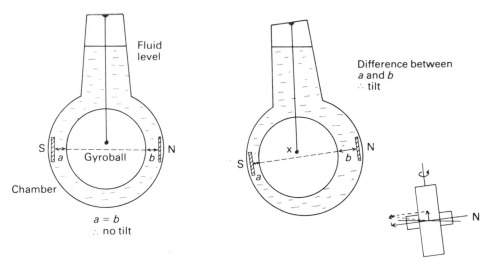

Fig. 8.28 A simplified version of the action of the gyroball inside a gyroscope

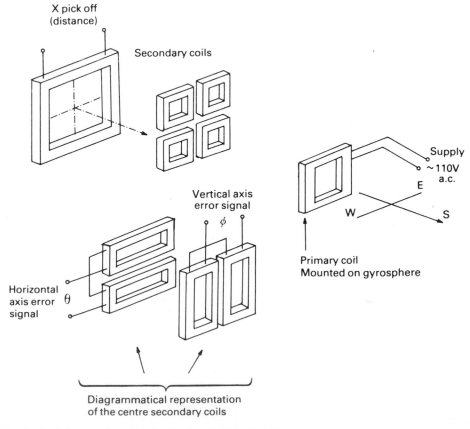

Fig. 8.29 Follow-up pick off coils (Courtesy of Sperry Ltd.)

One or more of the three output signals is produced by relative movement of the gyrosphere. In the figure,

X = a signal correspoonding to the distance of the sphere from each secondary coil

ϕ = a signal corresponding to vertical movement

θ = a signal corresponding to horizontal movement

Figure 8.30 illustrates the SR220 follow-up system. The horizontal servo mechanism, mounted on the west side of the horizontal ring, permits the sensitive element to follow up the gyrosphere about the horizontal axis. This servo operates from the difference signal θ produced by the secondary pick off coils. Difference signal ϕ is processed to provide the amplitude required to drive the sensitive element assembly in azimuth by rotating the phantom yoke assembly in the direction required to cancel the error signal. In this way the azimuth follow up circuit keeps the gyrosphere and sensitive element chamber in alignment as the gyro precesses.

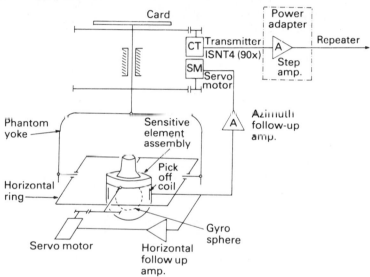

Fig. 8.30 The SR220 follow-up system (Courtesy of Sperry Ltd.)

8.5 Principles of the S. G. Brown MK.1 model 5 (C) gyrocompass

The central gyroscopic element of the system is called the "sensitive" element and is illustrated in figure 8.31. It is convenient to compare the sensitive element components with those of a free gyroscope on which the system is based (see figures 8.1 and 8.32).

Free Gyroscope	Sensitive element
The gyro spinner	The rotor of an induction motor with a heavy spinner attached at each end of the shaft
Horizontal and vertical axis pivots	A pair of torsion wires on each axis
Balanced gimbal assembly	The alloy gimbal and support torsion wires
Mounting platform	The tank case

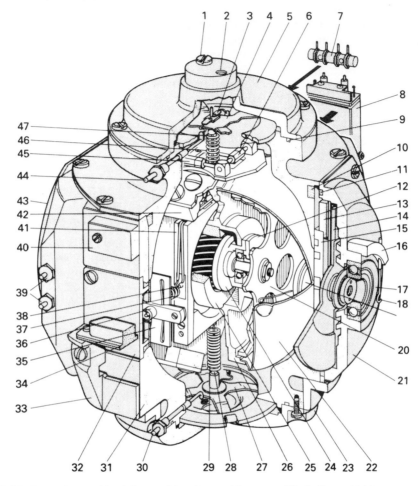

Fig. 8.31 General assembly of the sensitive element (Courtesy of S. G. Brown Ltd.)

1. Filler screw or plug
2. Breather (linen filter)
3. Flexible connection (terminal lug)
4. Top cruciform (support spring)
5. Tank top cover
6. Adjustable weights
7. Terminal block
8. Pendulum assembly
9. 'O' ring – medium
10. 'O' ring – large
11. 'O' ring – medium
12. Adaptor and plate (motor bearing housing)
13. Pick-up coil clamp
14. Rotary damp disc
15. Pick-up coil
16. Brush block

17. Ballrace (north)
18. Brush
19. Magnet assembly
20. Gyro wheel (one of two)
21. Cover
22. End bell (one of two)
23. Tank bottom cover
24. Rotor
25. Stator
26. Wheel case
27. Bottom cruciform (support spring)
28. Bottom vertical torsion wire
29. Bottom flex current – vertical
30. Terminal E3
31. Tank body
32. Adaptor stop
33. Bracket

34. Terminal block
35. East horizontal spring
36. East (stop)
37. East horizontal torsion wire
38. East horizontal flex current
39. Terminals E9, E10
40. Balance weight
41. Primary gimbal
42. Weight
43. Rotary damp
44. Terminal E4
45. Weight (adjustable)
46. Top flex current – vertical
47. Top vertical torsion wire

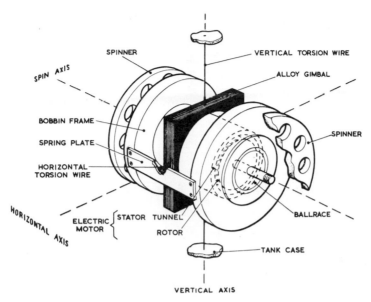

Fig. 8.32 The gyroscopic element. Compare with Fig. 8.31 for the equivalence of gyroscope components (Courtesy of S. G. Brown Ltd.)

The entire sensitive element is contained within a pair of thin walled aluminium hemispheres joined as shown in figure 8.33, to form the "gyroball". At the heart of this ball is a 3 phase induction motor, the rotor of which protrudes through the central bobbin assembly but is able to rotate because of the high quality support bearings. At each end of the rotor shaft, a heavy rimmed gyro spinner is attached to provide the necessary angular momentum for gyroscopic action to be established. Rotational speed of the induction motor is approximately 12 000 r.p.m.

The gyroball is centred within the tank by means of two vertical and two horizontal torsion wires which form virtually friction free pivots. The torsion wires permit small controlling torques to be applied in both the vertical and the horizontal axes to cause precessions of the axes in both *tilt* and *azimuth*. Additionally the torsion wires are used to route electrical supplies to the motor. The gyroball assembly is totally immersed in a viscous fluid called Halocarbon Wax, the specific gravity of which gives the ball neutral buoyancy, at normal operating temperatures, so that no mass acts on the torsion wires.

The tank containing the gyroball sensitive element is further suspended in a secondary gimbal system, as shown in figure 8.34, to permit free movement of the spin axis. This axis is now termed the "free-swing axis" which under normal operating conditions is horizontal and in line with the local meridian. The secondary gimbal system also permits movement about the east/west axis. Each of the movable axes in the secondary gimbal system can be controlled by a servo motor, which in turn provides both *tilt* and *azimuth* control of the gyroball, via a network of feedback amplifiers. An electromagnetic pick-up system initiates the signal feedback system which maintains, via the secondary gimbals and servo motors, the gyro free-swing (spin) axis in alignment with the north/south axis of the tank. If there is no twist in the two pairs of torsion wires, and no spurious torques are present about the spin axis, no precession of the gyroball occurs and there will be no movement of the control servo motors. As can be seen in figure 8.33 the gyro spin axis is in line with a magnet mounted in each hemisphere of the gyroball. Pick-up coils are mounted on the north/south ends of the containment tank and are arranged so that when the gyro-

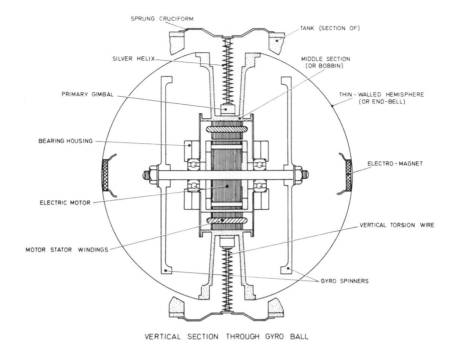

VERTICAL SECTION THROUGH GYRO BALL

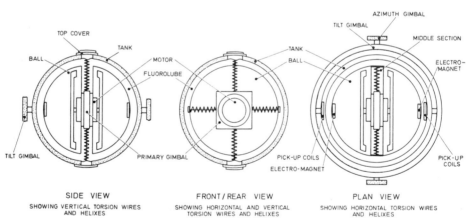

| SIDE VIEW | FRONT/REAR VIEW | PLAN VIEW |
| SHOWING VERTICAL TORSION WIRES AND HELIXES | SHOWING HORIZONTAL AND VERTICAL TORSION WIRES AND HELIXES | SHOWING HORIZONTAL TORSION WIRES AND HELIXES |

Fig. 8.33 Arrangement of the gyroball (Courtesy of S. G. Brown Ltd.)

ball is in alignment with the tank, no output from the coils is produced. If any misalignment occurs, output voltages are produced, from the fixed coils, which are proportional to the displacement in both *tilt* and *azimuth*. The small e.m.f.s. thus produced are amplified and fed back as control voltages to re-align the axis by precession caused by movement of the secondary gimbal system. The amplified *tilt* and *azimuth* voltages produced are used to drive the secondary gimbal servo motors in such a direction as to cancel the sensor pick-up voltages and so maintain the correct alignment of the gyroball within the tank.

With a means of tank/gyroball alignment thus established, controlled precessions are produced as follows: (see figure 8.35), to precess the gyroball in *azimuth* only, an external signal is injected into the *tilt* amplifier. The null signal condition of the pick-up coils is now

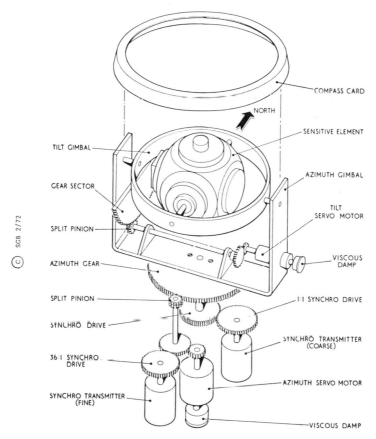

Fig. 8.34 Schematic arrangement of the S. G. Brown MK.1 model 5 (C) secondary gimbals

unbalanced and an output is produced and bed back to drive the *tilt* servo motor. This in turn drives the *tilt* secondary gimbal system to a position in which the *tilt* pick-up coil misalignment voltage is equal and opposite to the external voltage applied to the amplifier. The *tilt* servo feedback loop is now nulled, but with the tank and gyroball out of alignment in a *tilt* mode. A twist is thus produced of the horizontal torsion wires, producing a torque about the horizontal axis of the gyroball and causing it to precess in *azimuth*. As *azimuth* precesion occurs, *azimuth* misalignment of the tank/gyroball also occurs but this is detected by the *azimuth* pick-up coils. The *azimuth* servo motor now drives the secondary gimbal to rotate the tank in *azimuth* to seek cancellation of the error signal. Since the *azimuth* secondary gimbal maintains a fixed position relative to the gyro spin axis in *azimuth*, a direct heading indication is produced on the compass card which is mounted on this gimbal.

Control of the sensitive element in *tilt* is produced in a similar way. Therefore signals injected into the *tilt* and *azimuth* servo loops, having a sign and amplitude that produce the required precessional directions and rates, will achieve total control of the gyrocompass.

It is relatively simple to further control the gyroball by the introduction of additional signals because each of the feedback loops is essentially an electrical loop. One such signal is produced by the "gravity sensor" or "pendulum unit". The pendulum unit replaces the liquid ballistic system favoured by some manufacturers to produce gravity control of the

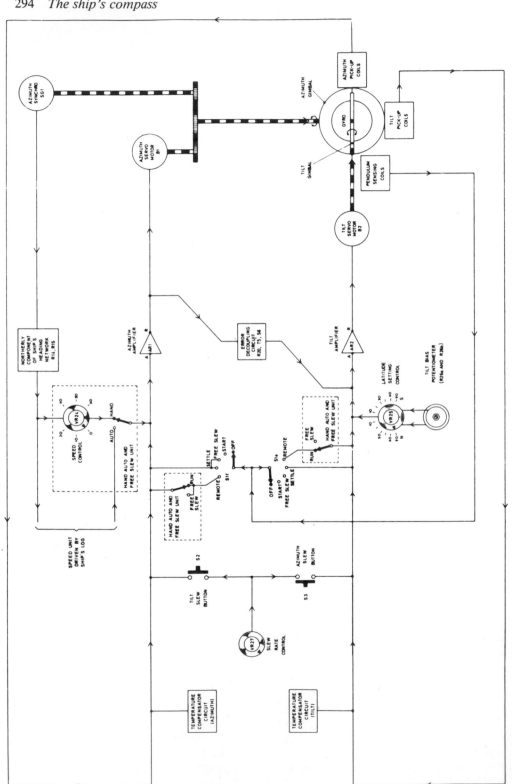

Fig. 8.35 The S. G. Brown MK.1 5 (C) compass circuits – schematic

gyro element in order to make the compass north seeking. To produce a north seeking action the gyroscopic unit must detect movement about the east/west (horizontal) axis. The pendulum unit is therefore mounted to the west side of the tank, level with the centre line. It is an electrically operated system consisting of an "E-shaped" laminated transformer core, fixed to the case, with a pendulum bob freely suspended by two flexible copper strips from the top of the assembly. The transformer (figure 8.36) has series opposing wound coils on the outer "E" sections and a single coil on the centre arm. The pendulum bob centres on the middle arm of the "E" core and is just clear of it. The whole assembly is contained in a viscous silicon liquid in order to damp the short term horizontal oscillations caused by the vessel rolling. Quiescently the bob will centre in the middle of the "E" core, but if the gyro tank tilts, the bob will offset causing the normally equalized magnetic field to be unbalanced and produce a stronger field on the outer arm towards which it is offset. The result is that a *tilt* signal, of correct sense and amplitude, is produced. This signal is fed to the *tilt* and *azimuth* amplifiers as required.

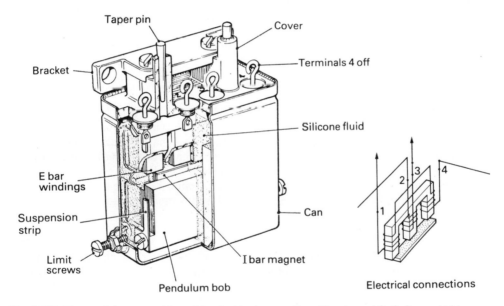

Fig. 8.36 The pendulum assembly and its electrical connections (Courtesy of S. G. Brown Ltd.)

The output signal of the pendulum unit is also used to enable the gyro to settle in the meridian and become "north settling". A small carefully calibrated portion of the output signal is applied to the *azimuth* amplifier to cause *azimuth* misalignment of the gyro tank and hence a twist of the vertical torsion wires. The result is a tilt of the sensitive element, the direction of which depends on whether the gyro spin axis is north or south end up with respect to the horizontal. The amplitude of the pendulum signal fed to the *azimuth* amplifier will determine the settling period of the gyro. In the S. G. Brown MK.1 model 5, this period is approximately 40 minutes.

Loop feedback versatility is again made use of by applying signals in order to achieve the necessary corrections for latitude and speed errors. The injected signals result in the required precessional rates in *azimuth*, for latitude correction and in *tilt*, for speed correction.

Speed correction

A signal which is proportional to the ship's speed, and the cosine of the ship's course, is coupled back to the *azimuth* amplifier to cause the gyroball to *tilt* in opposition to the apparent *tilt* caused by the northerly or southerly component of the ship's speed. The signal will therefore be maximum in amplitude when the course is due north or south, but will be of opposite sense. If the course is due east or west no correction is necessary. The system uses a 1:1 ratio *azimuth* synchronous transmitter SG1, which is mechanically driven by the *azimuth* servo motor gearing, and a balanced star connected resistor network as shown in figure 8.37. Alternatively an external signal derived from the ship's speed log may be used. In figure 8.37 the error for a ship sailing due north is maximum and therefore the feedback signal produced across RV24, by the currents flowing through SG1, S1 and S2 coils, will be maximum. A portion of this signal, dependent upon the speed setting of RV24, is fed to the *azimuth* amplifier to produce a *tilt* of the gyroball. For a course which is due south, the signal is again maximum, but is of opposite phase to the northerly signal. This will cause an opposite *tilt* of the gyroball to be produced. With the ship sailing due east, the synchronous transmitter SG1 is in a position which will produce a zero signal across RV24 and no correction signal is applied to the *azimuth* amplifier irrespective of the speed setting of RV24. Any intermediate setting of SG1 will produce a corresponding correction signal to be developed across RV24.

Latitude correction

The latitude correction circuit provides a signal, which is proportional to the sine of the vessel's latitude, to cause the gyroball to precess in *azimuth* at a rate equal and opposite to the apparent drift caused by the rotation of the earth. This signal will be zero at the equator and maximum at the poles. It must also be of opposite phase for north or south latitudes. VR25, the latitude potentiometer, derives its signal from the 24V centre tapped secondary winding of a transformer and therefore has signals of opposite phase at either end. This control sets the amplitude of the correction signal and is manually adjusted.

Temperature compensation

Both the vertical and horizontal torsion wires may twist with a change in ambient temperature. A corrective signal is produced in each of the *tilt* and *azimuth* temperature compensation circuits to counteract any precession of the gyroball caused by a change in temperature. The corrective signals are produced in the compensation circuits and connected to the *tilt* and *azimuth* amplifiers in such a way that both signal amplitude and sense will cause torques to be produced which are equal and opposite to those produced by twisting of the torsion wires. The effect of ambient temperature of the torsion wires is therefore cancelled.

Error decoupling circuit

The accuracy of a gyrocompass can be seriously affected by violent movement of the vessel, particularly heavy rolling caused by severe storms and rapid manoeuvring. A carefully calibrated error signal is derived from the output of the *azimuth* amplifier (which will be present due to misalignment of the tank and gyro spin axis during such conditions) and applied to the *tilt* amplifier to control the *tilt* gimbals. The system will provide partial and adequate compensation for errors which arise due to violent rolling conditions. The correction system is more than adequate for fittings on vessels of the Merchant Navy which would rarely be subjected to rapid manoeuvres.

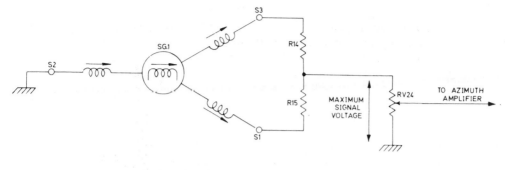

(a)   SHIP SAILING NORTH

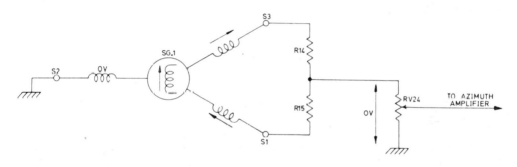

(b)   SHIP SAILING EAST

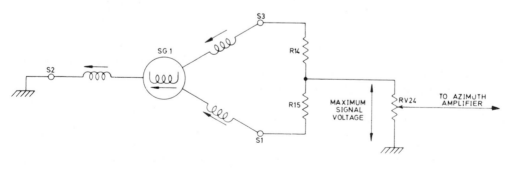

(c)   SHIP SAILING SOUTH

NOTE :-

ARROWS DENOTE INSTANTANEOUS
CURRENT FLOW

Fig. 8.37 Signal output of synchro SG1 for different headings (Courtesy of S. G. Brown Ltd.)

Slew rate

The purpose of the slew rate control VR27 is to rapidly level and orientate the gyro during the start-up procedure. The potentiometer VR27 is connected across the 24V centre tapped secondary winding of a transformer and is therefore able to produce an output of opposite phase and varying amplitude. The signal voltage level set by VR27 may be applied to the input of either the *azimuth* or *tilt* amplifiers separately by the use of push buttons. The buttons are interconnected in such a way that the signal cannot be applied to both amplifiers at the same time. If the output of VR27 is firstly applied to the *tilt* servo amplifier (by pressing the *azimuth* slew button) the gyro will precess towards the meridian. If the *tilt* slew button is now pressed, the gyro will be levelled by applying the output of VR27 to the *azimuth* servo motor. The slew rate control VR27 adjusts the *rate* at which the gyro precesses and *not* the extent of precession which is a function of time. It is essential that this control is centred before either slew button is pressed otherwise a violent kick of the gyro ball will occur in one direction making compass alignment more difficult to achieve. The selector switch S1 must be in the 'Free Slew' position during this operation.

Starting the compass (see figure 8.38)

The following sequence of operations will enable the compass to be run-up and aligned correctly.
1. Set the LATITUDE control to within 5° of the local latitude.
2. Centre the SLEW RATE control.
3. Set the SPEED control to zero.
4. Set the selector switch to START. The top of the gyro tank will be seen to 'kick' towards the spirit level bracket.
5. Wait 5 minutes for the gyro to run-up to speed.
6. Set the selector switch to FREE SLEW, then press the AZIMUTH SLEW button and, while keeping it depressed turn the SLEW RATE control so as to cause the compass card to rotate in the required direction towards the meridian. A clockwise rotation of the control causes the compass card reading to increase.
7. As the compass card approaches the estimated meridian, the SLEW RATE control should be slowly rotated in the reverse direction so that the compass card comes to rest on the vessel's heading with the control centralized.
8. Push the TILT SLEW button and turn the SLEW RATE control slowly to centre the bubble in the spirit level. Clockwise rotation of the control causes the north end of the tank to tilt downwards. As the tilt is equalized (as indicated by the spirit level), slowly rotate the control in the reverse direction so that the spirit level indicates that the gyro tank is level with the SLEW RATE control in its central position. The TILT SLEW button should not be released until this has been achieved.
9. Wait a further 2 minutes, for the pendulum bob to settle in the vertical plane.
10. Set the selector switch to SETTLE. The gyro will now rotate slowly on the meridian and after a period of 25 minutes will produce an accurate reading. This 25 minute settling period can be reduced if the vessel's course to which the compass is slewed is known to be correct to within 1°.
11. When the gyro has settled, set the selector switch to REMOTE. Set to RUN on the remote unit.

Notes:
1. The LATITUDE control should be kept to within 5° of the local latitude.
2. The SPEED control must be set to within 5 knots of the vessel's speed. (An error here of 5 knots causes an error of aproximately 0.5°.)

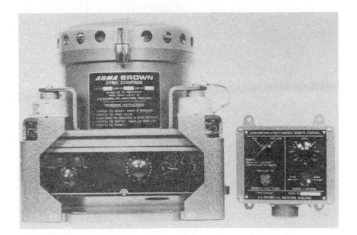

Switching Off

4.

(1)   Switch off all power supplies to the compass.

(2)   Set the Selector Switch to OFF.

(3)   Turn the SPEED control to zero.

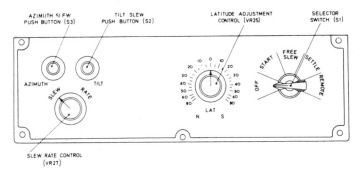

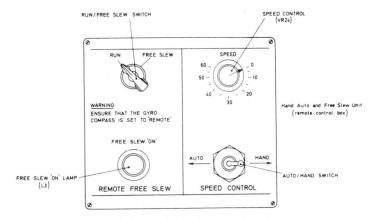

Fig. 8.38 The S. G. Brown gyrocompass MK.1 model 5 (C) front panel controls

3. The compass seeks and settles in the meridian more quickly when set in the SETTLE mode than in the REMOTE (RUN) mode. However, in the SETTLE mode the compass may be thrown off the heading. For this reason, the selector switch must not be left in the SETTLE position during operation of the gyrocompass.

8.6 Compass repeaters

Remote analog compass repeaters are simply mechanized compass cards driven either by a stepper motor or a synchro bearing transmission system. Digital heading displays can also be produced by digitizing the stepper "grey code" waveform before applying it to a suitable decoding system. The main disadvantage of the digital display of ship's heading is that it prevents the taking of bearings by sights. This section deals with the most popular bearing transmission systems.

Stepper

Figure 8.39 shows an early mechanical switching stepper system used by Sperry for bearing transmission to remote repeaters. The rotor of the transmitter is geared to the azimuth ring gearing of the master compass. The transmitter is a multi-contact rotary switch which completes the circuit for current to flow through the appropriate repeater motor coils. The transmitter rotor has two rotating arms spaced at 165 degrees to each other. Each rotor arm makes contact with copper segments arranged in four groups of three, each segment being wired to its corresponding number in the other three groups.

The gear ratio of transmitter rotor to azimuth gear is 180:1 therefore:

$$180 \text{ rev} \equiv 360 \text{ degrees}$$
$$1 \text{ rev} \equiv 2 \text{ degrees}$$
$$12 \text{ seg} \equiv 2 \text{ degrees}$$
$$1 \text{ seg} \equiv 2/12 \text{ degrees or } 10 \text{ minutes of arc}$$

The rotating arms make 12 steps per revolution. Each step therefore corresponds to 1/6th of a degree or 10 minutes of arc on the compass card because of the 180:1 gear reduction.

A simplified step by step receiver is shown in figure 8.39. Three pairs of coils are wound, and located at 60 degree intervals, on the stator assembly of the receiver. The rotor is centrally located and capable of fully rotating through 360 degrees. With the switch in the position shown, current flows through the series connected coils (1) and, under the influence of the magnetic field produced, the rotor takes up the position shown. As the switch moves to position 3, its make before break action causes current to flow through both coils 1 and 3 and the rotor moves to a position midway between the coils – due east/west. The next movement of the switch energizes coil 3 only causing the rotor to line up with this coil. In this way the rotor is caused to rotate one revolution in 12 steps. The stepper motor may also be used as part of a "direct digital control" (d.d.c.) system in which signals may be generated digitally to control movement of the repeater. A stepper system utilizes a cyclic binary code or gray code for its operation. The gray code is easily produced using shaft or disc encoders geared to the compass azimuth gearing. It follows therefore that future transmission sysems will be digitally encoded possibly using fibre optics for interconnection between transmitter and repeater.

Synchro

A synchro is a device which uses the basic principle of a single phase transformer with magnetic coupling between a rotating primary (rotor) and a number of secondaries

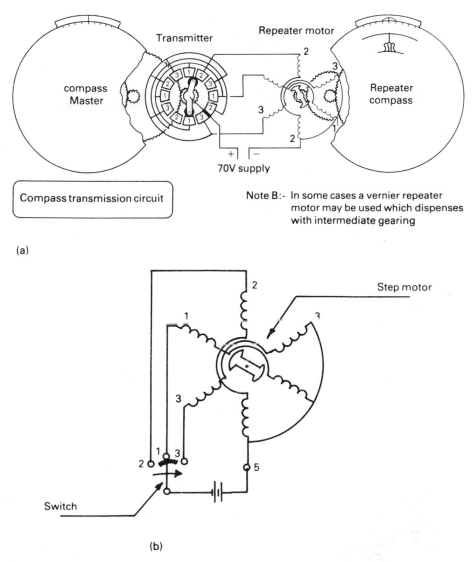

Note B:- In some cases a vernier repeater
motor may be used which dispenses
with intermediate gearing

(a)

(b)

Fig. 8.39 Stepper repeating system (a) Early mechanical switching system (b) Diagrammatic representation of a simple step motor receiver (Courtesy of Sperry Ltd.)

(stator). For the purpose of this description three secondaries are located at 120 degree intervals on the stator. The rotor may be rotated through 360 degrees within the laminated stator assembly holding the three secondary windings. The primary coil is energized by a low frequency a.c. applied via slip rings located on the main shaft. The magnitude and phase of the secondary induced e.m.f.s. are dependent upon the relative position of the rotor in relation to the stator windings.

Synchro repeater system

Figure 8.41 illustrates a synchro repeater system using the basic "synchro error detecting" method of operation common to many control applications. the rotor of the synchro

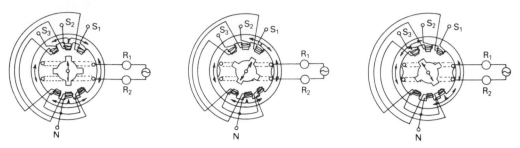

Fig. 8.40 The construction of a step motor

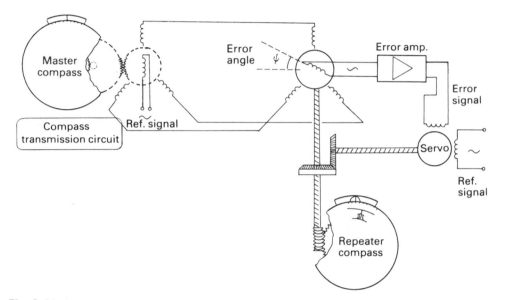

Fig. 8.41 A synchro bearing transmission system

transmitter is reduction geared to the azimuth ring of the gyrocompass. A reference low frequency a.c. supply to the transmitter rotor coil couples with the three secondaries to produce e.m.f.s. which cause current to flow around the three circuits. Each current flow produces a magnetic field around the corresponding receiver secondary and a resultant error signal is induced in the receiver rotor coil. No error signal is produced if the system is in the synchronous state with the transmitter and the receiver rotors at 90 degrees to each other. The error signal present, when the rotors are not synchronized, is directly proportional to the error angle ψ existing between the horizontal and the plane of the rotor. This error signal is amplified to the level required to drive a servo which turns the compass card. Also mechanically coupled to the servo shaft is the receiver rotor which turns to cancel the error signal as part of a mechanical negative feedback arrangement. The receiver rotor will always therefore line up (at 90 degrees) with the transmitter rotor to produce the synchronous state.

8.7 The magnetic repeating compass

A magnetic compass can be converted into a repeating compass by the addition of a flux gate assembly, which will produce output pulses to drive remote repeaters. A flux gate element is effectively a magnetometer which is used to detect both the magnitude and direction of a magnetic field. Flux gate elements in common use are of the "second harmonic" type, so called because if excited by a fundamental frequency "f", an output voltage will be generated which varies in both phase and amplitude, depending upon its position within the magnetic field, at a frequency of $2f$.

Construction

The basic flux gate consists of two thin wires of mumetal or permalloy, each wire contained in a glass tube, around which is wound a coil. Two such assemblies are used and are mounted side by side and parallel to each other. The two coils are connected in series so that their magnetic fields are in opposition when a low frequency a.c. (typically 2 Hz) is applied to them. Mumetal is used for the wire cores of each of the coils because of its property of magnetically saturating at very low levels of magnetic flux. (Mumetal magnetically saturates at a field strength of approximately 8 ampere turns per metre compared to approximately 250 000 ampere turns per metre for steel wire.)

A secondary coil, wound around the whole assembly, provides a mutually induced e.m.f. for the output voltage. Figure 8.42 illustrates the basic construction of a simple flux gate. Note that the primary coils are connected in series. In a practical unit a balancing system would be included to ensure that in the absence of any externally produced magnetic field, the magnetic field produced by the two primary windings would cancel and no output would be generated. If the current in coil A changes (see figure 8.43), the magnetic flux it causes will correspondingly change either in value or direction. Any change will produce a self induced e.m.f. in coil A and a mutually induced e.m.f. in coil B. Illustrated in figure 8.44 above is a cross section of a complete flux gate with coils A and C forming the primary function and coil B the secondary output coil.

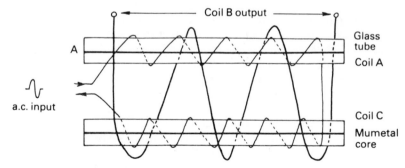

Fig. 8.42 The basic flux gate with primary windings of equal turns around tubes A and C. Secondary coil B is wound around the whole assembly

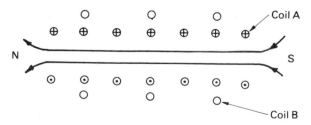

Fig. 8.43 Flux gate operation

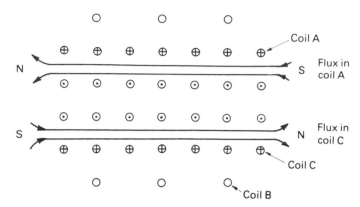

Fig. 8.44 A cross-section of a complete flux gate

If the magnetic fluxes produced by both coil A and C are of the same value but of opposite polarity, there will be no mutually induced e.m.f. in coil B. This is because the two magnetic fields linking with the turns of coil B will be effectively zero. This state can only exist if the two coils A and C are connected in series as shown in figure 8.42 causing the current flow through the two coils to be the same value at any instant. When this is the case the system is said to be balanced and the output voltage across coil B will be zero .

Figure 8.45 shows the currents and flux saturation levels for both coil A and coil C when the assembly is balanced. If a permanent magnet is placed in proximity of the flux gate as shown in figure 8.46 its magnetic field will have effects which tend to cancel out.

In the parts of the cores which carry flux in the same direction as the magnet, the core will saturate with a lower value of coil current. In the other half of the same core the two fluxes will oppose so that this part of the core does not saturate until a much larger current is flowing. These two effects will therefore not affect the balancing of the core fluxes as shown in figure 8.46 so there will be no mutually induced e.m.f. in the secondary coil B. If the permanent magnet is now placed parallel to the two cores of the flux gate as in figure 8.47 an imbalance occurs. The flux due to the magnet will now be in the same direction as that due to the coil current in one core but in the opposite direction in the other. The magnet will cause one core to saturate with a lower value of coil current and the other to require a larger value of coil current for saturation to occur. Figure 8.48 shows how the permanent magnet flux affects the flux produced in each core by the low frequency a.c. primary current on each half cycle of input voltage.

Figure 8.49 shows that the value of the a.c. induced into coil B is twice the frequency of the energizing supply, but depends upon the value of the permanent magnet field. The output also varies as the cosine of the angle between the line of the magnet and the flux gate. The a.c. output is then amplified and used to drive a servo motor which will rotate the gate until the output is zero. This corresponds to the magnet being at an angle of 90 degrees to the gate elements.

Practical flux gate systems

There are currently two main methods of using a flux gate to produce a repeating compass. The simplest of these uses a flux gate in conjunction with an ordinary magnetic compass (see figure 8.50) and will be described first.

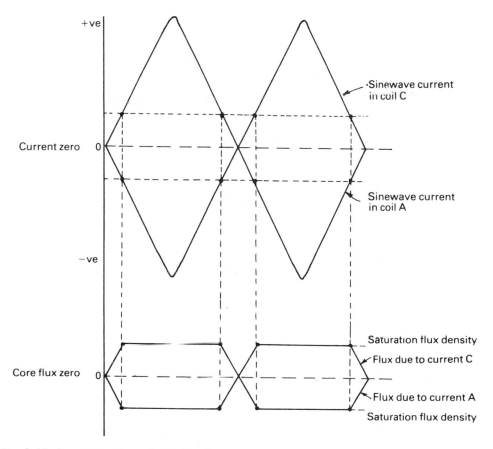

+ve

Current zero   0

−ve

Core flux zero   0

·Sinewave current in coil C

Sinewave current in coil A

Saturation flux density

Flux due to current C

Flux due to current A

Saturation flux density

Fig. 8.45 Currents and flux saturation levels

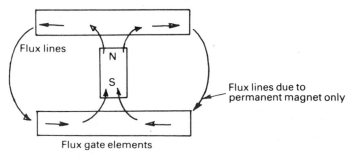

Flux lines

N

S

Flux lines due to permanent magnet only

Flux gate elements

Fig. 8.46 An illustration of flux lines caused by the addition of a permanent magnet to the flux gate

A flux gate in conjunction with a magnetic compass

A standard marine magnetic compass utilizes the north seeking property of a permanent magnet. A flux gate mounted on a rotatable platform is mounted in the compass bowl below the compass card. The core elements of the flux gate will therefore come under the influence of the permanent magnetic field produced by the compass pointer. As previously

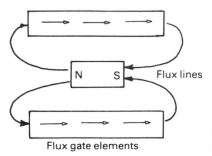

Fig. 8.47 Flux lines with the permanent magnet in line with the flux gate

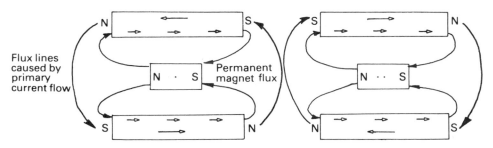

Fig. 8.48 The intensity of the magnetic flux in each core is changed on each half cycle of primary a.c.

shown the magnetization will have maximum effect when the flux gate and the compass magnet are parallel and zero effect when they are at 90 degrees to each other. This point will be referred to as the NULL point. The resultant output voltage from the secondary winding of the flux gate varies as the cosine of the angle between magnet and flux gate. Output from the flux gate secondary winding is amplified and its frequency divided by two before being applied to the control winding of a servo motor. This servo, which is mechanically coupled to the flux gate platform, drives the whole assembly towards a null point. Assuming the flux gate and magnet are not at 90 degrees to each other, an output from the flux gate secondary is produced which after processing is fed to the control winding of the servo motor. The reference winding supply is taken directly from the low frequency oscillator. This ensrue that correct phasing of the servo motor is achieved and that the flux gate will always be driven towards the correct null point. When the null point is reached, the servo amplifier input falls to zero causing the servo to stop. The flux gate is therefore always kept in correct alignment with the compass magnet.

Dual axis flux gate compass
As an alternative to using a flux gate in conjunction with a magnetic compass, it is possible to use a dual axis magnetometer to sense the earth's magnetic field to produce an indication of direction. The earth's magnetic lines of force are not horizontal to the earth's surface thus, it is necessary that the angle between the lines of force and the earth's surface be resolved into both vertical and horizontal components as shown in figure 8.51.

If we assume that a vessel is heading due north as shown in figure 8.52 the two horizontally orientated flux gates sense the magnitudes of the earth's horizontal magnetic flux lines diminished by sine and cosine functions of the heading. The resulting outputs produced, designated *HL* and *HA*, are derived as shown in figure 8.52.

A simplifed system is shown in figure 8.53. Flux gate 1 is mounted along the fore and aft line of the vessel and flux gate 2 athwartships. The fore and aft line component of the earth's magnetic field causes flux gate 1 to produce an output voltage proportional to the

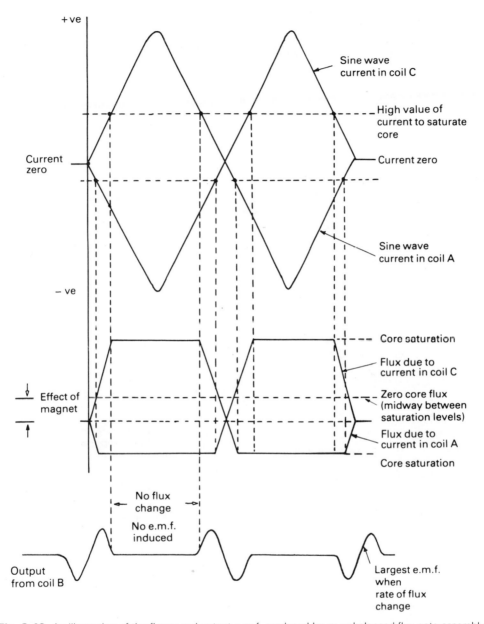

Fig. 8.49 An illustration of the fluxes and output e.m.f. produced by an unbalanced flux gate assembly

amplitude of this component. Similarly, gate 2 produces an output proportional to the athwartships component. Both signals are coupled to the stator coils of a synchro, which produces two magnetic fields proportional to the amplitude of the original fields acting upon the flux gates. The line of the resultant field within the synchro is the same as the direction of the earth's magnetic field *He*.

Output from the rotor of the synchro is connected, via a servo amplifier, to drive a servo motor which rotates the synchro rotor mechanically until it is at 90 degrees to the resultant

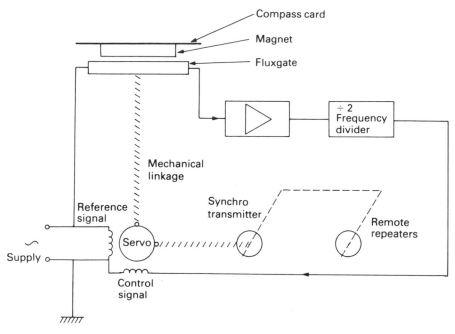

Fig. 8.50 A flux gate system in conjunction with a magnetic compass

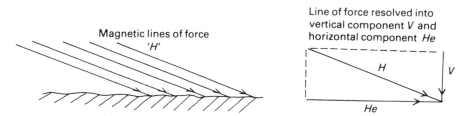

Fig. 8.51 An illustration of how the lines of force of the earth's magnetic field may be resolved into vertical and horizontal components.

field, at which point output from the rotor is zero and the servo stops. The synchro rotor is thus kept in alignment with the resultant direction of the magnetic field within the synchro, which in turn depends upon the direction, relative to both flux gates, of the earth's magnetic field. A compass card is directly driven by the rotor of the synchro. Remote repeaters can be fitted as illustrated in the previous case by the use of a synchro transmission system. A compass has thus been produced which eliminates the conventional pivoted magnet arrangement to provide an indication of magnetic north electrically. This is but a simple explanation of a system which is undergoing considerable research particularly in the field of small boat technology.

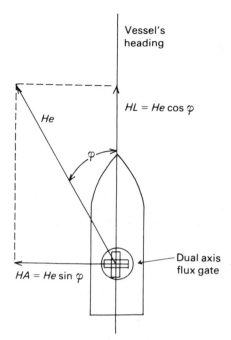

Vessel's
heading

$HL = He \cos \varphi$

He

φ

Dual axis
flux gate

$HA = He \sin \varphi$

Fig. 8.52 The vessel's course as a cosine function of He –
the direction of the earth's magnetic field

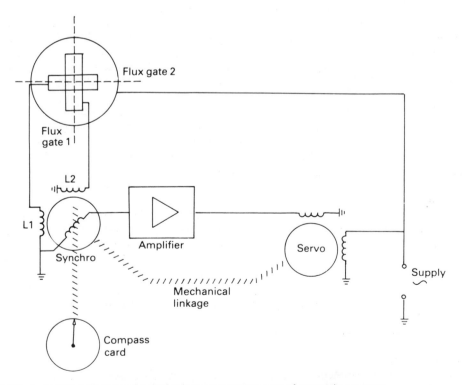

Flux gate 2

Flux
gate 1

L2

L1

Synchro

Amplifier

Servo

Mechanical
linkage

Supply

Compass
card

Fig. 8.53 A simplified diagram of a dual axis magnetometer type of magnetic compass

9
Automatic steering

9.1 Introduction

It has already been implied that a modern merchant vessel must be cost effective in order to survive the ever increasing pressure of a financially orientated industry. A good automatic pilot can improve the profit margin of a vessel in two ways. Firstly, it enables a reduction to be made in the number of ships' personnel and secondly a considerable saving in fuel can be achieved if the vessel makes good its course with little deviation. This chapter deals with the principles of automatic pilots to enable the reader to understand the electronic systems and all the operator control functions.

Early autopilots were installed in the wheelhouse from wherre they remote operated the vessel's helm via a direct drive system as shown in figure 9.1. Although efficient, the main drawback with the system was the reliance on a hydraulic telemotor unit. This unit may develop a leak permitting air to enter the system, thus causing uneven control and loss of motion. The loss of motion means that the efficiency of the system is downgraded and accurate steering is no longer possible. To overcome inherent inefficiencies in the telemotor unit a better type of autopilot has been developed. An electrical system now replaces the inefficient telemotor. The autopilot control system is still fitted in the wheelhouse but the power drive unit is now situated in the engine room close to the steering engine valves it operates directly. Before considering the electronic aspects of an autopilot system it is worthwhile to briefly consider some of the problems faced by an automatic steering device.

In its simplest form an autohelm (trade names 'Autopilot', 'Gyropilot') compares the course to steer data, as set by the helmsman, with the vessel's actual course data, as derived from a gyro or magnetic repeating compass, and applies rudder correction if an error is detected between the two input signals. Since the vessel's steering characteristics will vary under a variety of conditions, additional facilities must be provided to alter the action of the autopilot parameters in a similar way that a helmsman would alter his actions under the same prevailing conditions.

In order that a vessel holds a course as accurately as possible, the helm must be provided with data regarding the vessel's movement relative to the course to steer line. "Feedback" signals provide this data which consists of three sets of parameters:

(a) Position Data.   Information providing positional error from the course line.

(b) Rate Data.   Rate of change of course data.

(c) Accumulative Error Data.   Data regarding the cumulative build up of error.
Three main control functions which act on one or more of the data inputs listed above are: proportional control, derivative control and integral control.

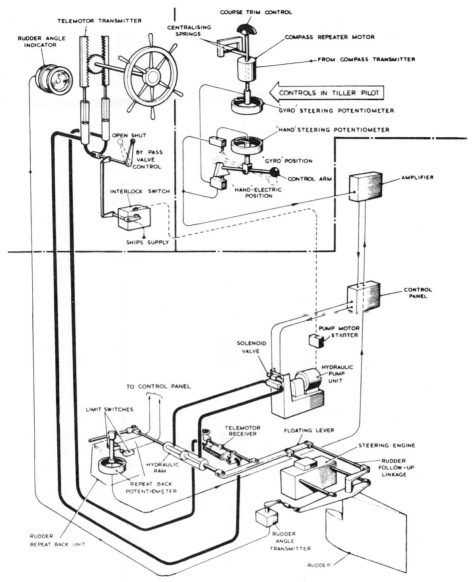

Fig. 9.1 Early manual/autohelm system using telemotors (Courtesy of Sperry Ltd.)

9.2 Proportional control

This electronic control signal causes the rudder to move by an amount proportional to the positional error from the course line. The effect on steering when only proportional control is applied is to cause the vessel to oscillate either side of the required course as shown in figure 9.2.

The vessel would eventually reach its destination although additional time and fuel would be expended on the voyage. Efficiency would consequently be downgraded and rudder component wear would be unacceptable. At the instant an error is detected, full

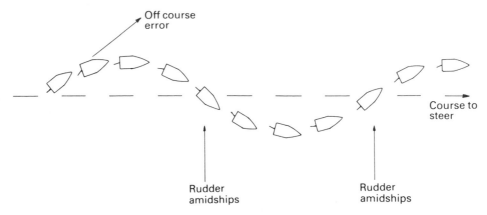

Fig. 9.2 The effect of proportional control only. The vessel oscillates about the course to steer

rudder is applied, bringing the vessel to starboard back towards its course (figure 9.2). As the vessel returns, the error is reduced and autopilot control is gradually removed. Unfortunately the rudder will be amidships as the vessel approaches its course causing an overshoot resulting in a southerly error. Corrective data is now applied causing a port turn to bring the vessel back onto course. This action again causes an overshoot producing corrective data to initiate a starboard turn in an attempt to bring the vessel back to its original course. It is not practical to calculate the actual distance of the vessel from the course line at any instant, therefore the method of achieving proportional control is by using a signal proportional to the rudder angle as a feedback signal.

9.3 Derivative control

With this form of control the rudder is shifted by an amount proportional to the "rate of change" of the vessel's deviation from its course. Derivative control is achieved by electronically differentiating the actual error signal. Its effect on the vessel is illustrated in figure 9.3. Any initial change of course error is sensed causing corrective starboard rudder to be applied. The rate of change of course decreases with the result that automatic rudder control decreases and, at point X, the rudder will have returned to the midships position. The vessel is now making good a course which is parallel to the required heading and will continue to do so until the autopilot is again caused to operate by external forces acting on the vessel.

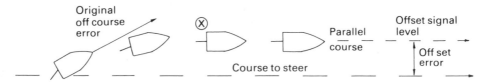

Fig. 9.3 The effect of derivative control only

An ideal combination of both proportional and derivative control produces a more satisfactory return to course as shown in figure 9.4.

The initial change of course causes the rudder to be controlled by a combined signal from both proportional and derivative signals. As the vessel undergoes a starboard

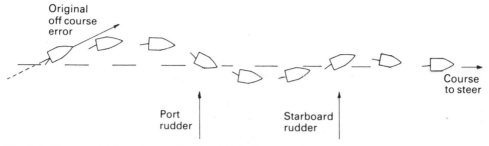

Fig. 9.4 The combination of proportional and derivative controls

turn (caused by proportional control only) there is a change of sign of the rate of change data causing some counter rudder to be applied. As the vessel crosses its original course, the rudder is to port, at some angle, bringing the vessel back to port. The course followed by the vessel is therefore a damped oscillation. The extent of counter rudder control applied is made variable to allow for differing vessel characteristics. Correct setting of the counter rudder control should cause the vessel to make good its original course as shown in figure 9.4. Counter rudder data must alays be applied in conjunction with the output of the manual ''rudder'' potentiometer, which varies the amount of rudder control applied per degree of heading error. Figures 9.5(a) and (b) illustrate the effect on vessel steering when the counter rudder and rudder controls are set too high and too low respectively.

(a)

Fig. 9.5(a) 'Counter rudder' and 'rudder' controls set too high. Severe oscillations are produced before the equipment settles

(b)

Fig. 9.5(b) 'Counter rudder' and 'rudder' controls set too low. Little overshoot with a sluggish return to course

9.4 Integral control

Data for integral control is derived by electronically integrating the heading error. The action of this data offsets the effect of a vessel being moved continuously off course. Data signals are produced by continuously sensing the heading error over a period of time and applying an appropriate degree of permanent helm. In addition to proportional control, derivative control and integral control, auto pilots normally have the yaw, trim, draft, rudder limit, and weather controls, which will be dealt with in more detail later in this chapter.

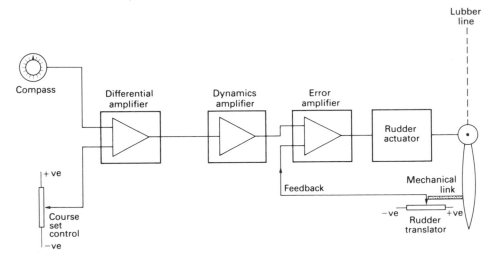

Fig. 9.6 A simple autohelm system

9.5 Basic autohelm

The simplest form of autohelm is that shown in figure 9.6. An output from a gyro or magnetic repeating compass is coupled to a differential amplifier along with a signal derived from a manual course setting control. If no difference exists between the two signals, no output will be produced by the amplifier and no movement of the rudder occurs. When a difference is detected between the two sources of data, an output error signal, proportional in magnitude to the size of the difference, is applied to the heading error amplifier. Output of this amplifier is coupled to the rudder actuator circuitry which causes the rudder to move in the direction determined by the sign of the output voltage. The error signal between compass and selected course inputs produces an output voltage from the differential amplifier which is proportional to the off course error. This type of control only therefore is termed *proportional* control. As has previously been shown, the use of proportional control only causes the vessel to oscillate either side of its intended course due to inertia producing overshooting.

With a Proportional, Integral and Derivative steering control system, the oscillation is minimized by modifying the error signal (ψ) produced as the difference between the selected heading and the compass heading. Figure 9.7 shows that a three input summing amplifier is used, termed the Dynamics Amplifier, which produces a resultant output signal equal to the sum of one or more of the input signals. The Demanded Rudder Error signal (ψ) is inspected by both the differentiator and the integrator. The differentiator determines the rate of changes of heading as the vessel returns to the selected course. This sensed rate of change, as a voltage, is compared with a fixed electrical time constant and if necessary a counter rudder signal will be produced. The magnitude of this signal slows the rate of change of course and thus damps the off course oscillation. Obviously the time constant of the differentiation circuit is critical if oscillations are to be fully damped. Time constant parameters depend upon the design characteristics of the vessel and are normally calculated and set when the vessel undergoes initial trials. Additionally a "counter rudder" control is fitted in order that the magnitude of the counter rudder signal may be varied to suit prevailing conditions.

Permanent disturbances of the course due to design parameters of the vessel must also

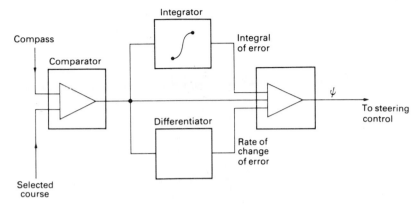

Fig. 9.7 Error signal summing circuit

be corrected. These long term errors, typically the shape of the hull or the effect of the screw action of a single propeller driving the ship to starboard, may be compensated for by the use of an integrator. The integral term thus produced is inserted into the control loop offsetting the rudder. This permits proportional corrections now to be applied about the mean offset course (the parallel course shown in figure 9.3). The offset signal amplitude causes a permanent offset error angle of the rudder. Output of the Dynamics Amplifier is now the total modified error signal (ψ) which is regulated by the "rudder" control to determine the amount of rudder correction per degree of heading error to be applied.

An overall simplified diagram of an Autohelm is shown in figure 9.8. The Rudder Error Amplifier is provided with variable sensitivity from the "weather" control, which in effect varies the gain of the amplifier by varying the feedback portion of the gain determining components. In this way the magnitude of the heading error signal required before the output from this amplifier causes the rudder to operate may be varied. Using this control a delay in rudder operation may be imposed if weather conditions cause the vessel to yaw due to a heavy swell aft of the beam. Under certain conditions, mainly draft and trim of the vessel, a degree of permanent rudder may be required. The "permanent helm" control provides an input to the Rudder Error Amplifier which may be positive or negative depending whether the rudder needs to be to starboard or to port. Since the effect of rudder movement does not influence the setting of this control, the rudder will remain permanently in the position set by this control (assuming no other control signals are produced). Permanent helm will also be applied automatically by sensing the build up of heading error in the integrator circuit.

In the system described control relays RLA and RLB are used to switch power to the steering gear contactors which in turn supply power of the correct amplitude and polarity to the prime rudder mover. As the rudder moves, a mechanical linkage drives the slider of a potentiometer to produce the rudder feedback signal. Output from this "rudder translator" potentiometer is normally used to indicate the instantaneous rudder angle. Excursions of the rudder may be limmited by the manually operated "rudder limit" control which fixes the maximum amount by which the rudder may move from the midships position.

An off-course alarm circuit senses the error signal at the output of the Heading Error Amplifier and causes an audible alarm to be sounded when a signal amplitude outside pre-determined limits is detected. A manual off-course limit control (not shown) is provided to enable an operator to select the point at which the alarm will sound.

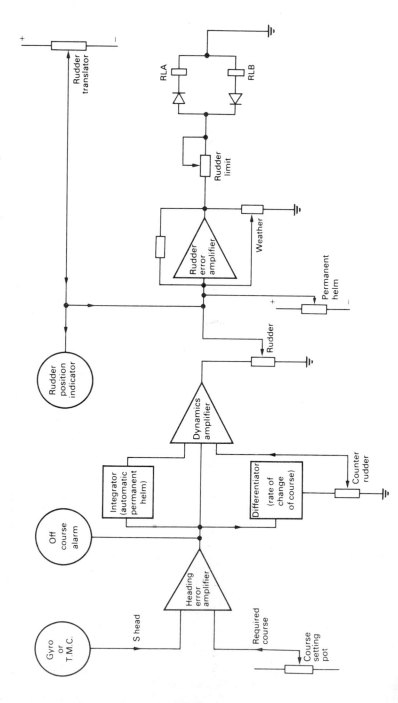

Fig. 9.8 Simplified autohelm diagram

9.6 Manual operator controls

Permanent helm

This control is intended for use when the vessel is being driven unilaterally off-course by a cross-wind. Its function is to apply sufficient permanent rudder angle to offset the drift caused by the wind, thus holding the vessel on the required heading. Permanent helm is also applied automatically when the steering system is in the automatic mode of operation.

Automatic application of permanent helm makes no use of the permanent helm control. The degree of rudder offset required for course-holding is now electronically computed and applied automatically. Since the computing process involves the charging of a capacitor, the required degree of permanent helm is built-up gradually over a period of minutes. This period may be changed by altering the charging time of the capacitor.

Rudder limit

This control sets a finite limit on the rudder angle obtained irrespective of the angle commanded by the automatic control circuitry. Obviously if the rudder was permitted to exceed design parameters severe damage may be caused.

Rudder

The rudder potentiometer enables the ship's steering characteristics to be modified in accordance with the changing requirements caused by loading and speed factors. This control determines the absolute degree of rudder command obtained for every degree of steady-rate heading error. For example, if this control is set to "2", the rudder will move through two degrees for every degree of heading error.

Counter rudder

The counter rudder control determines the degree of opposite helm to be applied if this be demanded by the control circuit. The control permits daily adjustments to be made as dictated by loading conditions.

Weather

The effect of weather and sea conditions can be effectively counteracted by the use of this control. The circuits controlled by this switch progressively densensitize the control amplifier which in turn causes an increase in the deadband width. The control also imposes an increasing time delay on the rudder command signal in order that the ship will recover naturally when under the influence of repetitive yaw. This means that the steering gear is not subjected to continual port/starboard commands. Thus the higher the setting of the weather control the wider will be the deadband. This increases the amplitude of yaw that can be tolerated before the steering gear is enabled.

Non follow-up mode (NFU)

Rudder control is by means of two position port/starboard lever switches. These switches will energize the directional valves on the hydraulic power unit directly thus removing the rudder feedback control. In this mode the normal autopilot control with repeat back is by-passed and the rudder is said to be under 'open loop' control. There is no feedback from the rudder to close the loop. The helmsman closes the loop by observing the rudder angle indicator and operating the NFU control as appropriate.

Follow-up mode (FU)

In this mode the FU tiller control voltage is applied to the error amplifier (Figure 9.9) along with the rudder feedback voltage. Rudder action is now under the influence of a single closed loop control.

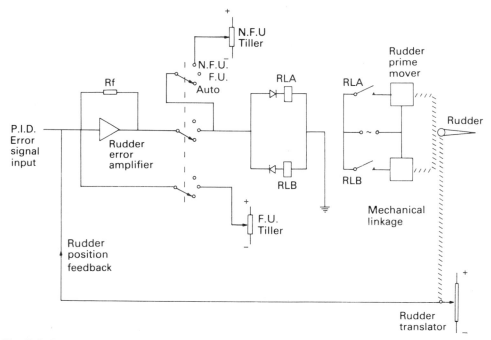

Fig. 9.9 FU and NFU control of tiller operation (Courtesy of Racal Marine Controls)

Deadband

This is the manually set bandwidth in which the rudder prime movers do not operate. If the deadband is set too wide the vessel's course is hardly affected by rudder commands. With the deadband too narrow the vessel is subjected to almost continuous rudder action causing excessive drag.

9.7 Overshoot

For optimum course keeping performance it is imperative that the autopilot operates with as narrow a deadband as possible. All steering systems suffer a degree of inherent overshoot. The effect of this overshoot on the stability of the rudder positioning system can be graphically represented as shown in figure 9.10. Two scales have been plotted on the vertical axis, the first being the rudder angle in degrees with respect to the midships position and the second, the voltage corresponding to that angle produced by the rudder translator.

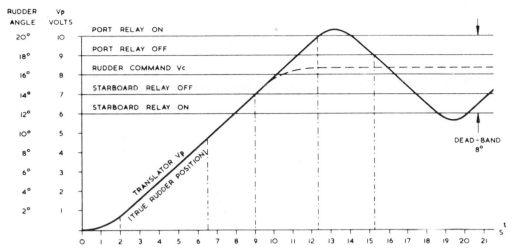

Fig. 9.10 Effect of overshoot on control system stability (Courtesy of Racal Marine Controls)

With reference to figure 9.10, it is assumed that a starboard rudder command is applied to the autopilot at time $t = 0$ seconds, and as a result the starboard rudder pulls in to activate the starboard pump causing the rudder to move to starboard. Since most hydraulic system pumps take a finite time to develop full stroke, the rudder does not reach its terminal velocity until $t = 2$ seconds. At time $t = 9$ seconds, the position feedback signal (Vp) crosses the release threshold of the starboard relay. Prime power is now removed from the steering gear pump. Because of inherent overshoot, caused by inertia, the rudder will continue to move to starboard as shown by the solid line. If the overshoot is of sufficient magnitude, it will cause the position feedback signal to cross the operating threshold of the port relay ($t = 12.5$ s), and thus set the rudder moving towards the midships position. When, at $t = 15.25$ s, Vp crosses the release threshold of the port relay power is again removed from the steering gear. Overshoot now carries the Vp signal back through the operating threshold of the starboard relay and the rudder once again moves to starboard. The control system is now described as unstable and the rudder is caused to oscillate or hunt. The dotted curve in figure 9.10 illustrates the operational characteristics of a stable system. Here, overshoot does not cause the port relay to be activated and thus the rudder arrives at the commanded position in one continuous movement.

One method of stabilizing an unstable system is to decrease the sensitivity of the rudder amplifier. This solution is not satisfactory because it has the effect of increasing the distances between the 'operate and release' thresholds of the steering relays thus producing a wider deadband and a degradation of the steering performance and efficiency.

A better solution is to remove power from the steering gear at some determinate time before Vp crosses the release threshold of the starboard relay. The extent of this predetermined release time must be dependent upon individual steering gear overshoot characteristics. In figure 9.10, if power was removed from the steering gear at $t = 6.5$ s (a time advance of 2.5 s), the inherent overshoot would not now carry vp through the operating threshold of the port relay and rudder movement would follow the dotted line illustrating a stable system. This principle is an outline of the Racal Decca Phantom Rudder system incorporated in the control amplifier circuitry of their autopilot units.

9.8 Phantom rudder

Dependent upon the setting of the "Phantom Rudder Speed" control, a determinate d.c. voltage is applied to an integrator input resistance with the result that the circuit commences to generate the positive going ramp voltage Vp defined by the solid line in figure 9.11. It should be noted that the polarity of the integrator output is the reverse of that of the translator output (Vt), hence the provision of separate voltage scales on the y-axis of the graph. It is arranged so that the slope of Vp and Vt are equal. On the assumption that the steering gear takes one second to run up to speed, the phantom output establishes a lead of approximately 0.75 volts (1.5 degrees) during this period. At time $t = 2.4\,s$, the phantom output, which functions as a position feedback signal, arrives at the release threshold of the starboard relay, one contact of which removes the -15 volts input from the integrator causing the output to halt at $+3$ volts. It is arranged that at this time a second input is applied to the phantom rudder circuit integrator which now produces a negative going ramp. The slope of this ramp is made to be gradual by limiting the amplitude of the signal applied to the integrator.

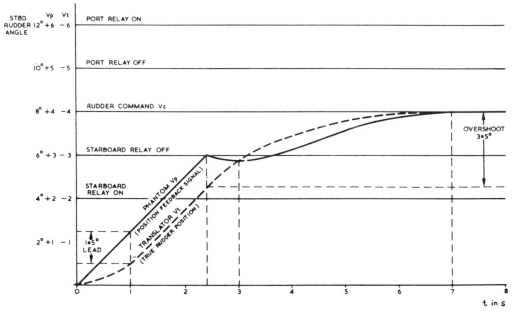

Fig. 9.11 Phantom rudder circuit, operational principle (Courtesy of Racal Marine Controls)

At time $t = 3\,s$, the phantom (Vp and translator (Vt) outputs will be equal and of opposite polarity causing the output from the integrator (Vp) to stop increasing. This condition is not stable because as Vt is carried progressively more negative by rudder overshoot, the integrator generates a positive going ramp of low slope. Output from the integrator will now continue to rise, and the slope will gradually decrease as the positive potential of Vp approaches parity with the negative potential of Vt. Ultimately at $t = 7\,s$, Vp will be equal to Vt. Since no input is now applied to the integrator, its output Vp will be held at the attained level, and the hypothetical position of the phantom rudder will be the same as that of the true rudder.

In the foregoing example, the lead of the phantom rudder on the true rudder was obtained purely as a result of the slow take-off of the steering gear. In practice, it is desirable that the phantom rudder speed output be set some 20% higher than that of the true rudder. Since with this arrangement the phantom rudder output will continue to increase its lead on the translator output so long as the steering gear is energized, some means has to be provided to limit the lead that the phantom output is permitted to build up. This function is performed by the "Steering Gear Overshoot" control which in effect limits the rise time of the integrator causing Vp to level off in stages as illustrated in figure 9.12.

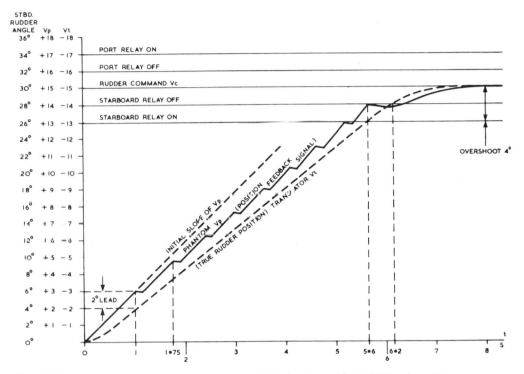

Fig. 9.12 Practical operation of phantom rudder circuit (Courtesy of Racal Marine Controls)

9.9 The adaptive autopilot

Autopilot systems so far described have operated under various command functions, the origins of which have been small signals produced by feedback loops. The rudder command loop signals have been further modified by the Proportional, Integral and Derivative terms which form the nucleus of the P.I.D. autopilot systems. The adjustment of operator controls on the P.I.D. autopilot requires considerable expertise if the system is to operate efficiently. It is not feasible to continually reset the potentiometers during constantly varying weather conditions, thus the system cannot be absolutely efficient. It has already been stated that the P.I.D. autopilot was developed in an effort to enable a vessel to follow a course as accurately as possible by reducing drag caused by excessive rudder angles whilst limiting rudder excursions to a low level in order that wear on the steering gear is minimized. Considerable research has been undertaken into the effects of the ship's natural yaw action in relation to the course to be steered. It has now been found that a straight course is not necessarily the most economical and that the ship's natural yaw action should not be smoothed out.

Operating parameters for modern adaptive autopilots (AAPs) have been developed by a number of notable design engineers over the past two decades. Probably the most influential of these is N. H. Norrbin who, in the early 1970s, derived a performance index relating to added resistance due to imperfect steering control. This he produced in the measurable term of *the square of the average heading error*. Most modern AAP controllers use this index as the fundamental control term. In addition to the fact that a straight course is not the most economical course it was decided that steering control should always be optimized with respect to the prevailing environmental conditions and a low bandwidth should be used to minimize losses. It should be obvious therefore that the two main factors which affect the steering control are:

(a) The complex characteristics of the vessel. Its handling parameters will be different for each vessel, even of the same type, and will change with the loading factor.

(b) Environmental influences, namely wind and tide which will be constantly shifting and introducing instantaneous variable course errors.

Obviously ship characteristics can be programmed into a standard autopilot system and their effects counteracted. This has been standard practice for many years. Environmental effects can, to some extent, be counteracted by the helmsman. It would, however, require a helmsman with the ability to instantaneously predict all ship and environmental effects before applying corrective rudder if course steering is to be optimized. Such a helmsman would be a treasure indeed. It is more logical to replace the helmsman with a computer which is able to react more quickly to constantly changing parameters.

The AAP is, in its simplest form, a good quality autopilot apparatus with the addition of a digital control system (microcomputer) producing the final rudder command signal. Contained in the microcomputer is data relating to the dynamics of a "model ship" which is analysed in order that rudder commands for the actual ship may be predicted.

It is evident that the dynamics of this model ship are critical to the AAP operation. In practice model ship dynamics are accurately set for the vessel on which the AAP is fitted. The AAP systems of two major companies both of which have considerable experience in the field of automatic steering control will now be described.

Sperry Ltd

Sperry designed their adaptive autopilot model ship dynamics around the following criteria:

(6a) Ships operating envelope; the vessel's speed, load factor and external environmental conditions,

(b) Precise dynamics of the vessel which relate to its steering control,

(c) The dynamics of the ship's steering system,

(d) The dynamics of the gyrocompass,

(e) The dynamics of the seaway.

It was then necessary to define the principle modes of operation which required specific performance criteria for each mode. The most used of these modes is open sea course keeping where optimized steering can lead to potentially large savings in fuel oil.

Open sea course keeping

Fuel consumption is affected by a number of factors such as engine performance, trim and the condition of the hull below the water line. These factors are, however, predictable and can be counteracted. Excessive rudder movements will introduce drag which causes fuel loss. It is essential that the computer is able to distinguish between ship/engine loss parameters and rudder movements and apply corrective rudder only when course keeping is affected by environmental conditions and not by the natural yaw of the vessel. Various mathematical formulae have been developed to analyse the AAP integral term to optimize rudder performance. Thus the AAP system automatically minimizes propulsion losses and is termed an adaptive control system (figure 9.13). The term adaptive is used because the mathematical parameters of the model ship have been "adapted" to match those of the actual vessel.

The performance criterion, when reduced to a form suitable for online evaluation on board ship, may be represented as

$$J = \int_0^T (\lambda\psi^2 + \delta^2)\,dt.$$

where ψ = ship's heading error,
δ = rudder angle and
λ = weighting factor derived from analytical expressions of drag forces due to steering.

Obviously the adaptive autopilot must be able to detect that a course change has been commanded. This is the function of the course changing control circuitry.

The course changing controller
When changing course it is standard practice to consider three phases of the manoeuvre: the start of the turn, the period of steady turn and the end of the turn. The amount of rudder applied determines the rate of turn and also the peak roll angle. In practice therefore the maximum roll angle is determined by the maximum permissible rudder limit. Proportional and rate gains can be obtained for each vessel and load condition as a function of speed. In the AAP gains are chosen based on the optimized results of the simulated model of the turn. The primary concern of the AAP in confined waters must be safety in manoeuvres. Course changes in confined waters are controlled by the confined waters controller, in figure 9.13, which is the same as that used for course keeping.

Confined waters mode
Cross-track error in confined waters must be minimized for safe pilotage. Since the microcomputer cannot determine cross-track data an alternative mathematical concept is used. Cross-track ddata for the computer are derived from balancing the heading error against the rudder rate.

$$J = \int_0^T (\lambda\psi_e^2 + \delta^2)\,dt$$

The main difference between the open sea course keeping controller and the confined waters controller is that the gaim of the latter is varied only as a function of the ship's speed.

Figure 9.13 is a simplified block diagram of the Adaptive Steering Module (ASM) which may be fitted to the popular Sperry Universal Gyropilot. This arrangement has also been used to develop a new generation of AAPs which is headed by the "SRP 2000 Ship Control System".

The SRP 2000 could justifiably be called an integrated navigation system because not only is it an AAP but it also utilizes inputs from other navigational aids to produce an accurate navigation fix. The system, the main control console for which is shown in figure 9.15, uses a new approach to autopilot design by employing the versatile CRT display. This display is able to provide the navigator with a large amount of data simply at the push of a button. The display, in its Navigation Mode is illustrated in Figure 9.16, where not only standard heading, rate and rudder angle terms are displayed but also, by scrolling the

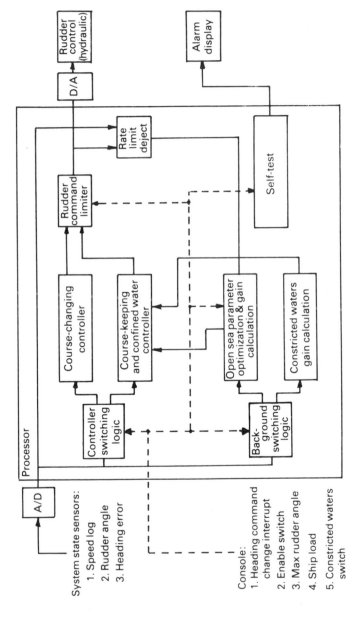

Fig. 9.13 Block diagram of a digital adaptive steering control system (Courtesy of Sperry Ltd.)

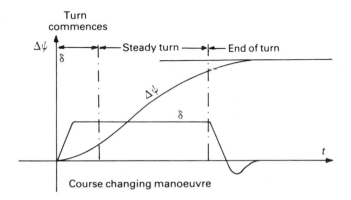

Fig. 9.14 Graph of a ship's heading error vs time in a course changing manoeuvre

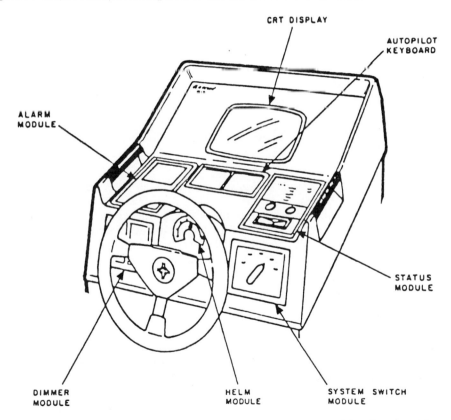

Fig. 9.15 SRP-2000 ship control system: Control console and indicator modules (Courtesy of Sperry Ltd.)

system, navigational data, waypoints, CMG (Course Made Good) etc. can be displayed. Other data pages available to the helmsman are: Instruction Page, Index Page, Emergency Mode, Helm Mode, Remote Mode, Gyro Mode, Turn Rate Mode and Calibration Page. When any of these pages is selected the linear displays of Heading, Rate and Rudder Angle are always available.

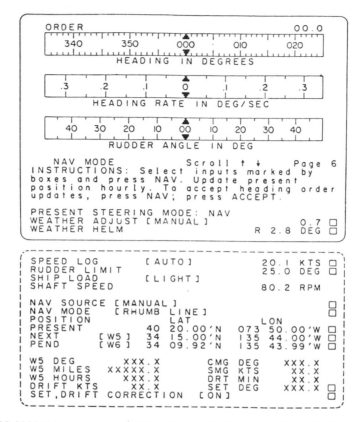

Fig. 9.16 SRP-2000 ship control system: Navigation mode (Courtesy of Sperry Ltd.)

Figure 9.17 shows the alarm/heading module which is independent of the main CRT display. Rate of turn, course error and heading display are accurately displayed in case of failure of the main CRT display. Additionally there are alarm indications for various critical parameters. As with most modern microprocessor controlled equipments a BITE system is inbuilt which will monitor critical parameters and produce warnings of error as listed in Table 9.1.

Racal Decca Marine Controls Ltd

Racal Decca's DP780 adaptive autopilot and steering control system will already be familiar to some readers. Figure 9.18 shows the basic system with the "model ship" concept clearly defined. The automatic autopilot has been designed as has previously been stated, to limit drag effects caused by ship characteristics and weather. As the weather progressively deteriorates rudder demands increase and fuel economy falls. Racal Decca have produced the characteristics of a "second order non-linear electronic ship model". This is actually a source of electronic signals which mirror the dynamic behaviour of the actual ship in every way. The model is capable of reacting to steering activity exactly as the ship herself does in calm weather. With these parameters accurately identified it is possible to identify the quite separate effects which environmental conditions have on the ship's steering characteristics. The model ship has been programmed with three parameters.

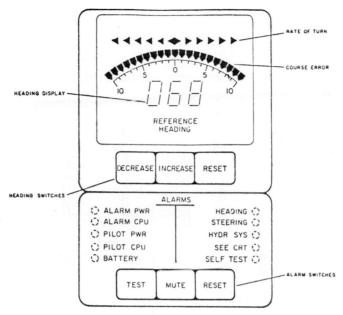

Fig. 9.17 SRP 2000 ship control system. Alarm/heading module (Courtesy of Sperry Ltd.)

Table 9.1

Message order	Message
1	Ship speed out of range
2	Analog/digital converter failure
3	15V Supply failure
4	Eeprom checksum failure
5	No CRT heartbeat
6	No ASM heartbeat
7	Hydraulics system 1 failure
8	Hydraulics system 2 failure
9	Hydraulics system 3 failure
10	Hydraulics system 4 failure
11	Steering system 1 failure
12	Steering system 2 failure
13	Autopilot failure
14	Rudder control unit failure
15	Heading change must be accepted
16	NAV source out of range
17	NAV message format error
18	NAV type not valid
19	Waypoint required
20	Invalid compass step data
21	Synchro converter error
22	Replace eeprom chip
23	Power failure
24	Common memory checksum failure
25	Waypoint cannot be reached

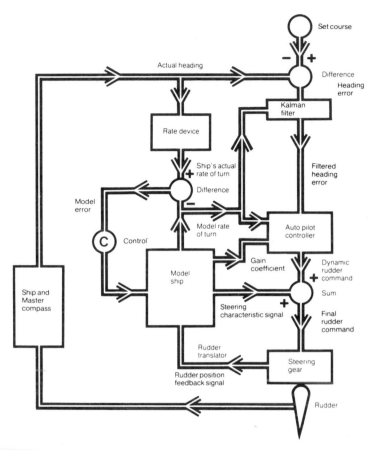

Fig. 9.18 Adaptive autopilot loop (Courtesy of Racal Decca Marine Controls Ltd)

1st parameter: (the only manual preset)
"Tau" setting. Derived from the ship's length and normal cruising speed, the speed factor is thereafter continuously updated by input from speed log or engine revolution indicator.

2nd parameter: (adaptive)
"Gain coefficient" setting. This parameter covers the ship's response (in rate of turn) to rudder movements.

3rd parameter: (adaptive)
"Ship Characteristics" setting. The parameter covers the ship's response to its own inherent ability to increase or decrease its own rate of turn, without any rudder movement.
  Both the adaptive parameters are achieved by comparing the model's response to the ship's rate of turn with an applied rudder angle (for gain coefficient setting) and without an applied rudder angle (for the ship characteristics setting). After a few manoeuvres, the model will have aligned itself and be in harmony with the actual ship i.e. it will have *adapted*.

Operation
Initially the AAP is programmed with the ship's characteristics. The voyage beings with

the "ship model" controlling the rudder activity. As the weather deteriorates the ship starts to yaw producing rudder demand signals, which are smoothed by the Kalman filter, bringing the ship back to its correct heading. The "ship model" in the microprocessor will be producing a rate signal based only on the vessel's initial movements in calm weather. The difference between the two rate command signals, that of the ship model and that of environmental effects, is entirely due to the influence of weather conditions. As has previously been stated it is *not* necessary for the AAP to keep the ship constantly on course because the vessel's natural yaw action will effectively negate the need for large rudder movements. Except in exceptional sea conditions the weather is allowed to act freely on the hull with little rudder movement produced. The actual heading will oscillate to one side or the other of the desired course although the ship itself averages a straight line supported by the permanent helm part of the "Steering Characteristic" parameter of the microprocessor. The Kalman filter, in the AAP controller, will smooth out large course offsets and average them out over a period of time.

In addition to wheel and auto steering the DP780 includes the auxiliary inputs "Rate Steering" and "Navigation Computer". Rate steering is a form of control, which is especially valuable in pilotage waters, utilizing inbuilt rate devices and the AAP electronics. The helmsman can cause the ship to turn at a specific rate-of-swing simply by using the wheel. The rate indicator and control panel is shown in figure 9.17. An indication of the rate of swing in degrees per ships length has been provided as a more meaningful indication of ship movement than the normal degrees per minute devices. The navigation computer input enables the AAP to accept programmed data from a navigation computer or integrated navigation system.

The two AAPs briefly described are representative of the range of modern autopilots which have been produced to improve fuel economy whilst maintaining safe pilotage. Autopilot design in the future will continue to improve steering characteristics by improving microprocessor software, and it seems likely that hardware design techniques will change little.

10
Radio direction finding

10.1 Introduction

Maritime radio direction finding is undoubtedly the oldest of the electronic navigation systems still in use at sea. However, when used by a competent operator it is most certainly one of the best systems for localized navigation. Martime RDF is unique amongst the position finding systems because it is the only one which is capable of determining the bearing vector from the receiving vessel of any transmitting station. This could be a vessel in distress and thus two receiving ships could pinpoint the distress position by producing cross vectors from two known positions. Modern apparatus permits bearings to be taken automatically, even when the receiver is unattended, providing that the unit is capable of receiving an international distress frequency. Such a system is obviously invaluable under the conditions where a vessel has been unable to transmit a position before the crew were forced to abandon ship. It is not surprising therefore that an approved RDF is currently a mandatory fitting on all vessels over 1600 g.r.t. The system can also be very inexpensive which makes it very attractive to the small boat owner. Consequently a direction finder is to be found on most small craft.

The RDF was extensively used throughout the last war for locating the source of radio transmissions because of its versatility. The principle of operation of the system has changed little since those days and is well documented. Its description in this book has therefore been simplified. However, the standard of the receiving apparatus has improved considerably, with automatic direction finderse now dominating the field. The second part of this chapter describes two such equipments.

A manually operated RDF is basically a superhet receiver with modifications to the antenna system. The receiver must be capable of selecting the required frequency band into which the received transmission will fall. The band for maritime radio beacons is 285 to 315 kHz. In practice most direction finders are able to tune over a much larger frequency band and thus improve the receiver's versatility. Frequency selection is a function of the radio frequency amplifier of any receiver. Prior to this stage comes the antenna stage which is the main feature of an RDF.

10.2 Radio waves

A propagated radio wave (figure 10.1) contains both electrostatic and electromagnetic fields of energy. The plane of the electrostatic field is used to denote the polarization characteristic of the propagated wave. A vertical electrostatic field denotes a vertically polarized transmission. An RDF utilizes the horizontal magnetic field produced by a vertically polarized wave at 90 degrees to the vertical plane. The ground wave of such a transmitter radiates omnidirectionally from the antenna with the base of the wave travelling along the surface of the earth. This will however restrict the range of transmission because the wave is rapidly attenuated by its contact with the ground. The useful range of bearings for a given radio beacon is therefore limited.

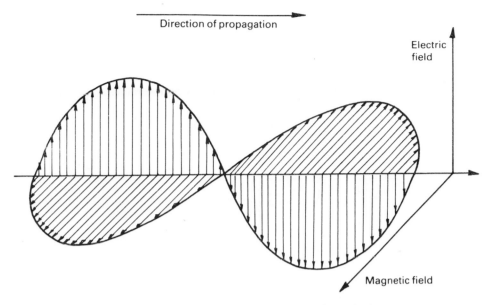

Fig. 10.1 The propagated radio wave illustrating the relationship between both fields of energy and the direction of propagation

10.3 Antenna

The electromagnetic component of the wave travelling horizontaly to the earth's surface will induce small voltages termed e.m.f. (electromotive force) into any vertical conductor in its path. If the conductor is a single vertical wire or antenna, a small current will be caused to flow along its length under the influence of the induced e.m.f. The amplitude of the current will depend upon a number of factors, but for a transmitter with a constant power output it is basically governed by the distance between the transmitter and the receiver. The frequency of the induced e.m.f. will be the same as the transmitted frequency. A vertical antenna possesses the ability to transmit or receive equally well in all directions and is therefore termed omnidirectional. If a transmitter is arranged to describe a circle at a constant distance from a vertical receiving antenna the induced e.m.f. will be constant for all vectors. A polar diagram (which illustrates the receptive properties of an antenna) for a vertical antenna is shown in figure 10.2. The length of the vectors drawn correspond to amplitude and therefore the strength of the signal produced at the speaker will be constant throughout 360 degrees. A polar diagram can be produced for any antenna simply by measuring the induced e.m.f. for all receiving vectors. Many antenna are carefully designed to be highly directional. An example of this is a basic television receiving antenna. In theory such an antenna could be used to determine the baring of the transmitting station. For maritime use however, a simple loop antenna is used. The loop consists of two vertical conductors closed at the top and base to permit current to flow. The shape of the loop is unimportant and for convenience it is often circular. Figure 10.3 shows two vertical antenna joined at the top and at the base via a coil to enable the antenna to be coupled to the input of a receiver. The distance between the vertical conductors must be less than one wavelength of the received frequency, a factor which presents no problem on the medium frequency band used at sea. The centre frequency of the maritime beacon band is 300 kHz, the wavelength of which is 1000 metres. If we assume the distance between the vertical arms to be half of one wavelength (although clearly this would also be

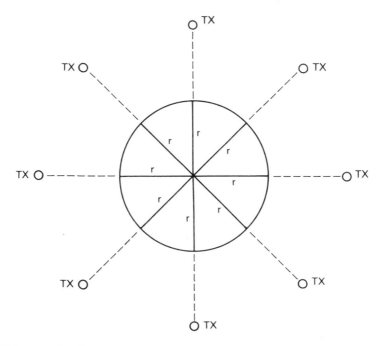

Fig. 10.2   Polar reception diagram of a vertical antenna

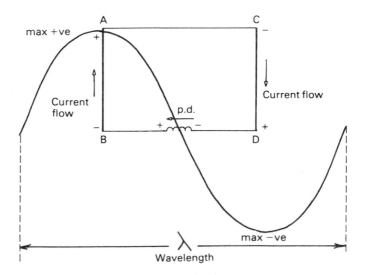

Fig. 10.3   The effect of one wavelength of the groundwave on a loop antenna

impossible in the maritime field) and the direction of propagation as shown in the diagram, then maximum e.m.f.s will be induced in both arms AB and CD. The e.m.f.s will be in antiphase and will cause current to flow through the coil under the influence of an e.m.f. equal to e.m.f. AB plus e.m.f. CD. The resultant current will be at its greatest and therefore if the direction of the received wave is in the plane shown, or 180 degrees away from it, a maximum signal input to the receiver will result. The single electromagnetic wavelength shown will be at 90 degrees to the vertical antenna arms.

With the transmitter at any angular position from the loop, e.m.f.s will be induced in both vertical arms. The relationship between the plane of the loop and the wavefront will determine the polarity of the induced e.m.f.s which in turn determine the direction and amplitude of the resultant current flowing through the inductor. For convenience we shall consider the plan view of the loop and the wavefront of the progapated signal.

Figure 10.4 illustrates that when the wavefront is parallel to the plane of the loop the e.m.f.s induced in both arms AB and CD will be of equal amplitude and the same polarity.

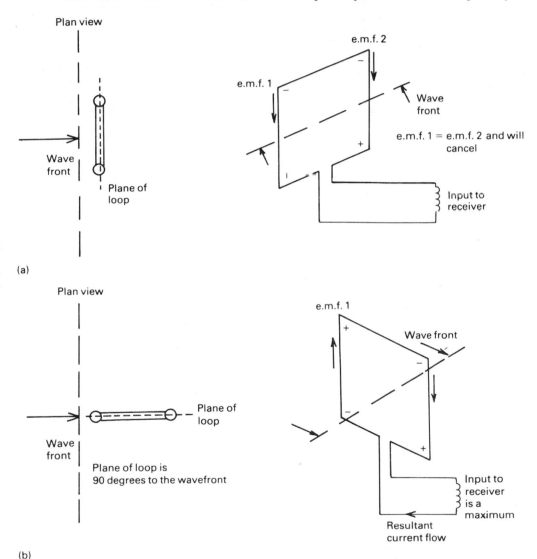

(a)

(b)

Fig. 10.4(a) The resultant output is zero if the plane of the loop is parallel to the received wavefront
(b) The resultant output is maximum if the plane of the loop is at 90 degrees to the received wavefront

The two will therefore cancel producing no resultant current flow in the inductor and hence no input to the receiver. This is termed a NULL position. Clearly there will be a second NULL position 180 degrees away from the first. If the loop is now rotated through 90 degrees so that its plane is now 90 degrees with respect to the wavefront, two e.m.f.s will again be induced in both vertical arms. In this case however, they will be of equal amplitude but opposite polarity and will cause a maximum circulating current to flow thorugh the coil. The situation corresponds to a maximum input to the receiver. Once again there will be a second maximum 180 degrees away from the first, the only difference being that the resultant current will flow in the opposite direction through the coupling coil. The polar diagram produced by such a rotating antenna is shown in figure 10.5 and for obvious reasons is called a "figure of eight" polar diagram. The resultant e.m.f. applied to the receiver from the loop will be 90 degrees out of phase with the received signal. A transmitter bearing north or south produces a resultant NULL output. A transmitter bearing east or west produces a resultant maximum output. Figure 10.6 illustrates the resultant loop e.m.f. produced by moving the loop through one wavelength of the input waveform. The 90 degree phase shift error produced by the loop antenna is eliminated by mounting the relative bearing pointer at 90 degrees to the plane of the loop.

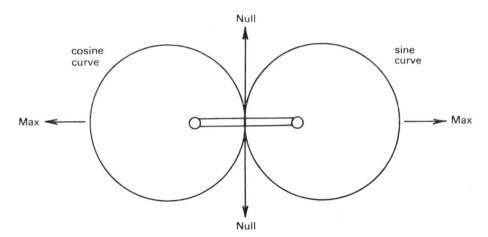

Fig. 10.5 A figure of eight polar diagram for loop antennae

10.4 Sense determination

The minima or NULL positions of the figure of eight polar diagram have been chosen to indicate the direction of the bearing because the human ear is more responsive to a reducing signal than to one which is increasing. There are however two NULL positions, one which indicates the relative bearing and the other the reciprocal. In most cases this poses no problem because the relative bearing position will be the one which lies in the expected bearing quadrant. However when taking the bearing of another vessel it is not known in which quadrant the bearing will lie and therefore a second input to the receiver is required in order that the reciprocal NULL position can be eliminated. The second input is derived from a vertical or sense antenna. The result of adding the vertical antenna signal to the resultant loop signal is yet another polar diagram, called a cardioid, is produced as shown in figure 10.7. The cardioid is produced by adding the figure of eight loop signal to the vertical antenna sense input. The two sine curves add radially, AB + AC = AD. The cosine curve is subtracted radially from the sine curve of the vertical antenna,

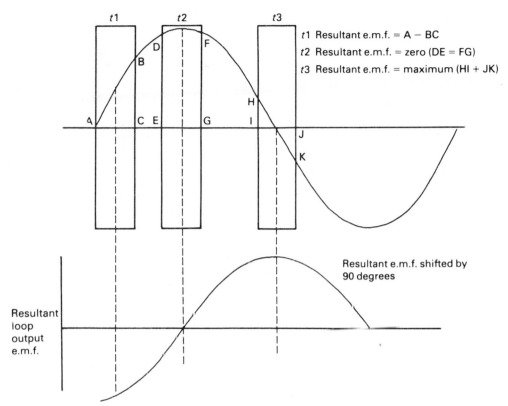

Fig. 10.6 The effect of moving a vertical loop through an electromagnetic waveform. The electromagnetic-wave is at 90 degrees to the vertical conductors

AE − AF = AG. Unfortunately the new single NULL position produced has yet again been shifted by 90 degrees. To compensate for this a second shorter pointer is fitted to manual direction finders at 90 degrees from the relative bearing pointer. Compensation is achieved by a phase shift circuit in an automatic direction finder.

With the exception of equipment designed for small craft, the rotating loop antenna system is no longer used and has been replaced by the superior fixed loop antenna "Bellini Tosi" system.

10.5 The Bellini Tosi system (BT)

The basis of the BT system is the two permanently fixed loop antennae, one mounted on the fore and aft line and the other on the port and starboard line of the vessel. The two loops are mounted on the same pedestal at 90 degrees to each other. Each precisely mounted loop is connected to a pair of fixed coils in a goniometer at the input to the receiver as shown in figure 10.8. The fixed Bellini Tosi loops are connected to corresponding fixed loops in the same plane inside the goniometer. Output from the search coil is tuned to the incoming frequency by the tuning capacitor or C. The resultant circulating current flows through the primary winding of T2 to provide the input to the receiver. The vertical antenna is coupled to the circuit via T1. The switch S1 is biased to the d.f. position to provide a second input when taking bearings for zero sharpening. The goniometer in

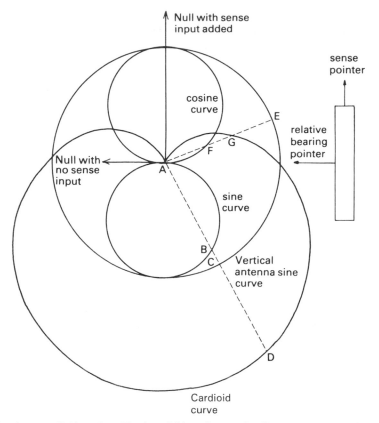

Fig. 10.7 Resultant cardioid produced by the addition of two polar diagrams

effect creates a miniaturized version of the rotating loop antenna system without its disadvantages.

Induced currents flowing in each loop are caused to flow through corresponding fixed field coils in the goniometer. The amplitude and phase relationship of each of the currents will depend upon the relationship between the plane of each fixed loop and the wavefront of the received signal. Each current will cause a magnetic field to be created around the fore and aft and port and starboard field coils of the goniometer. A fully rotatable search coil is inductively coupled to each of the field coils. In this way the mutual inductance between the search coil and the field coils follows a true cosine law for any angular position of the search coil to the field coils through 360 degrees of rotation. If the search coil is rotated fully the input to the receiver will consist of a varying signal producing two maxima and two minima positions. Basically a figure of eight polar diagram has been created artificially in the confined environment of the goniometer. Obviously the construction of the goniometer is critical. Modern manufacturing techniques are able to produce a small compact unit with a search coil able to be rotated by a small servo motor. Such a goniometer has led to the introduction of automatic direction finders.

Errors

The whole RDF system is fraught with errors to an extent that an uninformed operator may consider the bearings taken to be unreliable. This is not so. If a fixed loop RDF

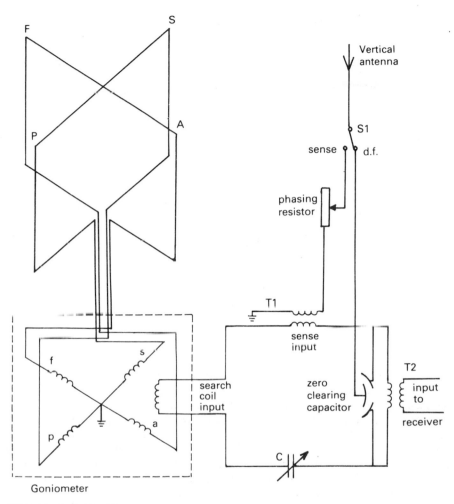

Fig. 10.8 The Bellini Tosi Systems

system is correctly installed and accurately calibrated errors can be reduced to virtually zero. However to understand the system fully one must also appreciate the error causes and cures. The major error factors are listed below.

Quadrantal error

This error is zero at the compass cardinal points rising to a mzximum at 045, 135, 225 and 315 degrees. Each maximum error vector falls into a quadrant and hence the error is termed Quadrantal. The cause of the error is a re-radiated signal produced, mainly along the fore and aft line of the vessel, by the ship's superstructure receiving and re-radiating the electromagnetic component of the signal. All metallic structures in the path of an electromagnetic wave will cause energy to be re-radiated. In this case the re-radiated signal is in phase with the received wave. The two signals arriving at the loop will be of the same frequency and phase and will therefore add vectorially causing the relative bearing to be displaced towards the fore and aft line of the vessel as shown in figure 10.9. The new

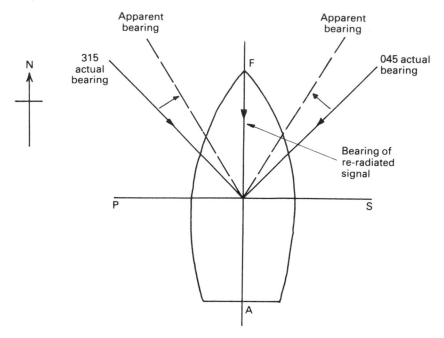

Fig. 10.9 The effects of quadrantal error

bearing is a vector sum of the received and re-radiated signals. The magnitude of the error will depend mainly upon the vessel's freeboard and the position of the loop antenna along the fore and aft line. For a loop mounted in the after quarter of the vessel, the effect will be greatest in the two forward quadrants, and vice versa for a loop antenna mounted in the forward quarter. Fortunately the error, for a given mounting position, is constant and can be virtually eliminated. For a Bellini Tosi system the fore and aft loop antenna will be under greater influence from the unwanted signal than the port and starboard loop antenna. Quadrantal error correction is therefore achieved by placing in parallel with the with the fore and aft loop goniometer coil a quadrantal error corrector coil. The effect of varying the inductance of such a coil during calibration is to reduce the signal pick up along the fore and aft line of the vessel. Modern apparatus also includes a smaller compensation coil across the port and starboard loop circuit. Correct setting of the coils will reduce the effect of quadrantal error to vitually zero. To fully eliminate the error, a site error correction chart as in figure 10.10, is compiled during calibration. The chart is used thereafter enabling corrections to be applied to each relative bearing taken. For modern vessels carrying deck containers a family of such curves is produced to indicate corrections to be applied under different deck cargo loading conditions.

Semi-circular error

As with quadrantal error, semi-circular error is caused by a re-radiated signal arriving at the loop antenna at the same time as the radio wave. In this case the re-radiated signal is produced by vertical conductors in the vicinity of the loop antenna. The re-radiated signal from such conductors will be out of phase with the primary signal and will therefore cause an error which rises to a maximum in two semi-circles. Conductors which produce an out of phase re-radiated signal possess a resonant length which is close to the half

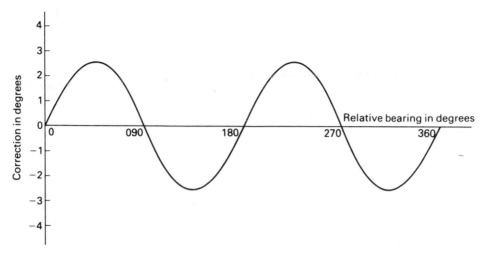

Fig. 10.10 Quadrantal error correction chart

wavelength of the received signal. The most obvious of these conductors are the vessel's various antennae, but wire stays will also produce the same effect. For re-radiation to take place, induced current must be able to flow in the conductor. To prevent this from happening and thus prevent re-radiation, it is simply a matter of isolating all the antennae not in use. The antennae must not be earthed, otherwise current will flow; they must be isolated by disconnection whilst a bearing is being taken. Both a sense antenna and an antenna for the automatic receiving aparatus must be left operational, however, and some re-radiation will result. Wire stays can be isolated by inserting insulators along their length. The small amount of re-radiated signal which still exists after these precautions have been taken, will cause a blurring of the NULL position when attempting to take a bearing. To counteract this all modern equipment is fitted with a zero sharpening or zero clearing control which enables the operator to reduce semi-circular error effect and produce a clear NULL position.

Polarization error or night effect

The RDF system works on the principle that the electromagnetic component of a propagated ground wave will cause small e.m.f.s to be induced in the vertical arms of a loop antenna. The horizontal portions of the loop antenna are not affected by the electromagnetic component of the vertical polarized wave, because the magnetic lines of force lie parallel to the horizontal parts of the loop. Under some conditions propagated radio waves are refracted by the ionosphere and will return to earth some distance away from the transmitter. The "skip distance" as the surface range between the transmitter and the received wave is known, depends upon a number of factors. Two of these are
(a) the frequency of the propagated wave, and
(b) the density of the ionosphere.
The frequency of the radio wave is a constant, but the density of the ionosphere is far from constant as it depends upon radiation from the sun. If an ionospherically refracted radio wave, from the same transmitter as the received ground wave, arrives at the loop, small e.m.fs will be generated in the horizontal portions of the antenna. Under such conditions it will not be possible to determine the direction of the transmitting station by rotating the

loop or search coil because the angular position of the horizontal portions of the loop with respect to the sky wave cannot be changed. Additionally the ground wave and sky wave arriving together at the antenna, may be in or out of phase and will cause fading to occur.

The relationship between the ground wave and the sky wave will be constantly changing in phase, amplitude and polarization which in turn will cause considerable fading and NULL position shifting to occur when attempting to take a bearing.

There is no cure for night effect. However, the effect is most prevalent one hour either side of the time of sunrise and sunset when the ionosphere will be most turbulent. It is advisable therefore not to attempt to take RDF bearings during these times.

Vertical effect

The error caused by vertical effect has been virtually eliminated by the careful construction of loop antenna. The error was caused by unequal capacitances between the unscreened vertical arms of the loop antenna and the ship's superstructure. The effect produced an imbalance in the loop antenna symmetry. This in turn produced errors which varied in each of the quadrants depending upon the ship's superstructure. The effect has been eliminated by mounting the loop conductors inside an electrostatic screening in the form of a tube. As shown in figure 10.11, the loop conductors are mounted precisely in the centre of the tube which has the effect of swamping the imbalance of the external capacitance. The loop screening tube is earthed at its centre and is supported at the pedestal by two insulation blocks. The blocks are in position to prevent the electrostatic screen from becoming a compelte circuit. Then it would become an electromagnetic screen preventing the passage of electromagnetic waves and causing the input to the receiver to fall to zero.

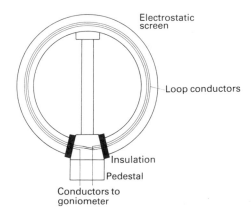

Fig. 10.11 Electrostatic screening of a single loop to minimize vertical error.

Coastal refraction

Maritime RDF utilizes the ground wave, the velocity of which is influenced by the conductivity of the surface over which the wave is travelling. As the ground wave crosses from ground to water an uneven change in velocity will occur. If the wave crosses at an acute angle, the extreme edge of the wavefront will be increased in speed causing refraction to take place as shown in figure 10.12. The refracted radio wave will arrive at the loop antenna on a bearing vector which could be in error by several degrees. To counteract the effects of this error, maritime radio beacons are contructed as colse to the coastline as possible in

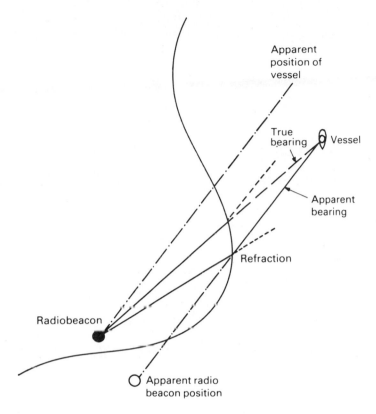

Fig. 10.12 The effect of coastal refraction

order to propagate the ground wave directly onto one medium. However, in some cases a vessel may take a bearing of a radio beacon across a peninsula. In this case coastal refraction will produce an error. The beacons which suffer from coastal refraction in these situations are well documented and error correction figures are listed.

10.6 An automatic direction finder using a servo system (figure 10.13)

The Lodestar III direction finding apparatus has for its heart a low power two phase servo which, via a mechanical drive mechanism rotates the goniometer search coil and bearing pointer. The servo derives its two a.c. inputs from a low frequency oscillator. One of the inputs is phase shifted by 90 degrees to satisfy the requirements of the servo system. Figure 10.14 illustrates the operational characteristics of the two phase induction servo used in this type of receiver. Two signals, a reference and a 90 degree phase shifted control signal, are applied to the two stator windings of the servo via power amplifiers. Current will flow through each of the coils causing magnetic fields to be created along the two axes shown. Each magnetic field causes small e.m.f.s to be induced in the squirrel cage rotor causing it to rotate under their influence. The relative bearing pointers shown above the two phase related signals in the figure, indicate the instantaneous position of the rotor at each of the 45 degree positions of one cycle of input. It must be remembered that the two waveforms are produced by an oscillator and will therefore never be stationary. The resultant

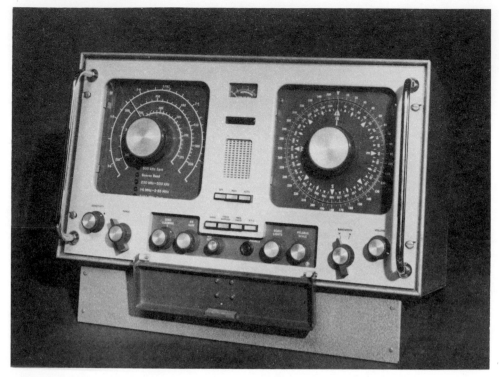

Fig. 10.13 The Marconi International Marine Co. Ltd. Servo automatic direction finder 'Lodestar' III

magnetic field produced by the two alternating currents will be continually changing in relationship and will produde a rotating magnetic field. The rotating magnetic field will cause the rotor to turn and will cause the search coil in the goniometer to rotate via the mechanical linkage. The search coil will continue to rotate as long as the two servo windings are under the influence of the phase quadrature signals. If one signal (the control) disappears the rotor will stop. If the phase relationship between the two signals changes the servo will again stop, unless the change is 180 degrees when the servo rotor will rotate in the opposite direction. This characteristic is used in the automatic direction finder apparatus where the control signal is coupled via the receiver circuits to the control winding of the servo. The control signal therefore is under the influence of the received resultant loop signal amplitude.

Basic system operation (figure 10.15)

Assuming that the search coil is stationary 90 degrees away from a bearing NULL position, a maximum output from the search coil to the loop amplifier will result. The loop signal is then phase shifted by 90 degrees to eliminate the error which will occur when the permanent sense input is applied at a later stage.

The low frequency servo signal produced by the servo oscillator is also phase shifted by 90 degrees. This phase shift is included to satisfy the phase quadrature requirements of the servo motor. The control signal is now applied to a Cowan modulator where both amplitude and phase modulation take place. The output waveform of the modulator has

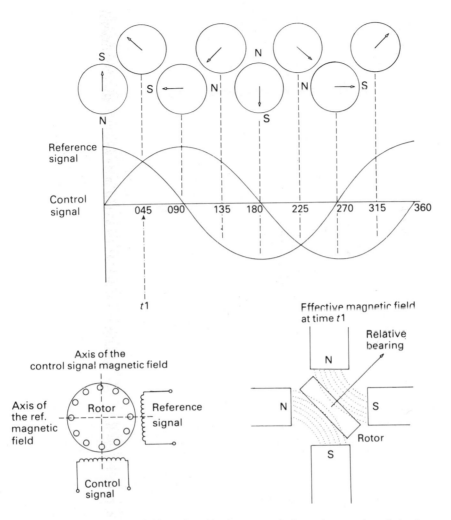

Fig. 10.14 The rotating magnetic field produced in the stator windings of a two phase induction servo

been alternately phase shifted by 180 degrees at the servo oscillator frequency as shown in figure 10.16. In the next r.f. amplifier, the vertical sense antenna signal is added to the output of the modulator causing the loop signal to be returned to its original phase. The signal is now an amplitude modulated radio frequency and is processed by the superhet receiver in the normal way. Chopping the loop signal in this way and then re-constituting it with the sense input signal ensures that the servo cannot rotate is the sense input fails. Thus a failsafe system has been introduced to eliminate the possibility that the servo would stop the search coil on the reciprocal NULL position of the realtive bearing if the sense antenna failed.

The servo detector circuit will detect the amplitude variation of the intermediate frequency and couple the resultant signal through a series resonant filter to the control winding of the servo. The filter ensures that only the low frequency servo signal is amplified as the servo control signal. The rotor will now rotate moving the search coil of the goniometer towards a bearing. This in turn will cause the loop signal to the r.f.

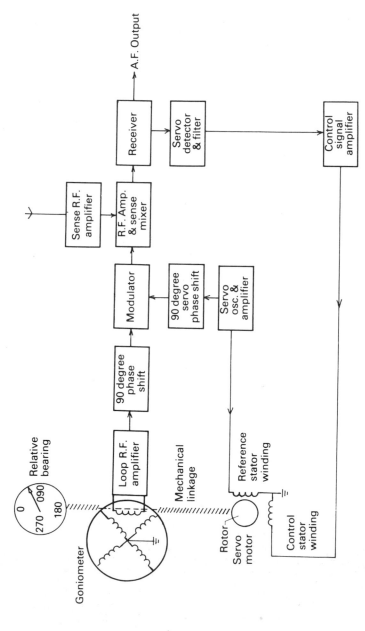

Fig. 10.15 Block diagram of an automatic direction finder based on a servo system

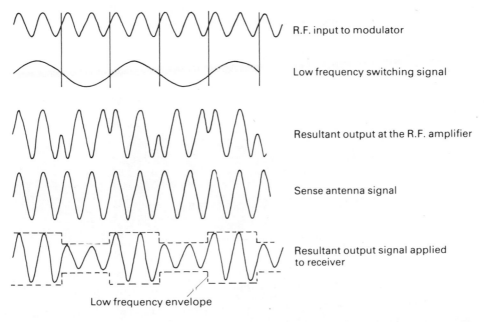

R.F. input to modulator

Low frequency switching signal

Resultant output at the R.F. amplifier

Sense antenna signal

Resultant output signal applied to receiver

Low frequency envelope

Fig. 10.16 Illustration of a waveform mixing to produce the servo signal envelope

amplifier to reduce in amplitude. The ouput from the modulator will therefore reduce causing the output from the servo detector to reduce. The control signal amplitude falls, the magnetic field created around the control stator winding reduces and the rotor will slow down. Eventually a NULL position will be reached where the loop signal falls to zero, no modulation takes place and the servo stops. Theoretically it is possible for the servo to stop on the reciprocal NULL position. In practice however, the reciprocal NULL position is very unstable due to noise and thus the system will only remain steady in the relative bearing position. To prevent NULL position overshoot, which could be produced by the torque of the servo as it swings rapidly towards a NULL, an opposing magnetic field is created within the servo, by a d.c, when the rotor has moved within prescribed limits of the NULL position.

Auto alarm mode

A small unit called "Autoguard" can be connected between the automatic alarm apparatus bells and the automatic direction finder servo system in order that automatic bearings may be taken on the 500 kHz international distress frequency when the receiver is left unattended. The "Autoguard" disables the servo system oscillator until power is received from the auto-alarm bells to lift the disable circuit. A relay in the "Autoguard" then switches on the servo oscillator for a few seconds enabling the system to indicate the bearing of the vessel in distress. The servo oscillator is again disabled before the automatic direction finder can take bearings of other vessels in the vicinity. Two vessels fitted with an "Autoguard" unit would be able to pinpoint the distress position accurately.

10.7 An automatic direction finder using a microprocessor

The STC ADF 790 (see figure 10.17) utilizes a crossed loop antenna with an integral sense antenna. Each loop signal output is coupled to a receiver via a switching system controlled by the microprocessor.

Fig. 10.17 The STC International Marine Company's ADF 790 Microprocessor based automatic direction finder

Receivers A and B are identical highly stable double conversion superhets. Receiver A however, is considered to be the primary receiver and has an automatic gain control circuit. Frequency stability of both receivers is maintained by the microprocessor which controls the frequency synthesizer to produce the required local oscillator frequencies. Frequency, phase and gain stability are of vital importance if errors are to be avoided.

Basic system operation (fig. 10.18)

The output signal amplitude of both loop antennae will vary with the angle of the received radiowave relative to the ship's heading. Figure 10.19 illustrates the resultant polar diagrams produced by the two loops for a transmission received on a relative bearing of 30 degrees. In this case the output from the fore and aft loop will be greater in amplitude than that from the port and starboard loop. The vector XY is an indication of signal amplitude corresponding to the relative bearing. Each loop signal is switched to a receiver and their amplitudes compared. The strongest signal, in this case the fore and aft loop resultant signal, is then switched to the primary receiver. Obviously the fore and aft loop polar diagram also indicates a reciprocal bearing NULL at 210 degrees. To remove this ambiguity the sense antenna is now connected to receiver B. The phase relationship between the fore and aft loop signal and the sense antenna signal is now compared in the bearing detection assembly board to determine the relative bearing. The process is extremely complex. It is controlled by the $\emptyset$ set (phase comparison initiation pulse) and the B sel line (bearing select) which both originate in the microprocessor. Basically the decoded phase relationship is used to clock up/down logic counter under command of the B sel line input. The output from the counters is then connected via an A to D converter to the interface circuits of the microprocessor.

The operation mode is selected using a key pad which employs a matrix to provide inputs to an encoder. The encoder produces a unique digital ouput code for each key pressed. The code is then coupled to the processor via the interface logic. Gyrocompass data are encoded into digital form in the interface circuit.

The microprocessor uses an 8 bit Central Processing Unit (CPU) which is fed with a clock control from the CRT logic board master oscillator. Address information, reset, read/write pulse, and latch enable pulse are all generated by the CPU in addition to the receiver control logic. The lower 8 bits, A0 to A7, of the CPU address are multiplexed with data and connected to IC2 which stores the data until required. IC2 is enabled by an address latch enable pulse as required. The CPU also provides I/O/$\overline{M}$, $\overline{WR}$ (write), and $\overline{RD}$ (read) which are gated via IC14 to provide four memory and port control lines $\overline{MEMR}$ (memory read), $\overline{MEMW}$ (memory write), $\overline{IOR}$ (input/output port read) and $\overline{IOW}$ (input/output port write). $\overline{MEMW}$ and $\overline{MEMR}$ are gated to IC19 to command both the EPROM and RAM memory capacity. Obviously there will be no write function to the EPROM memory. $\overline{IOR}$ and $\overline{IOW}$ are gated to IC18 which controls the three input/output ports.

The five EPROMs hold dedicated programs to control all the receiver functions and bearing calculations. Specific sections of EPROM memory are selected by the CPU under command of the keypad data. EPROM memory is selected by the $\overline{MEMR}$ line going to logic 0 to cause IC19 to decode the ADS BUS line A8 to A15 and produce an output on one of the lines 00 to 04. If all five EPROM outputs are required, the $\overline{MEMR}$ line remains low, the ADS BUS line A8 to A15 changes its 8 bit data encoding which in turn will produce a sequential output on lines 00 to 04 from IC19.

The two RAMs are commanded in parallel from the line 05 from IC19. Each RAM stores four bits of data (one RAM AD0 to AD3 and the second AD4 to AD7). Thus the RAMs are capable of storing 1024 eight bit words (4096 times two RAMs = 8192 bits). Data are written into the RAMs from the CPU or I/O ports when the $\overline{MEMW}$ line goes low.

Microprocessor operation in a bearing mode

Keypad commands are read onto the data bus via the I/O port IC7 which is enabled by holding the $\overline{RD}$ line low. The line 02 output from IC18 will also be enabled. The CPU now commands the receiver and bearing detection assembly functions to produce bearing data at the I/O port IC3. The bearing calculation program held in the EPROMs commands all the logic functions, via the CPU, during the operation sequence. Using the RAMs as storage, the CPU now inputs bearing and gyro data to complete the operation and produce the 8 bit data required to command the CRT logic. The CRT logic board converts the 8 bit data to produce display information and timebase requirements for the Visual Display Unit. Programs held in the five EPROMs make the equipment simple to operate and versatile.

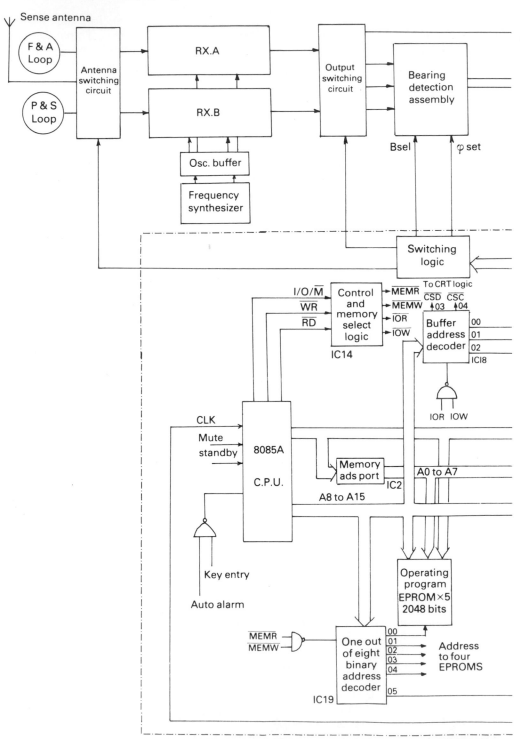

Fig. 10.18 The basic diagram of the STC International Marine ADF 790 Microprocessor controlled equipment

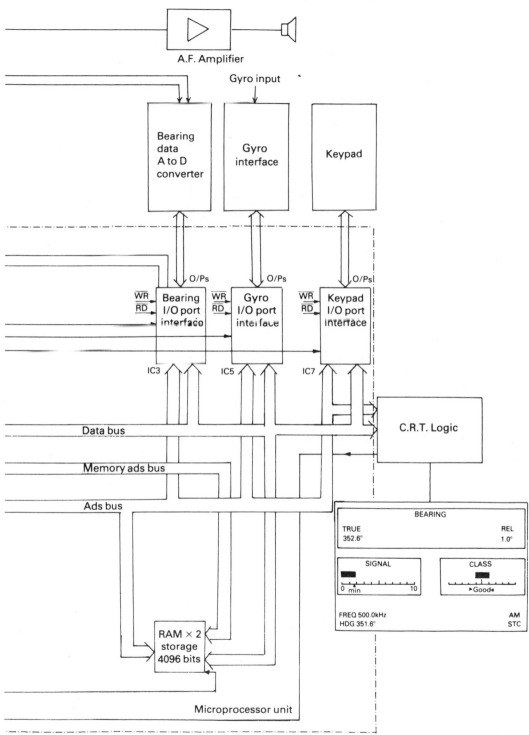

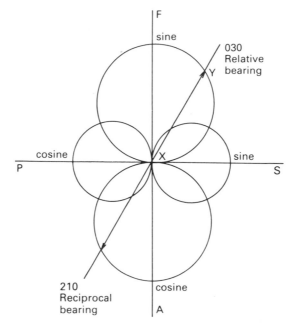

Fig. 10.19 The polar diagrams of a crossed loop system

Programs are included for:

Broadcast mode The receiver may be used for the reception of AM, CW and SSB signals.

Bearing mode As previously described.

Calibration mode To simplify calibration procedures.

Frequency sequential mode Enables bearings to be taken on three separate radio transmissions in sequence. The processor will continue to calculate and display bearings as shown in figure 10.20.

	Freq sequential			
Freq	True BRG	Rel BRG	Class	Sig
■ 500.0	106.3	99.3	2.1	32
2182.0	143.1	136.1	3.5	24
200.0	303.5	296.5	>5	05
Freq	500.0 kHz			AM
HDG	7.0°			STC

Fig. 10.20 Frequency sequential mode

Auto alarm mode If the equipment is ON or is switched to standby and an automatic alarm signal is received, the processor will automatically select 500 kHz, display a warning and continue to take bearings. Two consecutive "good" bearings will be frozen on the display.

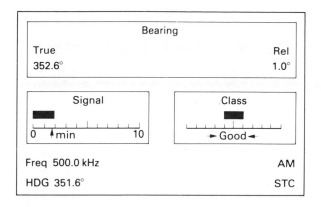

Fig. 10.21 Bearing mode display

Display As figure 10.21 illustrates, the display provides a continuous reading of the frequency selected, heading (derived from the gyro input), signal strength, class of bearing, true and relative bearings.

There is little doubt that RDF has a future in a world of instant navigation systems. However, that future must be dependent upon an automatic system such as one of the two described here.

11
Global maritime distress and safety system (GMDSS)

11.1 Introduction

It may seem a little strange to include a chapter concerning distress in a book dedicated to radio navigation. However, the Global Maritime Distress and Safety System is of prime importance to all maritime personnel as it is likely that elements within the system will affect each individual in the future. The GMDSS is being developed to provide mariners with a global communications and locating network, elements of which are capable of being operated by an individual with minimum communications knowledge and yet enable alerting and SAR (Search and Rescue) to be reliably controlled.

The present alerting distress and safety system, as defined in the International Convention for Safety of Life at Sea (SOLAS 1974) is built around the requirement that vessels at sea keep continuous radio listening watch on specified international distress frequencies. Depending upon the type of vessel and the length of the voyage undertaken radio equipment capable of transmitting over a specified range will also be carried. According to SOLAS 1974, the minimum range of communications which needs to be provided by shipboard equipment is 150 nautical miles. It may be thought that 150 miles is too small a distance over which to communicate a distress alert. It should be remembered however that a ship in distress requires immediate assistance which, by definition, can only readily be provided by ships in close vicinity to the casualty.

Traditionally ships subject to the SOLAS 1974 convention utilize two manually operated systems for distress alerting, which are:

(a) morse telegraphy on the Medium Frequency (MF) 500 kHz, and
(b) radiotelephony on the MF 2182 kHz or Very High Frequency (VHF) 156.8 mHz Channel 16.

There are major disadvantages with both of these systems. A highly trained morse operator is needed to handle morse telegraphy alerting and communications on 500 kHz, requiring ships to carry a specialized officer, with all subsequent ongoing costs. There is to be no place for the traditional morse radio operator in the new GMDSS operation and consequently morse telegraphy will cease to be used at sea after a transitional period. The limited range of communications using either MF or VHF can be tolerated and both frequencies will still be available in the GMDSS. Because ships at sea have always had some difficulty in communicating over long distances changes are rapidly being introduced. The advent of the satellite age and digital technology are both having a major impact upon GMDSS operation.

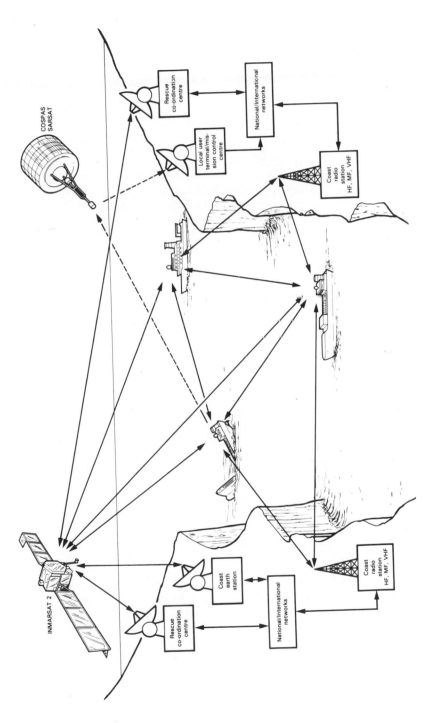

Fig. 11.1 General concept of the global system (courtesy I.M.O.)

11.2 The system

The basic concept of GMDSS is illustrated in figure 11.1. The diagram shows that a ship in distress is effectively inside a highly efficient radionet. If the casualty is correctly fitted with GMDSS equipment it will be able to alert and communicate with a wide range of other radio stations and through them initiate a coordinated search and rescue (SAR) operation based on a rescue coordination centre (RCC). The two satellite elements in the radionet are the International Maritime Satellite Organization's INMARSAT geostationary satellites and the Russian/French COSPAS/SARSAT satellites which are polar orbiting. Full details of the major global communications network provided by INMARSAT may be found in volume two of this publication – Electronic Aids to Navigation, Volume 2 Radar and Communications.

A navigation element of the GMDSS called NAVTEX will provide navigation data and meteoreological warnings. It is described later in this chapter and in chapter 12.

Whilst is should be remembered the the GMDSS is a global system it will not be necessary for all ships to carry a full range of communications equipment. The equipment to be carried will be determined by the declared area of operation of a vessel within the GMDSS radionet. Areas of operation have been designated as follows:

(a) Area A1: within the radio range of shore based VHF coastal radio stations. Typically 20 to 30 nmiles. Many countries will be unable to provide sufficient radio stations to produce an A1 area totally surrounding their coastline. For example the United Kingdom has declined to declare an A1 area around its coast. This means that ships will have to be fitted with radio equipment to satisfy A2 requirements for trading from the U.K.

(b) Area 2: within the radiorange of shore based MF coastal radio stations. Typically 100 to 150 nmiles.

(c) Area A3: within the coverage area INMARSAT satellites. Approximately the total surface area of the world excluding areas north of 70 degrees N and south of 70 degrees S.

(d) Area A4: all other remaining areas.

The first concern of any radio-communications operator during a distress is that of *Alerting*. Alerting SAR units to a maritime casualty must take precedence over all other communications. A GMDSS alert will normally be initiated and acknowledged manually. A manual alert is easily initiated by using Digital Selective Calling (DSC) or simply pressing the "red" button on an INMARSAT ship earth station (SES) unit, now known as a Mobile Earth Station (MES). If a disaster overwhelms a vessel before the DSC can be activated, a float free satellite emergency position-indicating radio beacon (EPIRB) is automatically released and activated. Under GMDSS regulations all vessels must be provided with two totally independent methods of distress alerting of which the EPIRB may be one.

The two traditional international distress communications frequencies 2182 kHz and Channel 16 on VHF will be retained for voice communications. A DSC distress alert will be transmitted on two additional frequencies, 2187.5 kHz and Channel 70 VHF. It is therefore necessary to have equipment which will maintain a dual listening watch on the appropriate frequency bands.

Once the Rescue Coordination Centre (RCC) for an ocean region has been advised of a distress alert it will use either terrestrial or satellite communications to alert other vessels in the area of the casuality. This again implies the use of DSC.

Because DSC forms such an integral part of GMDSS a description follows. Readers should remember that DSC is a highly complex electronic calling system and only a relatively brief organizational description can be provided here. Further in-depth technical information may be found in volume two of this work

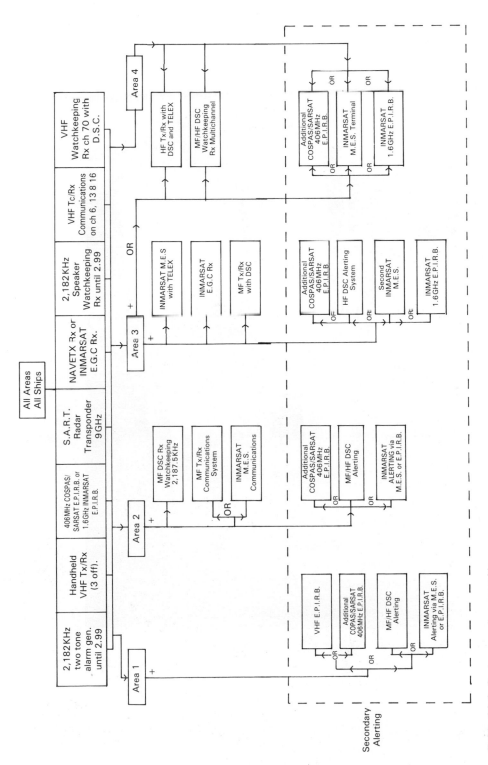

Table 11.1 Carriage requirement table

Fig. 11.2 Example of MF/HF DSC equipment (courtesy I.M.O.)

11.3 Digital selective calling (DSC)

Under international regulations all transmitting stations must identify themselves and consequently each station is provided with a selected code. This may simply be the station name as in the ship's name, or it may be the group of call letters or increasingly a group of numbers. The numbers will of course be decimal and in the case of ships form a group of nine numbers unique to a single vessel.

By using the ship's call number, a coastal radio station is able to call a selected vessel. Collective calls may also be made to all ships, or ships belonging to one company or trading in one area of the world. Selective calling is, depending upon radio wave propagational characteristics, a reliable way of automatically calling ships. Although the ship's call number is shown in decimal format, digital selective calling uses a sequence of seven unit binary combinations. It is only by the use of binary codes that true digital communications and hence reliability is achievable. Whilst DSC calls are of primary importance for distress alerting and acknowledgement, the system is capable of handling other more routine communications.

Figure 11.3 illustrates the sequence of distress call, relay and acknowledgement information which is transmitted. In the distress mode all messages will produce a hard copy on the associated printer. A distress call is initiated simply by pressing the "red" distress button. An incoming distress call will initiate the printer along with audio and visual alarms. The transmission speed of a DSC call varies depending upon the frequency band used. On MF and HF it is fairly slow at 100 bauds, but on VHF is 1200 bauds (the baud is the standard unit for expressing the speed of digital transmission). With all methods of automatic digital transmission it is necessary to include error correction coding in the transmission. This is to enable the receiving apparatus to identify errors and in some cases correct them. A DSC sequence transmits each single character twice and uses an overall message check at the end. A single call on MF or HF therefore varies between 6.2 and 7.2 seconds whereas on the faster baud rate of VHF it is between 0.45 and 0.63 seconds depending upon message content. In order to improve the chances of a DSC call or alert being received it is automatically transmitted for five consecutive attempts. Additionally when DSC alert is made on MF or HF it is transmitted up to six times over any or all of the frequencies available (one on MF and five on HF).

Once the DSC distress button has been activated the automatic transmission pattern shown in figure 11.3 is transmitted. The first two blocks are essential to permit the receiving DSC unit to synchronize with the incoming transmission.
Distress alert data:
(a) Format Specifier: A distress code will automatically be sent.
(b) Self identification: The unique nine digit number (in binary form) identifying the vessel in distress.
(c) Nature of Distress: This may be selected by the operator from one of nine codes, i.e. fire or explosion, flooding, collision etc. In the absence of a front panel input the system defaults to "undesignated distress".
(d) Distress Coordinates: Automatically included from the interfaced satellite navigation data or defaults to "no position" information.
(e) Time: The time at which the distress coordinates were valid.
(f) Telecommand: Indicates whether subsequent distress information will be by radiotelephony or Narrow Band Direct Printing (NBDP) telegraphy (a standard printer). The system defaults to radiotelephony.
It is evident that the future of GMDSS relies on the accuracy and reliability of DSC during alerting and communicating particularly for distress operations.

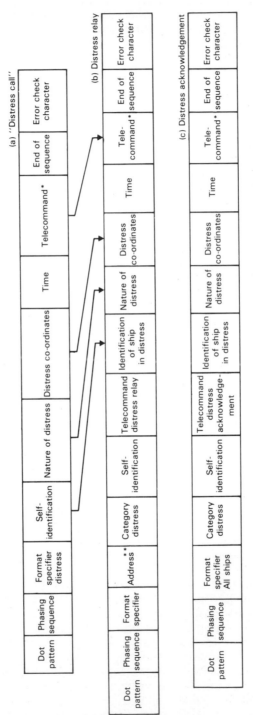

Fig. 11.3   Sequence of (a) "distress calls", (b) distress relay call and (c) distress acknowledgement

*Type of subsequent communication (radiotelephony or teleprinter)
**Address is not included if the format specifier is "all ships"
(courtesy I.M.O.)

Once a valid alert has been received and acknowledged by a regional Rescue Coordination Centre (RCC), Search and Rescue (SAR) operations will be initiated.

During this exercise radiocommunications will again be vital to the operation. On-scene communications are by definition short range and will normally take place on MF or VHF between the casualty and other ships or aircraft in the area using MF 2182 kHz and VHF Channel 70. Locating the casualty may be done using radiodirection finding or if the ship is in distress has activated an SAR 9 GHz transponder, the assisting unit's radar may be used. Bridge to bridge communications will of course be on VHF.

11.4 GMDSS space segment

Satellite communications plays a crucial role in the operation of GMDSS. Suitably equipped vessels can send a distress alert and receive an acknowledgement virtually instantly irrespective of their position in the world.

There are two satellite segments, the INMARSAT system and the COSPAS/ SARSAT system. The INMARSAT system uses four equatorial geostationary orbiting satellites whereas the COSPAS/SARSAT system utilizes polar orbiting satellites. Communication via the INMARSAT system is instantaneous and two way whereas via the COSPAS/SARSAT system communication suffers from some delay and is outward from the ship only.

11.5 COPAS/SARSAT

COSPAS/SARSAT (Space system for search of distress vessels/Search And Rescue Satellite-Aided Tracking) is an international satellite-aided search and rescue system established and operated by organizations in Canada, France, the USA and the USSR. Readers will now be aware of the system parameters and operation of the Transit satellite navigation network detailed in Chapter 6 of this volume.

COSPAS/SARSAT operates in a reciprocal mode to Transit satellites. Digital signals on 406 MHz (for maritime GMDSS EPIRBs) are transmitted upwards to be received and electronically processed by the satellite. Various parameters such as Doppler frequency shift are used to determine the position of the casualty which may be a maritime EPIRB, an aeronautical ELT (Emergency Locating Transmitter) or a PLB (Personal Locator Beacon). The data thus produced are transmitted to a Mission Control Centre (MCC) for onward transmission to an RCC when the satellite passes over an MCC. Depending upon the relative position of a satellite with respect to the casualty there may be some delay in downloading the information but this is insignificant when one considers that the system permits global distress alerting. The main elements of this alerting system are shown in figure 11.4.

11.6 INMARSAT

A brief outline description of the INMARSAT system follows in order to give the reader an understanding of INMARSAT's place in GMDSS. A full description of satellite communications and INMARSAT can be found in *Electronic Aids to Navigation: Radar and Communications*.

Forty-two countries are now signatory members of the International Maritime Satellite Organization (INMARSAT). Each member country appoints an organization to represent its investment and interests in INMARSAT. British Telecommunications International operates within this framework in the UK. INMARSAT provides the

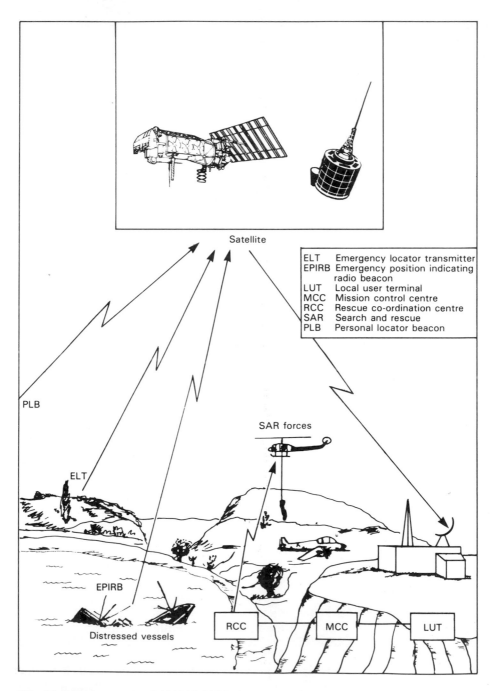

ELT   Emergency locator transmitter
EPIRB Emergency position indicating
       radio beacon
LUT   Local user terminal
MCC   Mission control centre
RCC   Rescue co-ordination centre
SAR   Search and rescue
PLB   Personal locator beacon

Fig. 11.4 Basic concept of COSPAS/SARSAT system (courtesy I.M.O.)

satellite capacity which in the first generation system consisted of leased transponders on Marecs and Intelsat vehicles.

INMARSAT signatories are responsible for the establishment and operation of coast earth stations (CES), now known as Land Earth Stations (LES), which form the landbased downlink from a satellite. Ship owners purchase mobile earth station equipment (MES) which has been constructed to INMARSAT approved standards.

INMARSAT's operations control centre (OCC) forms the nucleus of the system's control. The OCC is located near Euston railway station in central London from where technical operators monitor the network for all three ocean regions. Each of the ocean regions, Atlantic (AOR), Indian (IOR) and Pacific (POR) is served by one or more satellites in geostationary orbit approximately 36000 km above the equator. Currently there are four satellites in use each producing a coverage 'footprint' as shown in figure 11.5.

At the time of writing there are two main types of MES available. The largest of these is the INMARSAT A MES which is able to handle all forms of two way communications between ship and shore. Voice, telex, facsimile, data and slow scan television communications are able to be established using an INMARSAT A installation. This is easily recognized on board a ship by the large parabolic antenna enclosed inside a radome. A smaller and cheaper installation known as INMARSAT C MES is now available for use at sea. An INMARSAT C MES is not able to handle voice communications but provides two way communications via telex or computer data services. The unit is very small and uses a small omnidirectional antenna. Two further types of MES are under development, they are the INMARSAT B and the INMARSAT M units which will meet other needs.

Under GMDSS regulations an INMARSAT C MES is accepted as an alternative to an INMARSAT A MES or HF radio station on vessels trading in area A3.

The following services are provided by INMARSAT as part of the GMDSS radionet.

Ship to shore distress alerting

The INMARSAT system provides instant priority access to shore in emergency situations. The operator is provided with a red distress button which when activated instantly sends a distress request. The message is recognized at an LES and a priority channel is allocated. The system is entirely automatic and once activated will connect a ship operator directly with an RCC. If the MES is interfaced with the vessel's satellite navigation equipment, which is common practice, the geographical location of the distress will also be automatically transmitted. In addition, an L band EPIRB may be carried which will give access to the INMARSAT system should the beacon be activated in a distress situation. The beacon will not provide two way communications but a means of alerting only.

Shore to ship distress alerting

This may take one of three forms:
(a) An *All Ships Call* which is made to vessels in one ocean region.
(b) A *Geographical Area Call* which is made to vessels in a specific area. Areas used are based on the IMO NAVAREA system described later. A MES will automatically recognize and accept a geographical area call only if the operator has previously input a specific code.
(c) A *Group Call to Selected Ships* which will alert selected ships in any global area again providing specific codes have been input to the MES. Additionally shore to ship calls may in future be made via the Enhanced Group Calling (EGC) network.

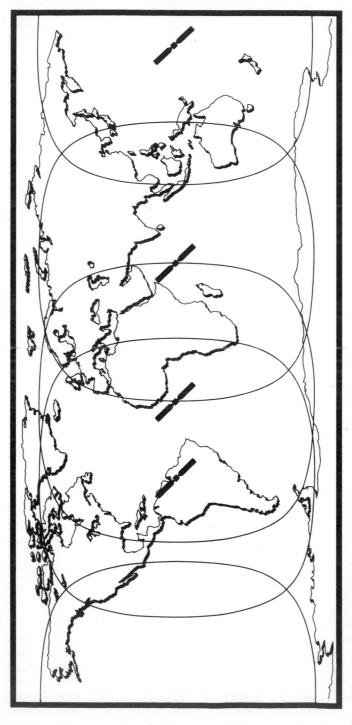

Fig. 11.5 INMARSAT four geostationary satellite configuration (courtesy Ocean Voice)

11.7 Enhanced group calling (ECG)

The EGC system has been designed by INMARSAT to provide a fully automated service capable of addressing messages to individual vessels, predetermined groups of ships or all ships in variable geographical areas. EGC alerts may be addressed to groups of ships designated by fleet, flag or geographical area. A geographical area may be further defined as a standard weather forecast area, a NAVAREA or other predetermined location. This means that in addition to efficient GMDSS shore to ship alerting, the system is able to provide automated urgency and safety information as well as fleet calls made by the owner.

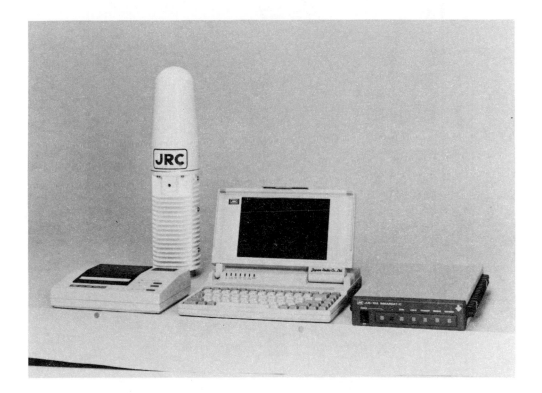

Fig. 11.6 JRC INMARSAT C equipment (Courtesy JRC Ltd)

Currently it is envisaged that an EGC receiver will be an addition to the INMARSAT C MES below decks equipment. Each satellite transmits a single carrier which will possess a higher radiated power (EIRP) than is required by the MES. This will enable future equipment to be developed which will be a broadcast receive only ship earth station (ROSES) unit dedicated to EGC operation. In the case of NAVAREA warnings, vessels could select the area for which they wished to receive messages. Figure 11.7 shows a transmission to NAVAREA II being received by ships heading for that area from NAVAREA IV.

As has been stated many times in this book, automated data transmissions must be provided with some form of error detection or correction system. The EGC service

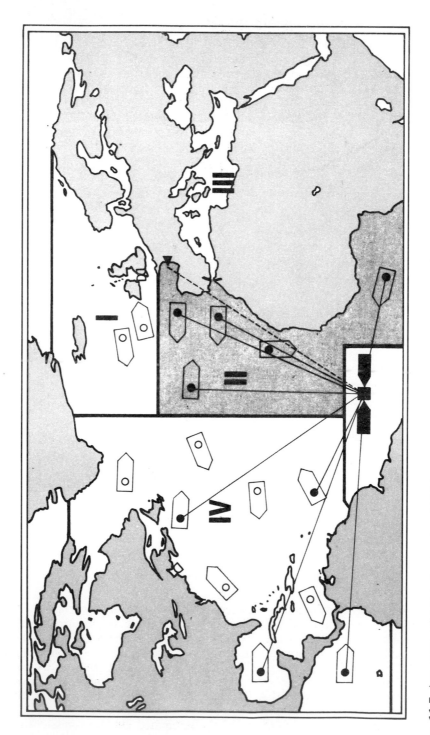

Fig. 11.7 Area group call addressing (courtesy I.M.O.)

is no exception. If the message possesses an unacceptable number of detected errors the message will not be printed. In practice the default figure is 4 per cent which in the INMARSAT system is extremely unlikely to occur. EGC calling may also supplement the NAVTEX service where areas of reception become difficult, using the NAVTEX 518 kHz transmission frequency.

12
The NAVTEX system

12.1 Introduction

The NAVTEX service forms an integral part of both the Global Maritime Distress and Safety System (GMDSS) and the World Wide Navigational Warning Service (WWNWS) which is provided by INMARSAT. These broadcast systems are designed to provide the navigator with up to date navigational warnings in English (the international maritime language). The systems are also able to provide a means of shore to ship alerting for distress and urgency message transmission. Whilst NAVTEX and NAVAREA message services require a number of different broadcasting arrangments, the two systems are essentially the same in many ways.

The WWNWS global service provided by INMARSAT is based on the International Maritime Organization (IMO) NAVAREAS shown in Figure 12.1. Messages within these designated areas are currently being transmitted on HF using morse telegraphy. However, regulations for implementing GMDSS clearly show that carrying a morse trained communications officer is not a requirement. It is therefore the intention of international authorities to continue this operation using automated broadcasts received by a Narrow Band Direct Printing (NBDP) unit fitted on board ships trading in the A3/A4 GMDSS areas. NAVTEX has been operating very successfully for a number of years using NBDP methods of alerting and message reception, even though NAVTEX range is limited beyond the coastal GMDSS areas A1/A2.

The NAVTEX service

NAVTEX uses the single frequency of 518 kHz with Frequency Shift Keying (FSK) on the FM carrier wave. The medium frequency 518 kHz propagates mainly by surface wave and therefore range is effectively determined by carrier power at the transmitter. Because all NAVTEX transmitters worldwide use 518 kHz, range must be strictly controlled. If two neighbouring transmissions were received by a single NAVTEX unit severe fading and signal degradation would occur with a consequent loss of data. An additional safeguard against this occurrence is the use of time division multiplex (TDM) techniques of the carrier frequency. A simple organizational matrix proposed for worldwide NAVTEX TDM transmission is shown in figure 12.3. Each NAVAREA is broken down into four groups of transmitters. Each of the four groups has six transmitters, each with a ten minute allocated transmission slot every four hours. It should be noted that the matrix is designed for broadcasts of routine navigational information and that a considerable amount of data can be transmitted in ten minutes at 100 bauds. Distress and vital warnings are transmitted upon receipt.

12.2 Receiver functions

A NAVTEX receiver is designed with the ability to select the messages to be printed. However, various messages including distress alerts cannot be excluded. The message

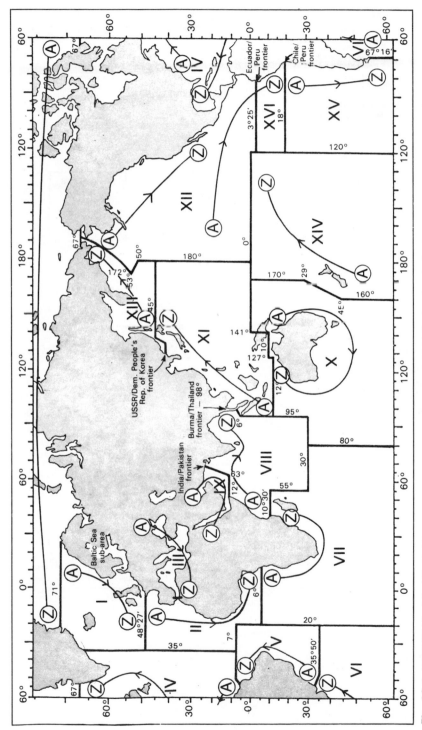

Fig. 12.1 NAVAREAS of the World Wide Navigational Warnings Service (WWNWS) showing the basic scheme for allocation of transmitter identification characters by IMO (courtesy I.M.O.)

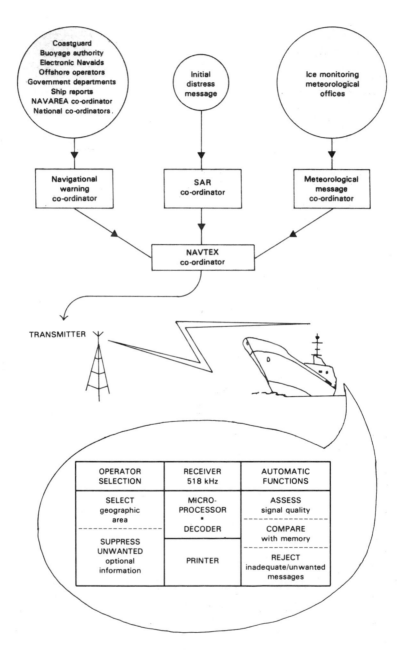

Fig. 12.2 Structure of the NAVTEX service (courtesy I.M.O.)

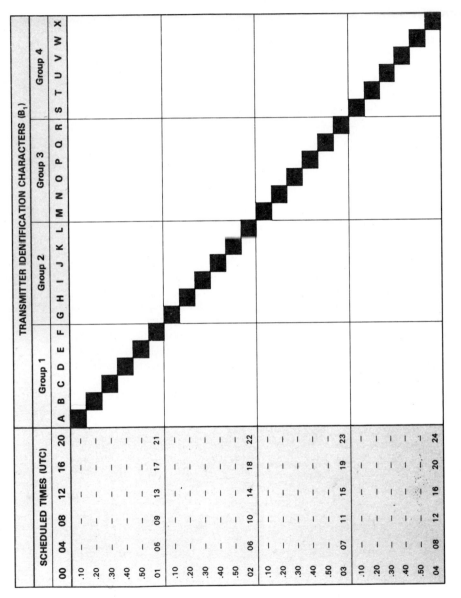

Fig. 12.3 Scheme for allocation of transmission schedules by the IMO (courtesy I.M.O.)

printed is determined by a technical code (B_1, B_2, B_3, B_4) which appears in the message preamble or may be selected by the operator. The technical letter B_1 is the assigned character which enables the operator to select a specific region. Figure 12.1 illustrates a plan for the allocation of transmitter identification character B_1 in order to prevent a receiver on the edge of a NAVAREA receiving two transmissions concurrently.

Subject indication character B_2 identifies the different classes of message available and permits the operator to reject unwanted data in order to conserve paper at the printer. The subject characters currently in use are:

A – Navigational warnings*
B – Meteorological warnings*
C – Ice reports
D – Search and rescue information*
E – Meteorological forecasts
F – Pilot service messages
G – DECCA messages
H – LORAN-C messages
I   – OMEGA messages
J   – SATNAV messages
K – Other electronic navaid messages
L – Navigation warnings additional to letter A*
*Messages which cannot be rejected by the receiver.

The characters B_3 and B_4 indicate the numbering of messages transmitted from 00 to 99. The use of the number 00 indicates a message which will be printed by all receivers within range of a transmitting station. This number is reserved for distress alerting.

Because the considerable cost of providing a NAVTEX service around the coastline of a country must be borne by the government of that country it is likely that some areas of the world will not be covered by the service. This is unfortunate because there is little doubt that the service along with INMARSAT's NAVAREA service will provide the mariner with distress, urgency, safety and navigational data to aid safe operation in a hostile environment.

A typical NAVTEX receiver is shown in figure 12.4.

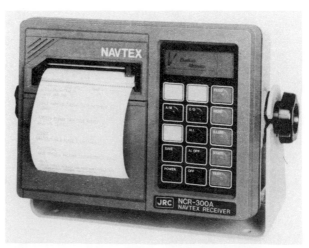

Fig. 12.4 A NAVTEX receiver

Appendix 1: Radio waves, propagtion and the ionosphere

The radio spectrum

Abbreviation	Band	Frequency Range	Wavelength
AF	Audio	20 kHz to 20 kHz	15 000 km to 15 km
RF	Radio	10 kHz to 300 GHz	30 km to 0.1 cm
VLF	Very Low	10 kHz to 30 kHz	30 km to 10 km
LF	Low	30 kHz to 300 kHz	10 km to 1 km
MF	Medium	300 kHz to 3000 kHz	1 km to 100 m
HF	High	3 MHz to 30 MHz	100 m to 10 m
VHF	Very High	30 MHz to 300 MHz	10 m to 1 m
UHF	Ultra High	300 MHz to 3000 MHz	1 m to 10 cm
SHF	Super High	3 GHz to 30 GHz	10 cm to 1 cm
EHF	Extreme High	30 GHz to 300 GHz	1 cm to 0.1 cm

Electromagnetic radio waves in the range 10 kHz to 300 000 MHz form the usable radio frequency spectrum, parts of which are used for broadcasting, communications and radio navigation sysems throughout the world. The velocity of electromagnetic radio waves is approximately 300×10^6 metres per second. This figure is important because it enables the wavelength of the transmitted frequency to be calculated. Thus a suitable transmitting antenna system can be designed for maximum efficiency.

$$\text{Wavelength } \lambda = \frac{300 \times 10^6}{\text{Frequency}} \quad \text{in metres}$$

Wavelength is also a measure of the distance travelled by a radiowave during one alternating cycle – peak to peak. The number of alternating cycles per second is a measure of the frequency.

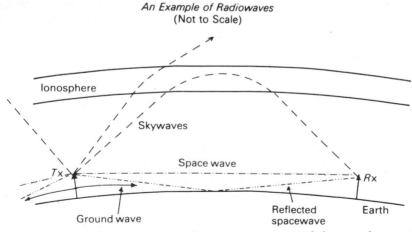

An Example of Radiowaves
(Not to Scale)

Radiowaves are transmitted (propagated) one one or more of three main wave forms: ground (Surface) wave, sky wave and space (Direct) wave. Intelligence is carried on one or more of these waves depending upon the carrier frequency which is used.

VLF (very low frequency)
VLF radio signals propagate using a combination of both the ground and space waves

which are guided, over great distances, between the lower edge of the ionosphere and the surface of the earth (see Chapter 5). Very large antenna systems are required to match the very long wavelength of VLF signals. With a wavelength of 30 km, at 10 kHz, highly efficient large antennae are only possible on land installations, often erected between mountain peaks.

LFC low frequency)
Communication is mainly by ground wave which suffers greater attenuation as frequency is increased. Range therefore depends upon the amplitude of the transmitted power and the efficiency of the antenna system. Wavelength has decreased to the point where suitable antennae of a practical size can be produced. Range of the groundwave for a given power is 1500 to 2000 km (Loran-C). The skywave is returned from the ionosphere, particularly during the hours of darkness, producing errors in some navigation systems.

MF (medium frequency)
Groundwave attenuation rapidly increases. Range, for a given transmitter power, is therefore reduced as frequency is increased. Groundwave range is typically 1500 km to under 50 km for a transmitted signal with a peak output power of 1 kW correctly matched into an efficient antenna system.

In the band below 1500 kHz skywaves are turned both day and night although comunication using these waves is unreliable. Above this figure the returned skywave has greater reliability but is affected by changes of the ionosphere due to diurnal changes, seasonal changes and the sunspot cycle. By taking these factors into account and carefully selecting the frequency, reliable communications up to a range of 2000 km can be achieved.

HF (high frequency)
This frequency band is widely used for terrestrial global communications. Groundwave range is insignificant being only a few km. For satisfactory communications using skywaves the frequency must be carefully selected. Skywaves of frequencies at the lower end of the band are absorbed by the ionospheric layers during the hours of daylight and are not returned to earth. Under these conditions communication can be established by selecting a frequency in the centre or upper end of the HF band. At night the lower frequency skywaves are returned, whereas the higher frequencies are not refracted sufficiently to be returned and are lost. The choice of frequency in this band for reliable communication over great distances is therefore a compromise.

VHF (very high frequency)
Both groundwaves and skywaves are practically non existent and can be ignored. Communication is via the space wave which may be ground reflected. Space waves effectively produce line of sight transmission and consequently the height of the antenna becomes important. The antenna may also be directional. Large objects in the path of a space wave will produce a blind spot in which reception is extremely difficult.

UHF (ultra high frequency)
Space waves and ground reflected waves are used with highly directional efficient antenna systems. Signal fading is minimal although wave polarization may be affected as the wave is ground reflected, resulting in a loss of signal strength. Blind spots are still a problem.

SHF (super high frequency)
Transmissions in this band have very short wavelengths and are known as microwaves. No skywaves exist, propagation is by direct and ground reflected waves. Wavelengths are in

centimetres, therefore compact highly efficient direction antennas can be used. This band is used for maritime radar and satellite communications.

EHF (extreme high frequency)
This band although at present not used in the maritime service forms the upper end of the usable radio frequency spectrum.

The ionosphere

At altitudes between 50 and 500 km above the earth's surface there exists a number of bands containing electrically charged atoms called ions. The ions may be negatively or positively charged by the loss or gain of a number of electrons. In the upper atmosphere, ions are formed by the action of ultraviolet light (u.v.). The extent of ionization depends mainly upon the intensity of u.v. light from the sun reaching our atmosphere. Ionization is therefore less during the hours of darkness and under constant change during the transitional periods of sunrise and sunset.

Four distinct ionized layers exist during the day reducing to two at night. Each layer has the property to attenuate and, under certain conditions, refract a radio skywave. Global communications rely on this phenomenon.

At the greatest distance above the earth's surface is the F layer, which during the day effectively consists of two levels of ionization designated F2 and F1. At night the two layers combine to form a single layer. At an altitude of approximately 90 to 150 km there exists a less intensely ionized layer called the E layer. This layer maintains its altitude throughout diurnal changes although at night it becomes weaker by a factor of two. Lowest and weakest of the layers is the D layer which disperses at night. It is this layer which is the principal source of absorption of HF radio waves. LF and VLF radio waves are reflected from this layer to provide long distance operations during the day.

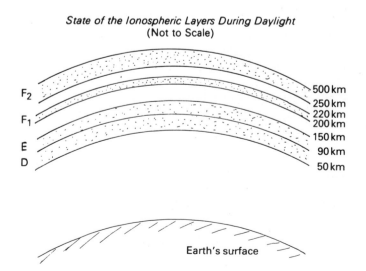

State of the Ionospheric Layers During Daylight
(Not to Scale)

Appendix 2: Doppler effect

In the early 19th century, Christian Doppler showed that the colour emitted by a star in relative movement across the sky appeared to change. Because light waves are part of the frequency spectrum it was later concluded that the received wavelength must change and therefore the apparent received frequency will change. This phenomenon is widely used in the field of electronics for the measurement of speed. The Doppler effect is used, in the text of this book, when describing the action of the Doppler speed log and for positional data in the Transit satellite navigation system.

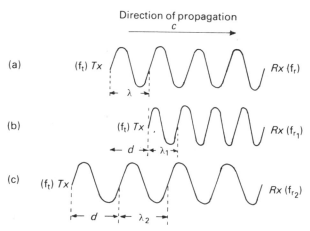

Wavelength (λ) is compressed in time for a transmitter moving towards the receiver (λ_1) and expanded for a transmiter moving away (λ_2). Consider a transmitter radiating a frequency (f_t). The velocity of propagation of radio waves in free space (c) is 300×10^6 metres per second. After a period of one second, the transmitted wave will occupy a distance of

$$\frac{c}{1} = C \text{ metres}$$

If the transmitter moves towards an observer at speed (v) it will, at the end of one second, have travelled a distance equal to (d) towards the receiver. Each transmitted wave has now been shortened because of the distance travelled towards the observer by the transmitter. Hence by definition a shorter wavelength defines a higher frequency (f_r). The shortened wavelength or apparently higher frequency, received is directly proportional to the speed of movement of the transmitter.

In figure (b) above the transmitter has moved towards the observer by distance (d). This is the distance travelled during the time of generating one cycle (T).

$$T = \frac{1}{f_t} \quad \text{and} \quad d = v \times T = \frac{v}{f_t}$$

therefore the apparent wavelength $\lambda_1 = \lambda - \dfrac{v}{f_t}$

$$\text{Frequency } f_{r_1} = \frac{c}{\lambda_1} = \frac{c}{\lambda - \dfrac{v}{f_t}} = \frac{cf_t}{\lambda f_t - v} = f_t \frac{c}{c - v} \tag{i}$$

For a moving transmitter which is approaching the receiver the received frequency is apparently increased. The reverse is true of a transmitter moving away from an observer, when the wavelength (λ_2) will be longer and the frequency decreased.

$$\lambda_2 = \lambda + \frac{v}{f_t}$$

$$\text{Frequency } f_r = f_t \frac{c}{c + v} \tag{ii}$$

If an observer moves, at velocity (v) towards a stationary sound source, the number of cycles reaching the receiver per second is increased, thus the apparent received frequency is increased.
The received frequency is:

$$f_r = f_t + \frac{v}{\lambda}$$

$$\frac{1}{\lambda} = \frac{f}{c} \quad \text{therefore} \quad f_t + \frac{fv}{c} = f_t\left(1 + \frac{v}{c}\right) = f_t\frac{c + v}{c} \tag{iii}$$

If the observer moves away from the stationary sound source the apparent received frequency is:

$$f_r = f_t \frac{c - v}{c} \tag{iv}$$

If, as in the Doppler log, both the observer and the sound source are moving towards a reflecting plane, the received frequency is:

$$f_r = f_t \frac{c}{c - v} \times \frac{c + v}{c} = f_t \frac{c + v}{c - v} \tag{v}$$

The Doppler frequency shift $f_d = f_r - f_r$ (or $f_t - f_r$)

$$f_d = f_t \times \frac{c + v}{c - v} - f_t$$

$$= \frac{cf_t + vf_t - cf_t + vf_t}{c - v}$$

$$= \frac{2vf_t}{c - v}$$

c is always very much greater than v, therefore the expression can be simplified to:

$$f_d = \frac{2vf_t}{c} \tag{vi}$$

where f_d = Doppler frequency shift in cycles per second
        v = Relative speed in the direction of the transmitted wave
        f_t = Transmitted frequency
        c = Velocity of propagation of radio wave

Appendix 3: Zilog Z80 terminology

$\overline{\text{CE}}$ CHIP ENABLE (input active low). When enabled the CTC/PIOs accept control words, interrupt vectors or time constant data words from the data bus during an I/O write cycle; or in the CTC transmits the contents of a down counter to the CPU.

CLK/TRG   EXTERNAL CLOCK/TIMER TRIGGER (input user selectable active High or Low). In counter mode, every active edge on this pin decrements the down counter. In timer mode the active edge starts the timer.

IEI   INTERRUPT ENABLE IN (input active high). A high indicates that no other interrupting devices of higher priority in the daisy chain are being serviced by the CPU.

IEO   INTERRUPT ENABLE OUT (output active low). Low when Z80 CTC channel that has been programmed to enable interrupts has a zero count condition on its down counter.

$\overline{\text{IORQ}}$ INPUT/OUTPUT REQUEST (input from CPU active low). Used with $\overline{\text{CE}}$ and $\overline{\text{RD}}$ to transfer data and channel control words between the CPU and the CTC. During a write cycle, $\overline{\text{IORQ}}$ and $\overline{\text{CE}}$ are active and $\overline{\text{RD}}$ inactive. In a read cycle $\overline{\text{IORQ}}$, $\overline{\text{CE}}$ and $\overline{\text{RD}}$ are active; the contents of the down counter are read by the CPU.

$\overline{\text{MI}}$ MACHINE CYCLE ONE (input from CPU active low). When $\overline{\text{MI}}$ and IORQ are active the CPU is acknowledging an interrupt. The CTC then places an interrupt vector on the data bus if it has highest priority and if a channel has requested an interrupt ($\overline{\text{INT}}$).

$\overline{\text{RD}}$ READ CYCLE STATUS (input active low). Used in conjunction with $\overline{\text{IORQ}}$ and $\overline{\text{CE}}$ to transfer data and channel control words between the CPU and the CTC.

$\overline{\text{INT}}$ INTERRUPT REQUEST (output active low). When a port requests an interrupt it puls $\overline{\text{INT}}$ low.

$\overline{\text{MREQ}}$ MEMORY REQUEST (output active low). This indicates that the address bus holds a valid address for a memory read or write operation.

$\overline{\text{RD}}$ READ (bidirectional active low). As an input this indicates that the CPU wants to read data from a memory.

$\overline{\text{MRD}}$ MEMORY READ (active low). CPU reads data.

$\overline{\text{MWR}}$ MEMORY WRITE (active low). CPU writes data into memory.

RFSH   MEMORY REFRESH (active low). Single transistor dynamic memory cells are used in each memory block. These cells must be "refreshed" to maintain memory storage. The action is an integral part of the main program and is accomplished by taking the $\overline{\text{RFSH}}$ line low at least once in each 2 ms period.

Appendix 4: Glossary of microprocessor and digital terms

This appendix is not intended to be a complte listing of terms relating to microprocessor and digital systems. The aim is to give a brief outline description of those terms found in the various chapters so that each section can be understood without the need to refer to specialist texts. Should the reader wish to go further than this then obviously text books dealing with these topics can be used.

Using the glossary

Many tems are referred to by an abbreviated form,or acronym, and where applicable the definition appears under this heading. The heading under the full version of the term will direct the reader to the acronym version.

Certain terms are included more than once, although under different headings, with cross references to link the headings. Cross references are only used when it is felt necessary, for easier understanding, to expand a particular definition.

ADC   Analog to digital converter. A device which samples an analog signal and converts the observed analog level to digital form. The digital form is made up from several binary digits, or BITS.

Active   A signal may be described as active *high* or active *low* to indicate which of the two logical levels (logic 1 or logic 0) causes the digital circuit to be enabled.

Address   A coded instruction which specifies the location in memory of stored data.

Algorithm   A set of rules laid out in a logical sequence to define a method of solving a particular problem.

Alphanumeric   A system where the required information is in a combination of alphabetic characters and numbers.

Analog   A system where the signal can be considered to vary continuously with time. A digital system on the other hand may be considered to consist of a finite number of discrete levels. The number of levels may only be two as in the case of a binary system.

Analog to Digital Converter   See ADC

AND Gate   For a description of a Gate see under that heading. An AND gate is an electronic circuit of two or more inputs which will only generate an output at logic 1 if *all* the inputs are at logic 1. All other combinations of input signals will give a logic 0 output. the performance of an AND gate may be defined in tems of a TRUTH TABLE which lists the output level for all possible input combinations. The truth table for a two input AND gate is:

A	B	F
0	0	0
0	1	0
1	0	0
1	1	1

where A and B are the inputs and F is the output.

ASC II   American Standard Code for Information Interchange. This is a common code which gives a 7-bit word to define letters, numbers and control characters.

Basic   Beginner's All-purpose Symbolic Instruction Code. This is a high-level language which enables the computer user to program the system using an easily understood set of instructions. Within the computer memory there is a 'translator' which converts the

BASIC language into the binary signals, or machine code, which the machine understands.

BCD   Binary Coded Decimal. A system of representing the numbers 0 to 9 inclusive by a binary equivalent. The relationship is as shown:

decimal number	binary coded value
0	0000
1	0001
2	0010
3	0011
4	0100
5	0101
6	0110
7	0111
8	1000
9	1001

Binary   A system of numbers using a base of 2 whereas the decimal system has a base of 10. The binary system only requires two symbols i.e. 1 and 0.

Bit   Contraction of *bi*nary digi*t*. A single bit may be a logic 1 or logic 0 and is usually represented by the presence or absence respectively of a voltage level.

Buffer   An electronic circuit connected between other circuit elements to prevent interactions between those elements. The buffer may also provide extra drive capability. A buffer may be used also as a temporary storage device to hold data which may be required at a later time while the computer is engaged on other tasks.

Bus   A collection of conductors used to transmit binary information in parallel around the system. For microprocessor applications there would be an *Address* bus used by the Central Processing Unit (CPU) to identify storage locations and a *Data* bus used for the transmission of data around the system.

Byte   A collection of 8 bits. In a microprocessor system using 8 bit data buses and a 16 bit address bus, then the data can be contained in one byte while the address needs two bytes to define it.

Character   The letters A–Z, numbers 0 to 9 and other special symbols used by a computer or microprocessor system and coded for use by the system.

Character Generator   The electronic circuitry required in order to prepare a character for display purposes. Such generators possess memory where the binary coded characters can be stored.

Chip Select   An input to an integrated circuit which, when active, allows the integrated circuit to be operative. If the input is not active then the integrated circuit is inactive. This control signal is sometimes called a *Chip enable* input.

Clock   A periodic timing signal used to control a system.

Code   A set of rules allocated to groups of bits. The combination of the bits in a group gives a unique meaning based on following the rules.

Coincidence Gate   An electronic circuit used to indicate by means of a certain output level, when two inputs are identical. When the inputs are binary in form then all bits of one input should be coincident with the corresponding bits of the other input before the required output level is generated. An Exclusive-NOR gate could be used for this purpose.

Command   A signal, or group of signals, used to begin or end an operation.

Complement   To 'complement' a number means to subtract that number from a specified value. In the binary case subtracting a binary number from 1 gives the 1's complement. In fact this gives a value where all bit values are inverted i.e. the 1's complement of 1011 is 0100. Many systems include a 2's complement facility and the 2's complement of a binary number can be found from the 1's complement simply by adding 1 i.e. the 2's complement of 1011 is 0100 + 1 = 0101.

Computer   In the case of a digital computer the basic system consists of a central processing unit (CPU), memory, input and output units and a control unit. The computer is able to perform such tasks as:
manipulate data, perform arithmetic and logical operations on data and store data.

Computer language   A set of conventions, rules and representations used to communicate with the computer system. The language may be low-level, such as assembler (uses mnemonics), or high-level, using user-orientated language like BASIC.

Converter   See under the headings of analog to digital converter (ADC) or digital to analog converter (DAC).

Counter   A circuit used to count the number of pulses received. The counter may be arranged to start from zero and count from there in increments of one (up-counter) or to start from the counter maximum capacity and decrement from that value one pulse at a time (down-counter).

CPU   Central Processing Unit. Part of a computer system which contains the main storage (registers), arithmetic and logic unit (ALU) and control circuitry. Sometimes referred to simply as the processor.

Daisy chain   A method used to indicate priority for several peripheral units requiring access to a computer system. The highest priority peripheral has first use of the data bus and when finished (or if use of the bus is not required), allows the next peripheral in the priority sequence use of the data bus.

Data   Information or signals, usually in binary form.

D-type Flip-flops   An electronic circuit which on receipt of a clock pulse will give an output logic level the same as that present at the input terminal prior to the arrival of the clock pulse. It is widely used as a data latching buffer element.

Decade Counter   A counter which has a maximum count capacity of ten.

Decoder   An electronic circuit which has several parallel inputs and the ability to 'recognize' one or more of the possible input combinations and output a signal when these combinations are received. All signal levels are binary.

Dedicated   A dedicated system is one designed to perform a specific operation i.e. a dedicated microprocessor system is programmed to perform only one specific task.

Demultiplexer   A device used to direct a time shared input signal to several outputs in order to separate the channels.

Digital Information in discrete or quantized form i.e. not continuous as in the case of an analog signal.

DAC Digital to Analog Converter. An electronic device for converting discrete signal levels into continuous form.

Disable A control signal which prevents a circuit or device from receiving or sending information.

Display A means of presenting information required by a user in visual form. Includes the use of CRT (cathode ray tube), l.e.d. (light emitting diode), liquid crystal, gas discharge and filament devices.

Driver An electronic circuit that provides the input for another circuit or device.

Enable A control signal which allows a circuit or device to receive or transmit information.

Encoder This is the inverse process of decoding. An encoder has several inputs but only one is in the logic 1 state. A binary code output is generated depending on which of the inputs has the logic 1 level.

EPROM Erasable and programmable read-only memory. A memory circuit with stored data which can be read at random. The data are capable of being erased and the chip reprogrammed with new data.

Exclusive-OR gate A circuit with 2 inputs and an output which can be at logic level 1 when either of the two inputs is at logic 1 and logic 0 if neither or both the inputs are at logic level 1.

Exclusive-NOR gate Since an NOR gate is an OR gate followed by an inverter then it follows that the exclusive-NOR gate has 2 inputs and an output which can be at logic 1 when neither or both the inputs are at logic 1 and logic 0 when either of the two inputs is at logic 1. This gate could be used as a coincidence gate.

Filament display A 7 segment filament wired element whereby an alphanumeric character may be displayed when certain of the filaments are caused to be lit.

Flag A flip-flop which can be set or reset to inform of an event that has occurred or a condition that exists within a system.

Flip-flop An electronic circuit having two stable states that can be used to store one bit. The circuit uses two gates, the output from each being cross-coupled as an input to the other. The output from one gate is usually referred to as the Q output while the output from the other gate, being the complement of the first output, is called $\overline{Q}$.

Gate This is a circuit with two or more inputs and an output which allows a logic level 1 to exisst at the output, or not, as the case may be, when certain defined criteria are met.

Hard Copy Printed or graphical output produced on paper by a computer system thus allowing a record to be kept.

Hex Gate A digital integrated circuit constructed so that there are six gates on the chip.

Highway A common path linking elements in a computer system along which data may travel.

Input/output ports These circuits allow external circuits to be connected to the computer internal bus system.

Integrated circuit (IC) A small 'chip' of silicon processed to form several elements directly interconnected to perform a given unique function.

Interface A common boundary between systems to allow them to interact.

Interrupt A computer input that temporarily suspends the main program and transfers control to a separate interrupt routine. Interrupt inputs to the microprocessor systems discussed in the main text are usually referred to by acronyms such as $\overline{\text{IRQ}}$ (interrupt request) and $\overline{\text{INT}}$.

Interrupt masking A technique which allows the computer to specify if an interrupt will be accepted. $\overline{\text{IRQ}}$ and $\overline{\text{INT}}$ are maskable interrupt inputs whereas NMI (non-maskable interrupt) is not.

Keypad (or Keyboard) A unit which forms part of an input device. This may have a full QWERTY type key layout or be a simplified arrangement to suit the needs of the system.

Language See computer Language.

Latch A temporary storage element, usually a flip-flop.

Logic Electronic circuits which control the flow of information through the system according to certain rules. These circuits are known as gates since the 'gates' are opened and closed by the sequence of events at the inputs.

Logic level Using binary notation the levels may be logic 1 or logic 0. According to the rules mentioned in the definition of logic, level 1 is taken to mean a logical statement is 'true' while level 0 means the logical statement is 'false'.

Magnetic tape A flexible, standard width, magnetic powder coated tape which can be used to store, and retrieve, binary based data.

Mask bit With reference to an interrupt request, an internal flip-flop in the MPU can be set to disable an interrupt (interrupt masked) or reset to allow the interrupt to be accepted.

Memory In a digital system, it is that part of the system where information is stored.

Microprocessor *See MPU.*

Monostable An electronic circuit which has only *one* stable state. The cirtuit is normally in the stable state and is triggered into the unstable state where it remains for a period of time determined by a CR time constant value of external components. After this period of time the circuit returns to the stable state.

MPU An IC that can be programmed with stored instructions to perform a wide variety of functions, consisting of at least a controller, some regisers and an ALU (arithmetic and logic unit). Thus the MPU contains the basic parts of a simple CPU.

Multiplexing A method of selecting one of several inputs and placing its value on a time shared output.

NAND Gate A gate that acts as an AND gate followed by an inverter i.e. the output logic level for any combination of inputs is the inverse of that and of the AND gate.

NOR Gate A gate that acts as an OR gate followed by an inverter i.e. the output logic level for any combination of inputs is the inverse of that of the OR gate.

NOT Gate   An inverter. A circuit whose output is high if the input is low and vice-versa.

Octal Latch   An integrated circuit package that offers eight separate flip-flop (or latch) circuits.

OR Gate   For a description of a Gate see under that heading. An OR gate is an electronic circuit of two or more inputs which will generate an output at logic 1 if any one or all of the inputs are at logic 1. Only when all inputs are at logic 0 will the output be at logic 0. The performance of an OR gate may be defined in terms of a *Truth Table* which lists the output level for all possible input combinations. The truth table for a two input OR gate is:

A	B	F
0	0	0
0	1	1
1	0	1
1	1	1

where A and B are the inputs and F is the output.

Port   Terminals (input and output) which allows access to or from a system.

Printer   The output peripheral of a computer system which allows a hard copy to be obtained.

Program   A sequence of instructions logically ordered to perform a particular task.

PROM   Programmable Read Only memory. This is the type of memory used to hold microprocessing instructions. It is a form of ROM which can be programmed by the supplier and not the user.

Pulses   Those signals used to energize a circuit digitally. There is a transition in signal level between discrete values and each level is maintained for a period of time.

Quad Gate   An integrated circuit package which offers four separate gate circuits of a particular type.

RAM   Random Access Memory. A memory that can be read from and written into.

Readout   A presentation of input information from a computer. It can be displayed on a screen, stored on tape or disc or be a hard copy when it is usually referred to as a printout.

Read/Write   Can refer to the type of memory element (RAM is sometimes referred to as read/write memory) or to the signal input line to a RAM chip, the logic level on which determines whether the memory is read or overwritten.

Register   A group of memory cells used to store groups of binary data in a microprocessor.

Reset   This could be an input to a flip-flop to bring the Q output to a logic 0 state or that facility which allows a microprocessor to be returned to a predetermined state. Where the point of return is situated in memory depends on the system.

Ripple counter   That form of binary counter where the output from the first flip-flop in the counter is used to trigger the second flip-flop. Sometimes called a ripple through counter since the carry bit from the first flip-flop seems to ripple through all the flip-flops of the counter.

ROM   A memory element containing information which cannot be altered under computer operation. The data can only be read by the computer.

Self-test   In some equipments this is a facility by which when power is first applied the system is checked by running through a special software routine. If a faulty area is found some indication is made to the user.

Sensor   A device, possibly a transducer, which converts physical data into electrical signal form. If digital in form the electrical signal can be processed by the computer directly while if analog in form, it requires analog to digital conversion (ADC) before being applied to the computer.

Seven-segment display   That form of display element comprising seven segments where each segment can be individually energized. The element is thus able to display a variety of alphanumeric characters depending on which segments are energized.

Shift register   A register in which the stored data can be shifted, a bit at a time, to the left or right.

Signal   An electrical variation, either continuously variable or variable between discrete levels, which can be interpreted as information.

Software   A program which can be loaded into a computer system and resides in RAM. Such programs can be loaded and changed at will.

Storage   A term used to describe any device capable of storing data. Memory elements are storage devices.

Subroutine   Part of a master program which can be entered frequently from the master program. Used to save programming space where a part of a program is repetitive.

Tape   The media, either paper or magnetic, used to store binary coded data for a computer system.

Test   The routine for establishing that a device or system is responding as it was designed to do.

Toggling   In a particular type of flip-flop when both inputs are held at logic level 1, the clock pulse always causes the output logic level to change i.e. if the original level was logic 1 then after the clock pulse it becomes logic 0 and vice versa. This automatic reversal of output logic level with clock pulses is called 'toggling'.

VDU   Visual display Unit. An input/output peripheral which has a keyboard for data input and a monitor screen for viewing both the input data and any outputted data. The system usually includes buffer storage facilities so that data may be loaded off-line. Often used to communicate directly with the computer in real time.

Index